FIFTH CENTURY STYLES IN GREEK SCULPTURE

FIFTH CENTURY STYLES IN GREEK SCULPTURE

By Brunilde Sismondo Ridgway

PRINCETON UNIVERSITY PRESS

PRINCETON, NEW JERSEY

Copyright © 1981 by Princeton University Press

Published by Princeton University Press, Princeton, New Jersey
In the United Kingdom: Princeton University Press, Guildford, Surrey

This book has been composed in Linotype Caledonia

Clothbound editions of Princeton University Press books
are printed on acid-free paper, and binding materials are
chosen for strength and durability

Printed in the United States of America by Princeton
University Press, Princeton, New Jersey

LIBRARY OF CONGRESS CATALOGING IN PUBLICATION DATA

Ridgway, Brunilde Sismondo, 1929-
    Fifth century styles in Greek sculpture.

    Includes bibliographies and index.
    1. Sculpture, Greek.   2. Classicism in art—
Greece.   I. Title.
NB90.R564   733′.3   80-8574
ISBN 0-691-03965-8
ISBN 0-691-10116-7 (pbk.)

Contents

List of Illustrations and Photographic Sources

1. Parthenon metope S 17 (photo DAI Athens)
2. Parthenon metope S 19 (photo DAI Athens)
3-5. Parthenon metope N 32 (photos DAI Athens)
6. Parthenon metope S 1 (photo Bryn Mawr College)
7. Hephaisteion metope, Theseus and Skiron (photo A. Frantz)
8. Hephaisteion metope, Theseus and the Marathon Bull (photo A. Frantz)
9. Hephaisteion metope, Theseus and the Minotaur (photo A. Frantz)
10. Hephaisteion metope, Herakles and the Lion (photo A. Frantz)
11. Rome, Villa Albani, metope (photo DAI Rome)
12. Thasos, Gate of Hera (photo courtesy French School in Athens)
13. Thasos, Gate of Zeus, fragment of Zeus (photo courtesy French School in Athens)
14. Thasos, Gate of Zeus, fragment of Hermes (photo courtesy French School in Athens)
15. Drawing of Gate of Zeus, by P. Rehak, after P. Bernard
16, 17. Sounion, Temple of Poseidon, figure from East Pediment (photos DAI Athens)
18. Parthenon, East Pediment, Figure D (photo British Museum, London)
19-20. Parthenon, West Pediment, torso H (photos British Museum, London)
21. Parthenon, East Pediment, torso H (photo A. Frantz)
22. Parthenon, East Pediment, Figures E-F (photo British Museum, London)
23. Parthenon, East Pediment, Figure G (photo British Museum, London)
24. Parthenon, East Pediment, Figures K-L-M (photo British Museum, London)
25. Rome, National Museum, Stumbling Niobid (photo Bryn Mawr College)
26-30. Ny Carlsberg Glyptothek, Copenhagen, Reclining Niobid (photos courtesy of the Glyptothek)

List of Abbreviations

Citation of bibliographical references for periodicals and standard works follows the guidelines and abbreviations set forth in *AJA* 82 (1978) 3-10 and *AJA* 84 (1980) 3. I have also used the following:

Agora Guide: *The Athenian Agora: A Guide to the Excavation and Museum*, American School of Classical Studies at Athens, 3rd ed., 1976.

Agora 14: *The Athenian Agora*, vol. 14, H. A. Thompson and R. E. Wycherley, *The Agora of Athens: The History, Shape and Uses of an Ancient City Center*, ASCSA, Princeton 1972.

Adam, *Technique*: S. Adam, *The Technique of Greek Sculpture*, BSA Suppl. 3, Oxford 1966.

Archaic Style: B. S. Ridgway, *The Archaic Style in Greek Sculpture*, Princeton 1977.

Ashmole, *Architect and Sculptor*: B. Ashmole, *Architect and Sculptor in Classical Greece* (The Wrightsman Lectures), New York 1972.

Bassai-Fries: Ch. Hofkes-Brukker and A. Mallwitz, *Der Bassai-Fries*, Munich 1975.

Berve and Gruben: H. Berve, G. Gruben and M. Hirmer, *Greek Temples, Theatres and Shrines*, New York 1962.

Bieber, *Ancient Copies*: M. Bieber, *Ancient Copies: Contribution to the History of Greek and Roman Art*, New York 1977.

Bieber, *Hellenistic Age*: M. Bieber, *The Sculpture of the Hellenistic Age*, rev. ed., New York 1961.

Blümel, *Berlin*: C. Blümel, *Die klassisch griechischen Skulpturen der Staatlichen Museen zu Berlin*, Berlin 1966.

Borbein: A. H. Borbein, "Die griechische Statue des 4. Jahrh. v. Chr.: Formalanalytische Untersuchungen zur Kunst der Nachklassik," *JdI* 88 (1973) 43-212.

Brommer, *Fries*: F. Brommer, *Der Parthenonfries—Katalog und Untersuchung*, Mainz 1977.

Brommer, *Giebel*: F. Brommer, *Die Skulpturen der Parthenon-Giebel—Katalog und Untersuchung*, Mainz 1963.

Brommer, *Metopen*: F. Brommer, *Die Metopen des Parthenon—Katalog und Untersuchung*, Mainz 1967.

Brouskari: M. S. Brouskari, *The Acropolis Museum: A Descriptive Catalogue*, Athens 1974.

Carpenter: R. Carpenter, *Greek Sculpture*, Chicago 1960.

Comstock and Vermeule: M. B. Comstock and C. C. Vermeule, *Sculpture in Stone: The Greek, Roman and Etruscan Collections of the Museum of Fine Arts, Boston*, Boston 1976.

Delivorrias: A. Delivorrias, *Attische Giebelskulpturen und Akrotere des fünften Jahrhunderts v. Chr.* (Tübingen Studien zur Archäologie und Kunstgeschichte, vol. 1), Tübingen 1974.

Despinis: G. Despinis, *Symbolē stē meletē tou Ergou tou Agorakritou*, Athens 1971.

Dinsmoor: W. B. Dinsmoor, *The Architecture of Ancient Greece*, London 1950.

Dohrn: T. Dohrn, *Attische Plastik vom Tode des Phidias bis zum Wirken der grossen Meister des IV. Jahrhunderts v. Chr.*, Krefeld 1957.

Festschrift Brommer: U. Hockmann and A. Krug, editors, *Festschrift für Frank Brommer*, Mainz 1977.

Final Programme: Eleventh International Congress of Classical Archaeology, London, 3-9 September 1978—*Final Programme*.

Fuchs, *Vorbilder*: W. Fuchs, *Die Vorbilder der neuattischen Reliefs* (*JdI—EH* 20), Berlin 1959.

GdD: Guide de Delos (Ecole Française d'Athènes), Paris 1966.

GettyMJ: J. Paul Getty Museum Journal, Malibu, California, 1974—

Hiller: F. Hiller, *Formgeschichtliche Untersuchungen zur griechischen Statue des späten 5. Jahrhunderts v. Chr.*, Mainz 1971.

Hausmann: U. Hausmann, *Griechische Weihreliefs*, Berlin 1960.

Hölscher, *Historienbilder*: T. Hölscher, *Griechische Historienbilder des 5. und 4. Jahrhunderts v. Chr.*, Würzburg 1973.

Hölscher, "Die Nike": T. Hölscher, "Die Nike der Messenier und Naupaktier in Olympia. Kunst und Geschichte im späten 5. Jahrhundert v. Chr.," *JdI* 89 (1974) 70-111.

Karouzou, *Catalogue*: S. Karouzou, National Archaeological Museum, *Collection of Sculpture—A Catalogue*, Athens 1968 (Greek ed., 1967).

Koch: H. Koch, *Studien zum Theseustempel in Athen*, Berlin 1955.

Kron: U. Kron, *Die Zehn attischen Phylenheroen* (*AthMitt—BH* 5), Berlin 1975.

Lauter: H. Lauter, "Die Koren des Erechtheion," *AntP* 16 (1976).

Leipen: N. Leipen, *Athena Parthenos: A Reconstruction* (Royal Ontario Museum), Toronto 1971.

Lippold, *Handbuch*: W. Otto, *Handbuch der Archäologie im Rahmen des Handbuchs der Altertumswissenschaft*, vol. 6:3,1, G. Lippold, *Die griechische Plastik*, Munich 1950.

Lullies and Hirmer: R. Lullies and M. Hirmer, *Greek Sculpture*, 2nd ed., New York 1960.

Magna Graecia: E. Langlotz, M. Hirmer, *The Art of Magna Graecia*, London 1965.

Moret, *L'Ilioupersis*: J. M. Moret, *L'Ilioupersis dans la céramique italiote* (Bibliotheca Helvetica Romana 14), Geneva 1975.

Morgan, "Friezes": Ch. Morgan, "The Sculptures of the Hephaisteion, II: The Friezes," *Hesperia* 31 (1962) 221-35.

Morgan, "Metopes": Ch. Morgan, "The Sculptures of the Hephaisteion, I," *Hesperia* 31 (1962) 210-19.

Morgan, "Pediments": Ch. Morgan, "The Sculptures of the Hephaisteion, III: The Pediments, Akroteria and Cult Images," *Hesperia* 32 (1963) 91-108.

Paribeni, *Catalogo*: E. Paribeni, *Catalogo delle Sculture di Cirene*, Rome 1959.

Pollitt, *Ancient View*: J. J. Pollitt, *The Ancient View of Greek Art: Criticism, History and Terminology*, student ed. (Yale Publications in the History of Art 26), New Haven 1974.

Pollitt, *Art and Experience*: J. J. Pollitt, *Art and Experience in Classical Greece*, Cambridge 1972.

Pollitt, *Sources: Greece*: J. J. Pollitt, *The Art of Greece, 1400-31 B.C.* (Sources and Documents in the History of Art Series), Englewood Cliffs, N.J. 1965.

Pollitt, *Sources: Rome*: J. J. Pollitt, *The Art of Rome, c. 753 B.C.-337 A.D.* (Sources and Documents in the History of Art Series), Englewood Cliffs, N.J. 1966.

Richter, *MMA Catalogue*: G.M.A. Richter, *Catalogue of Greek Sculptures in the Metropolitan Museum of Art*, Oxford, and Cambridge, Mass. 1954.

Richter, *Sculpture & Sculptors*: G.M.A. Richter, *The Sculpture and Sculptors of the Greeks*, New Haven 1950.

Robertson: M. Robertson, *A History of Greek Art*, Cambridge 1975.

Schuchhardt, *Alkamenes*: W.-H. Schuchhardt, *Alkamenes* (126 Winckelmannsprogramm), Berlin 1977.

Sculture Cirene: Sculture Greche e Romane di Cirene, ed. C. Anti, (Università di Padova, Pubblicazioni della Facoltà di Lettere e Filosofia, vol. 33), Padua 1959.

Severe Style: B. S. Ridgway, *The Severe Style in Greek Sculpture*, Princeton 1970.

Stewart: A. F. Stewart, *Skopas of Paros*, Park Ridge, N.J. 1977.

Strong: D. E. Strong, *Roman Imperial Sculpture*, London 1961.

Studies von Blanckenhagen: G. Kopcke and M. B. Moore, eds., *Studies in Classical Art and Archaeology—A Tribute to P. H. von Blanckenhagen*, Locust Valley, N.Y., 1979.

Travlos, *Pictorial Dictionary*: J. Travlos, *Pictorial Dictionary of Ancient Athens*, New York and Washington 1971.

Traversari, *Venezia*: G. Traversari, *Sculture del V°-IV° Secolo A. C. del Museo Archeologico di Venezia*, Venice 1973.

Wester: U. Wester, *Die Akroterfiguren des Tempels der Athener auf Delos* (Diss.), Heidelberg 1969.

Zanker: P. Zanker, *Klassizistische Statuen*, Mainz 1974.

Glossary

apoptygma   The upper part of a peplos or a chiton which is folded over, so that it creates the appearance of a valance or ruffle over the torso. It can also be called an *overfold*.

catenaries   Looping folds in U-shape, in the pattern produced by a chain (Italian *catena*) suspended from two points. They are used by sculptors to suggest that the underlying forms are rounded or cylindrical.

eye fold   A groove (within a primary ridge) ending in a wider loop resembling a buttonhole or an eye; usually meant to convey the response of soft cloth caught by a belt or a bend in the draping.

kolpos   From the Greek word for "gulf"; it occurs when material bulges over a belt, usually at the waist; the slack of cloth should allow freedom of arm movement; at the same time the kolpos follows the curve of the body, thus modeling the roundness of the stomach; usually the line of the kolpos runs parallel (or more or less parallel) to and below the edge of the apoptygma, but while the apoptygma consists of a single layer of cloth, the kolpos has no true edge, being formed by the material bent double.

modeling line   A fold or ridge carried across an underlying form so as to "model" it, therefore convey its shape despite its distance from the viewer or, in the case of relief, its relative shallowness.

motion line   A fold or ridge swinging away from the body so as to suggest that it is being displaced by rapid movement. Usually S-shaped, these lines impart a sense of motion to the figure even when the body is in a fairly static pose.

omega fold   The distinctive pattern that can occur at the edge of cloth when it waves and bends; a large pleat with ends bending under thus resembles the Greek letter Ω, hence the name. When the material forms a loop at each end of the central pleat, and the arch dips in the center, the resultant pattern resembles binoculars, and it is therefore called "binocular fold" or "butterfly."

press folds   A pattern of lines, usually crossing at right angles, engraved upon the surface and conveying the impression that a piece of cloth has been folded for a long time, so that when it is opened, the creases of the folding are still visible.

railroad tracks — Thin, ridgelike folds grouped in twos, so that they resemble train tracks; for the effect to be fully perceived, not only should the space between the two ridges be fairly flat and wide, but a much larger interval should occur between the "twin tracks" and the next set of them.

ribbon drapery — A pattern of drapery meant to convey the thinness of the material. The surface is covered with wide folds ending in sharp edges which lie flat over the body but are undercut, so as to give the impression that a series of ribbons is laid out over the surface of the cloth. Incision often accompanies this rendering.

rich style — The style of the period ca. 420-370 B.C., in which drapery is treated with great complexity, folds are flamboyant and largely decorative, and garments appear fluttering regardless of whether the figure is represented as static or in motion. I have tried to avoid this term in my text, since it defines a style that goes beyond the chronological range of my enquiry.

sanguisuga fold — A curving, hollow fold like an inflated sail, which seems created by an upswerving draft at edges of garments or overfolds. The name is derived from an early type of bronze fibula that resembles a swollen leech (Italian *sanguisuga*).

scratched drapery — A variety of ribbon drapery, from which it differs in that the "ribbons" are not undercut but simply scratched over the surface, giving the impression that the cloth almost penetrates the body underneath. There is little salience to scratched folds, which rely largely on incision rather than on ridges; the effect of transparency is not always satisfactory.

selvage, selvedge — The crimped edge on two sides of a woven cloth, which resembles pie crust and results from the looping threads of the woof as they turn around the vertical warp, to prevent unraveling along the sides.

swallow-tail motif — A typical pattern of Archaic drapery, like an inverted V, created when cloth cascades in zigzags on either side of a central pleat, thus resembling the forked tail of a swallow. This pattern is basically an extension of the omega fold, created by the lengthening of the pleating on either side.

tension folds — Sharp ridges branching off from a salience to suggest that the material is being stretched between two prominent points; the ridges are usually separated by deep valleys, with strong play of light and shadow.

transparent drapery — The effect obtained by carving very few ridges over an entire surface, so as to give the impression that the cloth adheres almost entirely to the body. The sculptor can then model the figure as if it were naked, adding a fold or two at wide intervals to betray the presence of the dress. This clinging drapery is also called *wet drapery*, and the trend has been defined *moist style* (W. Childs).

triangular apron   The draping of a mantle produced by folding over one edge as it crosses in front of the body from hip to hip, so that the hanging tip looks like an added apron. In the Fifth century the material usually seems to lie in only two layers, but occasionally, at the point of bend, folds gather into a *roll* for additional effects of light and shadow.

Venus rings   Thin lines incised on the necks of figures, especially young females, to suggest the softness of the flesh, or plumpness. Thought to occur only on voluptuous women (like a necklace of beauty—hence the name), it has now been noted also on children and young men.

Preface

THE incentive to write this book was provided by the encouraging reception students have been giving to my two previous surveys of Archaic and Severe sculpture. Despite the fact that the span of time covered by the present text produced some of the most famous monuments of Greek art, through my years of teaching I have found that no publication has yet satisfied the need for an analysis in depth, but that all available literature is either too general or too specific, as well as too abundant for students to encompass within a reasonable amount of time. In fact, there may be room for more books of this kind, one for each of the remaining centuries before Christ, if time will permit. At present I have stopped at the turn into the Fourth century, with only a brief excursus into the problems of Classicizing sculpture and of Roman copies.

Once again, the result is a cross between a handbook and a monograph. This time I was particularly helped by the recent appearance of Martin Robertson's monumental work *A History of Greek Art*, with its up-to-date bibliography. Although my own footnotes and bibliography do not consistently refer to it, its existence is being taken for granted, and students who wish for a concise summary of all pertinent facts and of recent opinions recast into a personal vision should always consult Robertson first. I have instead conceived of my task as that of concentrating exclusively on sculpture rather than on the many manifestations of Greek art, and of delving into the complexities of style rather than of providing basic information. Thus not all Fifth century monuments have been discussed, and those included are not all discussed to the same extent. I have, however, returned to the format of *The Severe Style*, which allows me to append to each chapter encapsulated comments on additional monuments.

One other major work is taken for granted in my analysis: Rhys Carpenter's *Greek Sculpture*, with its magisterial explanation of styles. Many of what I consider my own ideas are in fact only Carpenter's teachings developed in slightly different forms and directions, and the echo of his words can often be detected in my own phrasing.

It is certainly a result of my apprenticeship with Rhys Carpenter that I, like him, do not believe in the fruitfulness of attempting to reconstruct the oeuvre and style of single masters. Recent scholarly opposition to Carpenter's theories of logical development and anonymity of Greek craftsmanship has been strong; only one other voice was raised in implicit support, that of Ranuccio Bianchi Bandinelli, and in his case personal sociological and political ideologies may have rendered his arguments less impartial or at least less convincing. The majority of works being written at present follow in fact the tradition of focusing on the few great names of Greek sculptors that the ancient sources have preserved for us, thus increasing for students the difficulty of charting a safe course through the complexities of divergent attributions. In my efforts to counterbalance this tendency I may seem to have overstated my case against the Great Masters, despite the many friends who have tried to argue me out of my position—especially J. J. Pollitt, who so kindly read and criticized my first chapter. To be sure, as Martin Robertson has reiterated to me, individualism was paramount in the Greek way of life, and a sense of self-worth is implicit in the many signatures of ancient artists that have been found not only on statuary but also on vases, mosaics, and occasionally even architecture. Some commercialism (as an ancient form of advertisement) may perhaps be read into this practice, but no such materialistic motivation should underlie the competitive efforts of contemporary athletes, dramatists, and philosophers. I do concede that some sculptors of antiquity may have excelled over the others, but I suspect that their greatness remained within the confines of tradition, and that their own contribution may have been less startling to their contemporaries than it is to us today. Personalities probably became more colorful in the individualistic climate of the Fourth century, but at least for the period under review my position may be partly defensible. In addition, the present nature of our sculptural evidence is such as to warrant a largely anonymous treatment until further discoveries may force a revision of this approach.

Some may argue with my attempt to assign precise chronological brackets to certain stylistic phases. One of the characteristics of Greek sculpture during the second half of the Fifth century is in fact the coexistence of several modes of aesthetic expression, and toward the end of the century the so-called Rich style acquires such popularity that it is impossible to be sure whether a work belongs just before or just after 400 B.C. The inclusion of debatable pieces within this survey is therefore meant to suggest recognition of Fifth century style rather than an absolute Fifth century date.

My stylistic analyses may appear too detailed and pedantic, but it has been my experience that sculpture must be looked at repeatedly and closely before it is actually seen. In analyzing the behavior of muscles and folds, their ability to convey motion or structure or simply richness and elegance, I have tried to focus the reader's attention on details that can be taken in at a glance but are not truly perceived except as a total impression. I have purposely avoided generic descriptions of ethos and beauty in the sculpture under review, not because these qualities do not exist, but because I prefer to help dissect the concrete details that contribute to this greater effect. Thus I take style to be the specific way in which the carver renders facial features, bone structure, anatomy in all its parts, stance and balance, and especially drapery with all the intricacy of its many patterns and folds. No two renderings are alike, and thus we can distinguish separate hands as we could distinguish individual voices, but at the same time similarities of artistic idiom or at least of intent in expression can be noted, and thus we discern style. Since description of stylistic traits is difficult and its terminology may be variously understood, I have included a glossary of terms with my own definitions of them.

I have used the same approach to illustrate my text, trying to include as many close-ups of details as possible. In this I was greatly helped by the availability of Rhys Carpenter's photographic collection at Bryn Mawr College, for which I am most grateful. I have also relied heavily on the availability of many excellent plates: in Lullies and Hirmer, *Greek Sculpture*, in the series *Antike Plastik*, and especially in the great photographic commentary on the Parthenon sculptures provided by Frank Brommer. I have included, however, pictures of some monuments to facilitate reading and encourage visual analysis.

My students have provided the inspiration for this book; the opportunity to write it was provided by the University of Pittsburgh, which invited me to spend the winter term (January-April 1978) as Andrew Mellon Distinguished Visiting Professor in their Department of Fine Arts. The reduced teaching load, the office facilities, and the freedom from housekeeping chores were too tempting to resist, while the warm reception and the stimulating response of my Pittsburgh colleagues and students were too flattering to discount. The first five chapters of my text were written while in Pittsburgh, with occasional trips to the Bryn Mawr College Library; the rest of the main text was completed after my return to my home institution, by the end of August 1978. In September of that year, however, I attended the eleventh International Congress of Classical Archaeology in London, where many of the papers touched upon topics I had covered in my book; in addition I profited from discussion with many of the foreign scholars who attended the Congress. Upon my return to Bryn Mawr I tried to incorporate some of this new material into my text; I was therefore compelled to make frequent reference to the only printed account available at present: the summaries of the papers published in the *Final Programme* of the Congress. Although most readers will not have access to this booklet, they should be able to read these abstracts virtually unchanged in the Acts of the International Congress, *Greece and Italy in the Classical World* (Litchworth 1979).

Additional revisions to my text were made possible by the inspiring presence of Erika Simon, who was Mary Flexner Lecturer at Bryn Mawr College from October to December 1978. With invariable enthusiasm she shared with me as with everybody her great scholarship, her unparalleled knowledge of bibliography and iconography, and her understanding of Greek art. My pages are heavily indebted to her lectures and seminar discussions.

Another person whose name recurs like a leitmotif throughout my text is Evelyn B. Harrison. Not only has she touched upon every aspect of Fifth century sculpture in her publications, she has also been unstinting in her sharing of unpublished manuscripts, generous with her time and knowledge in oral discussion and in written information, most helpful in providing bibliographical tools of difficult access, and open-minded in criticizing those of my theories which she does not accept. Since individual acknowledgments are not always feasible within text and bibliographies, I wish to record here my heavy indebtedness and warm gratitude to both these great scholars and friends.

A special kind of thanks goes to all my students, whose many reports on topics of interest they will recognize within this book, together with many of their questions and comments. I particularly want to mention the members of my Fifth century seminar (September-December 1977) at Bryn Mawr College: Gunlög Anderson, Janer Belson, Mary Brand, Joan Connelly, Katherine Dohan, Mark Fullerton, Bridget Hamanaka, Erika Harnett, Ronald Lacy, Elissa Lewis, Raymond Liddell, Clair Lyons, and Polymnia Muhly. Their stimulating contribution to my work cannot be overstressed. In particular, Mark Fullerton has given me the benefit of his thinking and criticism during a supervised unit in Greek sculpture during 1978-1979. In Pittsburgh a more art-historical but all the more provocative inspiration was provided by the graduate students in my seminar (January-April 1978): Carolyn Cohen, Argie Leech, Kathy Muenchow, Helen Scully, Vanze Beldecos, Ellis Vuilleumier, and Carol Solomon. My former student Anne Weis, who was one of my Pittsburgh colleagues, provided additional stimulation and perceptive questioning. Last but not least, another former pupil, Carlos Picón, has been invaluable in scrutinizing my text and in supplying advance information on bibliography from his vantage lookout post at Oxford. To all these friends I extend my affectionate thanks.

After the basic text was completed and submitted to Princeton University Press, additional changes and revisions were made possible by a visit to the Ny Carlsberg Glyptothek in Copenhagen. I am grateful to the Director, Dr. Flemming Johansen, for his invitation and for lengthy discussion in front of the Niobids in his collection; my thanks go also to my friend Professor Carl Nylander, who suggested my visit.

That my text was accepted for publication is due largely to the support expressed by the three readers for the Press: Professors Evelyn B. Harrison, J. J. Pollitt, and Martin Robertson, whose helpful comments and corrections were gratefully incorporated. The staff of Princeton University Press in general, and my editor, Robert Brown, in particular, deserve my sincere appreciation and thanks for their continuous efforts on my behalf and their unfailing patience and cooperation.

Finally, a special word of gratitude goes to my family, who have learned to cope with a writing mother, and to my husband, who has not only tolerated but actively supported and encouraged my work, thus making it possible.

Brunilde Sismondo Ridgway

Bryn Mawr College
March 1980

FIFTH CENTURY STYLES IN GREEK SCULPTURE

CHAPTER 1

Greek Sculpture in the Fifth Century

DEFINITION AND CHRONOLOGY

STRICTLY speaking, the term Fifth century applies to the period between 500 and 400 B.C., and by extension to all its manifestations. In art-historical language, however, the definition is capable of greater refinement, since that time span involves at least three different stylistic phases, each with its own individuality, as well as many ramifications and subsidiary trends. Although these chronological divisions are largely set by modern convention, it is usually agreed that from 500 to 480 we have the last expression of the Archaic style proper, from 480 to 450 we witness the flourishing of the Severe, and from 450 to 400 that of the Classical; in addition, Archaistic, Lingering Archaic, and Lingering Severe exist side by side with the main stylistic currents, and the Classical style proper takes many forms for which separate terms will have to be established. Here we shall be concerned exclusively with Greek sculptural creations from ca. 450 to 400 B.C.

Since more than one style evolved during these fifty years, our chronological limits cannot be defended on the basis of a single, unified production. Nor can they be directly connected with major historical events that provide convenient fixed points in our chronology. The upper limit can, however, be justified on the basis that it is reasonably close to the inception of the Periklean Parthenon, in 447 B.C.: undoubtedly the great sculptural demand originating in that building program was responsible for a quickened pace in stylistic developments. The lower limit is less defensible, although it, too, is only a few years away from a major Athenian event, the defeat at Aigospotamoi in 405 B.C. Thus our treatment of the Fifth century seems bracketed in terms of Athenian history, a procedure which may be misleading but which may find some justification in actual events, as we shall discuss later.

This relatively brief chronological span is perhaps one of the most important for the history of Western culture. We think of it as the Classical period par excellence, when Athens achieved that peak of eminence which marked her as "the school of Hellas" for all future generations. The adjective *classicus* was already used in antiquity (for instance, by Aulus Gellius in the Second century A.C.), and was etymologically derived from *classis*, that is, the first class of citizens. Initially used to describe those authors who were considered the best and therefore worthy of being studied in school, the term was soon extended to include artistic manifestations. Today, in modern contexts, the expression "Classical art" has at least three meanings: it can apply to the whole of Greek and Roman art, as distinguished from that of other civilizations and ages; it can refer to the period of Greek art between the Persian wars and the time of Alexander the Great; finally it can be used to include only the second half of the Fifth century. Some scholars wish to stress

3

the importance of this last phase and refer to it as High Classical, while others reserve that definition for the Fourth century. Under the circumstances, I prefer to eliminate entirely these ambiguous terms. Although I consider the period 450-400 as Classical, I shall try to avoid calling it so, even if I am aware of the shortcomings of my own terminology, which calls Fifth century only its last fifty years.

Yet the term Classical should elicit one more consideration: regardless of its triple meaning, the word conveys a concept of excellence, and therefore of admiration, which prompted various "Classical" revivals through the ages. The first of these occurred under the Romans, who adopted Greek Fifth century style whenever they wanted to depict superhuman or mythical beings. Yet while these quotations from the Greek past can easily be recognized when they occur within a Roman historical context, they are not so clearly identifiable per se. One of the greatest problems facing modern art historians is therefore that of distinguishing between true Roman copies of Greek originals and Roman creations or adaptations in Greek Classical style; yet our awareness of the problem is relatively recent and in need of further refinement. Some scholars have focused on specific points or approaches. For instance, Paul Zanker, in *Klassizistische Statuen*, concentrates on nude male figures, especially those after Polykleitan originals, while Margarete Bieber, in *Ancient Copies: Contribution to the History of Greek and Roman Art*, has published her lifelong research which attempts to detect Roman works through misunderstandings in the rendering of Greek costumes. But results are uneven and understandably subjective, so that general agreement has not yet been reached over individual monuments. We shall have to discuss this problem in detail, both when dealing with attributions to specific masters and in the chapters on Roman copies and Roman creations.

Roman interference is not simply limited to the question of copies and adaptations: inevitably, through our literary sources, we tend to see with Roman eyes. Our main information on ancient sculpture comes from Pliny, who lived in the Flavian period, and from Pausanias, who traveled through Greece under the Antonines. Although these authors drew their information from earlier writings, they often interpreted them in contemporary terms or used their own judgment as conditioned by their traditional environment and by the stylistic tendencies of their own day. Thus Pausanias, invaluable as he is for our knowledge, frequently omits information which we would consider essential, while giving details that are for us of only secondary importance. It is often noted that he did not comment on the continuous frieze of the Parthenon; it should instead be stressed that he mentioned none of the temple friezes: in Athens those of the Erechtheion, the Nike Temple, the Ilissos Temple, and the Hephaisteion;[1] elsewhere at Bassai; and of course no mention is made of Sounion, which Pausanias did not visit. Yet in many buildings he pointed out the beauty of their stone ceilings! Since the periegetes usually gives the themes of pediments and sometimes also of metopes, one cannot assume that he was totally oblivious to architectural sculpture. Were it purely a question of interest in the subjects rather than in the decoration per se, certainly many of the continuous friezes depict topics

[1] Doubts have once again been raised as to the correctness of calling this temple the Hephaisteion (e.g., E. Harrison, *AJA* 81 [1977] 137-39, 421-26). On the other hand, to refer to it as the so-called Theseion, or "Theseion," is cumbersome and perhaps equally misleading. I have therefore retained the standard terminology of the majority of publications, without, however, wishing to imply a particular stand in this argument.

of mythological and historical import. It is perhaps more accurate to assume that to a person of Pausanias' time a continuous frieze was little more than a glorified molding, as indeed many of the Roman friezes were during the Second century of our era.

The Problem of Masters

Conversely, in a period dominated by the strong personalities of emperors and political figures, and certainly characterized by active collecting and antiquarian interests, it is perhaps logical that the history of Greek art should have been written around major masters. Although Pliny used many Greek sources, these in turn belonged largely to the Hellenistic period, equally aristocratic in outlook. In addition Pliny seems to have been greatly influenced by Varro (116-27 B.C.), an antiquarian who also thought in terms of "who, where, when, and what," and who published himself fifteen books on portraits of famous men. But is it safe to assume that individual artists were so prominent during their own lifetimes and specifically in the Fifth century B.C.?[2] Can we be sure that their reputation in Roman times corresponded to an equal fame in the Greek period and, most of all, that this fame was acquired because their individual styles were different and innovating in comparison to those of their contemporaries?

We are so accustomed to thinking in terms of great artistic personalities that we find it normal to do the same for the Greek period. If documents are not as abundant or detailed as those available for the Renaissance or later periods, we blame the chances of preservation or the different habits of the times. Yet when records survive from the Fifth century, they often list names of masters who find no mention in the ancient literary sources, and who seem to work on commission with little information supplied on subjects and poses. The best known example is that of the Erechtheion frieze, which consisted of separate marble figures fastened to a background of different stone; the building accounts for 409-405 B.C. show that the sculptors were paid by the figure, each defined rather vaguely as "youth beside the breastplate" or "chariot and youth with two horses being harnessed." Obviously such listing may simply mean that a minimum of description was required for payment, without precluding the possibility that elaborate models or drawings were furnished to the carvers. Yet the names of the actual carvers are not recorded elsewhere, nor do we ever hear of a famous sculptor connected with the building, except in other contexts (for instance, Kallimachos for a golden lamp in the interior of the Erechtheion[3]). The resultant picture is that of a group of artisans, not even affiliated in a workshop; yet the surviving fragments are of excellent workmanship and exemplify several stylistic traits which we usually attribute to great masters.

There are two possible answers to the problem. Either the major sculptors were only

[2] That even the Romans may not have thought so highly of the masters themselves, but rather of their creations, is shown by Plutarch *Life of Perikles* 2, and Lucian *Somnium* 6-9. The passages are collected and translated in Pollitt, *Sources: Grece*, 226-27.

[3] S. Karouzou has suggested (*AthMitt* 69-70 [1954-55] 79-94) that the technical similarity between the Erechtheion frieze and the statue base found within the Hephaisteion may result from common authorship: Alkamenes would therefore be the master who conceived the Erechtheion frieze. But no literary source or building account confirms this suggestion, and E. Harrison has even argued (*AJA* 81 [1977] 138-39, 265-87) that the cult statues by Alkamenes could not have stood on the base in question.

responsible for the general conception of a building's sculptural program, and the execution was left to competent but unoriginal artisans who worked through models or cartoons while the great master concentrated on the cult statue (like Pheidias for the Parthenon): thus only insignificant names would occur in the lists of payments. Or the Fifth century Greeks did not think in terms of artistic genius, and many stone carvers of the time could achieve equal levels of competence and ability; thus only the relative importance of the commissions, for instance the aura attaching to a cult statue, would be primarily responsible for the survival of the master's name in later sources. The result of the first hypothesis would be to admit that whatever remains of Greek originals, being mostly architectural sculpture, is the product of laborers which only remotely reflects the ability of the famous masters, and it is purely our modern mind which marvels at the excellence of the execution.[4] The second hypothesis would instead lead us to the realization that we cannot expect to recognize personal styles, that no single man of genius suddenly altered the course of sculpture to impose new forms and approaches of his own, and that the emphasis on a few names is largely the result of the slant in the extant Roman sources. In support of this second version of events one can add that Fifth century authors, such as playwrights or philosophers, never mention contemporary masters,[5] that all or most of the anecdotes referring to them seem to be later fabrications,[6] and particularly that the names which survived into the Roman period are often connected with the writing of specialized treatises which probably did no more than codify current artistic theories.[7] Thus, to take examples from another field, Hippodamian town planning is now known to have existed long before Hippodamos of Miletos, yet it was named after the man who presumably set down in writing its basic principles; similarly Vitruvius credited the Hellenistic Hermogenes with the invention of the pseudodipteral temple plan, which is clearly attested since the Sixth century B.C., even if on a different conceptual basis.

Were we to take this line of reasoning to its extreme consequences, several assumptions could be made. For instance, we could—to a great extent—discount the concept of ancient originality and artistic personality, and think largely in terms of general stylistic trends shaped and shared by all alike.[8] In effect, it has often been pointed out that different

[4] The comments by Brommer, *Giebel*, 135, on the relatively minimal echo found by the Parthenon sculptures in ancient literature could indeed be extended to all other Fifth century architectural sculpture.

[5] One exception to this statement is the passage in Plato's *Protagoras* (311C) in which both Polykleitos and Pheidias are mentioned as sculptors; yet the reference is more to their profession than to their art, which is not commented upon in any form. However see also Isokrates, *Antidosis* 2.

[6] A different position is taken by T. Hölscher, "Die Nike," 92-98, who believes that each anecdote contains a core of truth and that much of Fifth century art depended on the originality and even eccentricity of the artists. I would not exclude the possibility that more definite artistic personalities emerged in the Fourth century, in keeping with the more individualistic climate of the times and their art. In addition J. J. Pollitt has pointed out to me that

the Hellenistic writers on art were particularly interested in artists who could be considered the originators of some stylistic or technical feature, or in artists who served as analogues for developments in literature. The Peripatetic model for scholarly research projects, established by Aristotle and descending into the Hellenistic period through Demetrios of Phaleron, also contributed greatly to enshrining certain artists as "masters."

[7] Certainly a sculptor who could write a treatise on art-historical principles must have been a man of a certain education and intelligence. The above comments do not, however, imply that all masters were ignorant carvers, but simply that they did not play that *primadonna* role implicit in the extant Roman accounts. Single aesthetic contributions were still possible within this traditional framework.

[8] This position is typified best by Carpenter's *Greek Sculpture*. See in particular his introductory comments (p. v) where Greek sculpture is essen-

renderings, not just different hands, can be detected in the Parthenon sculptures; one of the pedimental statues has even been called "the reclining Doryphoros," yet Polykleitan influence could hardly be postulated at that time and place, where Pheidias should have reigned supreme.[9] We could also understand the strong influence that painting and engraving could exercise on contemporary sculpture, since often one master worked in more than one medium or one technique. Finally, if the major Greek names of our Roman sources are to be connected with written treatises, we could rely on a strong theoretical basis for all Classical art, though perhaps not consciously applied by all its practitioners. Thus progress would be along predictable and logical lines, and any major deviation from the norm, any stylistic leap that would seem to precede by several decades the general acceptance of a trend, should be viewed with suspicion and perhaps redated, rather than being considered the brilliant anticipation of a man of genius.

This position, which has occasionally been taken by some scholars, has been invariably criticized as forcing Greek sculpture into too confining a straitjacket of conformism and anonymity, implying a development of almost biological uniformity. Yet as philosophy and science in antiquity sem to have proceeded step by step, building on the discoveries or the premises of the previous generations, so artistic problems seem to have occupied all artists from time to time, to be solved gradually and thus to free the way for the next interest or technical accomplishment. That this conception is not entirely a modern fabrication can perhaps be shown by the fact that a coherent sculptural development can be plotted out from the beginning of the Sixth to the end of the Fourth century B.C., yet cannot be formulated for the Hellenistic period when all technical secrets had been mastered and no guiding philosophy seems to have informed sculptural production. But the Hellenistic is a period of artistic reminiscences, either consciously expressed or baroquely exaggerated out of all proportions. Art during the Fifth and Fourth centuries is instead forward-looking, with few lingering traditions.

For the other side of the question, to be sure, militates the obvious consideration that not a single developing style, but many, can be detected within the Fifth century. This statement applies in two ways: on the one hand different renderings appear on contemporary monuments, as already mentioned for the Parthenon itself; on the other hand, a division could almost be established at mid-period, perhaps around 425, when the stately

---

tially defined as "an anonymous product of an impersonal craft." A strong argument along the same lines has been made by P. Bruneau, "Situation methodologique de l'art antique," *AntCl* 44 (1975) 425-87. An intelligent summary and criticism of the available ancient sources and their limitations can be found in A. F. Stewart, *Skopas of Paros*, 1-4, although the author believes that the attempt to reconstruct artistic personalities should nonetheless be made; see also his addendum on p. 150. On more general, sociological terms, see the interesting discussion by R. Bianchi Bandinelli in a lecture delivered on Jan. 22, 1957: *ArchCl* 9 (1957) 1-17, reprinted with additions in R. Bianchi Bandinelli, *Archeologia e Cultura* (Milan and Naples 1961) 46-65.

Martin Robertson reminds me that each artistic

change must actually be made by an individual. I do not mean to argue against *all* artistic individuality; my position is mostly a question of degrees, of the forms of expression of such artistic assertiveness and of the relative importance of expressive media in ancient times.

[9] The tradition of a Polykleitan stay in Athens is based on debatable passages in literary sources: the Kleiton with whom Sokrates talked (Xenophon *Memor.* 3.10.6) and who was indeed a sculptor, but need not have been Polykleitos, and a mention in Plato (*Protagoras* 311C) that refers definitely to the Peloponnesian master but does not specify his location at the time. The allusion in Aelian (*VH* 14.6) seems anecdotal in character and, since it refers to a missed commission for a portrait of Kallias, need not imply that Polykleitos was in Athens.

7

and logical Parthenonian drapery style is supplanted by a flamboyant and far richer version. It is perhaps significant that the change is virtually epitomized for us in the Nike of Paionios, by a master with an obscure birthplace,[10] whose career cannot be traced despite recent efforts, and whose name has come down to us through inscriptions (which were also read and mentioned by Pausanias) but is otherwise not recorded by Pliny or other Roman sources. Yet his monument in Olympia remains one of the most spectacular originals we possess from the entire Fifth century.

Modern Literature

The emphasis on artistic personalities has also been abetted by modern writers. The very extensive literature on Fifth century sculpture concentrates largely on individual masters, an approach which was made authoritative by A. Furtwängler and was standard for early Twentieth century scholarship but has received further impulse in recent years with the brilliant identification of Agorakritos' Nemesis by G. Despinis. Methodologically it is of course expedient to group comparable works around famous names, but the procedure has at times taken the opposite course of starting from the attributions made by the ancient sources and trying to identify the monuments intended among the copies present in our museums. Though both approaches are open to question, it is clearly the second which presents the greatest dangers, not the least being that the Roman sources are at times contradictory and attribute the same work to different masters; in other cases, the subject is described in such vague terms that it is impossible for us to identify it with certainty. The first approach is also problematic, because stylistic affinity need not imply common authorship, especially when such affinities are determined on the basis of Roman copies. We possess, in fact, so few originals from the Fifth century that some of the very masters considered most important by both ancient and modern sources would not be represented were we to exclude Roman replicas. Yet undeniably, studies on Pheidias, Polykleitos, Agorakritos, Alkamenes, Kalamis, and others have greatly contributed to our understanding of Fifth century sculpture and can be consulted with profit as long as the premises for each assertion and attribution are critically examined in the light of new discoveries and present knowledge.

A variation of both approaches has consisted in trying to define not the masters themselves but their schools, again largely on the basis of Pliny and other early writers. The school of Polykleitos has received particular attention in German studies of the last two decades, and somewhat the same attempt has been made for Pheidias, although more in terms of subsequent generations than of pupils. Among the various publications special mention should be made of Tobias Dohrn, *Attische Plastik vom Tode des Phidias bis zum Wirken der grossen Meister des IV. Jahrhunderts v. Chr.*; his stylistic analyses are perceptive and illuminating, but his consistent effort to lower the entire chronology of late Fifth century sculpture has not met with general approval.

Another, and perhaps more fruitful, aspect of research has concentrated on individual monuments. Thus we now have Frank Brommer's trilogy on the Parthenon sculptures,

---

[10] Mende, as mentioned in the inscription of the Olympia pillar. Pausanias (5.26.1, and 5.10.8) adds that Mende is in Thrace, but a Mende in Chalkidike is also known and is favored by some scholars as Paionios' birthplace.

which takes advantage of all the accomplishments in modern photography and printing. Other architectural sculpture has been treated in equal detail, and many individual statues in the round, both originals and copies, have been the subject of recent monographs. Evelyn B. Harrison, in the course of preparing the catalogue of all sculptural finds from the Athenian Agora, has touched upon, and discussed in either article or lecture form, virtually every major monument or topic of Fifth century art, making considerable contributions to our knowledge of that phase; but her publications focus on individual problems and even her catalogue, when completed, will necessarily center on the excavated material. Few scholars have tried a synthetic approach to the entire production of the Fifth century, and even those who concentrate on surveying certain aspects or topics in Classical sculpture are inevitably limited by the nature of the inquiry. Worthy of specific mention are the article by Hilde Hiller, "Statuenstützen im fünften Jahrhundert v. Chr.," *AntK* 19 (1976) 30-40, and the difficult book by Friedrich Hiller, *Formgeschichtliche Untersuchungen zur griechischen Statue des späten 5. Jahrhunderts v. Chr.* In general, however, to find a total picture of Fifth century sculpture one must turn to handbooks, where information must often be excerpted from more general treatments of the whole of Greek art. Even Martin Robertson's monumental *History of Greek Art* discusses Fifth century works in several places rather than in one comprehensive chapter, and other handbooks are shorter and therefore inevitably more limited. Werner Fuchs's *Die Skulptur der Griechen* (Munich 1969) deals with the evolution of types (e.g., the male standing figure, the female figure, the seated figure), and therefore does not isolate specific periods. Georg Lippold's *Griechische Plastik*, which is arranged both chronologically and geographically, is still fundamental but out of date and in process of revision as part of a general reprinting of the *Handbuch der Archäologie*.

Even Lippold's listing of Fifth century sculpture, moreover, gives a misleading impression. It treats the topic at length, thus suggesting that we both have and know a great deal; yet, on second examination, it is apparent that the majority of the monuments included come from Athens or its vicinity; when they come from elsewhere, they are usually under Attic influence. If they belong to entirely different areas and masters, they are mostly known through statue bases and mentions in the literary sources; or regional attributions are made on the basis of style, since no provenience is attested for many statues in our museums. Finally, in several cases, works that had been traditionally dated within the Fifth century are now known to be later.

Particularly important among them are the Nereid Monument in Xanthos, Lycia, and the Heroon of Gjölbaschi Trysa in the same region, which have now been convincingly assigned to the 370s. Their redating is especially significant because their traditional chronology had been partly determined on historical grounds. It had in fact been generally assumed that the Attic overtones in some of the friezes were due to the presence in Lycia of Attic masters, or at least of carvers who had been trained in the school of Athens and the Parthenon and had then fled abroad when the disastrous outcome of the Peloponnesian War had deprived them of profitable commissions within the impoverished city. This theory is now automatically invalidated by the thirty-year span that separates the presumed exodus and the erection of the Lycian monuments. On the other hand another, and more interesting, problem is created, since the Attic similarities in iconography and style have now to be explained on other grounds, such as the existence and use of sketches or pattern books. Somewhat the same situation applies to the frieze of the temple of Apollo at Bassai, which I, among others, would tend to date at the very end of the Fifth century, if not later. Finally, even the chronology of the Argive Heraion has been lowered to a similar limit not only because the connection between its chryselephantine cult statue and the famous Polykleitos has been questioned, but also on architectural grounds.

The Role of History

The desire to connect artistic production with historical events is understandable and useful; but it is also dangerous. Aside from Thucydides' famous remark as to the misleading inferences to be made from the physical appearance of Sparta and Athens respectively, the entire post-Periklean building program stands in defiance of reason. Some structures have been attributed to years marked by peace treaties or by relative quiet in Athens; yet it is undoubted that work was progressing on the Akropolis in the blackest period of the Peloponnesian War, just before the final demise, as attested by the Erechtheion building accounts. In addition, the so-called Ilissos Temple, which used to be assigned to 449, has now been convincingly dated later, to the early 420s, that is, shortly after the devastating plague and during the first phase of the Peloponnesian War. A one-to-one correspondence between peace and art, or war and artistic sterility, should therefore be avoided.

There is, however, one historical factor that should receive greater emphasis than heretofore: the negative influence of Athens' control over her allies. A geographical survey of sculptural productivity in the Fifth century shows very little activity in the prosperous cities of the coast of Asia Minor even after peace with Persia had been achieved. The islands present the same general picture, and even Delos seems to prosper exclusively through Athenian benefactions. It may be exaggerated to speak of "The Shadow of the Parthenon," but it is remarkable how little we know about the Fifth century outside of Athens, and one may conclude that there is not much to be known. Pausanias, to be sure, mentions several monuments set up in Delphi and Olympia during the period under consideration, but they are often Athenian donations, or victory statues erected by individual athletes.

Cult Statues

More important is the emphasis on cult statues, several of which are named as having been made by Pheidias or other masters. This demand for divine images is something new, which may have started toward the end of the Archaic period, but certainly not on a scale comparable to the Fifth century development. It can perhaps be connected with renewed building activities, but not all the images mentioned by the sources coincide with the erection of a new temple. In addition, statues were also made for places where an earlier cult image did exist and which, we presume, continued to be the main object of veneration. This is certainly the case in Athens with the Athena Parthenos, and it is improbable that many cults with earlier histories should have waited until the Fifth century to obtain a divine image. This was most likely a propagandistic, rather than a purely spiritual, need, prompted by increased prosperity or by greater aesthetic sensitivity in the masses, since the early idols were notable for their mysterious and legendary origin rather than for their attractive appearance. Undoubtedly a certain element of emulation and outright competition had always existed among cities, as well as some desire to account for, or even show off, accumulated wealth. It is certainly important, however, that man is now consciously making his own gods, no longer as votive offerings but as cult statues in precious materials and on a vastly superhuman scale.

This phenomenon is important for several reasons. Aside from the philosophical shift in humanistic values (man now is truly measure of all things), it must have been largely responsible for the degree of idealization and aloof serenity that pervaded sculpture at this time, almost in open contradiction to the expressionistic tendencies of the Severe period. On the other hand, these divine images were often made of precious material and, even when in bronze or marble, were rendered relatively inaccessible by their cult purposes or by their colossal size. Thus we have no definite replica of the chryselephantine Zeus created by Pheidias for Olympia, and the reproductions of the Parthenos remain remote echoes of the original, often ranking at the level of touristic souvenirs in terms of aesthetic appeal. Yet this great production of cult statues and divine images not only set the style for future representations (the so-called religious conservatism of Greek art nearly always recalls a Fifth century prototype, since Archaic turns into Archaistic), but, as already mentioned, it had a strong impact on the later Romans, who took the images of their gods from the Greeks and therefore largely from the Fifth century.

It has been said that if Pheidias, with his powerful artistic personality, had not changed the course of Greek art toward an idealizing direction, the Severe style would have developed into the Hellenistic, that is, into its aesthetic equivalent at a much earlier date. One may wonder whether the change was dictated, not purely by the inclinations of the master (since it is dangerous to ascribe such a major influence to a single personality), but primarily by the nature of the commissions. Greek beliefs, popular but devout, were turning into state religion, official but cold.

Together with the cult statues, another genre entered Greek sculpture: that of the elaborately decorated statue bases. With images larger than life-size, bases had to be commensurate and therefore offered ample scope for additional narrative and decoration. The result was veritable friezes, some of which were made by applying separately carved figures against an independent background. This technique seems more closely connected with the minor arts than with major sculpture, yet these statue bases were more readily accessible to the viewer than architectural friezes or the cult statues themselves, and this eye-level perspective seems to have influenced sculptural reproductions and diffusion of motifs first established in this genre.

Particularly influential was the composition on the shield of the Athena Parthenos which, despite its large size, was equally related to metal chasing and repoussé work, and therefore to the minor arts; yet the Amazonomachy on that shield seems to have had the strongest possible impact on major monuments such as the Nike Temple frieze and later architectural sculpture—if architectural sculpture is indeed to be considered a major form of art. The very introduction of motifs that might have seemed "improper" for official sculpture in the round may have been promoted by the relative license allowed to the minor arts. To be sure, this distinction between major and minor forms of artistic expression may be purely artificial and conditioned by our modern mind, yet many subjects and compositions first attested on vases and then on reliefs and architectural friezes did not find translation into three-dimensional terms for more than a century. Or again, as mentioned above, it could be argued that all these two-dimensional renderings are simply reflections of lost monumental paintings, a major genre that reached considerable prominence within the Fifth century and exercised indisputable influence on the Parthenon sculptures and other contemporary monuments. This very fact is of considerable importance for our understanding of the Fifth century.

Change in Content

Together with this demand for cult statues and statue bases decorated with mythological subjects we witness another phenomenon difficult to interpret. While the subject matter of most architectural sculpture during the Archaic or the Severe period can be understood on the strength of our knowledge of Greek myths alone, the same cannot be said for that of the Fifth century. Cases in point are the East frieze of the Hephaisteion, at least the East if not all four friezes of the Nike Temple, certainly the Ilissos frieze, and even the Parthenon frieze, which has lately aroused a new spate of articles discussing its subject matter. This list could be considerably expanded if less well preserved sculptures were included, and in this connection it is important to remember that the subject matter of the very Parthenon Pediments would be incomprehensible to us in their present state of preservation were it not for Pausanias' information. While the Parthenon Pediments, however, simply depict well-known myths in an usual form, the other examples cited do not fall into this category. We should therefore consider the possibility that new interests and new, more "human" conceptions are reflected in this line of Fifth century production, a fact which is in itself of interest for our understanding of the period.

TRAITS

It seems therefore expedient to outline here what I consider the basic traits of Fifth century sculpture apart from those of the preceding and succeeding phases. Since several styles can be isolated within the period, either concomitantly or successively, the traits must be defined in the most general terms, so that they may apply to the entire sculptural production everywhere within the Greek world. It should also be stressed once again that Lingering Severe and Archaizing elements can be detected in many works of the time, although they will not be treated separately in this context.

1. *A representational, seemingly naturalistic approach to the human figure in its most perfect form.* Emphasis is on articulation and structure, and anatomical details are selected for their value as vertical and horizontal accents on the whole, almost like moldings on a building. Thus certain elements in the male nude are particularly emphasized or even exaggerated to increase their tectonic appearance, such as the groin and hip muscles or the pectorals; often an unnatural break is added at the waist level, marking the lower edge of the rib cage. Proportions tend to be heavy but without the blockiness of the Severe period. Female bodies are opulent and powerful. Heads are large, with large individual features, especially the eyes which sometimes seem almost bulging. Depictions avoid the extremes of youth and old age, children are simply shown smaller, without specific characterization. In keeping with this trait, and almost a corollary, is the following:

2. *Idealization.* Not only is the human figure represented at its best, it is also shown devoid of emotions, in ideal beauty and composure. Moods are conveyed through poses rather than through facial expression. Thus faces may appear vacant and remote or at best serene. Heroic quality is suggested by nakedness, especially in battle contexts where armor is unrealistically limited to token elements. Over-life-sized statues, which seem less numerous after the early Archaic period, now return into fashion, and some works reach gigantic proportions. Figures smaller than life-size continue to be made.[11]

3. *Interest in balance rather than in motion.* Although the Severe period had attempted to capture the human figure in split-second action, the Fifth century is more concerned with static equilibrium and quiet poses, at least in sculpture in the round. In narrative contexts motion is conveyed primarily through drapery or through what has been called "the heroic diagonal," but, with few exceptions, no great display of musculature under stress is attempted. Ponderation attracts considerable attention but almost as a mathematical formula, on theoretical principles. This trait is reinforced by:

4. *A theoretical approach to drapery.* For all its natural appearance, drapery is rational rather than realistic; it is not depicted per se but utilized and even exploited to express motion (motion line) or to model the human figure that it is supposed to cover (modeling line). Different textures are conveyed but under implausible circumstances; yet the renderings are so aesthetically pleasing and convincing that any illogicity goes unquestioned. The sculptor's control of folds becomes so complete that eventually it results in highly decorative and baroque renderings, as if in a tour de force to be unreal while representing a definite (material) aspect of reality. Attention to detail is so great that selvage (selvedge) is consistently shown, that is, a crimped edge on cloth, which resembles pie crust and, in weaving, results from the looping threads of the woof as they turn around the vertical warp, to prevent unraveling along the sides. This rendering is so often found that it can be considered a hallmark of the period.[12] After 400 the motif occurs sporadically, almost as an antiquarian trait.

5. *Ideological and humanistic content.* For all its emphasis on divine dignity, the Fifth century has a new conception of human worth, which finds expression in a greater focus on the individual. The first portrait statues are made, though character is depicted rather

[11] Size manipulation by sculptors deserves attention. While a figurine is easily understandable both in terms of technique and economy, statues well over—or somewhat under—life-size imply a conscious decision on the part of their maker, since neither is part of his everyday experience. A gigantic statue presents technical rather than conceptual problems, because an anthropomorphic vision of the gods would naturally tend to find expression in magnification of the human features. This step was reached virtually at the dawn of Greek sculpture, probably under foreign influence and technical teaching, but the practice of making such large statues seems to have diminished in the course of the Archaic and Severe periods except perhaps within the field of architectural sculpture, where size was conditioned by external circumstances. The widespread resumption of such practice in the Fifth century is therefore important, especially in its em-

phasis (cultic rather than votive statues). More difficult to understand is the creation of *under-life-sized* statues, which are nevertheless considerably larger than statuettes and which imply sophisticated thinking. They become popular during the late Archaic period and continue throughout Greek art. Of course, this type of statuary can be found in other ancient cultures, but its rationale is largely symbolic, and therefore mostly different from the representational approach of the Greeks.

[12] One particularly fine example of selvage occurs on a Severe original, the Nike from Paros (*Severe Style*, figs. 56 and 58, pp. 36-37). Since not all the Parthenon sculptures seem to show this detail consistently, the trait could be a Parian (Ionic) invention that was introduced into Athens via the island masters (the gang who came with Agorakritos, who is assumed to have worked on the building).

than physiognomy. History, as the deeds of men, becomes a subject of artistic expression, both symbolically and overtly, if generically, and patriotism is extolled. Human compassion is shown in the motif of the combatant helping a wounded comrade. Attic grave stelai return, even if without emotional overtones, and the dead is depicted at the height of human dignity.

It now remains to isolate these traits in our survey of Fifth century sculpture. Since so many of the monuments under discussion are well known, I shall attempt to comment rather than to describe, and to achieve a broad perspective that includes geographical differences. Since Roman copies are questionable as genuine examples of Fifth century styles, we shall begin our survey with architectural sculpture, which preserves for us undoubted Greek originals and has often the advantage of being dated within a fairly limited span of years. We shall treat each type of architectural decoration separately, beginning with metopes.

BIBLIOGRAPHY 1

FOR PAGE 3

For definitions of "classical" see B. Ashmole, *The Classical Ideal in Greek Sculpture* (Lectures in Memory of L. T. Semple, University of Cincinnati 1964) 3; *EAA*, s.v. Classicismo (R. Bianchi Bandinelli); Pollitt, *Art and Experience*, 1-2 (see his p. 80 for Fifth century = High Classical).

FOR PAGE 5

On Varro and his influence on Pliny see, e.g., Pollitt, *Ancient View*, 80 and n. 24; id., *Sources: Rome*, xx; also *OCD*, s.v. Varro; and Bieber, *Ancient Copies*, 187.

On the Erechtheion building accounts see ch. 4.

On the positions of masters in the Classical period, besides the references given in nn. 6 and 8 see also H. Lauter, *Zur gesellschaftlichen Stellung des bildenden Künstlers in der griechischen Klassik* (Erlanger Forschungen 23, 1974), which, however, does not address our particular concern; N. Himmelmann, *JdI* 94 (1979) 127-42.

FOR PAGE 6

On Hippodamos of Miletos: J. R. McCredie, in *Studies presented to George M. A. Hanfmann* (Cambridge, Mass. 1971) 95-100.

FOR PAGE 7

For criticism against a linear development of Greek art see, e.g., P. Devambez, *CRAI* 1976, 165 and 167; id., *RA* 1976, 272 n. 5; Robertson, 297. In favor: Carpenter, 135 and passim.

FOR PAGE 8

For recent bibliography on the major masters see chs. 7 and 8.

FOR PAGE 9

Redating of the Nereid Monument and Gjölbaschi Trysa: W.A.P. Childs, *OpusRom* 9 (1973) 105-16; id., *RA* 1976, 281-316; id., *The City-Reliefs of Lycia* (Princeton 1978), passim.

FOR PAGE 10

Bassai frieze: see ch. 4.

Argive Heraion, lowering of date on architectural grounds: G. Roux, *L'Architecture de l'Argolide aux IVe et IIIe siecles avant J.C.* (Paris 1961) 58; on sculptural grounds: P. Amandry, *Charites, Festschrift Langlotz* (Bonn 1957) 79-82; A. Linfert, *Von Polyklet zu Lysipp* (Diss. Freiburg, pub. Giessen 1966) 2 and passim.

Ilissos Temple: C. A. Picón, *AJA* 82 (1978) 47-81.

Peter Green's *Shadow of the Parthenon* (Los Angeles and Berkeley 1972) refers tangentially to what I mean by the expression. For the impact of historical events on art see Hölscher, "Die Nike" and *Historienbilder*.

For the emphasis on cult statues see also Robertson, 294, who stresses the novelty of the enormous scale.

FOR PAGE 11

Pheidias responsible for new artistic direction: G.M.A. Richter, *Three Critical Periods* (Oxford 1951) 7.

On statue bases see ch. 7. For comments on the minor-art aspect of the technique: Dohrn, 30-31 (although not all the examples he quotes are correct).

FOR PAGE 12

For the influence of monumental painting on the Parthenon, see, e.g., Robertson, 305 and passim.

The obscurity of themes in Classical art has been noted by Robertson, 349.

FOR PAGE 13

"Heroic diagonal" was coined by Kenneth Clark, *The Nude* (Bollingen Series 35:2, 1956) 187-91; see also Robertson, 316.

CHAPTER 2

Architectural Sculpture: Metopes

THE PARTHENON METOPES

For several reasons, I begin by discussing the Parthenon metopes. In the first place, they are among the earliest sculptures to have been made for the Parthenon, since they were in position by 442, or 438 at the latest, as indicated by the building accounts. Although individual details may have been added in situ, the greatest amount of carving was obviously done on the ground, as shown by the height of the relief and by the fact that cuttings had to be made into some triglyphs to accommodate the projecting sculpture. Not only are the metopes the earliest Parthenon feature: it has even been suggested that some of them were made for an earlier, Kimonian Temple, in which case they would date from the Severe period. Although this theory has been generally rejected on several grounds, it is certainly true that most of the South metopes, coincidentally also the best preserved from the entire building,[1] retain distinctive traits of the Severe style. This feature is best explained, however, in terms of lingering tradition, and it is quite possible that the various Fifth century styles developed in the process of carving, since highly advanced details can be noticed in whatever remains of some other metopes, or, for that matter, in some of the South series as well.[2] It is nonetheless improbable that judgment was passed on the reliefs once they had all been carved, so that the least progressive could be relegated to the relatively unexposed South side: numerical reasons alone automatically exclude an alternate position on either façade, and the relative importance of the themes would seem to require that the Centauromachy be planned for the South side. If this arrangement was determined a priori, it is equally illogical to assume that older masters, locked in the ways of the past, would be assigned to the task, since experience was probably valued over youth, in which case the more visible North frieze, rather than the South, would have been given to them. Were it not that the West metopes are so badly damaged as to make judg-

[1] It is generally assumed that Christians defaced all metopes on East, West, and North sides (except for N 32, which was taken for the Annunciation), but that they left the South metopes intact because the centaurs had been accepted into Christian iconography. G. W. Ferguson, *Signs and Symbols in Christian Art* (New York 1961) 8, states that the monsters symbolized "savage passions and excesses, especially the sin of adultery" as well as brute force and vengeance, the heretic, and man divided between good and evil. It may therefore have appeared providential to the early Athenian Christians that the Lapiths seem to lose their battle against the centaurs, and the whole metopal series might have been meant as an admonition against sin. I owe this reference to Carol Solomon. D. T. Bryant, Jr., has called to my attention that *Physiologus*, compiled in A.D. 200, already gives a similar meaning for the Centaurs several centuries before the Parthenon was converted into a Christian church; cf. Broadway translation (London and New York, n.d.) 207, and K. Weitzmann, *Ancient Book Illumination* (Cambridge, Mass., 1959) pl. x, fig. 20.

[2] N. Himmelmann has recently advocated that the South metopes are in fact the latest on the building: *Stele*, Memorial volume for N. Kontoleon (Athens 1980), 161-71.

ment impossible, we would probably find as many Severe traits in them as in some from the South side. Therefore, through these ninety-two reliefs we witness the genesis of Fifth century styles.

Another reason to begin with the Parthenon metopes is that we are so accustomed to them and their remarkable profusion that we fail to realize how unusual carved metopes are, not only in general but especially for Athens at this time. Except for the Athenian Treasury at Delphi, which probably adopted the feature in imitation of neighboring buildings, these are *the first* sculptured Athenian metopes, since none have been found in Athens from earlier periods. The metopes on the Hephaisteion, as will be argued later, were probably introduced under the influence of the Parthenon, although they may be largely contemporary with the Akropolis panels. It is also remarkable that the Parthenon master[3] elected to decorate the entire perimeter of the temple, since earlier examples elsewhere limited relief metopes to the inner porches or to short returns beyond the façade, and only treasuries had ever been entirely decorated with carved metopes, probably because of their very nature as votive offering and their more limited size.[4] Despite the imposing scale of the Parthenon, there is in its overwhelming sculptural program a touch of the excessive which is hardly in keeping with other manifestations of Athenian taste, and which in fact has prompted some scholars to suggest that the Parthenon is not a temple in the true meaning of the word but rather an oversized treasury.

Meaning and Subject Matter

If we are correct in stressing the uniqueness of this arrangement, which was indeed never again to find a parallel in Attica, nor, as it seems, elsewhere, we can only assume that the

[3] The expression "the Parthenon master" is used here to avoid naming the person(s) responsible for the planning of the entire building. Plutarch tells us that Pheidias was the overall supervisor, but architectural details such as a continuous Ionic frieze and carved metopes would seem to lie within the jurisdiction of the architect. On the other hand Iktinos, especially if he was a Peloponnesian as suggested by his name, would have been more accustomed to carved metopes only over the porches, if at all. It is more logical to assume that Perikles himself was responsible for this grandiose conception, and that it was he who had both the culture and the power to guide architect and sculptor. In this connection it is worth recalling that Perikles was an Alkmaionid on his mother's side and that the link with Delphi would have been to him natural and obvious. The main themes in the Parthenon sculptural program could then be seen to carry a *generic* message of Athenian victories, both in allusion and in actual content, since even the Ilioupersis saw the rescue of Theseus' mother, Aithra, by her grandchildren Demophon and Akamas, an episode which was probably depicted in one of the now missing North metopes. Other evidence of Perikles' influence on the Parthenon program may be seen in the many allusions to celestial phenomena (see ch. 7). The statesman's guidance could indeed be compared to that of a medieval abbot building a cathedral, or, conversely, to that of Peisistratos on the Sixth century Akropolis. On Peisistratos' iconographic guidance see J. Boardman, *RA* 1972, 57-72, and *JHS* 95 (1975) 1-12; on the role of the patron on Greek buildings see J. J. Coulton, *Ancient Greek Architects at Work* (Ithaca, N.Y., 1977) ch. 2. This "tyrannical" approach may have contributed to making Perikles' building program so open to attack by the opposition; on the other hand, N. Himmelmann has recently made a strong case against Plutarch's statement and Perikles' involvement, in the light of Fifth century inscriptions and democratic practices: *Bonner Festgabe J. Straub* (*BonnJbb* Beiheft 39, 1977) 67-90.

[4] Only one possible temple, the so-called Treasury at Foce del Sele, ca. 560 B.C., seems to have had all its metopes sculptured; however, the parallel is so remote, both in date and in location, that no connection can be assumed with the Parthenon. Of successors to the Parthenon, only the Argive Heraion, built after the fire of 423, offers a slight possibility of having had carved metopes all around, but even this theory is disputed and, in the light of the general evidence, it will be here considered unlikely.

visual association with the Delphic Treasury was intentional and would have been apparent to contemporary Athenians. Perhaps this very resemblance added to the political message supposedly conveyed by the various sculptural themes and linked the two buildings as comparable manifestations of triumphant democracies or prosperous states. It is important to note that the Athenian Treasury is also the first *mainland* building we know to employ unity of subject matter within an entire metopal cycle, although only the Geryonomachy of its West side and the Amazonomachy of its East side are strictly comparable to the Parthenon program. The depiction of Amazons on the treasury, both as part of the metopes and as akroteria, underscores the value of the theme for the Athenians before it had acquired its symbolic meaning of victory over an Eastern enemy.[5]

That the Parthenon topics were selected to convey this message after the peace with Persia has been often repeated. Certainly in the victory of the Gods over the Giants, the Lapiths over the Centaurs, and maybe even the Athenians over the Amazons,[6] one sees the triumph of the forces of order over the chaos represented by brutish or at least unnatural opponents. But the Gigantomachy was traditionally embroidered on the peplos given quadrennially in the Panathenaia to the venerated wooden statue of Athena,[7] and the subject had already found expression on the pediment of the so-called Peisistratid Temple in the late Sixth century, as well as on the Temple of Apollo at Delphi. The Centauromachy in its turn had received monumental treatment both in sculpture at Olympia and in Mikon's painting in the Theseion. These are therefore traditional myths, of pan-Hellenic rather than exclusively Athenian significance. But the Ilioupersis of the North side seems a less understandable choice.[8] Here only the eastern ethnos of the enemy could have been conveyed, certainly no notion of brutishness or barbarism, since the Trojans were considered related to the Greeks[9] and worshipers of Athena. The specific depiction of the events is also surpris-

---

[5] For the Athenian Treasury, I accept the date suggested by E. Harrison, in the 490s, which would make the building predate the Battle of Marathon. It has often been argued (most recently by H. H. Büsing, in *Studies von Blanckenhagen*, 29-36) that the treasury dates after 490 and that the Amazonomachy there is also an allusion to the victory over the Persians. In such case, the meaning of mounted Amazons as akroteria to the building would still have to be explained. The Amazonomachy had also received pictorial treatment before its appearance on the Parthenon: Mikon had painted it in the Stoa Poikile (Paus. 1.15.1) and we know that he had also depicted the women on horseback, as on the Parthenon metopes: Aristophanes *Lysistrata* 678-79 and scholiast (Pollitt, *Sources: Greece*, 106).

[6] Brommer, *Metopen*, 191-95, is very scrupulous in interpreting evidence. He leaves open the question whether the West metopes depict Amazons or simply people in Oriental costume, since their sex can no longer be determined in their present damaged state. However, the recurrence of the theme on the shield of the Athena Parthenos makes the supposition plausible. Similarly, on the basis of the metopes interpolated into the South sequence and

of their difficult interpretation, Brommer assumes that the Centauromachy represented may be different from the traditional; he therefore avoids the term Lapith for the human opponents, to include the possibility that the metopes depicted an Attic myth (*Metopen*, 238-40). Here, however, the term will be used for expediency, although Brommer's point is well taken. The correlation between the South metopes and the topic depicted on the Parthenos' sandals should also be noted. The possible connection with the pediments of the Nike Temple as recently reconstructed by G. Despinis will be discussed in ch. 3.

[7] I cannot accept Parke's argument that the peplos was given to the Pheidian statue after its erection (H. W. Parke, *Festivals of the Athenians* [Ithaca, N.Y., 1977] 38-41).

[8] R. Hampe (*GGA* 215 [1963] 145) has noted, however, that Gigantomachy and Ilioupersis were often associated in major monuments: on the Corfu Pediment, the Argive Heraion, the Olympieion at Akragas. See also above, n. 3 and below, comments on the metopes from the Argive Heraion.

[9] Moret, *L'Ilioupersis*, 152, notes that Attic representations of the story do not distinguish between

ing, with considerable toning down of the brutal element inherent in the subject, at least in the present depleted state of the North series. Were it not for the distinctive scene of Helen being protected from Menelaos by Aphrodite and Eros (N 25), one would tend to doubt the traditional interpretation. Here again, pictorial prototypes for the entire topic are known, not only that in the Stoa Poikile, but also that in the Lesche of the Knidians at Delphi—yet Knidos could imply no specific allusion to Persia. I suspect that too much has been made of this underlying meaning of Western victory in the Parthenon program, especially since all but one of the motifs occur again in the rendering of the Athena Parthenos within the cella, where the allusion is bound to be more generic and timeless, as befits a cult statue. Perhaps only a major gathering of famous mythological themes was intended for the architectural sculpture, of the kind that would allow multiplying the episodes and therefore would fill the unprecedented number of fourteen and thirty-two metopes per side, respectively. To be sure, new meaning could have been added to old stories as events unfolded,[10] and different visitors to the Parthenon "read" its message according to their own level of sophistication; but a word of caution should perhaps be here introduced in our all-too-pat explanations.[11]

This point is perhaps reinforced by the peculiar intrusion that the Carrey drawings attest to for the center zone of the South metopes. That area was most heavily damaged by the explosion in 1687, and therefore the missing fourteen metopes cannot be examined directly for possible clues. What remains of metope S 16 is still obscure, and the only posi-

---

Trojans and Greeks in terms of attire or weapons, contrary to practices in South Italian vases, and also to Attic renderings of Persians.

[10] This is actually suggested by T. Holscher, *Jdl* 89 (1974) 80 and 87, who sees political implications added to myths after the end of the Sixth century. J. Boardman has written several articles (e.g., *RA* 1972, 57-72; *JHS* 95 [1975] 1-12) on the political meaning of some Archaic representations. To the contrary Moret, *L'Ilioupersis*, 297, assumes that allegorical understanding of myths was limited to philosophers and did not extend to Fifth century representations.

[11] In the new spiritual climate of the Fifth century one may even wonder whether the message of the Parthenonian Ilioupersis was not already one of human concern and admonition, as—later—in Euripides' play *The Trojan Women*, written after the Athenian atrocities on Melos (416 B.C.). Indeed, to the Greeks the Trojan events were history rather than myth, although part of the remote past, and certainly as historical as Theseus, whose bones could be recovered by Kimon. It is therefore difficult for us to draw lines between pure myths and events which the Greeks themselves might have considered historical. That the escape of Aineias should be depicted in the Parthenon cycle (if N 28 is correctly interpreted) may then seem a reminder to the Athenians about the pains of exile and the founding of new states. Certainly the message seems both sim-

pler and more complex than traditionally believed. Peter von Blanckenhagen has theorized that, to some people at least, the temple and its cult image conveyed the supreme indifference of the gods toward man, and that only the monstrous Centaurs, in their interaction with the Lapiths, showed some "humane" feelings (for a summary of these unpublished lectures, see *Die Interpretation in der Altertumswissenschaft*, Fifth Congress of the Fédération Internationale des Associations d'Etudes Classiques, Bonn 1971, p. 111). In his extensive discussion of the theme in *L'Ilioupersis*, Moret has pointed out that in traditional iconography the emphasis was placed not on the fighting but on the killing of women and children and on key scenes such as the Murder of Priam and the Rape of Kassandra (pp. 53-55). According to his statistics, moreover, the subject enjoyed its greatest popularity on Attic vases between 500 and 450 B.C. After that date, only two examples of the subject are extant (p. 54) despite the fact that the Parthenon metopes could have provided renewed impetus for the iconography. To Polygnotos' originality in depicting the subject in the Knidian Lesche Moret ascribes the fact that the painting seems to have had so little influence on vases (p. 59). In either case, it seems surprising that vase painters should have virtually abandoned the subject at a time when victory over Persia and the existence of two major monuments should have promoted an even greater exploitation of the theme.

tive statement that can be made is that the struggle—if struggle it is—takes place between two human beings, not between a Lapith and a centaur. Although recent attempts have been made to explain the intrusive subject, none of them is entirely convincing. To visualize the scene as a flashback to the myth of Ixion and Nephele, which stood at the origin of the centaurs and the ancestry of Peirithoos, seems peculiar in a Classical context and more appropriate to oral narrative or to modern film.[12] By contrast, the intrusive centaurs that early drawings had attributed to the North metopes, thus supporting the theory of interpolated subjects on both long sides, have now been convincingly explained away as an antiquarian misunderstanding and repetition of some metopes from the South, so that the unity of subject matter for the North cycle cannot be questioned on their basis.

Composition

Stylistic comments should start with composition. Each side presents a different arrangement, but in all cases, as far as we can see, the architectural frame is not so much ignored as unutilized. One may recall the difference with Olympia, where Kerberos emerged from behind the triglyphs, Herakles (in the Augian Stables myth) seemed to pry them loose and, together with Athena (in the Atlas metope), appeared to support the roof. In the Parthenon, by and large, all figures stand well within the center of the panel, and only occasionally does some detail of the composition overlap the upper fascia (e.g., W 1).[13] More frequently (e.g., E 1, S 28) the relief is so high that the figures rest on the epistyle, vaguely anticipating the evasion from sculptural space of the Pergamon Gigantomachy, but some details, those farther from the viewer, may be barely raised over the background plane and would have been visible only through the enhancement of paint. Usually action is confined to the single panel, with the total series needed to get the sense of the theme; however, individual metopes could be eliminated, at least from W and S, without affecting com-

[12] The theory of the genealogical flashback is by E. Simon, *JdI* 90 (1975) 100-120. It has since been criticized by J. Dörig, *MusHelv* 35 (1978) 221-32, who proposes instead to see in these metopes not a unified subject but several dramas of royal families alluding to Athenian relationships with Thrace, Thessaly, and Lemnos. Specifically, he compares the pensive woman on S 19 with the Prokne by Alkamenes, which he considers an original, carved by a Lemnian as illustration of a Lemnian myth. A further response to Simon has been given by E. B. Harrison, who would interpret the interpolated myths as the subject of the song by the musician on S 17. Thus metopes S 17-20 would still belong to the cycle of Peirithoos' wedding feast, metopes 13-16 would be two blood crimes rather than one: Boutes raping Koronis in the presence of the young Dionysos (S 13-14) and Ixion killing a young relative while Helios in his chariot witnesses the deed, as already suggested by Simon. A different theory is proposed by M. Robertson, who does not believe that S 16 represents a fight, and would like to read in the reliefs the story of Daidalos in Athens (S 13-14), in flight (15-16) and in Crete (17-18). The two remaining metopes (19-20) should also belong to the same cycle but their interpretation is more problematic. For Harrison's and Robertson's theories see *Studies von Blanckenhagen*, 91-98 and 78-87, respectively.

[13] To be sure, when the metopes were seen from ground level in their pristine state, almost all heads would have given the impression of overlapping the upper fascia because of the angle of vision. Weapons and other objects added in metal may have overlapped the triglyphs. However, J. Hurwit (*AJA* 81 [1977] 1-30, and especially 12-13) gives a different reading. According to him, "no other series . . . displays so effective and conscious a denial of all limits and constraints." Yet his basic point, that the Parthenon metopes evade their frame, does not contradict my statement that they leave it unutilized. A possible exception may be E 14, where the chariot emerges from the base line.

prehension. In a few cases (E 11-12, N 24-25) the action seems to extend across the triglyph, but never to involve more than two panels.

In the combat scenes, the hair-pulling motif, which had already appeared at Olympia, occurs at least once (W 14) as part of a popular trend that will continue for centuries.[14] Figures on horseback loom victorious over their unmounted opponents, and thus compositional lines alone seem to give the upper hand to the centaurs, who are perennial riders by nature. Through his analysis of holes for metal attachments, Brommer has demonstrated that some centaurs may be in more dangerous situations than it now appears, since weapons have corroded away. Yet no centaur was shown dead while at least one Lapith is positively represented as lifeless (S 28).[15]

This is one of the most interesting metopes for several reasons. In its present damaged state, its triumphant message is nonetheless conveyed by the animal skin with its powerful paws and grinning mouth pointing downward toward the defeated youth. More than stomping on the victim, the centaur seems to be prancing with joy, while parts of the hide-mantle radiate behind him to indicate motion. The skin itself is rendered with remarkable skill in suggesting the arm beneath it, fist wrapped and pulling forward, thus creating tension lines. The dead Lapith lies over his left arm, still partly covered by the mantle, and the supporting left shoulder makes the body arch, so that it is fully visible from below. This same position, unnatural at eye level, occurs in the two fallen figures on the East frieze of the Hephaisteion and is often used for corpses in architectural sculpture, obviously for optical reasons. The centaur's tail looks unnatural and was perhaps recut in antiquity. Several metopes seem in fact to have been retouched in later times, perhaps during the Antonine period when some of the pedimental statues were copied and probably even replaced or repaired. The square outline of the break on the man's neck makes me wonder whether a beard was represented, but this would be unusual. Indeed, one marvels at the youth of all Lapiths, since men must have been present at the wedding feast as well. Probably human youth was emphasized—regardless of plausibility—as a means of contrast with the centaurs, who are all shown fairly old, some of them to the point of caricature.

Composition utilizes many motifs familiar from previous periods, for instance that of the flying leap (S 3,[16] perhaps also S 2), the crossing diagonals (S 27), and the pyramidal schema which balances opposing forces (e.g., S 1, S 26). Outlines convey fighting but execution varies so that S 31 is almost a ballet figure rather than a death struggle,[17] and the

---

[14] For a lengthy discussion of this motif, from Geometric times onward, see Moret, *L'Ilioupersis*, 193-205 and especially 203. Although vases illustrate the action at least as early as the Eighth century, the earliest monumental example seems to be the Amazon's metope from Temple E at Selinus.

[15] Perhaps the depiction of a dead centaur was avoided because of the inevitable but difficult foreshortening required by the pose. The Bassai frieze, which attempted the feat, produced a very pictorial, but also peculiar, figure. The result of this technical difficulty is, however, that the centaurs are not shown truly defeated, and at best, compositions convey a stalemate situation between man and monster;

only the centaur on S 2 seems to have lost the battle.

[16] The Lapith in S 3 looks like Superman, an anachronistic comment that is meant to emphasize the effectiveness, hence the continuity, of certain patterns down to our times. The same could be said of the man in S 7; by contrast, the centaur opposing him is poorly rendered: his back curves almost to the point of deformity, since torsion is not well conveyed, and his head sits strangely over his shoulders.

[17] It has been pointed out to me that the peculiar tiptoe position and bent left knee of the Lapith in S 31 are required by the raised right leg pressing against the centaur's chest, and the same comment

centaur in S 30 looks more patronizing than threatening. The most daring composition seems that of S 9, where the centaur lifts the left leg of a Lapith, who has lost his balance by falling backward over a large vessel lying on the ground. The Lapith, though obviously in midair, tries to retaliate by jabbing his left thumb into the centaur's eye. The momentary pose of both combatants and the twirling motion suggested by the centaur's action recall the violent and freer scenes of the Hephaisteion metopes, especially that of Theseus and Skiron, as Brommer also noted.

Drapery is turned into a device. In several places it fills a rather empty metope (e.g., W 1), in others it creates a textural, certainly a chromatic, backdrop for a naked body, such as the marvelously theatrical mantle of the Lapith in S 27. That the garment could not possibly drape in such graceful catenaries without slipping through its own weight is not immediately obvious, and second consideration may decide that the rendering is needed to suggest the split-second timing of the pose.

So little can be seen of the metopes on the other three sides that few comments can be made. Brommer has suggested that a free hand was given the sculptors of the West series, and that the monotonous alternation of figures on foot with figures on horseback is the result of limited oral directives from the main master. A better state of preservation might have elicited more favorable judgment. The question should here be raised nonetheless as to what form assignments took for the various metopes. As already remarked for the South panels, compositional lines often seem effective even when the actual carving fails to convey struggle. Could the individual stone carvers have been given outline sketches that they were free to flesh out according to their own ability? That considerable freedom for personal expression was allowed is shown by the differences in the rendering of the centaurs, for whom no true model could be found in nature: some have long hair, some short hair; some have a masklike ugliness, while others look human and almost compassionate; some have a smooth transition from human torso to equine rump, while others have a peculiar projection at the juncture, which cannot be an exaggeration of withers but resembles the hump of zebu cows.[18] On the other hand, some poses are virtually duplicated in different contexts, with a monotony that a single designer might have avoided.

The metopes of the East façade seem by far the most pictorial in character, especially E 6, with its enormous rock on which a figure kneels, while his opponent seems to be framed by the opening of a cave. If this is indeed Poseidon, he cannot be throwing Nisyros at his enemy, at the most he could be pushing it against him; Brommer leaves the identification open and wants instead to recognize Poseidon in E 14. This last metope too has pic-

---

applies in reverse to S 26. Yet realism is here at the expense of aesthetic validity, since greater balance and struggle would have been conveyed by a straight weight leg or even by a more diagonal stance. Conversely, the position of the centaurs looks plausible, yet no horse could really support itself as shown on these metopes. Note, by contrast, how much more effectively the same motif has been handled in S 1, because of the more inclined and torsional pose of the Lapith. On the other hand the dancelike pose with bent knee has an old history, since it appears in the early Sixth century on a shield strap from

Olympia (K. Schefold, *Frühgriechische Sagenbilder* [Munich 1964] pl. 80).

[18] In one centaur (S 10) the hump has hair, as if representing the termination of an otherwise invisible mane. Note that many of the Bassai frieze centaurs have a similar rendering, probably inspired by the Parthenon (for comments on the hair motif see B. Shefton, *Hesperia* 31 [1962] 339-40 n. 43). It is impossible to tell at present how the centaurs' bodies were painted, but certainly the animal parts would have had the same coloring as natural horses. See now V. Bruno, *AJA* 85 (1981) 1-11.

torial elements: the fish carved against the chariot, near the wheel axle, and the figures emerging from what must obviously have been meant as the sea surface, a motif that recurs on the East pediment. The surprising metope with Dionysos and the panther (E 2)[19] would have been even more unusual in its original state, with a metal snake fastened to the background. Athena being crowned by a hovering Nike in her moment of victory (E 4) is another pictorial touch (which will provide inspiration for many Roman historical reliefs), and so is Eros (E 11) shooting into the distance, across the triglyph, to protect his mother.[20]

Style

From the standpoint of style, let us begin by isolating the traits that have often been considered Severe: the impressionistic rendering of the hair on the Lapiths and on the puzzling humans of S 16; the low foreheads; the heavily-lidded eyes; the pronounced jaw lines; the use of the drill, or at least of rounded forms, in some hair renderings;[21] the inclusion of veins (e.g., S 7). Drapery appears doughy and in places collapses inorganically when it meets an obstacle: for instance, the vase in S 9 or the ground in W 14.[22] Male anatomy appears built up in sections, especially in the area of the torso, and very seldom does musculature reflect strain. In some figures the pubic hair has the pointed triangular shape that recalls late Archaic renderings (e.g., S 26). Expressions are still rendered, and with the same linear devices employed on the Olympia pediments: furrowed brows, open mouths, wrinkled noses and dilated nostrils. But many features are definitely Classical.

Drapery seems to run the gamut from pure Severe texture and behavior to the most elaborate and rich Fifth century style. We have already mentioned the Severe plasticity of the garment in W 14: note also its evenly spaced ridges. Eye folds and Archaic zigzags occur, for instance, in the mantle of S 26. The erratic behavior of cloth in S 10 and S 8 shows that their carvers had not yet mastered the modeling line. The woman's right leg on S 10 is positively flattened, rather than brought out by the pattern of folds. Somewhat comparable is also the rendering of the chlamys over the right arm of the Lapith in S 2. Contrast S 7, where somewhat angular catenaries impart a sense of depth and volume and, less effective, a similar attempt in S 9.

The central female figure in S 20 wears a peplos Olympia-fashion: short, squarish, and rather flat overfold, short kolpos that runs horizontally parallel to the waist line with no

[19] A late Archaic prototype for this composition has now been suggested by W. Fuchs in a three-figure metope from the Temple of Apollo on Aigina: *Boreas* 1 (1978) 26-27.

[20] If Eros is correctly identified in E 11, he is smaller than the other deities but larger than a child. He also appears as a youth on the East frieze, next to Aphrodite, where the identification cannot be doubted. On the other hand, his size is diminutive in N 25, where he perches on Aphrodite's shoulder. A distinction was probably intended between Eros as a god in his own right and the *effects* of Eros, conceived almost like *eidola* or souls. On vases several small Erotes can in fact be shown fluttering around to suggest an aura of love.

[21] Maybe here, as at Olympia, hair that was

painted black or blond/red on youthful figures could be rendered impressionistically as a smooth surface, while white hair, as a sign of old age, needed the chiaroscuro punctuation created by drill holes to be properly discernible from a distance.

[22] By contrast, note the rendering on S 27. The Lapith's mantle is deflected by the centaur's torso, but the edge waves and wreathes instead of collapsing flat under its own weight. That some masters did not really know what to do with drapery alone, away from the supporting human body, is also shown by the peculiar massing of the mantle under the right foot of the Lapith on S 8. The rendering is so ineffective that what should be cloth looks instead like a sponge or a rock; cf. Brommer, *Metopen*, pls. 190, 192:3.

curve to suggest the roundness of the stomach. By contrast S 17 has a most sophisticated rendering of a thin garment (fig. 1): the deep and narrow valleys separating the high ridges are further articulated by incision or by very thin folds at their bottom; the ridges themselves are flattened and almost concave, each split further by more than one diagonal channel, with a resultant twisting effect. This is a fractioning and belaboring of surface that effectively conveys fine texture. The thinness of some ridges almost equals that of the incisions. We may see here the beginning, or at least a form, of the so-called ribbon drapery.

"Scratched drapery" is perhaps a more accurate definition for the rendering on the female figure of S 29. Its sculptor has adopted the same compositional principles, but the result is too fractioned, so that the garment seems to hang in shreds from her right shoulder and the engraving tool has penetrated, as if wounding, into her thigh. Somewhat the same rendering, though perhaps more skillfully executed, occurs on the highly fragmentary S 19 (fig. 2); whatever is preserved of the female figure shows a thin, ribbonlike chiton with short apoptygma and deep pouch overlapping a heavy mantle worn doubled at the waist so that it forms a short triangular apron. This way of wearing the mantle is certainly "Classical," and so is its texture, with sharp edges to pouches and folds, which have almost entirely lost the doughiness of the Severe style. In terms of stylistic iconography this is perhaps the most important among the Parthenon metopes.

One of the most admired is the best preserved panel from the North side (N 32) (figs. 3-5), and certainly the foamy richness of its garments attests to superior carving techniques. But in terms of stylistic development this rendering is not quite as advanced as that of S 17, S 19, and perhaps even the less skillful but more "Classical" S 29. The costume of the seated Hera (?) is like that of S 19, and texture is clearly differentiated from chiton to himation. However, the latter is still somewhat doughy, the triangular overfold behaves peculiarly over the left hip and manages to hide rather than to convey the contour of the body, perhaps because of the difficulty of the pose. The tip of the mantle falling from the left shoulder is carefully cut as if to avoid symmetrical zigzags, but its pattern is not far from Archaic prototypes like Antenor's kore. Even the chiton folds betray uncertainty over the breasts and at the neckline. As for the standing figure, the basic pattern of her belted peplos has not progressed far from that of Angelitos' Athena, with its lack of a kolpos at the belt and a straight hem to the overfold. Only the saillike mantle, so cleverly carved away from the background, adds vivacity to the whole, as well as the slightly provocative detail of the naked leg and torso showing on the right side. Indeed it is remarkable how daring the Parthenon metopes are in revealing the female body. The disarray of several figures on the South metopes is justified by their struggle with the centaurs, a solution for which the Olympia pediment had prepared the way; even so, the totally bare breasts of S 21 are surprising, and Carrey's drawing attests that no chiton was indicated in paint, at least by 1674.

It may be coincidence, but the presence of selvage on mantles always seems to go with the more advanced renderings; its absence in N 32 may confirm our analysis of its style. The conception of that billowing mantle is, however, quite advanced, certainly more successful than any of the flying drapery preserved elsewhere on the metopes. Yet one fragment may suggest an even more daring conception in the metope with the descending Selene, N 29. The peculiar projection in the upper right corner of the panel has been interpreted as a moon crescent on close analogy with vase painting, but the explanation seems unlikely because the stone appears to thicken at one end. Could it represent the tip of a flying mantle, worn scarflike around Selene's arms? Her right hand probably held up one end of such mantle, her left presumably held the reins, but the drapery could have been wrapped around the forearm and flung against the background, where its tip still adheres. If this were so, here would begin a rendering that found much favor in later times and was consistently employed by the Romans to indicate celestial deities.

Another flying mantle, that of the rider on W 1, shows one more motif with a Classical future: the so-called omega fold. It is formed by a wide pleat in the center of the cloth: at the hem its edges curve and bend under, to touch a short distance below the bottom of the pleat itself. The resultant pattern resembles a capital omega, hence the nickname. The motif was well known in the Archaic period, when it occurred usually at the center of a cascade of zigzags on either side (the swallow-tail motif). In the Severe period the omega fold began to appear alone, as a corollary to the modeling line, and the Fifth century seems to continue the trend, not only as a convenient way to suggest softness and layering of cloth but also as an interesting decorative pattern. As the flamboyant traits of the period increase, omega folds may appear illogically divorced from drapery lines, and the elaboration of their curves makes them resemble the lenses of a binocular, hence another popular nickname. To grasp the difference between the early and the advanced Classical style, compare the flying mantle of W 1 with that of Dexileos on his famous gravestone which, since he died in 394, is chronologically close to the end of the previous century. In Dexileos' mantle there are two such omega folds, and the pleats from which they originate point downward, so that the motif is visible from its most decorative angle. While the Parthenon cloak looks heavy and leathery, stretching out horizontally behind the rider, on the stele the garment curls upward gracefully; its folds are so full that they show nicks and bends like a lead pipe. The Parthenon mantle is both a hieroglyph for speed and a functional item of clothing; Dexileos' chlamys flutters illogically as if it were both light and heavy, and serves an almost purely decorative purpose.

The same stylistic diversity observed in the drapery of the Parthenon metopes has been pointed out in the rendering of the centaurs. A few details of anatomy may receive brief comment.

In both centaurs and Lapiths great attention is paid to the area of the abdomen and the rib cage. In a few instances the male figure is shown as if holding his breath, so that a peculiar horizontal accent forms midway between pectorals and navel (e.g., S 6, S 8, S 27). As already mentioned, some torsos appear built up in sections and thus recall the Apollo from the West pediment at Olympia, but the hip muscles and digitations are more pronounced. Male bodies are lean and youthful, and therefore, when poorly executed, dry. Women, by contrast, are monumental, far too powerful for the centaurs who struggle with them (S 10, S 12), and only one seems small enough to be lifted and carried away (S 29); this peculiar discrepancy may derive from the sculptor's inability to convey a woman's body (although this is rather a question of size than of rendering), or from his latent sense of humor. Centaurs are usually muscular and physically more mature than the Lapiths, with the possible exception of that in S 6, who shows no abdominal detailing but only a few engraved lines around the navel. Is the sculptor trying to suggest a rounded belly? Wrinkles and lines at the waist appear also on lean Lapiths, and not always because of their poses, so we may have here a stylistic mannerism, with a possible ancestry in Myron's Diskobolos.

Among all Parthenon metopes the most famous is S 1 (fig. 6), which therefore needs no description. However, it may bear repeating, in this context, that the most striking element of style is the fact that the sculptor has been willing to hide part of the centaur's face, thus making the monster all the more formidable in the viewer's imagination. Earlier monuments had also attempted comparable renderings: for instance, Herakles the Archer from the East Pediment at Aegina, but there the face is complete and only the angle of vision masks it. In S 1 the face melts into the background when seen from the side, and it was obviously not thought out in its entirety, a most unusual approach for the Classical period. It is difficult to portray a centaur from the back, given his dual nature as man and horse; this metope, the only one to attempt it, succeeds in presenting a most powerful, if seemingly short-waisted, creature in a convincing though superficial penetration of background space. Even now that Brommer has shown how precarious the Centaur's stranglehold is, with a long skewer penetrating his groin, we cannot fail to gasp with the limp Lapith, doubting that his rubbery (and overlong) fingers can release the grasp. The long hanging mantle with its downward pull emphasizes the helplessness of the youth and forecasts his fall, once the vise opens. Yet the youth's face is virtually unmarked by his predicament, and it is his pose that elicits our response.

THE HEPHAISTEION METOPES

Because of the unusual wealth of carved metopes on the Parthenon, the more limited number on the Hephaisteion (ten on the East façade and four on each of the long sides) has often prompted some justification. It has also been suggested that the order of the reliefs as it now appears on the building is not that originally planned by the master, but represents a second-best solution adopted when lack of funds and time demanded a speedy completion of the building, with whatever carvings were already at hand being placed in the most prominent positions.[23] Finally, the date of the temple, its cult and its relationship to the Parthenon are difficult and disputed problems, which show no immediate prospect of satisfactory solution. Here only sculptural comments can be advanced, and of a rather general nature, without new supporting evidence; conclusions should be taken as tentative, more as suggestions than as answers.

The date of the temple has been based on that of pottery found to the south and west of the building together with marble chips that probably came from the temple fabric; tests in the interior and the foundations of the temple itself were made inconclusive by the great number of alterations introduced by later periods, with consequent elimination of

[23] Morgan has pointed out the peculiarity of having the Fight with Geryon occupy two of the front metopes when already the limited number of panels available resulted in a curtailment of the entire cycle of Herakles' Labors. However, the Labors were not made canonical for a long time, even after the strong influence of Olympia had established a fixed number of twelve. Note, for instance, that according to Pausanias (9.11.4), Praxiteles decorated the pediment of the Herakleion at Thebes with "most of Herakles' twelve labors" although the Stymphalian Birds and the Cleaning of the Augian Stables were omitted and the Wrestle with Antaios was included instead. It has also been suggested that only nine Labors were shown on the Athenian temple in order to balance the nine deeds of Theseus: eight on the side metopes and one on the East frieze (*Agora Guide*, 49).

stratigraphy and evidence. The diagnostic pottery has been dated no later than ca. 450 B.C., and thus it is generally assumed that work on the temple began at that time or shortly thereafter.[24] It has however been pointed out that while all moldings up to and including the horizontal cornice are in keeping with such a date, the profiles of raking cornice and sima appear to be at least twenty-five years later or more, thus suggesting different phases of construction. Those scholars who accept this chronological dichotomy also tend to assign different dates to the sculptural decoration of the building, but by and large all agree that the metopes are earlier in style than the friezes; as for the pedimental statues, revisions have been made to some earlier attributions, and it is now agreed that all sculptural decoration on the building was in Parian marble. The two continuous friezes will be treated in a later chapter, but it is important to establish here their relationship to the metopes in terms of spatial arrangement. The stylistic position of the metopes should also be determined vis-à-vis the Parthenon.

Rather than pointing out how few the Hephaisteion metopes are in comparison with the Akropolis temple, we should stress how remarkable it is to have carved metopes at all, in Athens and elsewhere. The Hephaisteion has been convincingly grouped with three other Attic temples which clearly betray the same architectural style. In all four buildings the plan places special emphasis on the front pteron and its relationship to the pronaos, but only the Hephaisteion metopes are sculptured.[25] Other Doric structures erected at this time have plain metopes: the Propylaia, the Telesterion at Eleusis, the Temple of the Athenians at Delos, to mention only Attic buildings. Elsewhere in the Greek world, none of the many Sicilian and South Italian temples erected at this time has carved panels, in an area where they seem earlier to have been most at home.[26] The few instances of relief metopes known

[24] Note that Dinsmoor's dating of the Hephaisteion to 449-444 was based largely on a mathematical division of the span 449-432 for the four temples by him attributed to the same architect. The lower date was reached on the grounds that the Rhamnous temple was left unfinished, therefore in the same state as the Propylaia on the Akropolis and perhaps for the same reason (war and plague). These speculations were then supported with astronomical calculations to determine the very day of the temple foundation. Despinis (55-61; 68-70 and passim) has now suggested that the Rhamnous temple, after a construction phase from 436 to 431 (Dinsmoor's dates) and an interruption, was then completed around 423 and later, since its akroterion is to be placed ca. 420-410. Yet he dates the cult statue ca. 430, but its base after 423.

[25] It has been suggested (A. J. Dinsmoor, *Rhamnous* [Keramos Guides 1972] 11-12; W. B. Dinsmoor, *Hesperia* 30 [1961] 195-203) that the façade metopes of the temple at Rhamnous were (or at least were meant to be) carved, because they consist of thin slabs rather than thick blocks like those on the other three sides. But no plausible candidates have yet been found for the spot. If the architect had indeed planned to use sculptured metopes and then desisted, we might have one more indication

of his reluctance to adopt relief panels, perhaps in accordance with general taste. The unfinished state of the temple may also account for this omission. For the suggestion of carved metopes on the Temple of Ares see now K. Stähler, *Boreas* 2 (1979) 185-88, pl. 17; G. Despinis, *Stele* (Athens 1980) 491-96.

[26] Four badly defaced panels and two attributed fragments have been considered repairs and replacements for some of the carved metopes of the second (late Archaic) Temple of Hera at Foce del Sele. However, their date remains uncertain; it had first been given as ca. 400, but the excavators modified their theory after more extensive study of the sculpture from that area, and finally published a suggestion that at least one of these replacements should be dated to the mid-Fourth century. Even if the earlier chronology were correct, statistically these metopes are unimportant, since they represent a repair to a preexisting series and therefore cannot reflect either a continuous or a renewed interest in this form of architectural sculpture. See *NSc* 1937, 350-54, pl. 14 and fig. 96 on p. 353; *EAA*, s.v. Silaris; *Heraion alla Foce del Sele* vol. 1 (Rome 1951) 187-90. Note that Lippold, *Handbuch*, 211 n. 13, records one metope as coming from Paestum, but his reference to the *NSc* volume makes it clear that Foce del Sele is intended.

at present seem to occur at the very end of the Fifth century, if not already in the Fourth,[27] and remain remarkable for their isolation, since the pattern of largely uncarved metopes continues in later times. The temples in question are that of Apollo at Bassai (relief metopes only over the porches) and that of Hera at the Argive Heraion (probably from both façades, though the evidence is controversial). To a little-known temple near Amphipolis in Thrace two metopes can be attributed, one found in situ and another in Rome that corresponds to the first in dimensions and style. Finally, the Villa Albani in Rome houses one additional metope which has not been conclusively assigned to a known building. To be sure, it is the occurrence of carved metopes, not the actual preserved number, that counts, but only a total of four structures can be named, regardless of other considerations.

More significant is perhaps the fact that *no Doric temple* built in Athens or Attica—except for the Parthenon and the Hephaisteion—ever had carved (narrative) metopes, to my knowledge. Were we to extend our search elsewhere, the entire Fourth century only adds the carved metopes of the Tholos at Delphi and those over the porches of the Temple of Athena Alea at Tegea; for the Hellenistic period only those of the Athenaion at Ilion come readily to mind.[28] By and large it looks as if carved metopes were a feature of the Archaic period, and with a limited distribution at that; Olympia and Athens produced two spectacular examples in the Fifth century and therefore a few other temples followed suit, but the practice was never widespread; by the Fourth century new areas and forms of decoration were found for the Doric order, and the carved metope receded to a mere repetition of patterns (like the rosettes of the tholos at Epidauros, the boukrania and tripods of the Hellenistic proskenion at Delos, or the boukrania and stylized poppy flowers of the Lesser Propylaia at Eleusis), shifted to funerary structures (like the Belevi Mausoleum or the Lefkadia Tomb), or disappeared entirely. It is against this general background that the Hephaisteion metopes should be examined.

It would then seem reasonable to assume that the Parthenon influenced the Hephaisteion rather than vice versa. Excavation of the temple's foundations has shown that the alignment of the pronaos antae with the third column of the peristyle on the sides was planned from the beginning; we can therefore infer that emphasis on the front pteroma was a basic feature of the plan, but we have no way of knowing whether carved metopes were originally intended, as well as a carved frieze. Since the architect found different solutions in his buildings elsewhere, one may justifiably suggest that carved metopes were for him the exception rather than the rule, especially in the light of the background sketched above. Independent development of the two structures could be argued, but since the Parthenon's proportions and internal arrangement can be shown to have influenced the Hephaisteion architect, as postulated on the basis of modifications to the setting of cross-walls and the

---

[27] An earlier example, from Crete, may conversely still belong to the Severe period: see Appendix 2:1. Note the relief of a horse to left, probably from a quadriga, in the Delphi museum, labeled "late Fifth Century B.C. metope."

[28] One more Hellenistic metope (a Centauromachy) occurs on Thera: F. Hiller von Gaertringen, *Thera* 3 (Berlin 1904) 121 and fig. 96. Delos has some badly effaced metopes from the Monument of the Bulls: J. Marcadé, *BCH* 75 (1951) 55 n. 4; latest discussion of the monument, J. Coupry, *Etudes Deliennes* (*BCH* suppl. 1, 1973) 147-56. The so-called Temple of Peace in the Forum of Paestum is now considered the Capitolium of the Roman colony founded in 273 B.C. within the Lucanian city, so that its carved metopes can hardly be counted among the Greek examples.

addition of interior supports, it is equally possible that the Parthenon's carved metopes affected architectural elements which came, after all, rather late in the building sequence.[29]

If this theory is correct, the Hephaisteion metopes should reflect a sculptural style no earlier than 447 and preferably later, even after 438. It is obviously impossible to date sculpture with such precision, especially in its present weathered and damaged conditions and without direct observation. On the basis of photographs, however, the following can be stated (figs. 7-10).

In terms of subject matter, the Hephaisteion metopes represent a return to Archaic or Severe prototypes: a series of episodes distinct in time and therefore conveniently isolated by the triglyphs, with the recurrence of the same hero providing the only link between panels.[30] By contrast, the Parthenon had established a sort of bird's-eye view over events occurring simultaneously and seen as if through a series of windows opening onto the same scene.[31]

Compositionally, the Hephaisteion metopes rely on the same patterns employed by the Parthenon and, earlier, by the Athenian Treasury: the Olympia discoveries seem to be bypassed or ignored. In their present state the metopes show a surprising amount of empty background, hardly more crowded even when the sculptures were intact. The figures are placed well in the center of the panel and the architectural frame is largely ignored. The relief is very high with some parts fully in the round (fig. 7). A few details suggest landscape but seem less pictorial than in the Parthenon and function largely as props for the action and identification for the figures: thus Kerberos has its own rock from which to emerge and Sinis his tree. But most striking in these metopes are the violent poses, more appropriate to painting than to sculpture. Animals are small, and the Marathon Bull (fig. 8) is nowhere near as powerful as the surging beast of the Olympia metope; the Krommyon Sow looks almost like a begging pet. The human opponents, however, struggle and the Minotaur (fig. 9) fights back, so that the outcome of the contest is left in balance, settled only in the viewer's mind. Movement is conveyed through poses rather than through drapery: a Severe trait. Yet some of the action is surprising for any period, with figures upside down or in revolving motion. Bodies are lean, hard, and predominantly naked with only an occasional mantle. Against that empty background the total effect is stark and sober.

Stylistic details are hard to pinpoint. Since there is so little drapery, a proper analysis of folds is impossible. The Athena on the panel with Herakles bringing back the Apples of the Hesperides wears a peplos that looks uncompromisingly Severe in its straight horizontal

---

[29] Theoretically, but less probably, the influence may also have come from Delphi. In either case, however, if our suggestion corresponds to facts, it would seem as if the architect, not the sculptor, had the final say on the Hephaisteion program. No major sculptural name is associated with the building by the literary sources, regardless of its identification. Alkamenes is thought to have made the cult statues of Athena Hephaistia and Hephaistos, but the building accounts date them to 421-415, therefore well after the initial planning for the Hephaisteion, and Harrison has recently argued that the statues did not stand in that building (*AJA* 81 [1977] 137-39, 422-26). As for the temple, which she assigns to Artemis Eukleia, she recognizes two periods of construction and places the metopes (and perhaps also the west pediment) in the 450s, before the Parthenon metopes. She dates the two friezes (and possibly the East Pediment and the akroteria) between the Parthenon frieze and the Nike Temple frieze, around 430: *Final Programme*, 65.

[30] The only exception to this rule is the Geryonomachy stretching over two metopes of the façade: see above, n. 23.

[31] I am not convinced that a temporal progression may have been shown in the North metopes of the Parthenon, as some scholars claim (summaries in Brommer, *Metopen*, 216-17).

and vertical accents, but no more so than that of the female figure on the Parthenon S 20. In the metope with the Marathon Bull, Theseus' mantle has a definite selvage, and it forms V-folds rather than catenaries in the panel with the Krommyon Sow. Herakles' pose, in handing the Apples to Athena, is chiastic and Polykleitan, and the abdominal wrinkles in the Minotaur and other figures resemble those on the Parthenon metopes. Heads are badly damaged or entirely missing; hair, where preserved, seems to be treated impressionistically as a smooth calotte, but the same treatment occurs in the Lapiths of the Parthenon. The head of an old man, which had been attributed to Eurystheus in the metope of Herakles and the Boar, has now been reassigned to the pediments, which may therefore imply an even later date despite its resemblance to the Olympia seer. All in all, nothing seems to preclude a date contemporary with the Parthenon metopes or even slightly later.

Two final comments. As already mentioned, and despite the similarity in subject matter, the Hephaisteion metopes are remarkably different from those at Olympia, even if still somewhat Severe in style. Particularly noticeable is the difference in the moment chosen, which at Olympia is often just before or just after a deed, while in Athens it is usually in the midst of the action, with the outcome still somewhat in balance (fig. 10). Characterization is minimal, and Theseus seems to have the short hair of an athlete, not the rolled up coiffure of a hero, which may also be a chronological indication. Herakles wears the lion skin, which was so conspicuously absent at Olympia, but Athena has no aegis and was probably identifiable only through spear and context; at some point she had in fact been mistaken for one of the Hesperides.[32]

The second comment concerns the architectural arrangement. Dinsmoor's hypothesis still seems the best: the architect wanted to emphasize the front pteroma and therefore enclosed it in a three-sided box of carved metopes on the exterior, with the continuous frieze forming the fourth side on the interior. At Sounion he chose to emphasize only the internal space by carrying a continuous carved frieze around all four sides of the front pteroma, therefore as a backer for the plain metopes of the Doric frieze on the exterior. Why the architect was so concerned with that specific area, especially at Sounion, where no specific angle of vision from below (as for the Hephaisteion) can be established, is now all but impossible to fathom. The very fact that in the Hephaisteion he considered the inclusion of a continuous frieze from the beginning (as shown by the foundations) may imply that he was familiar with the projected Parthenon frieze, or that he was inspired by the so-called Peisistratid Temple of the late Sixth century, if indeed, as I believe, that building possessed such a sculptured feature.

OTHER METOPES

Next in time comes the metope in the Villa Albani in Rome, which has not yet been convincingly attributed to any building (fig. 11). It had once been suggested that it belonged to the Temple at Rhamnous, but measurements proved it too small. Its style

[32] Fifth century architectural sculpture is not well enough preserved to allow safe generalizations, but by and large personages (on metopes, friezes, and pediments) seem to be characterized by their personal ethos rather than by the external attributes so well liked during the Archaic period. Were it truly so, this fact would be in marked contrast with the plethora of symbolic attributes given to Classical cult statues, as mentioned in the literary sources.

is said to be Attic, but the rounded faces of the two goddesses remind me of the Bassai frieze, and their drapery could be Boeotian. That the marble seems to be Pentelic may speak in support of an Attic provenience, but identification of marbles is notoriously dangerous.

The metope is filled by two large female figures wearing two different versions of the peplos; one woman is in active motion to the left while the other stands still at the right-hand margin. The active figure is identifiable as Artemis, because she is extracting an arrow from the quiver over her shoulder and traces of a metal bow appear in her left hand. By association, the quieter goddess must be her mother, Leto. The metope has been dated to ca. 420, and indeed the rather conventional drapery pattern may support this chronology. Yet the resemblance with the Bassai frieze could bring the date down; in particular, the relative heaviness of the figures and the uneven rendering of their drapery makes me think of Boeotian grave stelai, or perhaps of provincial art in general. Note, for instance, the rather flat, very shallow relief of the mantles against the background, and their swirling patterns of folds, which find close echoes both in the Bassai frieze and the Dexileos stele (dated 394); yet compare with this rendering the heavy, almost columnar massing of folds over Leto's right leg. The same figure shows a peculiar system of folds between the breasts and her belt, in a mixture of tension folds and modeling lines that again seems rather advanced and also artificial enough to come after the extravagant Attic renderings of the late Fifth century. The belt is revealed in the center, but the slack of the overfold comes down steeply over both hips, yet without the richness of some Athena figures of the mid-twenties. The same contradiction is visible in the Artemis: her right leg is shown naked, emerging from her swinging skirt, which in turn has the same long S-folds that appear in Figure G (fig. 23) of the Parthenon East Pediment. But her mantle is much more lively and hints of transparent drapery are given over the breasts and the left leg. In the face, her eyes seem almost melting and slightly concave, as in Fourth century heads. All in all, the work is difficult to assess stylistically and could be as late as ca. 400.[33]

This is the date assigned to another metope in Rome, which retains the torso of a warrior fighting against a now-missing opponent. The developed body with its massive proportions has led some scholars to believe that it might be the product of a Peloponnesian school, or at least of masters under Polykleitan influence, but the discovery near Amphipolis (Thrace) of a similar metope, with the same dimensions (as large as those of the Parthenon panels) and with a closely comparable group of two fighting figures, suggests that the metope found in Rome in 1890 had been taken there from Northern Greece.[34]

The Bassai Metopes

More important are two major buildings in the Peloponnesos, the Temple of Apollo at Bassai and that of Hera at the Argive Heraion. Both series belong to highly controversial

[33] To my knowledge only F. Hiller (55 n. 120, 63, 69) has placed this metope between the Erechtheion frieze and the Delphi tholos, after the turn of the century.

[34] It would be important to know, were the connection between the two metopes assured, whether the one in Rome reached Italy during Roman times or later, through the early travelers. In the former case, we would have positive proof that the Romans looted architectural sculpture even from Doric friezes, and not only from among the more easily removable pedimental statues.

architectural structures, and debate over their chronology has been lively. The Bassai metopes, though quite fragmentary, have been discussed in several articles, and attempts have been made to reconstruct their composition and identify their style. The carved panels decorated the Doric frieze over the porches, while the outer metopes were left blank and the pediments empty. The peculiar interior plan of the temple, the possibility that the inner continuous frieze was set up twice, perhaps with considerable modification of the original sequence, and Pausanias' attribution of the construction to Iktinos, have lent credit to the theory that the temple was begun as early as ca. 450 and was continued after an interruption, perhaps around 425 or later. Recent testing in the foundations has shown that the building was intended to have its distinctive interior arrangement from the very beginning, and pottery from the foundation fill can be dated to the last quarter of the Fifth century, so that the time of construction should be lowered to that same period.

The metopes can probably be assigned to ca. 400, almost contemporary with the frieze although perhaps of better quality and closer to Attic style. They present problems of interpretation, and previous reconstructions as well as early joins can be questioned. Some figures are shown in active poses, one with castanets may be dancing. The torso of a citharode draped in an overfolded peplos with a broochlike Gorgoneion has been identified as Orpheus, but this attribute for the singer remains unparalleled and unexplained; in addition the face once attached to the head is smaller in scale and does not belong to it. The so-called Dionysos-and-Ariadne metope may also need revision: the thumb of the hand behind the woman's head appears on the left side of her neck, so that the action may be more violent than affectionate. In terms of style there are several examples of transparent drapery, "railroad tracks" folds, and the woman with castanets wears a garment which clings to her body with a thinness that belies the presence of an overfold. The edge of the latter rises and bends over with a mannerism intended to indicate clearly that the underside of the cloth is being shown and which occurs also in some figures on the frieze. This is definitely a late trait.

The Argive Heraion Metopes

The metopes from the Argive Heraion are also preserved in fragments, partly because of their high relief, and have not been intensively restudied in the light of new knowledge, together with the remains of the pedimental sculpture. The only fixed chronological point is that of the fire in 423 which destroyed the earlier Heraion, but, since another terrace was chosen for the replacement, work on a new temple could have begun before the destruction. On the other hand, the shortened plan of the new building, and details of its elevation, have prompted a dating at the very end of the Fifth or the beginning of the Fourth century. We cannot even be sure of the exact position of the relief panels. The excavators stressed that some fragments were found along the North and South sides of the temple, but Pausanias (2.17.3) mentions two epic subjects per façade ("above the columns") as if he were listing what he saw on each pediment and on the immediately underlying metopes. Even this interpretation is not certain, although it is improbable (even if not impossible) that a single pediment depicted two different myths simultaneously.[35]

---

[35] For the Labors of Herakles depicted on a single pediment by Praxiteles, see Pausanias 9.11.4. J. Mar-   cadé, *AntK* 21 (1978) 111-12, has recently argued that the outer metopes of the Delphic Tholos illus-

As a third possibility, the metopes could have decorated the entablature over the two porches.[36]

Pausanias states that one side showed the Birth of Zeus and the Gigantomachy, the other the Trojan War and the Ilioupersis. Since some fragments undoubtedly depict Amazons, perhaps the Amazonomachy *at Troy* was represented, thus explaining Pausanias' statement.[37] The Trojan War was of particular interest to the people at Argos, since it was fought by their great epic heroes, yet some obvious connection exists between the topics of the Parthenon and those of the Heraion, despite the fact that relationships between the two respective states were not particularly friendly. On a wider plane, Amazonomachy and Ilioupersis occur again together on the pediments of the Asklepieion at Epidauros (ca. 375),[38] while the Amazonomachy and the Centauromachy were carved on the Bassai frieze. It seems therefore as if the Amazonomachy had lost both its Oriental and its Attic symbolism by the early Fourth century, even if the artistic prominence of the Parthenon was the main reason influencing the choice of such subjects.[39]

Stylistically, the metopes of the Argive Heraion show at least one example of that transparent drapery virtually engraved over the figures, which is the ultimate stage of the "ribbon" style. Other renderings are equally transparent, using few folds in order to denote the twisting and straining of thin material. Bodies are clearly modeled, with garments adhering to them over large areas; breasts and stomachs are outlined by deviated folds that stem from a few prominent points. Lines are almost never straight but swirl and sway both on and off the bodies, and edges wave upwards in a variety of bizarre motifs. The preserved heads show great variety of forms, but some foreheads are triangular and eyes are deeply set at the inner corner, thus foreshadowing some trends of the advanced Fourth century.[40] The same comments apply to the relatively round and small shape of the faces, and the wavy outline of the hair on a male head. Finally, the use of the drill for speed in carving

---

trated both Amazonomachy and Centauromachy, therefore two subjects within one frieze, but the round structure may have made this arrangement feasible.

[36] This opinion has been expressed recently both by M. Robertson (397) and R. Tomlinson, *Greek Sanctuaries* (New York 1976) 92. Ch. Waldstein (*Argive Heraeum* 1 [Boston and N.Y. 1902] 147) specifically states that a number of metope fragments were found at the North and South sides and that some had crashed through the roof of the South stoa, where they "were deposited on the floor" and covered anew when the stoa was destroyed. One questions whether this reconstruction of events is plausible, or if the sculptures had been taken into the stoa intentionally at some later time.

[37] That the Ilioupersis was the subject of the (West ?) pediment is proven by a fragment in the round showing an archaistic idol encircled by a human arm, and therefore depicting either the rape of Kassandra or Helen at the Palladion. A second idol, in xoanon form, also comes from the temple. The Amazonomachy is firmly connected to the metopes by the relief technique of many fragments.

For the theory of the Amazonomachy at Troy see Karouzou, *Catalogue*, 59, no. 3500.

[38] A similar combination, Gigantomachy on the East Pediment and Ilioupersis on the West, is recorded by Diodoros (13.82) for the Olympieion at Akragas, but there the allusion could have been to the victory over the Carthaginians at Himera in 480, especially since the temple was erected by the labor of the prisoners taken in that battle.

[39] Besides the Amazonomachy on the Delphic Tholos (ca. 380), in the later Fourth century the subject occurs again, not only on the Mausoleion at Halikarnassos, therefore on the tomb of an Oriental if Hellenized ruler, but also on a funerary monument from Athens, the virtually still unpublished Kallithea tomb: *AAA* 1 (1968) 108-109; 4 (1971) 108-10.

[40] Close to renderings on the Argive metopes are some fragmentary heads with inserted eyes attributed by E. Raphtopoulou, *Deltion* 26 (1971) 264-75 and French summary on pp. 329-31. It is remarkable that such complicated technique should be used for marble sculpture in the round. Is this a trait of Lingering Severe or a Peloponnesian peculiarity?

and in detaching parts of the relief from the background may also speak for a rather advanced date. The male bodies are lean though muscular, and the best preserved one shows less fractioning of the torso than customary in Attic monuments, almost as if a younger age were depicted. Under the circumstances it is difficult to accept the claim that the influence of Polykleitos and his school is obvious in all the carvings.[41] The same suggestion has been made for the metope in Rome now known to be from near Amphipolis, and one can perhaps doubt the validity of these attributions.

SUMMARY

In synthesis, Fifth century metopes present a surprising picture, albeit one conditioned by the chance of the finds and unbalanced by the Parthenon. On the one hand, they provide an almost textbook demonstration of the development of Classical style, moving from Severe traits to ever-increasing understanding of modeling and motion lines. On the other hand, they appear unusual and mostly limited to the Parthenon and its imitators. Bassai, given also the location and the originality of the yet undetermined subject, may have used carved metopes in the Olympia tradition, but the Argive Heraion, in its selection of themes, may reflect Parthenonian influence. The Hephaisteion, in effect contemporary with the Akropolis temple, is a more direct and immediate example of the impact of that building, even if the Hephaisteion reliefs exhibit a different style.

Chronologically we miss the intermediate stages: from an abundance of riches (because of the sheer number of the Parthenon metopes and the considerable contribution of the Hephaisteion) during the first decade of the Classical period, we move to the very end of the century, or at least to its last decade; we therefore go from the relatively simple style of the beginnings (449-440) to the rich extravagance of the end (410-400). The Albani metope could belong to the 420s but is more likely to be a late "provincial" work. The presence of carved metopes in Thrace is remarkable, their absence in Magna Graecia surprising, given the many Fifth century Doric buildings and the earlier predilection for carved metopes in the area. The most important contribution of this survey is that it stresses the originality of the Parthenon and undermines the notion that carved metopes should be taken as the norm. Their disappearance could be the direct consequence of stylistic development: as poses became freer and actions more integrated in terms of groups and total composition (that is, the depiction of simultaneously occurring events), the restrictions imposed by the metopal frame may have been felt as hampering and confining. In addition, the relative lightness of the superstructure in developed Doric, and a progressive interest in the interior rather than in the exterior of the building, may have encouraged the elimination of carved elements from the outer frieze. Yet it is surprising that a new spurt of interest in figured metopes should have occurred just when these

---

[41] Waldstein was convinced of such influence especially because of the rendering of the mouth, with a thickened upper lip, in the heads from the metopes. Yet this trait cannot be definitely assigned to Polykleitan works. It is also understandable that Polykleitos' name should have been made for the architectural sculptures, since the master is said by Pausanias to have made the chryselephantine cult statue for the Heraion. However, this may have been a younger master by the same name and not the famous Fifth century sculptor, therefore comparisons with Doryphoros and Diadoumenos are not very helpful. In addition, at least one scholar has claimed Pheidian influence on the metopes: A Laurenzi, *EAA*, s.v. Argo.

stylistic trends were beginning to develop, around 400. It is also interesting to note that the Fourth century introduced the figured coffer: an equally confining space and frame with the added complication (or challenge) of a difficult point of view.[42]

[42] The persistence of iconographic traditions can be exemplified by a recent find: some as yet unattributed relief panels excavated near the Agora gate at Aphrodisias illustrate the Gigantomachy, the Amazonomachy and the Centauromachy. They have been dated to the Second century A.C.: K. Erim, in M. J. Mellink, *AJA* 82 (1978) 325.

1. *Metope from Knossos, Herakles and the Boar.* This fragmentary panel (press H. 0.69m, W. 0.72m, relief H., 0.05m) has received little attention since its publication by S. Benton, *JHS* 57 (1937) 38-43, pl. 3. It was found in 1903 near Knossos, reused as a drain cover near a Roman road, badly weathered and broken across, both its upper corners missing. Herakles is depicted moving to right, holding a boar upside down over his left shoulder. In the lower right corner of the field, over the rim of a large pithos, Eurystheus' head and outstretched right arm appear. The scene is traditional, although the boar has not yet been tipped forward toward the cowering king and Herakles' pose is therefore not as threatening as in other renderings. The hero is shown bearded, with short hair and long moustache; his right ear is swollen, as befits a wrestler. Benton speaks of a Myronian type.

Despite the lack of an upper fascia, this panel has been considered a metope and attributed to a conjectural Classical phase of the Archaic Temple of Apollo Delphinios at Knossos, known to have been Doric on the evidence of a column. Because of its similarity to Olympia and the Hephaisteion, this relief has been dated between the two, ca. 455-450, and in fact the cubic rendering of Herakles' head is in keeping with the Severe style. However, other details still legible on the panel, the pose, and the findspot suggest that a date after the mid-century is more likely. Note that for a metope the relief height is relatively low.

Benton compares the Knossian panel with a relief in Athens (Nat. Mus. 43, Benton p. 40, no. 3, fig. 3 on p. 41) which she considers votive because of its plain and steep pediment and the lack of Eurystheus in the scene (this opinion is repeated in Karouzou, *Catalogue*, 42). It is remarkable, however, that the animal's legs and Herakles' club overlap the gable and that the lower half of the slab is broken along two slanted lines, which duplicate in reverse the outlines of the pediment, so that a hexagonally shaped stone results: a later recutting? I suspect that the "pediment" may in fact be the upper fascia of a metope which probably included also Eurystheus in its original state, since the Knossian panel proves that the horizontal position of the boar is

still compatible with the story: examples on Attic vases attest to the schema with the animal carried tail first. The interest of this late Archaic (or Archaistic?) relief lies primarily in the fact that it was found (in 1839) near the Hephaisteion (pres. H. 0.76m).

2. *Metope from Elis, combat scene.* Panel bordered by an upper fascia, broken on the left side and at the bottom. A youth, holding a round shield and a chlamys, which flutters behind him to left, stretches his right arm to push away an opponent (now missing) who has grasped his head from the rear. A hole in his right side suggests a spear thrust. Since the relief was found reused in a Byzantine building and no Classical temple has as yet been located in Elis, style provides the only chronological indication. The metope was published as "perhaps still Fourth century," but the composition, especially the parallelism of the arms, reminds me of the Bassai frieze, and the youth's wide face is not incompatible with a late Fifth century date. See J. Keil and A. von Premerstein, *ÖJh* 14 (1911) Beibl. cols. 115-16, fig. 63, and discussion on cols. 107, 113; mentioned by K. Stähler, *Boreas* 1 (1978) 85 n. 67.

3. *Relief of Athena with inserted eyes, Basel Mus. BS 228.* Although the background is entirely broken away, the flat rear of the figure speaks for its being a relief, presumably architectural. E. Berger (*AntK* 10 [1967] 82-88, pls. 22, 23.1-4, 6) has suggested that it may originally have been a metope, a pedimental figure, even part of a statue base or of a monument comparable to the Nike Balustrade. The Athena, preserved to just below the knees, is about half life-size (pres. H. 0.53m). She wears a peplos belted over a wind-blown apoptygma and perhaps a small mantle only partly suggested by unclear traces near the arms. Her left arm, broken off above the elbow, held a shield against the background, inner face showing; the line of the shoulder may indicate that her missing right arm was raised, holding a spear. Berger points out the peculiar rendering of the aegis worn along the V-neckline with a pendantlike Gorgoneion, the lively drapery, the vast amount of metal attachments, especially in the helmet. He considers the Athena Ionic in style, either from the islands or Asia Minor, and

dates her around 420 or shortly after. Berger notes that inserted eyes are more appropriate for sculpture in the round (p. 83), but some reliefs with the same technique are known: an Archaic horse's head, perhaps from the Peisistratid Temple (Brouskari, 52, fig. 92, Akr. 1340), a youth on a fragmentary stele, perhaps from Megara (Richter, *MMA Catalogue* 18, no. 22, pl. 22c). The engraved lines on the Athena's drapery, which occur within flat areas bordered by sharp ridges, remind me of the Bassai frieze or the Villa Albani metope, and the gathering of the garment between the legs seems a sign of later date, perhaps closer to 400. Note the selvage, with particularly long incisions marking the crimping, rather than modeling: it could already belong to the Fourth century. The head has been reattached and is of a different color, but is said to belong. The peculiar "break" at the eyes, prolonging the line of the outer corners, and the bulging lid muscles may indicate a viewpoint from below.

4. *Sculptured Gates of Thasos* (figs. 12-15). Although these reliefs cannot be considered metopes in the proper sense of the term, and some of them resemble votive reliefs or grave stelai within a naiskos frame, their connection with the gates, of which they decorated the monolithic jambs, and therefore with a larger architectural whole, makes them part of architectural sculpture, while their compositional limits are akin to those of metopes. Unique within the Greek tradition, the use of divine figures carved on city gates has been considered of Oriental inspiration, although it has also been suggested that at least some of the reliefs may have been carved for other locations and then transferred to their findspot. Since the gates closed beyond the jambs, the reliefs would have been visible only from outside the walls; the motion patterns of the compositions varied from gate to gate.

When first published by Ch. Picard (*Etudes Thasiennes 8, Les murailles, I: les portes sculptées à images divines*, Paris 1962), only six panels were known (one through a drawing) and were assigned to different periods, beginning around the end of the Sixth century, with the latest identified as an Archaizing representation of Zeus and dated around 411. The subsequent discovery of a matching panel from the same gate, undoubtedly showing an enthroned Zeus, has relabeled the former Hera, but the late date has been confirmed (P. Bernard, *BCH* 89 [1965] 64-89).

These two late Fifth century reliefs have several points of interest. The seated Hera undoubtedly wears Archaistic dress: a long diagonal mantle with elaborate ruffle and central pleat, over a sleeved chiton. A standing Iris (?) next to her combines fairly transparent, Classical drapery with upcurving, Ionic wings, the farther one drawn in perspective as background to her head. The Zeus panel, of which only four fragments remain, retains the head of Hermes with petasos and a seminaked, mantled Zeus in pure Classical style. Under each of the two seats stands a youth in motion. These small figures have been described as dancers and considered filling ornaments, since they seem to have no direct relationship to the frame of the chair (Bernard, 81-82). However, athletic statues as supports are known from Pausanias' description of the throne of Zeus at Olympia, and appear in Attic vase painting. Specifically, a Red Figure amphora by the Nikoxenos Painter (Munich 2304, *ARV²* 221, 1; *CVA* Munich 4, Germany 12, pl. 180.1) provides a good parallel for the Thasian youths, as well as for the sphinx ornament in the Zeus panel, which at present seems restored too low (Bernard, 70, fig. 2). The Thasian figures are probably athletes, the one under Hera's seat perhaps a pugilist tying his thong or an akontist testing the string of his javelin. The figure under Zeus' throne is too fragmentary for precise identification but conforms to athletic renderings.

For recent bibliography on the Thasian gates see *BCH* 102 (1978) 807-10; also *BCH* 91 (1967) 469-72 and pls. 9-15. I thank Gloria F. Pinney for the vase painting reference, and Paul Rehak for the drawing of the Gate of Zeus (fig. 15), which he made after the photographs of the fragments and the drawing in Bernard.

FOR PAGE 16

The most comprehensive recent account of the Parthenon metopes is Brommer, *Metopen*, who also discusses methods of installment (176-77). Other recent articles include M. Tombropoulou-Brouskari, *AthMitt* 80 (1965) 127-42; W. Schiering, *JdI* 85 (1970) 82-93; M. Wegner, *RA* 1968, 119-30; M. Moltesen, *AA* 1976, 53-58. See also M. Weber, F. Brommer, J. Frel, *GettyMusJ* 5 (1977) 5-20.

Kimonian phase: R. Carpenter, *The Architects of the Parthenon* (Penguin Books 1970). For some critical reviews of this work see, e.g., W. B. Dinsmoor, Jr., *AJA* 75 (1971) 339-40; I. M. Shear, *Phoenix* 26 (1972) 192-94.

FOR PAGE 17

On carved metopes during the Archaic period and their uneven distribution see *Archaic Style*, ch. 7.

The Parthenon as a treasury: V. Bruno, *The Parthenon* (Norton Critical Studies in Art History, New York 1974) 67, with earlier bibliography in n. 12. See also pp. 91-92 for the standard view on the meaning of the Parthenon program.

FOR PAGE 19

On the Ilioupersis by Polygnotos in the Stoa Poikile in Athens: Pausanias 1.15.3; in the Lesche of the Knidians at Delphi: Pausanias 10.25.2. On the Ilioupersis as history see Hölscher, *Historienbilder*, 70-73. I have not been able to consult E. Thomas, *Mythos und Geschichte—Untersuchungen zum historischen Gehalt griechischer Mythendarstellungen* (Cologne 1976). Cf. also Moret, *L'Ilioupersis*, 275-78.

On the Carrey drawings in general, Th. Bowie and D. Thimme, *The Carrey Drawings of the Parthenon Sculptures* (Bloomington 1971).

FOR PAGE 20

Centaurs within North cycle: F. Brommer, *JdI* 80 (1965) 266-79.

FOR PAGE 21

For possible damage to the Parthenon in the Antonine period see J. Binder, in *Festschrift Brommer*, 29-31, esp. 31. See also infra, chs. 3 and 7.

FOR PAGE 22

Metopes S 9 compared to the Hephaisteion: Brommer, *Metopen*, 90-91.

Freedom of artists who carved West metopes: Brommer, *Metopen*, 180 (oral instructions).

FOR PAGE 23

Various opinions on the style of the metopes are listed in Brommer, *Metopen*, 229. Cf. also *Severe Style*, 100. A "severe" head in the Ny Carlsberg Glyptothek has recently been attributed to S 15: M. Moltesen, *AA* 1976, 53-58.

FOR PAGE 24

Metope N 32; the seated figure may be Themis, because she wears the chiton/himation combination rather than the peplos as customary for Hera in the Parthenon sculpture: E. Simon, *JdI* 90 (1975) 109-11; for the shoulder-cord of Themis see E. B. Harrison, in *Festschrift Brommer*, 155-61, who does not mention this example.

Antenor's kore: *Archaic Style*, figs. 57-58.

Angelitos' Athena: *Severe Style*, fig. 39.

FOR PAGE 25

Representations of Selene on vases: see, e.g., an oinochoe in Florence, in the manner of the Aegisthus Painter, *EAA*, s.v. Selene, p. 169, fig. 217. For a Roman example as late as the time of Constantine, see ibid., p. 170, fig. 219.

Omega folds: Adam, *Technique*, 51.

Dexileos' stele: Lullies and Hirmer, pl. 192.

FOR PAGE 26

The disparity in the facial renderings of the centaurs has been highlighted by G. Rodenwaldt, *Köpfe von den Südmetopen des Parthenon* (*AbhBerlAk* 1945-46) (Berlin 1948).

Herakles the Archer, Aegina: D. Ohly, *Die Aegineten*, vol. 1 (Munich 1976) pls. 30-34.

Hephaisteion metopes: H. Koch, *Studien zum Theseustempel in Athen* (Berlin 1955); Morgan, "Metopes," suggests that the order of the metopes is not as originally planned. See also *Agora* 14, 142-47, and E. B. Harrison, as cited in ch. 2, n. 29.

For the dating of the Hephaisteion and the attribution of other temples to the same architect see Dinsmoor, 180-82; note a different opinion by H. Knell, *AA* 1973, 94-114. The latest discussion is in R. E. Wycherley, *The Stones of Athens* (Princeton 1978) 69 and n. 90.

FOR PAGE 28

The Bassai metopes, those from the Argive Heraion and from near Amphipolis are discussed later in the chapter.

Villa Albani metope: see infra.

Metopes from the Delphic Tholos: latest discussions in B. Vierneisel-Schlörb, in *Festschrift für Gerhard Kleiner* (Tübingen 1976) 80-84, with additional bibliography; Stewart, p. 87; J. Marcade, *AntK* 21 (1978) 111-12.

Metopes from the Temple of Athena Alea at Tegea: Stewart, 30-32, 57-58, 62-66.

Metopes of the Athenaion at Ilion: B. M. Holden, *The Metopes of the Temple of Athena at Ilion* (Smith College, Northampton, Mass., 1964); H. Jucker, *AA* 1969, 248-56.

Tholos at Epidauros: Berve and Gruben, fig. 97a.

Hellenistic proskenion at Delos: *Guide de Delos* (Paris 1966) pl. 9:1 and pp. 47, 158.

Eleusis, Lesser Propylaia: G. E. Mylonas, *Eleusis and the Eleusinian Mysteries* (Princeton 1961) 158. This building, erected ca. 50 B.C., carries carved decoration on the triglyphs as well, in a final disruption of the Doric frieze.

Belevi Mausoleum: the final publication is still pending; on the chronological controversy see most recently W. Alzinger, *Final Programme*, 74; also S. Buluç in *X International Congress* (Ankara 1978) 1085-92.

Lefkadia Tomb: Ph. Petsas, *Ho Taphos ton Leukadion* (Athens 1966) 100-107. This Centauromachy is only painted, but with shading suggesting high relief; see V. Bruno, *AJA* 85 (1981), 1-11.

For the influence of the Parthenon on the Hephaisteion plan see, e.g., *Agora* 14, 144, and W. B. Dinsmoor, *Hesperia* suppl. 5 (1941) 154-55.

FOR PAGE 30

Head of "Eurystheus": Morgan, "Metopes," pl. 76. Changed by Delivorrias, 30-33; accepted by E. B. Harrison, *AJA* 80 (1976) 210.

Athena as one of the Hesperides: see bibliography in H. A. Thompson, *AJA* 66 (1962) 340 n. 7.

Metope in the Villa Albani: W. Fuchs in Helbig⁴, no. 3308 (dated ca. 420 and connected with the school of Agorakritos); *EA* 3582; *Hesperia* 30 (1961) 199-203; *AthMitt* 77 (1962) Beil. 50:1; F. Hiller, 55 n. 120, 63-69.

FOR PAGE 31

For Boeotian grave stelai see W. Schild-Xenidou, *Boiotische Grab- und Weihreliefs archaischer und Klassischer Zeit* (Athens 1972), and infra, ch. 6.

Metope in Rome, Conservatori Museum: W. Fuchs in Helbig⁴, no. 1659. Found in Rome NE of Forum Pacis; *NSc* 1890, 239; *Hesperia* 29 (1960) pl. 71; O. Broneer, *Isthmia* 1 (Princeton 1971) appendix 2. Fuchs considers the style Peloponnesian, under influence of Polykleitan school.

Metope from near Amphipolis: Kavalla Mus. no. Λ 425. The label lists provenience from near the village of Aedonochorion of Strymon (ancient Tragilos). D. Lazaridis, *Odigos Mouseou Kavalas* (Athens 1969) 143 and pl. 54; Broneer, *Isthmia* 1, 182-83.

For a list of Greek originals found in Rome see E. Paribeni, *8° Convegno di Studi Magna Grecia 1968* (Naples 1969) 83-89. I have not been able to consult M. Pape, *Griechische Kunstwerke aus Kriegsbeute und ihre öffentliche Aufstellung in Rom* (1975).

Bassai metopes: Ch. Hofkes-Brukker, *BABesch* 38 (1963) 52-83, dated 425-420; B. Vierneisel-Schlörb, in *Festschrift Kleiner*, 78-79, nn. 57-60.

FOR PAGE 32

Testing in the Bassai foundations: N. Yalouris, *AAA* 6 (1973) 39-55; F. Cooper, *Final Programme*, 58-59.

The removal of the face from Metope B.M. 510 is due to C. A. Picón; an article is forthcoming in *BSA*. For the identification of sculptural fragments from the Bassai metopes see N. Yalouris, *ArchEph* 1967, 187-99. A new study, by B. Madigan, is in preparation.

Metopes from the Argive Heraion: B. Vierneisel-Schlörb, in *Festschrift Kleiner*, 68-70 and n. 17 with bibliography. The original publication remains the most detailed description: Ch. Waldstein, *The Argive Heraeum*, 1 (Boston 1902) 144-47. Some additions have been made by E. Raphtopoulou, *Deltion* 26 (1971) 264-75, and French summary on pp. 329-31. See also Stewart, 85-87.

CHAPTER 3

Architectural Sculpture: Pediments and Akroteria

PEDIMENTAL decoration had enjoyed a great vogue in Athens during the Archaic period; it would therefore be reasonable to assume that all the new Attic temples built during the Fifth century had sculptures on their gables. But this is not entirely the case. The Parthenon, as part of its general decorative program, had impressive pedimental statuary, which survives to some extent. The Hephaisteion, which seems to have been under the influence of the Parthenon, also featured sculptures on both façades, but the remains are fragmentary and have not yet received final publication.[1] Although both the Temple of Ares and the Nike Temple had the cornice prepared to receive sculpture, in the case of the former, it is not sure whether the project was ever completed. As for the Nike Temple, Despinis has recently identified nine fragments which belonged to its gables; the remains however are too scanty to allow extensive discussion.[2] Very little remains from the pediments of the Temple of Poseidon at Sounion[3] (figs. 16-17) and no pedimental sculpture seems to have been planned for the Rhamnous temple. One scholar has suggested that a large head of a goat at Brauron comes from the pedimental decoration of the Fifth century temple, but the piece remains unpublished and even the date of the temple is debated—it may be earlier than our period. One more temple, dedicated by the Athenians on Delos, had elaborate group akroteria but no sculpture on the gables, and in general it

[1] Both H. A. Thompson and Ch. Morgan have suggested possible topics and reconstructions of the pediments of the Hephaisteion, but both theories have been rendered obsolete by the realization that the pieces they attributed are in Pentelic, while the building had employed Parian sculptures. E. Harrison's theories have not yet been published, and she does not seem to favor those proposed by Delivorrias: see AJA 80 (1976) 209-10, and Final Programme, 65. Cf. also ch. 2, n. 29.

[2] G. Despinis, Deltion 29 (1974) [pub. 1977] 1-24, with German summary on pp. 273-75. The fragments have been convincingly attributed on the basis of their distinctive method of attachment to the gable floor, by means of rounded pins. Primarily on the strength of a male torso in fighting pose and of a female helmeted head, Despinis has suggested that the East pediment featured a Gigantomachy. Because of the appropriateness of the subject, he then surmises that an Amazonomachy appeared on the West gable, but this hypothesis remains purely conjectural. It is interesting to note that one of the fragments claimed by Despinis for the Nike Temple

Pediments (the lower half of a draped female figure in motion) had previously been assigned to the Erechtheion frieze, which should be at least one decade later than the sculpture of the Nike Temple.

[3] For the latest reconstruction of the Sounion Pediment, see Delivorrias; however, cf. also E. B. Harrison's review of his book, AJA 80 (1976) 209-10. Only one figure, a seated peplophoros, undoubtedly belongs to one of the gables (figs. 16, 17). Although the piece is headless and badly weathered, enough remains to show that the traditional dating of the temple, between 444 and 440, may be too high. The adherence of the costume to the torso, with a deep groove marking its contour, and the great transparency of the cloth over the legs would seem more in keeping with a date around 420. The lively course of the folds in the woman's lap and the deep pockets between the legs recall some figures from the Erechtheion frieze. Finally, the large areas of exposed flesh under the armpits strengthen the argument for a lower chronology, at least for the pedimental sculpture.

seems as if Fifth century Athenians came to prefer complex sculptures on the roof over pedimental compositions. Certainly many temples were built in Athens and vicinity during the time span under survey, and it is remarkable that only a few of them had decorated pediments, although the total picture is richer than that of carved metopes.

Elsewhere in the Greek world a few more examples of sculptured gables occur. The Argive Heraion, which dates from the very end of the Fifth, if not already from the Fourth, century, had the Birth of Zeus on one side and the Ilioupersis on the other.[4] The Metroon at Olympia (again a site with a tradition of pedimental decoration) has had at least one figure attributed to its gable, but the attribution is not confirmed and the date of the statue is given as early Fourth century. Similarly, some buildings traditionally dated before 400, such as the Nereid Monument in Xanthos with relief compositions on both pediments, have now been redated considerably later and therefore cannot be included. The Temple of Apollo at Bassai, to which sculptures had been assigned, has now been shown to have had no pedimental decoration. In some cases, statues attributed to temples are described as either pedimental or akroterial; for instance, the torso of a male figure in motion ascribed to the Temple of Zeus at Cyrene, and the elaborate group of two riders and a Nereid from the Marasà temple at Lokroi. Finally, literary sources mention that the Olympieion at Akragas had decorated pediments, and some relief fragments from them may have survived.[5] Given the enormous scale of the building, it is difficult to visualize the arrangement, and in any case the structure is too anomalous to be of statistical importance, especially in consideration of the many other Akragan temples without tympanal decoration.

Yet the tradition of sculptured gables may have been stronger than that of carved metopes, since a few more examples occurred during the Fourth century,[6] and the Hellenistic period witnessed a sporadic revival of the practice.[7] In addition, some Fifth century statues are preserved which, because of their narrow depth and one-sided composition,

---

[4] If F. Eichler is correct in reconstructing the double episode of Helen and Kassandra within the single pediment (as argued on the basis of fragments of two idols with traces of the suppliant's hand on them), the Argive Heraion would represent the first simultaneous occurrence of these iconographic motifs in monumental form: see Moret, *L'Ilioupersis*, 60.

[5] I owe this information to Malcolm Bell, who is conducting a major study of this temple. He tells me that the composition seems to have included landscape lines and that heads were inserted in marble, a technique known from the metopes of Temple E at Selinus. Professor Bell has also pointed out to me that Naevius describes the giants of the pediment as anguiped, presumably being so depicted for the first time in our knowledge; cf. J. C. Carter, in *Studies von Blanckenhagen*, 150 n. 45, for further comments and references on this point.

[6] Temples of Asklepios and of Apollo Maleatas at Epidauros, of Apollo at Delphi, of Athena Alea at Tegea; Temple at Mazi; Nereid Monument at Xanthos. Note also the decorated pediments of the Alexander Sarcophagus from Sidon, and the reclin-

ing Herakles in Athens, which may have belonged to the gable of a shrine for that hero: Travlos, *Pictorial Dictionary*, figs. 360-61. Other "floating figures" should be attributed to temples, for instance the "Dionysos" once connected with the Metroon at Olympia, and others to be discussed below. Some decorated pediments are only known through Pausanias and can no longer be visualized: the Twelve Labors of Herakles on the Herakleion at Thebes, for example, or those of the Asklepieion at Titane.

[7] Hieron at Samothrace, Temple of Dionysos at Teos, Temple of Poseidon and Amphitrite at Tenos; also many Italo-Etrusco-Roman temples with terracotta decoration. See also S. Lattimore, "A Greek Pediment on a Roman Temple," *AJA* 78 (1974) 55-61. Tarentine funerary naiskoi seem to have some form of pedimental ornament, as well as elaborate akroteria: J. C. Carter, *Sculpture of Taras* (Philadelphia 1975) 14-16. Some Hellenistic "floating figures" have also been considered possible pedimental candidates, e.g., Athens Nat. Mus. 3257, P. W. Lehmann, *Samothrace* 3:1 (Princeton 1969) 316 fig. 265, 317 and n. 151.

seem to demand a pedimental setting. Since several of them were found in Rome, and others are in modern museums without known provenience, attributions remain tentative but should be statistically taken into account.

Before discussing individual sculptures in detail, one more question should be raised. It has often been stated that, after the fluctuations of the early Archaic period, a "canonical" formula was reached by which one of the pediments, usually the East, represented the epiphany of the major divinity, in a quiet scene, while the rear pediment depicted a more violent subject of specific mythological content. Can this statement be supported by the evidence?

In the Parthenon, the Birth of Athena can be considered an epiphany of the goddess, while her Strife with Poseidon on the West gable has a more violent connotation; but it is incorrect to speak in terms of "quiet" versus "animated" since there is equal action on both sides, some figures running, others seated watching or awaiting the news. Even the newly born probably appeared in motion, rather than as a static apparition comparable to the Zeus from Olympia East or the Athena of Aegina West.

Too little is known about the Hephaisteion pediments to express an opinion. The chariots suggested by the floor cuttings in the East gable could imply arrival and therefore motion, but the scene itself might have been quiet; the West Pediment is usually believed to have depicted a Centauromachy, but published evidence is still missing. As for the other temples, too little is known, and recent reconstructions have not met with general agreement. Certainly the Fourth century does not seem to have adhered to this "norm," in that both pediments at Epidauros, as well as at Tegea, depicted violent scenes, while both those at Delphi were probably "quiet." All in all, it may be best to refrain from formulating rules which may not have applied in antiquity, given the scarce evidence at our disposal. Thus the Parthenon can neither be viewed as "canonical" nor as normative for future pediments.

THE PARTHENON PEDIMENTS

According to the building accounts, the Parthenon was finished by 433/2 and therefore by that date its pedimental sculptures were on the gables. It is more difficult to determine when they were actually carved, since work on such large and complex pieces could have begun as early as 447, when the entire Parthenon project was started. None of the statues could have been put in position before the erection of the entablature by 438, and in that year the accounts list again deliveries of marble to the workshops. It is therefore possible to assume that carving of the pedimental statues began only then and, computing from the record of wages, that it was carried out by ten masters. Quarrying, carting, and sculpturing of marble are recorded as late as 434/3, and indeed, given the scale of the entire project, it is amazing that work could be completed in such a short time. Thus the Parthenon sculptures remain among the most firmly dated monuments in antiquity whether we accept the shorter (438/7-433/2) or the longer span (447-432).

Because of their importance, the Parthenon Pediments have received a great deal of attention since their first display in England in 1807. Brommer's recent publication has given rise to a renewed spurt of interest in Parthenonian problems. The existence of such well-documented and beautifully illustrated studies eliminates the need for detailed description and presentation. We can therefore focus on the problems still extant and especially on analyzing stylistic traits.

Identification

Because of Pausanias' invaluable, albeit laconic, information, we know the subject of both pediments. As Brommer has correctly remarked, however, we would not have been able to identify the scenes in their present fragmentary state without that literary aid. The Birth of Athena is a topic well known from other depictions, and therefore only compositional problems remain to be solved. The Strife with Poseidon is more complex, since other extant representations are later than the Parthenon and no established account of the myth exists. Since the center portion of the pediment is sadly fragmentary and Carrey's drawings are of only limited help, it is impossible to determine whether the value of the individual tokens alone had to be judged by the spectators, or whether an element of race was involved, whereby the token stood not per se but as proof of arrival. One more theory has been recently advanced: that the thunderbolt of Zeus was depicted in the gable, settling the issue between the two contestants, but the supposition may require too abstract and pictorial a rendering for the time.[8]

Beyond the general question of explaining the themes, there remains the more specific task of identifying the individual figures, and here controversy is rife. Only the two corner figures of the East Pediment (Helios and Selene/Nyx with their chariots) can be considered certain; all the others have been variously labeled, on various grounds. In the West Pediment only the fragments of the two protagonists can be positively identified because of their scale and, for Athena, attributes. Next in plausibility is Figure O, the charioteer of Poseidon, as Amphitrite. Figure N, because of the cuttings on her back for the attachment of wings, could be Iris, since Nike had to be on Athena's side, but her connection with the West Pediment is occasionally still being challenged. All the others are uncertain, including "Kekrops and his daughter" (Figures B and C), since the snake lies between the figures, which are depicted as fully human. As long as firm identifications for the spectators drawn by Carrey cannot be found, we cannot even be sure that they are Attic heroes rather than gods, although the presence of so many children seems to weaken the second possibility.

Figure A, from the Northwest corner (our left) is usually called the Ilissos (or, alternatively, the Kephissos), that is, a river god who, together with a companion figure at the opposite end, would have given the topographical limits of the scene. This identification is based on the reclining pose and on comparison with similar male figures at the corners of the East Pediment at Olympia, which Pausanias identifies as the Alpheios and the Kladeos, the two local rivers. On the other hand, it has been argued that Pausanias either

[8] This theory, advanced by Erika Simon, has been briefly summarized in *AntK* 20 (1977) 144; however, I was able to hear the entire argument in a lecture delivered by her at Bryn Mawr College on November 1, 1978. Simon makes the interesting point that the moment depicted on the gable is later than usually believed. Poseidon, enraged by Athena's victory, is invading her territory and threatening to flood the land of Attica. This theory accounts for Poseidon's off-center position in the Carrey drawing, and for the recoil of Athena and the other figures on her side. Simon's article will appear in *Tainia*, a Festschrift for R. Hampe.

43

accepted or provided that explanation because, to him, a Greek of Roman times, the pose alone was sufficient to suggest a river god. A Greek of the Classical period would have needed more definite characterization or attributes to make a positive identification.[9]

Could the attributes alone have been sufficient to identify the Parthenon figures? Since hands and whatever they might have held are all missing, both at Olympia and on the Parthenon, the question remains open. The Parthenon master used the pictorial device of having Sun and Moon (or Night) set the chronology of the East scene, and he could therefore have employed a similar motif to set the topography of the West. In addition, he seems to have been reluctant to add identifying traits, witness the difficulty we experience in recognizing most of the pedimental figures as well as some of the gods on the East frieze, at least in their present state. Certainly, if Herakles or Theseus, Dionysos or Ares, had been traditionally portrayed in their physical appearance as well as in their accessories, we would not be still debating the identity of Figure D on the East Pediment, now that the attributes are lost. The same comment could apply to the reclining male of the West gable. The river-god identification is shaken, however, by the fact that the corresponding statue on the Southwest corner (Figure W) is a reclining female. Although the Nymph of an Athenian spring could be so depicted (Kallirhoe?), this iconography is probably less obvious; equally problematic is the pose of her neighbor, the kneeling youth V, which some scholars identify as the other Athenian river. Perhaps the most important point to be made from all these arguments is that the Parthenon figures seem to defy traditional iconography and that their identification must have rested almost entirely on their attributes, or on the specific knowledge of contemporary Athenians.

In the light of this difficulty, considerable importance attaches to a recent attempt to identify the occupants of the East Pediment on the basis of the location of their shrines within Athens. Although reconstruction and identification are first argued on other grounds, final confirmation for the proposed arrangement is sought in the fact that all the gods of the southern half of the pediment had Athenian sanctuaries to the south of the Akropolis, and those of the northern half had sanctuaries to the north of it. However, our knowledge of Athenian topography is still relative, and several divinities were worshiped in

[9] River gods are usually characterized by bull's horns and often hold a cornucopia. Since one of the Olympia reclining figures retains its head, which is obviously not horned, some scholars have tended to dismiss Pausanias' statement: the figures would then represent resting athletes, or even spectators at the race, in symbolic anticipation of audiences at future Olympic games. Yet this interpretation is equally open to dispute, since athletic events performed in a Greek stadium were watched from an upright or a sitting, never a reclining position, and therefore even that allusion would have been incomprehensible to a Fifth century Greek. Parallels taken from Etruscan painted tombs (M. L. Säflund, *SIMA* 27, pp. 120-21, fig. 83a-b, Stackelberg Tomb) are not convincing because the spectators reclining under the stands are not really following the games. R. R. Holloway, *AJA* 69 (1965) 344, has moreover pointed out how unusual such a covered stand would be in a Greek context. In addition, even taking into account conflicting identifications, at least one river god, the Kephissos, appears only in fully human form, without horns or other attributes, on the late Fifth century Xenokrateia relief, infra, ch. 6. Given the importance of Olympia and the impact of the Temple of Zeus on the Greek world, it is not improbable that the more humanized rendering of the river gods was sparked by its example. I therefore tend to accept Pausanias' statement for the Olympia Pediments. B. Ashmole (*Architect and Sculptor*, 35) believes that the two Olympia figures are further characterized by their difference in age, yet the seemingly more muscular and hence more youthful appearance of the right-hand figure (Kladeos) may be the result of its more torsional pose rather than of age. Both reclining men seem to me approximately coetaneous.

more than one location, so that the argument is not irrefutable. Another theory attempts to define the gods on the basis of their degree of participation in the central event, assuming that distance from Zeus implies topographical distance from Olympos. In contrast to the West Pediment setting, which legend and tokens clearly identify as the Akropolis, the East Pediment is seen as divided into zones: the peak of Olympos in the center, where the Birth of Athena is taking place, a border zone (the Cloud-sphere) at the foot of the mountain, and finally the zone of Okeanos, marked by Helios and Selene. Even this theory is tentative and in process of revision. The identification of the figures on both pediments must therefore for the moment remain open.

Composition

When the pagan temple was transformed into a Christian church between the Fifth and the Seventh century A.C., a large window was opened in the East Pediment to provide light for the underlying altar in the interior. The main sculptures were probably removed from the gable at that time and seem irrevocably lost. The situation is different for the West Pediment, which was still in a relatively good state of preservation in 1674 when Carrey drew it. Our main concern here is the recovery of the fragmentary statues and the identification of the various personages, but the general lines of the composition are clear. Athena and Poseidon in the center formed two strong diagonals springing away from the central axis, which might or might not have been marked by an olive tree with a coiled snake around it. Flanking the two major divinities were their chariots, each with charioteer and attendant, followed in turn by a series of seated or reclining figures down to the corners of the gable.

The idea of placing chariots on a pediment did not originate with the Parthenon, since we find it at Olympia, at Eretria and at Delphi, on the Siphnian Treasury (ca. 525). Even earlier, a single chariot had appeared on an Akropolis building in the so-called Hydra Pediment (ca. 560). Given the scale of the Parthenon gable, however, the feat is daring and the drawing seems to show the horses in motion, in far livelier poses than the meek animals of the Temple of Zeus. In this connection two interesting details transpire from Carrey's drawing: the horses of Athena are supported by a peculiar torso, half human, half rock, which was already headless in 1674; near the chariot of Poseidon is an unusual animal that looks like a toothed dolphin and obviously symbolizes the watery domain of the god. Although these features of Carrey's drawing had obtained little credence and had actually been misunderstood or disregarded, chance has preserved both items: the rocky torso has now been recognized in Akr. 879, and N. Yalouris has joined a porcine snout to a fish body thus unmistakably reproducing the peculiar creature of the drawing. These two sculptures are truly surprising. The fish, although understandable both as an image and a symbol, is somewhat strange on a pediment; the torso is more enigmatic, but presumably represented some creature of the earth (Harrison once suggested Kranaos) emerging under Athena's horses as if rising from the pedimental floor, in a pictorial touch comparable to the rising Helios in the East gable.

It has also been argued that Carrey's drawing includes a pool of water and small dolphins directly under Athena's chariot: the salt-sea which Poseidon produced with his trident and which, with its sudden appearance, has made the goddess's horses rear. No tangible evidence remains of this detail beyond the rather vague rendering of the drawing, and the lively pose of the horses may be explained by their racing. Even the snake and the olive tree have come into question, since the fragments traditionally attributed appear to be of Roman workmanship. They could be a replacement for an original feature, since the Parthenon seems to have undergone damage and repair, probably in the Antonine period; but they are probably from an entirely different context, since they were recovered near the Olympieion. Although the olive tree was Athena's token and the snake her animal, both familiar occupants of the Akropolis, we cannot be entirely sure of their presence on the pediment. If they did indeed appear, they might have emphasized the central axis of the composition while adding another pictorial detail to the whole.[10] From this dividing line in the center the motion would have spread diagonally toward the corners—variations in scale being admirably controlled by the poses—to end with the reclining figures. An unexpected element in the entire scene is the presence of so many children, some partly preserved and others attested to by the Carrey drawings. It is usually assumed that the Romans, not the Classical Greeks, included children in their representations; both the Parthenon West Pediment and the frieze belie this notion.

The East Pediment is more traditional in its composition in that its axis seems to have been occupied by a central figure. Here, however, our information is lacunose, and the preserved fragments cannot go beyond Carrey's drawing, which leaves the center empty. Reconstructions have been based on three types of evidence: (1) the floor markings left on the pedimental floor by the now lost statues, including the cutting for iron bars working as cantilevers under the heaviest pieces; (2) the echoes of the scene in later works, both vase paintings and Neo-Attic reliefs or Roman copies; (3) the identification and integration of fragments which seem stylistically related to the Parthenon sculptures although already missing from the gable in 1674. In this context, most important is the experiment being carried out at present by the Basel Museum. Lightweight replicas of all extant figures and casts of the pedimental blocks are being used to reproduce the available evidence; attributed fragments are also reproduced in casts and are being integrated by professional sculptors on the basis of Fifth century proportions and fashions. By dealing with easily movable materials, various combinations are made possible and several compositions have been tried out, but a completely satisfactory solution has not yet been reached. This system, however, is the only one likely to produce new results, short of some unexpected major find, which seems improbable at so late a date.

A major issue in filling the center gap is not the selection of the divinities involved—since Zeus, Athena, and Hephaistos are inescapable choices—but rather their positioning. Zeus must have occupied the center and is likely to have been seated, given his greater importance and therefore his greater size, as well as the markings on the pedimental floor. But a Zeus enthroned in profile, even if on a backless throne, divides the pediment in two, and this is not a satisfactory solution, although the so-called Introduction Pediment (ca. 550) had adopted it. A frontally seated Zeus requires more space than available on the narrow ledge; a foreshortened statue would have looked peculiar next to other seated figures shown

---

[10] E. Simon (supra, n. 8), while accepting the presence of an olive tree, would restore it in bronze, much smaller and fastened behind the legs of Athena's horses, thus removing it from the center of the composition. She argues that no snake could have appeared around it, since there was only one such animal on the Akropolis and the West Pediment already included it between Figures B and C.

in normal proportions, while a Zeus on a throne partly in relief would again contrast with the other pieces entirely in the round. A third solution, that of a Zeus diagonally seated, perhaps on a rocky elevation, is now being explored, but there is some difficulty in reconciling it with the floor markings. Another problem consists in locating Hera, a figure not seen by Carrey but which has been recomposed from two fragments of the body (the so-called Wegner Peplophoros) and a battered but once-bejeweled head. Its placement on the pediment depends on the height of the total figure, which has been variously restored with consequent difference in solutions. Nevertheless, it seems assured that the statue belongs, although Hera's presence at the birth of Athena has appeared questionable to some scholars on mythological grounds.

Several reconstructions of the central scene have been proposed in recent years, notably one in which two chariots flank the protagonists, as in the West gable. This theory is suggested on the basis of the floor markings, which seem to require heavy and angular loads comparable to the undisputed chariots of the West.[11] But these markings, though similar, are not identical; and the number of horses on one pediment would seem excessive, given the presence of Helios' and Selene's quadrigas at the corners. These latter provide an interesting pictorial touch to the composition, since the powerful figure of the Sun god is seen emerging from plastically rendered waves, only his muscular arms and shoulders visible above water level; similarly, Selene's horses are depicted as partly submerged, their heads overlapping the edge of the cornice in a suggestive downward movement.

Brommer's photographs have clearly demonstrated the freedom of these Parthenon statues in breaking through the limits of their frame, not only illusionistically, as if the cornice were penetrable, but also physically, with limbs projecting outside the invisible vertical plane sealing the gable.[12] Even statues completely contained within the pediment sit or lie at different angles, and therefore the composition is not paratactic but articulated so as to transmit movement from the center to the corners.[13] In contrast, the West arrangement seems to have had a more linear and clearer outline; but pictorial details are unmistakable in both.[14] One may therefore conclude that the composition of the two Parthenon

[11] A. Delivorrias has now attributed a horse's head in the Athens National Museum to the left chariot (of Hephaistos) on the East gable; the Wegner Peplophoros ("Hera") would be its charioteer. These and other suggestions, as well as a discussion of later repairs, are included in the summary of a paper that was to have been delivered at the Eleventh International Congress in London, *Final Programme*, 64. See also I. Beyer, *AthMitt* 92 (1977) 101-16.

[12] This freedom with the architectural setting seems in direct contrast to the approach noted for the metopes and the frieze. To be sure, our judgment may be affected by present conditions and by the difference between a view from the ground and observations made from photographs taken at eye level. Nonetheless, this variety may also be further proof of the many different minds responsible for the sculptural program of the Parthenon.

[13] Often noted, but worth repeating, is the Parthenon symmetry with variation: each corner of the

East Pediment is occupied by a chariot, one reclining and two seated figures. But on the left corner the chariot rises (with a male charioteer), the reclining figure is a naked male, detached physically and compositionally from the two seated goddesses, who are carved from one block of marble. In the opposite (right) corner, the chariot descends (with a female charioteer), the reclining figure is a heavily, if transparently, dressed female, who forms a tight group, physically and compositionally, with one of the two seated goddesses, while the other is separate and at a different angle. For a reconstruction based on such principles see now H. Walter, *Stele* (Athens 1980) 448-62.

[14] Robertson, 300, comments that in the "Ilissos" the left leg is carved as if partly sunk under the surface, but the rendering may be caused by the torsional pose. In general, the corner figures of the West Pediment are not so well balanced as those of the East: there are too many seated figures on the right corner, at least to judge from Carrey's

Pediments is so unified and aesthetically successful because it manages not only to utilize but even to eliminate the confining frame. In so doing, however, it ceases to be purely sculptural and comes into conflict with the architectural reality of the entablature, thus perhaps spelling the end of this type of pedimental decoration. Whatever can be inferred from later pediments seems to show a return to more traditional formulas in which the horizontal cornice functions as a veritable floor, impenetrable but supporting.

Style

Before embarking on an analysis of individual statues, it should be emphasized that no attempt will be made to identify specific hands or to make attributions to masters. This approach has been tried with such varied results that it hardly seems profitable to pursue this line further. Styles will therefore be described in general terms and similarities established without implying common authorship. It will be taken for granted that several sculptors worked on the pedimental statues, but the results will be studied as a whole, as representative of broad stylistic trends effective at the time.

Although the pediments were probably the last area of the temple to receive their sculptural decoration, their figures can be appropriately discussed after the metopes, with which they have in common both three-dimensionality and the high-relief effect of a unifying background. To be sure, in the metopes, poses could be explored that were technically impossible in statuary in the round, but since a statue in the round could be secured to the tympanon or to the pedimental floor, an almost equal freedom in composition was provided. That the metopes, at least those best preserved from the South side, seem earlier than the pedimental sculptures is here taken to mean not that they were carved by different masters but that styles developed very rapidly in the course of carving, given the unprecedented demand.

Anatomy

That more than one style is present on the gables is made clear by a comparison between the two reclining male figures, D from the East (fig. 18) and A from the West Pediment. Their dissimilarity is not caused by the different pose, loose and relaxed the one, alert and torsional the other; it is rather a difference in build. Figure D has been called "the reclining Doryphoros," as if Polykleitos' famous statue had magically been able to lie down. The resemblance is strong, as far as we can judge from the Roman copies of the Polykleitan bronze: the musculature is powerful, the proportions are heavy, the position of the limbs is in chiastic contrapposto. In fact, the propped left elbow pushes the shoulder up, while the right one is lowered and the entire right side is compressed as if the bent right leg were pushing against the ground. The left leg opens up at a wide angle and looks relaxed, with-

drawings and current attributions. On the other hand, the big child (Figure E) on the left corresponds to the big child (Figure S) on the opposite corner. To judge from Carrey's drawings, there is an abundance of female figures on this gable, thus recalling Varro's statement. He suggested (apud Augustine *De civ. D.* 18.9) that Athena won the contest with Poseidon because there was one more woman than the men among the judges: could he have been referring to the scene of the Parthenon Pediment?

out the tension at the knee so clearly expressed by the taut tendon on the right. If a certain sectioning is still apparent in the articulation of the torso (the wide pectorals, the prominent rib cage, the indentation at the waist), it is softened by the modulation in the transitions. West A is leaner, less muscular, yet tenser, fractioned into different planes rather than into parts. But the true difference may best be conveyed by a comparison of two modern physiques. East D has the longilineal and coordinated appearance of a modern athlete, preferably a North American, while West A has a short, lean, angular build typical of a Mediterranean man. It is obviously methodologically improper to comment on ancient Greek men, for whom little or no information exists, but the modern appearance of East D seems a perfect example of that idealizing approach to the human figure which relied on abstract formulas rather than on an accurate reproduction of reality. West A is probably as "unreal" but he seems closer to the Lapiths on the South metopes and therefore more directly developed from the canons of the Severe style. For all his torsion, his pose is still frontal and relatively shallow—an eloquent silhouette—as contrasted with the great freedom in space of East D.

Other examples of male anatomy are equally dissimilar. Torso H from the West Pediment (figs. 19, 20) has that emphatic division above the waist which suggests the intaking of breath; by contrast, the very powerful torso of Poseidon (Figure M) from the same gable shows perhaps more detail but less division; yet the salience of sternum[15] and clavicles, abdomen and digitations, combine to produce an even greater impression of physical effort as well as power. If torso H from the opposite (East) pediment (fig. 21) should also represent Poseidon, as some assume, it falls short of the impressive conception of that god on the West gable; the marked indentation at the end of the rib cage links East H with West H in style, though the rendering is perhaps more plausible in the former because of the raised arms.[16]

As for female anatomy, it is more uniform and truly heroic in scale; shoulders are large and straight, breasts full and high, thighs massive and hips wide. However, with few exceptions, the rendering of the female body is so conditioned by the covering drapery that the two are inevitably interconnected.

Drapery

Two basic styles of drapery are represented on the pediments: in simple terms, they can be called the heavy and the thin type, although the differentiation does not seem dependent on the actual consistency (texture) of the costume depicted. It is interesting that all three preserved female figures from the South (left) corner of the East Pediment may be wearing the peplos, while the three extant from the opposite (North, right) corner wear chiton and himation; this differentiation may stem from the preference of the various sculptors, or perhaps deeper iconographic meaning is implied.[17]

[15] Note a similar sternal projection in the Lapiths of South 26 and 31, but within a much slenderer, and therefore less powerful, torso. It may be argued that West M is simply shown as older than West H and that difference in age is the true reason for the difference in rendering. I believe, however, that we are dealing primarily with a matter of style.

[16] West B seems also physically comparable to West A and H.

[17] E. Harrison, *AJA* 71 (1967) 43, states that Figure F wears a peplos while Figure E wears a chiton with short overfold that does not cover the girdle in the back. To be sure, E's drapery below the mantle, over her feet, appears quite thin. On the

On E, F, and G (figs. 22, 23) the costume is treated opaquely, with flat folds over the chest that end in thin, almost metallic edges. The breasts are modeled under the drapery but not by the folds themselves, which actually disappear over the salience or cross it indifferently; V-folds between the breasts repeat the pattern of the neckline. Over the legs the mantle lies heavy and fairly flat, but the knees are taken as tension points from which long and sharp ridges can branch off, suggesting the pull of the body under the material. Note the strong diagonal from left knee to right ankle on E, a motif that will find great favor in standing figures of a later period (e.g., the Maussollos from Halikarnassos). The patterns of both kolpos and mantle over the lap of the seated goddesses are difficult to disentangle and were probably not clearly visible when the statues were in their proper position. But the strong play of light and shadow created by the deep cutting of all lower folds gives great relief to the pose, and must have counterbalanced the inevitable flattening produced by the angle of vision. Similarly, the sloping thighs accentuate tridimensionality and counteract the telescoping of the legs into the stomach when seen from below. This mantle drapery does not have the doughiness of the Severe style, but neither does it have the realistic details of selvage and weights. The carver seems to have been uncertain of his rendering where the lower garment reaches the feet, and the resultant folds are awkward and confused. E's skirt does indeed appear thinner than the upper part of her costume, but the main folds are equally flat and sharply edged, with inner detailing which produces an effect of torsion; the rendering and hence the level of "evolution" are comparable to those of metope S 17.

Figure G is running, and therefore her peplos behaves somewhat differently, but the approach to drapery is the same: V-patterns on the chest, folds crossing the breasts and twisting over the stomach as if a second, thin layer were superimposed over a thicker lower one.[18] The very long and deep S-curve starting at the waist and almost bisecting the figure is very effective in conveying motion, but the reality of the body beneath is diminished and distorted. It almost seems as if G's thighs begin immediately below the waist, and it is difficult to reconstruct the outline of her left leg from the front view, despite (or perhaps be-

---

internal evidence of the Parthenon sculptures, however, the main difference between a peplos and a chiton, aside from the relative heaviness of the material, seems to lie not only in the length of the overfold but in the presence or absence of sleeves. All three figures from the North (right) corner, K, L, and M, have the lower garment pinned in several places along the arms, and the contrast with the bare limbs of E, F, and G is obvious. Figure N on the West Pediment is equally sleeveless, although she is depicted in the thinner garment. Here, however, the difference may lie in the fact that this is a chitoniskos, therefore a shorter version of the fuller chiton. As for the overfold, it is fairly long on West N, and on East E the short hem makes a sudden dip toward the right hip (Brommer, *Giebel*, pl. 34:1-2), where it would have been visible from the ground; the shorter length over the left side may therefore be considered an economy at a point of least exposure. In addition, G's overfold over the back is

short enough to reveal the belt, yet there is no question the garment is a peplos. The rendering of F's garment over the back cannot be compared because it is covered by the heavy mantle. One more possibility should be considered: that the master who carved E either forgot, or was forced by a carving (or an iconographic) mistake to eliminate, the sleeves of what he had rendered as a thin chiton below the himation, over the lower legs; thus he made the upper part of his statue look as if it is wearing a peplos, the lower half as if wearing a chiton. Such dichotomies between the upper and lower part of a single figure occur also in the frieze, when something is interposed between the two sections: cf., e.g., W III:5.

[18] These confusing lines seem almost a direct derivation (in mirror image) from the equally uncertain pattern on the so-called Candia Type, of the Severe period (*Severe Style*, fig. 168).

cause of) the sharp fold which seems to terminate abruptly over her knee. The right knee, by contrast, is clearly defined, but it is not successful in creating those tension lines which are so effective in the seated figures. Here the repetitive waves rippling between knee and ankle manage to convey speed, but entirely flatten the body beneath. This peculiar wing-pattern becomes almost a hieroglyph for motion in later sculptures and in different positions, for instance, in the short skirts of East Greek figures.

Many other points on this figure deserve comment: the strongly undercut edge of the skirt, waving away from its plinth as if it were in metal (and G is the only extant figure to have a plinth, among all preserved pedimental statues from the Parthenon); the daring effect of the naked parts of the body along the left side, once obviously enhanced by the contrasting color of the garment; the billowing mantle, which forms a shell behind the figure and adds a saillike effect to the composition; the apoptygma, which flies out and up to meet the mantle, thus forming a useful bridge of stone between body and cloak. Without the drapery, this figure would seem rather static, her position closer to that of a gliding skater than to that of a runner; but then, it is difficult to visualize G itself without the garment.

Entirely different is the case of West N, both in pose and style. The sculptor has conceived first a strong body in motion, and has then "applied," as it were, drapery to it. Folds are rather flat, with only few definite ridges, all in lively motion. In between, engraved lines animate the surface and suggest the thinness of the material. The area of the stomach is seemingly free of drapery, since the salience separates the folds, which gather on either side as if to outline it. The modeling principle is comparable to that of applying an egg-and-dart pattern onto the surface of an ovolo molding to bring out the profile. On the statue transparency is carried to the point that even the prominence of the pubic area is apparent. U-lines separate the breasts and many but shallow folds cover them, so that their volume is undisguised. Indeed, the garment clings to the powerful torso and to the legs in the wide stride almost as if held in place by the statics of a synthetic material. Incision is here more important than undercutting, and the body, not the garment, conveys the pose. Similar, though not identical, "scratched drapery" covers the kneeling Figure C from the same pediment, but its state of preservation is poor. Perhaps greater understanding can be obtained now that C and her male companion have been moved from the gable to the Akropolis Museum. However, enough incision is visible over the left thigh to allow the comparison.

The most famous statues, from the East Pediment, are K, L, and M (fig. 24). For all their similarity in actual pose, K and L differ from E and F in the treatment of the drapery. The mantle here stretches from knee to knee, with horizontal tension folds that will appear a generation later on some standing figures of the Bassai frieze, with equally flattening effect. What saves the Parthenon statues from two-dimensionality are the angle of vision and the deep carving between the folds, with consequent gathering of deep shadows in the cavities. Mantles are more than ever rational rather than naturalistic. Each long ridge can be followed from its point of origin to that of end, as it loops around the body like a rope; yet no fold could ever be so continuous. The opaque surface of the mantles still manages to convey the outlines of the legs beneath because it contours the rounded forms, each fold forming a small horizontal ledge around calf and thigh (here again the contrast with E and F is revealing). Vertical edges have long flutings of selvage (Brommer, pl. 46:2). As for the upper torso, it is covered in all three figures by the thin, sleeved chiton with overfold. Thinness is rendered by separating each main ridge into smaller surfaces, but incision is not as prominent as in West C and N.

The mannerism of the "slipped strap," also but less conspicuously present in the metopes, begins here what will be a long-lasting career, becoming virtually the hallmark of Classical and Classicizing femininity. The material clings to the breasts in an unnatural manner, and Figure M shows one further refinement: the circular cutting enframing the breast as a very thin and sharp fold that seemingly flattens the rest of the cloth over the flesh and emphasizes its projection (Brommer, pl. 48:1-2). Somewhat the same motif occurs over M's stomach, but with more folds than on West N and therefore with less resultant transparency. Another mannerism of thin drapery on M, and to some extent also on her companions, is the duplication of ridges, which therefore run in twos like miniature tracks. L, in whose lap M reclines, has her chiton held by a shoulder strap crossing under the armpits and obviously (though invisibly) over the back.[19] K seems to have a selvage even at the edge of her overfold which falls in almost archaistic patterns. All three figures have been considered clothed in "drapé mouillé," as if the clinging effect of their garments were caused by wetness; they are, in other words, typical examples of Classical drapery: implausible under the circumstances but aesthetically convincing, logical but unreal.

All other female figures on the pediments range somewhere between these two styles. Only two comments need be added: (1) The Wegner Peplophoros, if it really belongs to the East gable, has unusually thick and static drapery, almost too columnar in the skirt, with the central fold split by a minor groove as if it were a measuring device on the statue's axis. Her short and only slightly curved kolpos, covered by an overfold where grooves and facets run irregular and uncertain patterns, recalls the Karyatids of the Erechtheion more than the other pedimental sculptures, yet she has no marked shift in balance, as one would expect. (2) The fragmentary torso of Athena from the West gable shows press folds, an unusual and realistic trait that we normally associate with the late Fourth century or even with the Hellenistic period. Could such details have been added during a refurbishing of the sculptures? A technical footnote may conclude this section. Even the most rigidly vertical folds, in a Classical and especially a Parthenonian statue, manage to avoid an effect of extreme stiffness. The secret lies in the carving, which is not limited to scooping out the marble in between the ridges but also undercuts them, so that if a section were taken of a fluted skirt, we would obtain a series of omegas rather than of simplified meanders. This latter is instead often the mark of a Roman copy, which therefore looks much drier than its Classical prototype.

In brief summary, the Parthenon Pediments can be said to be representative of two trends in drapery that future styles will develop almost to extremes: the heavy but animated drapery receptive to motion lines, and the thin transparent drapery aided by engraving and layering, highly effective for modeling. Motion and modeling lines can, however,

---

[19] The iconographic significance of this detail has recently received some attention: Berger interpreted it as the requirement for a figure of action, and therefore identified the goddess as Artemis. Harrison pointed out the similarity with later representations of Themis and opted in favor of that goddess. Since the cord appears also on Muses and even mortals, this detail, though significant, seems liable to other interpretations.

occur indifferently in both types and, at this point, with varying success. Drapery on male figures is so little preserved that not much can be said about it: the mantle around West C's legs has a selvage (Brommer, pl. 89:4), and that of West A collapses with almost Severe softness (Brommer, pl. 84:2). There is an abrupt ending to some of its channel folds, and a comparable approach appears on the animal skin under East D, though the total effect is different, more fractioned and angular. East H has some drapery over his left shoulder, at present invisible from the front but perhaps once extending to his hips and legs, and the same is true of West H, where a whole chlamys remains over the shoulders, undetected from the front. Since the backs of the statues were finished in approximate manner, as if to ensure the general correctness of the draping from all sides, but only in its perfunctory outlines in the rear, no more specific comments can be made.

Cloth of various kinds is used, as in the metopes, to provide a backdrop for the figures or to add realistic details: heavy folded blankets cover the chests on which E and F sit on the East Pediment; more drapery is festooned over the couch where M reclines, dissimulating the precise appearance of the support. The animal skin of East D and the mantle of West A, appearing just under the naked torso and in between the legs, provided an outline of color to the flesh. Was this contrast also one of texture? D. Haynes has pointed out that two protected areas of male flesh (on East A and West A) retain a polish which weathering has probably removed from exposed parts. He has therefore suggested that a shiny surface should no longer be considered an exclusively Roman trait but a technical feature used as early as the Fifth century B.C. The observation of polish is undoubtedly correct, but could this detail stem from a refurbishing of the statues in Roman times? Epigraphical evidence shows that monuments in sanctuaries were periodically cleaned and repainted, and we have some reasons to believe that the Parthenon was damaged and repaired at some point during the Antonine period, when casts of some pedimental figures were also taken. If the repairs extended to replacing certain damaged pieces, a more general polishing could have been carried out to eliminate too strong a contrast between the original and the new parts.

Heads

Only East D retains its head (fig. 18), and badly weathered at that. The heads of Hera from the East and of Athena from the West Pediment are sadly fragmentary and retain little of the facial features. Nonetheless, that of Athena is instructive, in that it shows engraved Venus rings on the neck, a feature which occurs already during the Sixth century on the female figures from the Didyma column drums, but seems to have had limited currency in Greece itself until the time of the Parthenon. Here, however, it appears not only on the pedimental Athena but also on some frieze figures, both male and female, so that this too can be considered a Parthenonian mannerism akin to the navel folds, and feigning realism. Finally, one more head has been attributed to the Parthenon, though not to a definite figure or pediment: the so-called Laborde Head in Paris. Even in its present restored condition the head is less weathered than that of East D; it too shows Venus rings on the neck, and continuous, almost semicircular wavelets of hair over the forehead which recall the rendering on the Hera; over the nape, the hair is pulled up so that the neck remains free. From the front, the face is wide if asymmetrical and was probably turned somewhat toward its right. The eyes are wide open and in profile appear triangular and rather deeply set. Both the Laborde and the Hera heads show that a good number of metal attachments once provided for elaborate jewelry, including earrings.

As for East D, it is dangerous to draw conclusions from its present damaged conditions, since the loss of the original surface adds a sfumato quality to the features that cannot have been part of the original look. There is still some animation to the forehead, and the eyebrows seem relatively sharp, overshadowing the deep-set eyes, of which only the proper right preserves a jutting lower lid, almost like a shelf. The outline of the cranium is rather flat on top, like the Doryphoros'. On the right side, once protected by the pedimental overhang, one can still see traces of engraved locks, belying the present appearance of an impressionistic hair rendering. An indentation over the nape, which occurs also on many ephebic figures on the frieze, may have suggested another naturalistic, if exaggerated, feature of human heads. The face is rather broad with heavy chin and massive cheeks, and it recalls that of some Lapiths on the South metopes. It is certainly youthful and unmarked, and at present unidentifiable.

In a general overview of the pedimental sculptures of the Parthenon, they truly appear as the most impressive display of Classical style. Individual renderings may be more or less successful, and the language of drapery is at times still confused, but the difference from the Olympia Pediments is striking; we tend to forget that no other pedimental experiments had intervened between the two. Whereas Olympia layered its horses and roughened the backs of many figures, the Parthenon statues are almost entirely complete, with only slight differences in finish distinguishing back from front. Since the scale of the individual figures is well over life-size,[20] and some complex groupings are cut from single blocks of marble, undoubtedly the carvers followed the outlines of preliminary models, of whatever nature and scale. Certain adjustments also had to be made, as some reworked areas show; but by and large these adjustments are so minimal, especially given the strict confines of the pedimental frames which could not be accommodated at will, that one tends to assume such preliminary models to have been in the round. Regardless of the incomplete state of our knowledge, it is perhaps legitimate to state that nothing equal to these sculptures was ever achieved by pediments in antiquity.

FLOATING PEDIMENTAL SCULPTURE

It is well attested that the Romans took away from Greece as booty several types of architectural sculpture, especially pedimental; yet some pieces found in Rome and assumed

[20] Ashmole (*Architect and Sculptor*, 99, 109) has strongly criticized the lack of uniform scale in those Parthenon sculptures which were immediately visually comparable, such as metopes and pediments. He assumes that an effort was made to carve the metopal figures as large as possible within the confines of the frame, yet the resultant effect must have still fallen short of the mark, since the pedimental statues are so much larger. He also criticizes the variation of scale among the pedimental figures themselves. Without necessarily agreeing with such strictures, it is important to note, with Ashmole, how different the scale was at Olympia, where the metopes, though visually removed from competition with the pedimental statuary, were larger than those of the Parthenon because of different proportions in the entablature. It is here again the time to ask whether major decisions of this nature were made by sculptor or by architect, or perhaps by a patron who wanted all possible areas of the Parthenon decorated, regardless of aesthetic consequences. On the problem of pronaos design see J. J. Coulton, *JHS* 95 (1975) 13-24.

to be of Greek workmanship are still debated as possible gable ornaments. Among these the most important are the so-called Niobids.

There are several of these figures, of different provenience within Rome itself and different location at present. Their dimensions vary, and they have been combined in so many ways that it is perhaps clearer to list them here in tabulated form.

(A) The "Stumbling Niobid" in the Terme, from the Gardens of Sallust. H. 1.49m, calculated to 1.60m in erect pose (Vierneisel). Back finished but somewhat perfunctorily (fig. 25).

(B) Reclining male Niobid, Ny Carlsberg Glyptothek, Copenhagen, cat. no. 399. From the Gardens of Sallust. Calculated H. 1 60m (Vierneisel); actual L. 1.65m, H. 0.62m (figs. 26-30).

(C) Fleeing female Niobid, Ny Carlsberg, cat. no. 398. From the Gardens of Sallust. H. 1.42m, calculated to ca. 1.60m in erect pose (Vierneisel). Back perfunctorily finished (figs. 31, 32).

(D) Apollo the Archer, Rome, Conservatori. From the area of the Temple of Apollo Sosianus. H. 1.52m (erect height not calculated). Reworked in antiquity.

(E) Fragmentary head of Artemis with inserted eyes. In Bonn, private collection, provenience unknown. Pres. H. 0.27m.

(F) Male wounded torso in Berlin; bought on the antiquarian market in 1956, provenience unknown. Restored H. ca. 1.35m, calculated to ca. 1.60m in erect pose (Vierneisel). Plinth, and tree trunk in back. Back of statue encrusted but well finished.

(G) Male head in Frankfurt, considered Apollo Citharode by Hafner, but generally rejected as forgery.

(H) Alba Youth, Ny Carlsberg, cat. no. 400. Probably to be dated to the Fourth century B.C. Presumably from Rome.

(I) Torso of a wounded male, Archaeological Museum, Sevilla. Provenience unknown but probably Rome. Pres. H. and L.: 0.86m and 1.10m; calculated H.: life-size or slightly over. Back roughly finished.

(J) So-called Smaller Niobid, Ny Carlsberg, cat. no. 304: running female figure. From Castelgandolfo, near Rome. H. 0.69m. Back finished, but attachment hole high on shoulders.

(K) Kneeling Youth ("Smaller Niobid"), Ny Carlsberg, cat. no. 399a. From Castelgandolfo. Pres. H. 0.37m. Attachment hole in weathered back.

(L) Helmeted head, Ny Carlsberg, cat. no. 107m. Acquired in Rome.

Of the statues listed above,[21] A, B, F, and I show arrow wounds and could therefore be Niobids. Also C, H, J, and K are usually thought to be, but the identification is based on their fleeing or ducking poses rather than on actual evidence of weapon marks. Only I, J, and K are surely pedimental because of tenon holes for attachment to a tympanon wall

[21] One more Niobid (?) may be preserved in a "Graeco-Roman creation based on a figure probably intended for a pediment or a group. The original was carved about 410 to 390 B.C." C. C. Vermeule, *Catalogue of the Ancient Art in the J. Paul Getty Museum* (Malibu 1973) 12-13, no. 22. For a Niobid torso see also K. Schefold, *Meisterwerke griechischer Kunst* (Basel 1960) fig. 311, ca. 380 B.C.

or the state of finish of their backs; A, B, C, D, F, and H are probably pedimental, but not all scholars agree. At least one of the surely architectural pieces gives fairly convincing evidence of being a Niobid, thus attesting to the use of that myth for a pedimental composition which is otherwise unrecorded by Pausanias or other literary sources. Yet, as it has been pointed out, the Killing of the Niobids would be most appropriate decoration for a temple either to Artemis or to Apollo.

Although the original grouping of some of these figures and the suggestion that they are pedimental go back to A. Furtwängler, W. B. Dinsmoor was the first to assign A, B, and C to the Temple at Bassai. This theory has now been made obsolete by the new architectural study of that building, which has shown that no pedimental sculpture ever filled its gables. However, the grouping has held and other figures have been attributed to it, notably D, E, F (Langlotz, Hafner, Vierneisel), and, much more tentatively, H (Fuchs). Another grouping has put together the "Smaller Niobids," J, K, and L (Hofkes-Brukker), while I seems to stand apart both in size and style (Wegner), though almost identical in proportions to the Stumbling Niobid in the Terme (A). Other scholars would accept that A, B, and C go together but reject the Apollo/Artemis connection (von Steuben). Finally, not everybody agrees that A, B, C, and even D are pedimental. Given the controversy, it seems impossible to reach final conclusions and only a few comments can be made.

Of all the statues listed above, A is undoubtedly the most interesting (fig. 25). Its style has been called Attic (Carpenter), Peloponnesian (Lullies), Ionic and Magna Graecian (Hafner). Its proposed date oscillates between 440 and 430, a rather limited span. A relatively close comparison—which was used to reinforce the attribution to that temple—can be made with a figure from the Centauromachy frieze at Bassai: a woman clutching an idol while a centaur pulls away her garment, thus revealing most of her body; however, the situation is different and the motif may have occurred spontaneously to a master, without direct inspiration from the Terme Niobid. This stumbling figure is conceived primarily for a specific point of view and appears unnaturally thin from other angles, hence the pedimental attribution. It has been pointed out, however, that the expression on her face and the details of her drapery would not have been visible from ground level, and that therefore the statue must have stood on a low pedestal, not on a building. Similar comments have been made for the two larger Niobids in Copenhagen, though with less force.

Several scholars agree in postulating a South Italian origin for the Large Niobids, but so little marble sculpture remains from Magna Graecia that close parallels for the Terme Niobid are difficult to find. If, moreover, a pedimental attribution is accepted, there is the further difficulty of assigning the statue to a temple, since no definite tradition of decorated gables existed in either Sicily or South Italy, despite the recent finds from Metapontion. The presence of an emphatic selvage and the clinging, collapsing drapery may perhaps reinforce a Parian, or at least an Ionic connection; certainly the extent of nakedness and the expression of pain conveyed by the open mouth and the more deeply set left eye are unusual. The strong and systematic asymmetry in the face corresponds to the formula analyzed by Schneider and in vogue at Olympia. Anatomically, the body is strong and almost masculine except for the addition of the breasts, but modeling and softness have been achieved around the hips as well as in the neck, which has no engraved Venus rings.

The garment has been carefully described as an unbelted and unpinned peplos, but the overfold is barely discernible on casual observation: could both pins have been lost in fleeing? Yet, if not a peplos, would the figure be shown wearing only a mantle? This solution seems unlikely, but perhaps the sculptor meant to convey something specific by the state of the girl's garment, something comparable to the slipping cloak of the hero taken by surprise. The garment, as rendered in the Stumbling Niobid, provides an excellent support for the unstable pose, and the arms strengthen both the neck and their own precarious thinness while suggesting the agony of death; these traits are the hallmark of the great master who finds compositional solutions to technical difficulties. The slight elevation of the plinth under the right foot adds a touch of landscape.

While the Terme Niobid conveys the unmistakable impression of a Greek original, the two figures in Copenhagen (B and C, figs. 26-32) seem vastly different. Even the advocates of the grouping speak of eclecticism and different masters. B and C have been restored, both in modern and especially in ancient times,[22] but evaluation is difficult even when these repairs are taken into account, nor can a Magna Graecian label explain away stylistic peculiarities. B's inserted nipples and the lively modeling of his torso suggest original Greek workmanship, but his pose is awkward even when visualized as a collapse after an attempt to rise: this explanation may account for the arched chest, but the rigid, parallel legs remain unclear. It is also difficult to explain why the plinth has been retained only down to the thighs, which leaves the lower legs suspended; that the plinth was not meant to be sunk into a corresponding cavity is shown by the drapery carved over part of it on the rear and by two cuttings, presumably for right-angled dowels, on the same side. Closer examination reveals that some folds of drapery occur between the thighs, under the right leg, in a rendering incompatible with the present course of the mantle and difficult to carve with the legs in their outstretched position. Since both lower legs are broken and mended (the right at the lower edge of the mantle, the left just below the knee) and their marble has a slightly different color from that of the other parts, the possibility remains that the original composition showed the youth with at least one leg partially bent and that the present appearance is due to later integration and alteration. Intriguing is also the detail of the unusually large hole in the back, between mantle and body, which presumably served for the fastening of a metal arrow. When a rod is inserted into the cavity, it slants toward the youth's right so that it could never have been reached by the raised hand unless broken and bent at an angle, a rather unlikely depiction for a lethal weapon. Perhaps the most plausible supposition is that a Greek original statue was extensively reworked and altered in Roman times to conform to a specific position and viewpoint; yet some peculiarities remain unexplained. In particular note the youth's hair, completely carved since entirely separate from the hand, although with a displaced central whirligig and a drilled curl

---

[22] This observation applies also to the Smaller Niobids in Copenhagen, especially for the separately attached parts; cf. Delivorrias, 88. K. Vierneisel (*Final Programme*, 68) delivered a paper in September 1978, suggesting that the traces of reworking visible on the Terme Niobid and on the two figures (B and C) in Copenhagen are closely comparable to those on the "Niobid" in Berlin and confirm that the four figures may have stood together, at least in Roman times, as part of a new setting. Whether the Berlin torso originally belonged with the others remains a problematic question. I would tend to doubt it. Note that the Stumbling Niobid in the Terme underwent the same reworking as the other figures, yet her appearance does not raise the doubts suggested by the two pieces in Copenhagen, which I was able to examine closely in March 1979.

which may be a *puntello*. The pattern of locks over the forehead is also unusual. The strong oval of his face contrasts with the wider shape of the Terme Niobid A.

It contrasts also with the face of the Fleeing Niobid C, which in its present, heavily restored state looks much like a Roman copy and strongly recalls the Olympia replacement figures at the corners of the West pediment. The groove on C's forehead is too sharp and linear, the face too narrow, the mouth too small, the chin line too flat; finally, the drilled centers of the curls overlapping the sakkos at the temples are either too early or too late to be in keeping with her drapery style. This, in turn, is incongruous and her costume is possibly misunderstood. In particular, the overfold, lifted like a mantle over the head in the rear, functions like a halo all around her waist, totally uninterrupted and artificial, without corner weights or selvage or opening of any sort. Were she to let the cloth fall, it would be much longer in the back than over the front, and certainly longer than the kolpos all around, with which the apoptygma seems to merge over the left side. C's drapery is more linear than A's, yet more adept at modeling the body; the transparency of the cloth over the left hand is worth noting, but the folds in the back are doughy, static, and perfunctory. As for the body, C's shoulders seem too narrow for the legs, her thighs too elongated, perhaps to counteract the automatic foreshortening of a high placement. All in all, I believe this figure is a Roman addition to a Classical group brought to Rome in incomplete conditions.

The remaining figures in our list can be discussed more briefly. The Apollo D is proportionately smaller than the Stumbling Niobid A. As for the Artemis, her inserted eyes make her so different from the other statues that a grouping seems unlikely. In his second publication of the head, Langlotz advocated that it came from the pediment of the Temple of Hera at Kroton, but he no longer associated her with the Apollo. The Berlin torso F has been recently joined to a fragmentary base with feet that have completely altered the pose as originally restored. The stance is now more convincing, but the pedimental connection may have been weakened by the presence of a tree stump on the base, which would have been unnecessary within a gable where fastening to the tympanon would have sufficed to keep the body safe. Many of the "Aeginetans," for instance, have similarly unbalanced lunging poses without need for extra supports. In addition, feet, base, and the beginning of the tree stump were worked separately and then attached to the body, a technique that seems unusual for a pedimental piece. Both wound and pose could be appropriate to a warrior, with pubic hair perhaps rendered in paint and helmet and/or shield added for characterization.

Basically, even fleeing female figures cannot be positively identified as Niobids unless wounded; they could be nymphs fleeing from gods or monsters, or women from centaurs. The so-called Smaller Niobid from Castelgandolfo (J) falls under these strictures, but at least she is definitely pedimental, together with the squatting (?) youth K, whose left arm at some stage must have held a complicated attachment. He could easily be understood as an archer rather than a ducking Niobid. With her thin drapery, the running girl J definitely dates from the late Fifth century, and some of the fold patterns, such as the upward wave of the kolpos over the left hip and the thin sharp ridges running parallel down from her raised right thigh, may even be found well into the Fourth. This date could fit also the youth. Together with the helmeted head L they have been attributed to Paionios, though perhaps to different pediments of an unspecified Magna Graecian temple; or the three pieces could fit together within an Ilioupersis. To group a head with two headless bodies on the basis of a common resemblance to the Bassai frieze seems dangerous, and to name a master on the same basis, when not even the Bassai sculpture can definitely be attributed to him, is equally questionable. Since J and K come from the same site and have approximately the same dimensions, they probably come from the same pediment, but what they represent and where their temple was is now impossible to fathom.[23]

On present evidence, therefore, only the Sevilla figure (I) may still stand the "pedimental" test for a Killing-of-the-Niobids theme, though he too does not unmistakably deserve the name and, perhaps, the Greek date. On the basis of his existence, and maybe also that of the Stumbling Niobid in the Terme (a sure identification), pedimental compositions with the Killing of the Niobids seem attested, perhaps around 430 or somewhat later, but their original location is still undetermined and a Magna Graecian provenience seems doubtful.

Other free-standing statues may be considered pedimental, but with similar uncertainty. Notable is the equestrian figure in Boston, from a group which included at least one fallen figure under the horse. This rider is so similar to the "Penthesilea" of the Epidauros Pediment, even to the detail of a dislocated left hip to fit the pose, that perhaps its architectural connection is assured. A recent theory considers it part of a polyandrion or state monument in the round, and indeed equal attention to finish prevails on both sides, but the anatomical peculiarity would seem to preclude the possibility. A fallen opponent acting as a support under the horse's body would make more sense for a pediment, since a similar free-standing group could more easily have been rendered in bronze, unless we assume that the use of that material was considered inappropriate for funerary monuments. The date of the sculpture oscillates on either side of 400 according to the various authors, and no guess can be made as to its provenience or sex.

AKROTERIA

Together with pediments and frieze areas, the apex and corners of a roof had represented traditional spots for sculptural decoration since Archaic times, and the popularity of

[23] The helmeted head L is problematic: Hofkes-Brukker considers it male but other scholars have described it as female, and indeed it resembles the so-called Athena Rospigliosi. The slightly pathetic expression, the twist of the neck, the modeling of eyes and brows, and especially the relatively narrow and delicate oval of the face suggest that this head may not even belong to the Fifth century. A fourth statue, a seated and headless woman now in Berlin (C. Blümel, *Berlin*, no. 116 [K 7] pp. 97-98, figs. 186-88), allegedly found on Monte Compatri near Tusculum, has been associated with J, K, and L on the basis of provenience, size, and technical similarities, such as the method of attachment for the separately carved head. The seated figure rests on an uneven plinth once inserted in a base, and has also been considered pedimental; it seems, however, more three-dimensional than the other pieces and has therefore been omitted from our list. It could hardly be earlier than ca. 420 and is possibly later, but the heaviness and relative simplicity of her mantle and chiton have prompted Blümel to compare it with the seated ladies of the Boston Throne. It is certainly not Attic work and may be Magna Graecian.

Another addition to the group has been made by Delivorrias (89-90): the fragmentary lower part of a running female figure now in Budapest but originally also from Castelgandolfo. The difficulty of deciding whether the complete statue could have stood on the West Pediment at Sounion or whether its height would require an akroterial position at the apex of a gable has forced Delivorrias to leave the question open, despite his inclination to attribute the Smaller Niobids to the Sounion Temple (86-90). Other recent suggestions for their attribution are there summarized.

complex akroterial forms seems to have increased in reverse proportion to that of pedimental sculpture, perhaps in avoidance of potential competition. Since in the Fifth century both gable statues and akroterial figures were carved in the round, and both types could be given a somewhat perfunctory treatment of the back, the difference between them should be primarily noticeable in the weathering, especially of the rear, which in the former is protected by the tympanon wall while in the latter is exposed to the elements. However, weathering can occur after a statue has left its original position, so that certainty cannot always be reached.

An interesting problem is presented by two groups, each comprised of a youth dismounting from his horse, which in turn is supported by a bearded Triton; since the two are mirror images, they would fit well on opposite corners of a roof. It has also been suggested that a Nereid formed part of the original composition, and that the riders were so close to her that cuttings for the horses' hooves were made into the figure's drapery. The total group would have occupied the center of a pediment on the so-called Marasà temple at Lokroi in Magna Graecia. By and large this suggestion has not found followers, especially since two comparable riders in terracotta, their horses supported by sphinxes, were definitely akroteria from an earlier temple also in Lokroi (Marafioti), where a tradition of such finials existed. If, on the other hand, the Marasà group were pedimental, one would have to visualize it as different from the narrative compositions of contemporary Greek gables: the two riders are the Dioskouroi, with a clear allusion to the help across the sea they had given to the Lokrians at the battle of the Sagra; but the effect would be symbolic and epiphanic, almost like a Roman pediment, while the corners of the gable would probably remain unoccupied.[24]

A complex group has been postulated for the apex of the Athenian Hephaisteion: two girls, one carrying the other on her back, which had first been interpreted as a game of *ephedrismos* or as Hesperides reaching for the apples. Even these figures, however, have been now attributed to a pediment. The scene would be one of rescue, as suggested by the angle of the lap of the lower (carrying) girl, which is not compatible with a standing pose. A head had once been attached to the same figure, but it has now been removed, so the date can be assessed only on the basis of drapery style. The "slipped strap" and ribbonlike chiton of the girl being carried suggest a post-Parthenon Pediment date, the peplos of the carrying woman has deeply cut furrows in coloristic contrast; both would be possible around 420.

That complex groups as akroteria did indeed exist during the Fifth century is attested not only by literary sources but also by actual examples. Pausanias (1.3.1) mentions "terracotta images standing on the tiles" of the Royal Stoa: Theseus throwing Skiron into the sea and Hemera carrying off Kephalos. Some fragments from these akroteria have been recovered by the Agora excavators. Other information may come from inscriptions listing gold for akroteria, which were probably in bronze overlaid with the more costly material; on the basis of these treasure records and of traces on the blocks forming the base for the central akroterion on the Nike Temple, a group of Bellerophon riding Pegasos and killing the Chimaera, balanced by single Nikai at the corners, has been hypothesized for that

---

[24] While the pedimental theory has been resurrected by Foti in 1965, support for a central and akroterial position has been sought by U. Wester (118-19) in the theory that the female figure was once surrounded by floral branches. The rider groups, facing inward, would have stood over the corners.

building. The complicated pose would have been quite possible in bronze and particularly attractive in that medium which allowed complexity regardless of the small scale required by the size of the building. On the other hand, another suggestion appeared in print almost at the same time, attributing to the Nike Temple three fragmentary pieces in marble: a headless peplophoros in active motion to the left (Athens, Nat. Mus. 3043, from the Akropolis), the upper torso of a similar woman in the same direction, hence from the opposite façade (Akr. 6463), and the so-called Finley Group in the Louvre, which preserves the upper torso of a female figure carrying a seminaked youth, of whom only the lower body now remains. Thus the central akroterion would have represented Eos carrying off Kephalos, with running figures at the corners. The figure in the National Museum seems undoubtedly to be an akroterion because of the method of attachment discernible from the back, but it is more likely to be of Roman date; the same is true of Akr. 6463. The base for the central akroterion of the Nike Temple, because of its fastening holes, appears indeed to require a metal sculpture.

A very beautiful group akroterion, though poorly preserved, is said to come from the Temple of Nemesis at Rhamnous. Some doubts have been expressed as to its true provenience, but the addition of other pieces has been argued to confirm it. Together with the lateral akroteria, it may have been the only sculptural adornment of that building. The scene represented a kidnapping, as shown by the interlocking of two female feet with one male foot, perhaps Boreas and Oreithyia. The lively hem of the peplos on the base has suggested a date ca. 420-410.

The most complex and best preserved group akroterion comes from the Temple of the Athenians at Delos, usually dated ca. 425-417. At first erroneously reconstructed as a four-figure composition (plus an animal), the central akroterion on the East side is now composed of a bearded and powerful Boreas, who resembles the Poseidon of the Parthenon West Pediment, lifting a thinly dressed Oreithyia, and between them the small horse that is perhaps an attribute of the North Wind, or, as Wester believes, a lion. The central akroterion on the West side was also a group, Eos kidnapping Kephalos (plus a hound), but is less well preserved. At the corners were fleeing maidens, connected by their terror to the central scene.[25] It is interesting to note that most of these group akroteria show kidnappings, since the compact interlocking of figures would provide maximum stability for the composition, together with clarity of outlines which almost appear as extensions of the raking cornices. The nonterrestrial nature of the protagonists (Boreas as the North Wind, Eos as a celestial divinity, even Bellerophon on a flying horse) would lend a certain degree of plausibility to the lofty positioning. The narrative involved in such groups, especially in correlation with the lateral akroteria, as well as the sculptural elaboration of the compositions, weaken or even replace the need for pedimental decoration, with which they would have come into visual conflict.

In terms of distribution, we are again better informed about Athenian practices than those from elsewhere. On the Akropolis the Parthenon had floral akroteria,[26] and probably

---

[25] The Nike (Delos 4285) traditionally assigned to this building has now been attributed to the Monument of the Bulls (early Third century B.C.): J. Marcadé, *BCH* 75 (1951) 82-87; Delivorrias, 187, no. 11. If this attribution is correct, it underscores the difficulty we experience in dating late Fifth century styles, as well as their revival in the Hellenistic period.

[26] However, Delivorrias now suggests (undelivered paper, *Final Programme*, 64) looking for female figures as lateral akroteria.

also the Erechtheion. We do not know whether the Propylaia received akroteria, and groups have been postulated for the Nike Temple but only their bases remain. The presence of figured akroteria is attested for the Archaic period and it therefore seems plausible also for the Classical, on the basis of the evidence from other Athenian shrines.

From the Agora come three striking examples of female figures. One has been associated with the Temple of Ares, near which it was found, and is probably the earliest of the three (figs. 33-36). It is not a Nike because it lacks wings, yet her pose is one of movement, as indicated by the flying overfold of her peplos and the way in which her drapery gathers between her thighs, as if pushed by the wind. In profile, the skirt is seen to move away from her feet, possibly balancing a slight tilt forward. Stylistically, note how the V-folds of the apoptygma turn into catenaries on the peplos itself, above the waist: this trait could suggest an earlier date than the rest of the drapery rendering. As a whole, however, this figure seems to fit in with the Nike Temple frieze and the uplifted overfold is a late trait, perhaps nearer 410.[27]

A second figure has been attributed to the Hephaisteion, although its style places it at the end of the Fifth century or, more probably, into the next. It is a headless woman (the Agora "Nereid") wearing a very thin chiton, which has slipped off her left arm revealing her breast; a mantle covers her raised right thigh and gathers in a massive bunch where the right hand probably held it in front of her pubes, with a deeply carved fold creating a pocket of shadow in its center. The chiton is virtually engraved onto the figure itself, so that the navel clearly shows through and the left leg appears naked; very few ridges alternate with wide smooth expanses, which suggest bare flesh. Long thin folds outline the torso, especially along the right side, thus emphasizing the contour of the body with shadow. This style strongly recalls the akroteria from the Temple of Asklepios at Epidauros, dated ca. 375; the pose is comparable to that of East Parthenon G with both knees bent, but more frontal.

By contrast, the third female akroterion (fig. 37), probably from the Stoa of Zeus,[28] seems to be almost in the old *Knielauf* pose: both her feet are off the ground and she is supported only by her dipping skirt. She wears a peplos with overfold belted high under her breasts and then again at waist level, with a kolpos forming in between the two belts; thus her overfold appears unusually long. The peplos has lost all its traditional volume and swings and moves as if much thinner, yet the selvage is conspicuously rendered along

[27] The upswing of the garment is attested as early as the Nike of Paionios (ca. 425) and, to some extent, it occurs also on Figure G of the East and Figure N of the West Parthenon Pediments. What is more striking is the rendering of the peplos over the back of the Agora akroterion, with rounded edge dipping low below the shoulder blades and leaving the upper torso uncovered. Wings may have originally been planned, to be attached separately. The unusual form of the garment could then be explained as an attempt to reconcile a realistic costume with unrealistic appendages (see also the comments on Nikai in ch. 5).

[28] H. A. Thompson stresses that stoas within the Agora were considered religious buildings—hence their sculptural decoration. That another companion piece for the Agora Nike may be the so-called Palatine Aura is suggested by E. B. Harrison, who is quoted by A. F. Stewart, *BSA* 70 (1975) 200 and n. 7. Harrison dates both figures to the 390s and leaves open the question of the building to which they belonged. For the Palatine Aura see Stewart, loc. cit., pl. 26; Helbig⁴, no. 2256. I would agree in dating this piece to the Fourth century, and would therefore dissociate it from the Agora Nike. For the Nereids riding dolphins as Athenian akroteria which were even copied in Roman times see S. Lattimore, *The Marine Thiasos* (Los Angeles 1976) 50-51; L. Beschi, *ASAtene* 50-51, n.s. 34-35 (1972-73) 488-92; *Deltion* 29.2:1 (1973-74) 2, pl. 6a; W. Fuchs, *Boreas* 2 (1979) 59-60.

her right side; the garment has slipped off the left shoulder, but it still clings to the breast, outlining it emphatically. Under this overlay of flamboyant drapery the figure's body is fully revealed in its healthy massiveness, down to the tense tendons of the thighs. Against the surviving left calf the cloth forms sharp ridges, which stand out like shelves. The mantle billowing behind her back and large wings would have added to the total powerful impression.

The face of this figure is damaged and only its lower half remains over the strong neck. Another head, attributed to a companion figure, is intact but seems less massive in the chin area and with a softer jaw line. Her hair waves in deep scallops over the forehead, with strong undercutting separating it from the face. It is a pleasant, if indifferent, serene head, which somehow does not convey the strength of what remains of the other figure. Both, however, appear to have drill holes at the corners of the mouth, which increase the undulating pattern of the upper lip. Given the flamboyant illogicality of the garment and its highly decorative approach, the figure should be dated very late in the Fifth century, probably in the very last years, when the Classical idiom seems to give way to baroque exaggerations.[29]

Only two more akroterial sets can here be mentioned, because of some features of interest. One is composed of two fragmentary terracotta figures, one male and one female, from the Sixth century Temple B at Himera. They have both been dated to the last quarter of the Fifth century, but on the basis of their style, the selvage in the peplos and the underlying chiton of the female akroterion, this chronology might even be lowered. It is interesting to note the widespread use of certain stylistic mannerisms, like the selvage, and the practice of making statues in contemporary style even when they adorned a building of much earlier date.

The second set has been attributed to the Temple at Bassai, but there is some evidence now that floral akroteria may have adorned its corners, so that a different identification must be sought for the two female figures in the Louvre. They are both headless and smaller than life-size, each with one foot raised in mirror image on a rectangular block of unequal height. The woman facing to the right is extensively repaired, including most of the upper torso, which is modern; but enough remains to show that she is wearing an overfolded peplos that opens on her right side to reveal most of her leg; a peculiar looping fold over her raised left thigh has been explained as the end of a chlamys coming from behind, but photographs at least seem to show continuity between this "loop" and the edge of the overfold. The second figure, facing to the left, is instead dressed in a very thin chiton with short overfold clinging unnaturally to her body and with similar loop on her raised right thigh. Because of the transparency in the rendering, and a certain similarity with some figures on the Bassai frieze, the two statues in the Louvre have been dated toward the end of the Fifth century, approximately contemporary with the Nike Balustrade. However, Picard, in discussing them, compared the chiton wearer to the Este Aphrodite, which is now usually considered a Hellenistic work. The comparison is indeed convincing; given the differences in costume and rendering of the two figures,

---

[29] These figures have been dated to the early Fourth century, but their drapery is a good example of the stylistic direction taken by the late Fifth. A youth with a mantle on his back, leaning forward, has been attributed to the Fifth century Ilissos Temple, though without much supporting evidence: A. Linfert, *AA* 1968, 433-34.

is it possible to assume that the woman facing right is a Greek original of the late Fifth century which was given a counterpart in later (Roman?) times when transported to Rome? In support of this hypothesis note, in the chiton wearer, the very long folds crossing the entire body at a diagonal and the excessive mannerism in the transparent drapery, especially the decorative motif at the neckline.[30]

SUMMARY

Our review of pedimental sculpture suggests that this form of architectural decoration was considerably more popular than the carved metopes, although we are unable to reconstruct many pedimental compositions, and some statues are at present "floating" without definite attributions. It should be noted that it has been impossible to determine a canonical form of pedimental embellishment, with distinction in mood and subject matter from gable to gable. The Parthenon once again stands out for its balanced compositions, its freedom with the pedimental frame, and the complexity of its groups, but it must be stressed that its sculptures represent the bulk of our evidence at present. Geographic distribution favors Attica, but sporadic occurrences in the Peloponnesos and Magna Graecia are attested. That pedimental statuary was carried off to Rome as booty, perhaps from South Italy, seems indisputable.

Stylistically, the Parthenon Pediments present the same variety noticed in the metopes, but with greater control of modeling and motion lines in drapery, as well as more developed anatomy. Akroteria are also important as our main examples of undoubted Greek originals of the period, and they represent a greater stylistic range than pedimental statues, since some of them can be dated to the very end of the Fifth century. They attest to an ever greater emphasis on transparent and flamboyant drapery, with the traditional peplos becoming thinner and thinner, almost like a chiton; yet chiton and peplos are often used alternately on associated figures, either for variety or for iconographic distinction. The baroque mannerisms of the late Fifth century seem to have been imitated in the Hellenistic and Roman periods, so that even figures traditionally dated within the Classical period may, at least in one instance, have to be down-dated. Complex group akroteria, especially kidnapping scenes, seem to become increasingly popular to the point of competing with pedimental decoration. Figured akroteria may be the only form of architectural sculpture present in all areas of the Greek world, with the exception of Asia Minor, which is conspicuously unrepresented for the entire period. Stylistic forms seem to be fairly uniform everywhere, with little regional distinction, especially toward the end of the century.

[30] F. Hiller, p. 71, n. 4, believes that the Este Aphrodite belongs to the early Fourth century and accepts its similarity to the "Bassai akroteria." To be sure, one female figure on the Bassai frieze (slab 524, Hofkes-Brukker, *Bassai-Fries*, p. 55, no. H4-524) has a similar long fold stretching from her right breast to her left ankle, but the total effect is entirely different.

Carlos A. Picón has noticed that the chiton wearer (Louvre 3516) was sketched by P. Jacques in Rome in 1576; the drawing is reproduced by S. Reinach, *L'Album de Pierre Jacques* (Paris 1902) 127, pl. 50, who gives the statue as lost. In his publication Picard has been able to trace the provenience of the piece only as far back as the early Nineteenth century, in the Villa Miollis in Rome. Jacques' drawing shows that the chiton wearer was known much earlier and almost assures us that the piece, whether Roman or Greek, is at least ancient and not a Renaissance or later counterpart for the other akroterial figure. Jacques' drawing shows the figure with raised right arm and a head, but it also indicates that the latter was separately attached.

1. *Metronomic Pediment, Ashmolean Museum, Oxford* (fig. 38). This small gable (calculated length, 2.05m) forms a perfect frame for the upper torso of a man with arms outstretched and head in profile to right. That no continuation with the lower body was ever intended is shown by the small border to the horizontal edge of the field. Above the man's right shoulder the impression of a right foot is outlined in such low relief as to suggest a footprint on a soft medium like sand or clay. The right corner containing the man's left hand, which appears joined to the rest of the gable in some photographs, has been recognized as a restoration of relatively recent date and has now been removed.

The pediment, once part of the Arundel collection, has been considered a votive relief, the ornament for an architect's tomb and a table of standard measures (see Robertson, 199 and n. 77 on p. 650). Both the earliest and the latest discussion of the pediment (A. Michaelis, *JHS* 4 [1883] 335-50, and B. Wesenberg, *MarbWinck-Prog* 1975-76, 15-22) have concentrated on the metrological value of the piece, which seems to represent units of measurements: the arm span (ancient *orgyia*) and the foot. But while the latter gives the Attic version of the measurement, the former seems based on the Ionic foot. Michaelis, who had recognized the difference, assumed that the relief belonged to an area where trade required knowledge of both systems. Other suggestions had included the enactment of an Attic decree requiring the adoption of the Athenian system by all their allies. But, as Wesenberg has pointed out, the foot unit seems of secondary importance to the primary image, and the arm span is not automatically broken down into foot-long segments, unless this indication occurred in the now-missing right corner.

The only traces of fastening are said to occur on the upper surface of the gable; the lower can no longer be examined in the present installation. It seems unlikely that the pediment may have crowned the official decree on Attic weights and measures, since the two depictions on the gable cannot be accurately used as canons. The pediment may have topped a funerary structure, and the style of the carving may support this suggestion: it has been considered Samian or Parian,

and it may well belong to Asia Minor, where the gabled tomb form was relatively common. Perhaps the owner of the grave was not an architect, as surmised, nor a sculptor (since the two dimensions do not seem to apply to a sculptural canon), but a philosopher who held man to be "measure of all things." This interpretation is more in accord with the evidence than the theory of an imaginative (anthropomorphized) but official measuring standard. Dates suggested for the relief oscillate between 460 and 425 B.C. (for the latter see, e.g., Lippold, *Handbuch*, 176 and n. 9). An Ionic provenience would explain the Lingering Severe style of the carving and accord with a date around 440-430.

The pediment has been most recently mentioned by A. Kostoglou-Despinis, *Problemata tes Parianes Plastikes tou 5ou Aiona p.Ch.* (Diss. Thessaloniki 1979) 159-60, pl. 52 and nn. 472-74. By comparison with the stele from Ikaria, the Parian style of the relief is accepted, and a date within the decade 460-450 supported. Although the theory that the relief surmounted a public edict on measuring standards is preferred, other possibilities are not excluded.

2. *Pediment with funerary banquet scene from Sardis.* Only the left half of this gable was found in 1969, reused in a Roman context. It was published by G.M.A. Hanfmann, *Mélanges Mansel* (Ankara 1974) 289-302, pl. 99, who calculated the total length as 4.60m (H. 0.58m) and attributed it to a shrinelike tomb. The missing right half has now been found, completing the composition: *AJA* 83 (1979) 340, pl. 54.3. The scene follows the schema of the Funerary Banquet reliefs: the main personage reclines on a couch surrounded by attendants and often by his wife and other members of the family. In the Sardis pediment the reclining bearded man, the seated wife, and two smaller seated figures occupy the left half; two standing servants and a low table supporting several vessels fill the right. Comparison with the East Pediment of the Nereid Monument is convincing and confirms the funerary/heroizing character of the Sardis relief. A resemblance to the late Archaic pediment from Corfu should also be noted: A. Choremis, *AAA* 7 (1974) 183-86; the latter, however, seems appropriate for a temple. The Sardis pediment is interesting on

two counts: the Greek style of the carving which, although water-worn, is said to be excellent, and the adaptation of the Funerary Banquet scene to a triangular frame, which should here be earlier than in Xanthos. Hanfmann has dated this gable to ca. 450-430. Note the wide spacing, the empty corners, the greater height of the seated figures on the left half, whose heads overlap the top molding, as contrasted with the servants on the right, whose heads are contained by it despite their standing position, and the frontal stance of the smaller attendants.

See additional bibliography in G.M.A. Hanfmann, N. H. Ramage, *Sculpture from Sardis* (Cambridge, Mass., 1978) 56-57, no. 18.

3. *Pediment in Zurich (Archaeological Collection of the University)*. This, too, is likely to have adorned a small funerary building and, like the Sardis Banquet, it uses wide spacing and leaves the corners substantially empty, probably because of the difficulty of maintaining a uniform scale at a small size (H. 0.25m). The best illustration is in K. Schefold, *Meisterwerke griechischer Kunst* (Basel and Stuttgart 1960), 83, 84, fig. VII 308 on p. 246, entry on p. 248. He considers the work Attic, ca. 400, although admitting that the lack of indication of any connection with stone members makes the postulated wood-and-mud-brick building unusual for Attic tombs. Other scholars prefer a South Italian provenience for the piece (e.g., Ch. Karouzos, in *Charisterion eis A. Orlandos* 3 [Athens 1966] 376 n. 2; dated at the end of the Fifth century). The scene has been described as Hermes introducing a woman to the Underworld, which is indicated as a rocky landscape surrounded on either side by the waves of Acheron in engraved lines. Certainly the male figure to the left of the central axis, with his arm on the shoulder of a standing woman, recalls the Hermes of the Orpheus Relief (cf. ch. 8). On either side of the two personages, a woman rests the right foot on an elevation; since they both face to right, they add a monotonous note and recall comparable poses near the gables of the Mourning Women Sarcophagus. This is perhaps a sign that the gable may come from Asia Minor and be later than ca. 400. For the most recent discussion see S. Karouzou, *ArchEph* 1974, 42 n. 4, with previous bibliography.

4. *Simkhovitch head, RISD Museum*. This life-sized female head (fig. 39), once adorned with metal jewelry, was probably fastened to the sof-fit of a raking cornice, as suggested by the large hole in the center of its crown and by the slightly unworked area around it. The pronounced asymmetry of the features, describing an open curve to proper right, also speaks for a definite viewpoint (from three-quarter left), as compatible with a pedimental function (see fig. 8c in B. S. Ridgway, *Classical Sculpture*, Catalogue of the Museum of Art, RISD [Providence, R.I., 1972] 28-30, no. 8). Shallow holes above the fillet and near the temples may have served as measuring points for a rudimentary copying system, and may support the architectural association: statues of considerable scale meant to be placed in a definite position within a gable must have been executed according to strict specifications and quite likely on the basis of preliminary models in the round. That the sculptor did not eliminate his points of reference may confirm his knowledge that they would not be visible once the statue reached its destination.

Stylistically the head, once in the collection of Professor V. Simkhovitch, belongs within the Attic sphere of ca. 420 B.C. E. G. Pemberton (*ArtB* 59 [1977] 626-28), although suggesting that it may be a copy, has compared it to the head Athens Nat. Mus. 4845 (Delivorrias, pl. 31), recently attributed to the Ares Temple. However the RISD lady has a narrower face, which appears distinctive even in comparison to other related pieces. Attribution to a specific pediment remains at present impossible. Note that the same museum owns one more fragment from a pedimental composition: the two male feet resting flat on a slightly sloping plinth (cat. no. 9, p. 31), considerably smaller in scale than the Simkhovitch head and equally unattributable with confidence, although probably contemporary (fig. 40).

5. *Pedimental seated female figure*. From three fragments (two from the Akropolis and one from the National Museum in Athens) a beautiful pedimental statue of the late Fifth century has been recomposed by A. Delivorrias (pp. 8-15) and assigned to the Temple of Ares, since its scale and style are not compatible with any Akropolis building known at present. Although the figure for the moment could be considered "floating," its pedimental nature seems undeniable because of the perfunctory carving of both sides and rear. Delivorrias reconstructs it as a figure at rest, her left hand lying relaxed on

her lap, her right supporting her head with elbow propped on the raised knee. The pose is complemented by the right foot on a stool as contrasted with the left on the ground, which causes the uneven alignment of the thighs. On the basis of the extensive weathering of the front, Delivorrias places the statue frontally within the gable, a second figure next to her at her left side, as indicated by some attachment holes near the arm and shoulder blade. However, the restless arrangement of the chiton folds around the woman's left foot is best seen from a three-quarter view from the left (cf. Delivorrias, pl. 4). The body (which appears static and frontal in the drawing of Delivorrias Folding Plate 1) from that angle acquires motion and interest, and the position of the left arm suggests impending action rather than relaxation. The woman seems about to leave her diphros, her left elbow moving backward and outward, her left leg dropping to the ground off the stool, her torso leaning forward.

The relatively shallow depth of the mantle folds, which do not form true tension lines in between the legs, the "slipped strap" effect that makes all chiton folds stem from the left shoulder, the ridges outlining the plastically conceived torso, suggest a date close to the Nike Balustrade. Delivorrias has noted that many breaks appear fresh; there remains some hope that missing elements may yet be recognized and joined.

6. *Male figure in motion, Milles Collection.* This headless torso striding to left with upraised right arm is obviously conceived for frontal viewing because of its limited compositional depth. It had first been published as an akroterion (A. Andren, *OpAth* 2 [1955] 1-3), but it was subsequently considered pedimental because its attire suggested identification as Hephaistos and its pose appeared suitable for a Birth-of-Athena context, probably in imitation of the Parthenon East gable (J. Marcadé, *BCH* 81 [1957] 92-94). The problem is still being debated. In a recent summary of the literature, Brommer (*Hephaistos. Der Schmiedegott in der antiken Kunst* [Mainz 1978] 99-100, no. 7, cat. p. 241) has only analyzed the identification, which can be neither supported nor refuted, but which he considers unlikely because of the running pose and the raised arm, not a normal gesture for the smith god. In his latest published account, Andren cautiously returns to the akroterial interpretation

and dismisses the divine identification: *EAA* suppl. (1970) s.v. Svezia, fig. 767. It is impossible to state definitely whether the statue is a Fifth century original or a copy, but a male figure, if representing a human being, would hardly be appropriate as the subject of an akroterion (although see Wester, 114-15), and the chitoniskos seem typical of Hephaistos. The pose need not indicate running as much as startled motion, and the god's lameness may not have been specifically stressed in a narrative context. A pedimental function would seem likelier than an akroterial one, but the question must remain open. If not Hephaistos, the figure could perhaps represent Odysseus, for whom the attire would be equally appropriate, but again within a narrative, therefore a pedimental, context.

7. *Leda (or Nemesis) and the Swan* (figs. 41, 42). Boston, Museum of Fine Arts; L. D. Caskey, *Catalogue* (1925) 52-55, no. 22; Comstock and Vermeule, 29-30, no. 37. Pres. H. 0.885m, L. 0.53m. The raised left foot, the one-sided composition with little depth, and the perfunctory carving of the proper left side suggest that this statue once adorned the left-hand corner of a gable; in fact, its similarity with the Louvre akroteria is striking and probably meaningful. The statue has been altered by reworking during the Renaissance, when it was transformed into a fountain (the water spouted from a bronze neck and head with which the swan had been provided). It adorned the Palazzo Farnese at Caprarola, near Rome, and it must have been found in that city, but its style has been considered Attic. It has been tentatively attributed to the Temple of Nemesis at Rhamnous because of the appropriateness of the subject, whence it was probably taken to Rome as booty (Comstock and Vermeule), but Delivorrias, perhaps significantly, mentions the Boston piece only in a footnote (n. 636 on pp. 148-49) and does not connect it with a specific building. Carpenter (155-56) attributed it to Master F of the Nike Balustrade, but the rather cylindrical, undifferentiated treatment of the right arm and the calligraphic rendering of the drapery may speak for a Peloponnesian or South Italian origin.

Points of interest: the extensive uncovering of the female body because of the unpinning of the peplos, which recalls the Terme Niobid (fig. 25); and the subject matter, appropriate for a free-standing group such as the Fourth century created, but more surprising for an akroterion. Since the specific mythological allusion should preclude a mechanical duplication of the figure in mirror image, it is legitimate to wonder what adorned the opposite corner. Perhaps only a Ganymede-and-the-Eagle could make a suitable pendant, but the diversity of the figures would still be unusual. The most recent treatment of the so-called Timothean Leda (A. Rieche, *AntP* 17 [1978] 21-55) does not discuss the Boston piece as a possible prototype.

FOR PAGE 40

Hephaisteion Pediments: Morgan, "Pediments"; H. A. Thompson, *AJA* 66 (1962) 339-47; Delivorrias, 16-60. Cf. also chs. 2 and 4 for a discussion of other sculpture on the building.

Temple of Ares: Delivorrias, 94-161.

Nike Temple: Despinis, *Deltion* 29 (1974, publ. 1977) 1-24, with German summary on 273-75. Delivorrias, 185-87, no. 10.

Temple of Poseidon at Sounion: Delivorrias, 61-93.

Temple of Artemis at Brauron: P. Themelis, *Brauron. Guide to the Site and Museum* (Athens 1971) 16.

Temple of the Athenians on Delos: see infra, section on akroteria.

FOR PAGE 41

The Argive Heraion: latest, Delivorrias, 189-91, no. 13; F. Eichler, *ÖJh* 19-20 (1919) 18-46.

Metroon at Olympia: W. Fuchs, *AthMitt* 71 (1956) 66-73; A. Mallwitz, *Olympia und seine Bauten* (Munich 1972) 160-63.

Nereid Monument redated: see ch. 1, bibliography for p. 9.

Temple of Apollo at Bassai: the information comes from F. Cooper, whose book on the architecture of the building is forthcoming.

Male figure from Cyrene, Temple of Zeus: considered pedimental in the caption to fig. 910, p. 681, in *EAA*, s.v. Cirene; Paribeni, *Catalogo*, 26, no. 33, pl. 38, considers the statue part of an akroterial group of Boreas and Oreithyia; cf. Wester, 114.

Lokroi Temple (Marasà): see infra, p. 60.

Olympieion at Akragas: Diodoros 13.82.

FOR PAGE 42

On pedimental compositions in general see E. Lapalus, *Le Fronton sculpté en Grèce* (Paris 1947) and, more recently but less thoroughly, W. Fuchs *Die Skulptur der Griechen* (Munich 1969) 384-96. Cf. also Delivorrias, 1-5.

On the Tegea Pediments see Stewart, pt. 1; the Epidauros Pediments will receive final publication by Yalouris; in the interim his views are expressed in *EAA* suppl., s.v. Epidauro. On the Fourth century pediments of the Temple of Apollo at Delphi see F. Croissant and J. Mar-

cadé, *BCH* 96 (1972) 887-95; Marcadé, *BCH* suppl. 4 (1977) 389-408; P. Themelis, *Arch-Eph* 1976, 8-11.

Parthenon Pediments: on the building accounts for the entire project see A. Burford in *Parthenos and Parthenon* (*Greece and Rome*, suppl. to vol. 10, [Oxford 1963]) 23-34, esp. 29-32.

On the sculptural decoration of the pediments, with the best illustrations, Brommer, *Giebel* (1963). Since its appearance an extensive bibliography has accumulated, of which only the most recent can be mentioned. Among the book reviews, note *Gnomon* 39 (1967) 156-72 (W. Fuchs); *AJA* 69 (1965) 184-86 (E. B. Harrison); and review articles: *BCH* 88 (1964) 623-46 (J. Marcadé); *ArchCl* (1965) 54-78 (G. Becatti). Also F. Brommer, *AthMitt* 84 (1969) 103-26. In general, bibliography through 1974 can be found in Delivorrias, 184-85. Interesting comments in Ashmole, *Architect and Sculptor*, 107-15.

FOR PAGE 43

Harrison's latest study, on the shoulder-cord of Themis (East Pediment, Figure L), is in *Festschrift Brommer*, 155-61. The most recent publication by Berger is in *AntK* 20 (1977) 124-41; cf. also *Final Programme*, 64-65.

Myth of the Strife of Athena with Poseidon; that no established account exists is stated by Brommer, *Giebel*, 158. For E. Simon's version see n. 8. For the element of race see J. Binder, as quoted by W. Fuchs, *AthMitt* 79 (1964) 134. See also J. Binder in *Stele* (Athens 1980) 487-90.

West N: recently challenged by Ch. Jeppesen, lecture 1978.

Corner figures not identifiable as river gods: R. M. Gais, *AJA* 82 (1978) 355-79, esp. 362.

FOR PAGE 44

East Pediment, identification of figures based on location of shrines: E. B. Harrison, *AJA* 71 (1967) 27-58 (reprinted in V. Bruno, *The Parthenon* [New York 1974] 225-311).

FOR PAGE 45

Identification based on distance from center: E. Berger, *Die Geburt der Athena im Ostgiebel des Parthenon* (Studien der Skulpturhalle Basel 1, Mainz 1975); reviewed in *AJA* 81 (1977) 118-20 (E. B. Harrison); *ArtB* 59 (1977) 124-25. See however Berger's more recent opinion in *AntK* 20 (1977) 134-40.

Akr. 879: Brommer, *Giebel*, pls. 141-42; as Kranaos: Harrison, *AJA* 69 (1965) 185-86; as autochthonous hero: *AJA* 71 (1967) 33 n. 45.

The possible marine elements in the Parthenon Pediments are summarized by S. Lattimore, *The Marine Thiasos in Greek Sculpture* (Monumenta Archaeologica 3, UCLA, Los Angeles, 1976) 81, with original bibliography. Yalouris' discovery is, to my knowledge, still unpublished; for the fish without snout see N. Yalouris, *Deltion* 29.2:1 (1973-74) 2, no. Θ, pl. 4.

FOR PAGE 46

Roman workmanship of olive tree and snake: Brommer, *Giebel*, 96-97; Harrison, *AJA* 69 (1965) 186; other authors concur.

On the Basel experiments, the various reconstructions of the Wegner Peplophoros and of the central composition, see bibliography for p. 45. Berger's book summarizes all previous suggestions. Wegner Peplophoros: Brommer, *Giebel*, pl. 136.

FOR PAGE 51

Wing pattern as drapery mannerism: see F. Hiller, 67-69, pl. 15; also C. A. Picón, *AJA* 82 (1978) 70 and n. 92. The trait occurs as early as the Running Girl from Eleusis, *Severe Style*, fig. 36. For its appearance in East Greek works see W.A.P. Childs, *RA* 1976, 296-300.

Modeling principle as compared to decoration of moldings: see R. Carpenter, *Greek Art* (Philadelphia 1962) 235.

FOR PAGE 53

Polish on statues: D.E.L. Haynes, in *Wandlungen* (Festschrift für Homann-Wedeking, Waldsassen/Bayern 1975) 131, pl. 28.

Hera head: Brommer, *Giebel*, pls. 134-35 (Marcadé had attributed this head to Helios, but probably erroneously).

Laborde Head: Brommer, *Giebel*, pl. 132.

FOR PAGE 54

For a list of Greek originals found in Rome (perhaps brought there as booty) see E. Paribeni, *8° convegno di studi Magna Grecia 1968* (Naples 1969) 83-89, who includes the Niobids.

FOR PAGE 55

Stumbling Niobid in the Terme: most recently H. von Steuben in Helbig[4], no. 2279; K. Vierneisel, *Pantheon* 32 (1974) 123-27; see also id., *Final Programme*, 68. A general discussion of the Niobids and their grouping can be found in G. Hafner, *Ein Apollon-Kopf in Frankfurt und die Niobiden-Gruppe des 5. Jahrhunderts —Griechische Kunstwerke aus Rom* (Deutsche Beiträge zur Altertumswissenschaft, vol. 17, Baden-Baden 1962).

Apollo the Archer, Rome: W. Fuchs in Helbig[4], no. 1642; *Severe Style*, 106-107 and passim; *Magna Graecia*, pls. 115-17.

Fragmentary head of Artemis: E. Langlotz, in *Studies Presented to D. M. Robinson* 1 (St. Louis 1951) 638-47; *Magna Graecia*, pl. 114 (caption suggests provenience from pediment of Temple of Hera at Crotone, and no longer associates it with the Apollo).

Male wounded torso in Berlin: Vierneisel, *Pantheon* 32 (1974) 123-27.

Male head in Frankfurt: Hafner, *Ein Apollon-Kopf*.

Alba Youth: BrBr 649; Stewart, 101-102, no. 1; *EA* 1789-92; for its connection with the Niobids see W. Fuchs, *AthMitt* 71 (1956) 70 n. 20.

Torso of wounded male, Sevilla: M. Wegner, *AntP* 15 (1975) 7-14.

Smaller Niobids in Copenhagen: J: BrBr 663; K: BrBr 771; tentatively connected by Despinis (165) with Temple of Nemesis at Rhamnous, by Delivorrias (86-90; see also p. 189) with Temple of Poseidon at Sounion. Connected with Paionios by Ch. Hofkes-Brukker, *BABesch* 42 (1967) 18-25, figs. 7, 9-11, 13-14.

Helmeted head in Copenhagen: Hofkes-Brukker, *BABesch* 42 (1967) 25-28 and figs. 15, 17, connected with Niobids and with a Magna Graecian temple.

FOR PAGE 56

Dinsmoor, on pediments of Bassai Temple: *AJA* 43 (1939) 27-47. Carpenter, on Stumbling Niobid: *MAAR* 18 (1941) 28-29; cf. also his *Greek Sculpture*, 132-33, 146, 217 (by a master connected with the Nike Balustrade?).

Lullies, on Stumbling Niobid: in Lullies and Hirmer, comments to pls. 174-77.

Figure on the Bassai frieze: *Bassai-Fries*, 55-56, slab H4-524.

Formula for facial asymmetry: L. A. Schneider, *Asymmetrie griechischer Köpfe vom 5. Jh. bis zum Hellenismus* (Wiesbaden 1973); for the Stumbling Niobid see his p. 105 and figs. 10-12. The two larger Niobids in Copenhagen and the Apollo in Rome are Schneider's nos. 77, 79, and 76, respectively, pp. 104-105. For the description of the Niobid's garment see Bieber, *Ancient Copies*, 59-60. Detail of face: Hafner, 54, fig. 21.

FOR PAGE 57

On the hero taken by surprise: B. Shefton, *Hesperia* 31 (1962) 356-60.

Copenhagen Niobid (B): detail of face, Hafner, 51, fig. 18; view of the back: text to BrBr 710-11, fig. 3.

FOR PAGE 58

Copenhagen Niobid (C): detail of face, Hafner, 52, fig. 19. For rear view of the Smaller Niobids in Copenhagen see Hofkes-Brukker, *BABesch* 42 (1967) figs. 11 and 14.

FOR PAGE 59

Equestrian figure in Boston: Comstock and Vermeule, p. 32, no. 42 (dated to the Fourth century). Among the most recent discussions, see Delivorrias, 154-55 (attributed to the pediment of the Temple of Ares), and K. Stähler, *AA* 1976, 58-72 (considered a free-standing funerary monument). For the latter possibility, see R. Stupperich, *Staatsbegräbnis und Privatgrabmal im klassischen Athen* (Münster 1977) 21. For a general treatment of classical akroteria see Delivorrias. Wester, after dealing with the akroteria of the Temple of the Athenians in Delos, appends lists of other pertinent parallels and examples (pp. 106-20).

FOR PAGE 60

Lokroi youths (Dioskouroi) from Marasà temple: *Magna Graecia*, figs. 122-23; S. Lattimore, *The Marine Thiasos in Greek Sculpture* (Los Angeles 1976) 14, pl. 3:3; Wester, 118-19; Delivorrias, 92; A. De Franciscis, *RömMitt* 67 (1960) 1-29; G. Foti, *Klearchos* 21-22 (1964) 21-26.

Marafioti Temple akroteria: *Magna Graecia*, fig. 124; *Archaic Style*, 218, 223.

Ephedrismos group: *Agora Guide* 195, with bibliography on p. 319; Delivorrias assigns it to the pediment: pp. 33-40, suggests that female head does not belong: pp. 28-29 and n. 112; pls. 9-11. Cf. also Morgan, "Pediments," 95 and appendix III, pp. 97-98.

Terracotta akroteria from the Royal Stoa: *Agora* 14, p. 85 and n. 10 with bibliography.

Nike Temple akroterion, Bellerophon and Chimaera: P. N. Boulter, *Hesperia* 38 (1969) 133-40.

FOR PAGE 61

Alternate suggestion for marble akroteria: A. Linfert, *AA* 1968, 427-34. Athens Nat. Mus. 3043 is considered an Attic work from around 410 B.C. also by Karouzou, *Catalogue*, 62; cf. also text to BrBr 766-67, figs. 8-11 (L. Curtius), and Delivorrias, 191-92. Akr. 6463 is considered by Brouskari, 171, part of a relief, perhaps from a Roman sarcophagus of the Second century A.C. Not all objects said to come from the Athenian Akropolis were excavated there, since the citadel served as a repository of finds from all over Athens during the Nineteenth century.

Rhamnous akroterion: Athens Nat. Mus. 2348; Delivorrias, 188. Some doubts as to the origin of the group have been expressed, e.g., by A. N. Dinsmoor, *Rhamnous* (Keramos Guides, Athens 1972) 11, but Despinis, 162, accepts the attribution and suggests that some fragments in the Rhamnous magazine may belong (p. 166).

Temple of the Athenians, Delos: Wester, with modifications in the interpretation of the associated animals, esp. 25-31, 98, for the East akroterion, and 17-21 for the West. For her attribution to the master of Figures A-F of the Parthenon West Pediment, and of metope S 29 see pp. 57-96.

Further comparison with the central Poseidon of the West Pediment: V. Bruno in *In Memoriam Otto J. Brendel* (Mainz 1976) 55-67. See also Delivorrias, 188.

Parthenon akroteria: J. Binder, in *Festschrift Brommer*, 29-31, with list of available fragments.

FOR PAGE 62

Erechtheion akroteria: Delivorrias, 191-92 (Roman copies?)

Agora figure associated with Temple of Ares: Athens Nat. Mus. 1732; *Agora Guide*, 106-108, bibliography on. p. 315; the main publication, pending Harrison's catalogue, is P. N. Boulter, *Hesperia* 22 (1953) 141-47.

Agora "Nereid": *Agora Guide*, 190, fig. 99, 191, bibliography on p. 319; Delivorrias, 45-47. Connected with Hephaisteion.

Nike from Stoa of Zeus: *Agora Guide*, 221, fig. 32 on p. 78; head of a companion piece: *Agora* 14, pl. 51c, p. 99. *Hesperia* 4 (1935) 374-75, fig. 4 for back view, fig. 5 for side view.

FOR PAGE 63

Himera akroteria: N. Bonacasa, *Archaeology* 29 (1976) 46.

Bassai akroteria: I owe the information on floral akroteria to F. Cooper, who will soon publish the evidence. The two statues in the Louvre were first attributed by Ch. Picard, *MonPiot* 39 (1943) 49-80; the attribution is accepted by Ch. Hofkes-Brukker, *BABesch* 40 (1965) 51-71, who publishes good photographs of the back views and adds an Apollo in Copenhagen.

CHAPTER 4

Architectural Sculpture: Friezes

THE most popular form of architectural decoration during the Fifth century seems to be the continuous frieze. This basically East Greek feature was introduced into the Greek mainland during the late Archaic period, but no examples of carved friezes, either in the entablature or elsewhere on a temple, are known from the Severe phase; only funerary buildings in non-Greek territory employed the form and perhaps even Greek workmen. The great Asia Minor temples, such as the Artemision at Ephesos or the Heraion at Samos, may have continued the actual carving of their architectural sculpture well down into the Fifth century, but the decision of placing a continuous frieze in certain key positions (e.g., the carved parapet-sima at Ephesos) had been made during the Archaic period and within an Archaic and local tradition of architectural decoration. Fifth century Athens brought the continuous Ionic frieze back into prominence, and in spectacular fashion.

All known Fifth century temple friezes occur in Attica itself, and the one exception, although in Arkadia, is still vaguely connected with Athens, either by popular belief or by historical circumstances. Of the Attic friezes, three are from the Akropolis (Parthenon, Erechtheion, Nike Temple), a fourth occurs on the so-called Ilissos Temple, usually attributed to the same architect of the Nike Temple, Kallikrates. The fifth example, the Hephaisteion, provides a link with the sixth, the Temple at Sounion, since they were built by the same man. The only non-Attic example occurs in the Temple at Bassai, which Pausanias ascribes to Iktinos, the architect of the Parthenon. This statement may not be correct, and recent evidence has shown that at any rate the Arkadian building postdates the Parthenon, since it was not built until after 425. On the other hand, it has been suggested that Pausanias is correct in stating that the temple was erected in gratitude to Apollo for freeing the Phigaleians from the plague. This assertion had been discounted since the famous disease which killed Perikles had not reached the Peloponnesos, but Cooper maintains that Apollo Epikourios was traditionally the patron of mercenaries, and that Arkadian soldiers had indeed participated in the Peloponnesian War at the time of the plague. Their deliverance from the disease may have prompted the thank offering. We may therefore assume that the returning soldiers had either derived their inspiration from, or had brought back with them, some of the masters once active in Athens.

We traditionally think of a continuous frieze in terms of later examples (such as that encircling the large Artemision at Magnesia), running above the architrave of a peripteral building. This supposedly canonical position appears, however, rather exceptional when reviewed against actual examples; although a few peripteral buildings may have employed the decoration in this fashion in earlier times, evidence is minimal and perhaps misleading. The only definite instances of entablature friezes on the exteriors of buildings occur on the Delphic Treasuries, which are small structures without peristyle, so that the carved band runs largely over solid walls. Around 520 B.C. the so-called Peisistratid Temple on the Athenian Akropolis may have introduced a new arrangement: an entablature frieze over the Ionic columns of prostyle porches to a Doric peripteral building. Whether the frieze extended over the cella walls or was limited to the porches alone is now impossible to tell, but the former arrangement seems more likely in view of the later examples. All known Fifth century friezes, in fact, seem to have been used specifically to delimit space or to tie together isolated architectural elements; in other words, the continuous band acted almost like a ribbon, either binding masses or defining an empty area.[1]

The Parthenon should be considered first, as being the earliest Classical example.[2] Here the frieze visually connects the prostyle porches to the cella, much as the Peisistratid frieze might have done, though the Parthenon uses Doric columns throughout. To be sure, prostyle columns in elevation do not look as separate from the rest of the cella building as they appear on plans;[3] nonetheless, the unbroken sequence of color and figures provided by a carved Ionic frieze might have had a more unifying effect than the chromatic alternation of triglyphs and metopes, which moreover, in the case of porches with columns in antis, never extend to the lateral cella walls.[4] The same connecting purpose was served by the friezes on the Ilissos and the Nike Temples, where the prostyle porches constitute the façades of the buildings and the only columns employed by them. Finally, even the Erechtheion, although anomalous in its symmetry, has a prostyle East façade and an even greater aesthetic need to unify its disparate elements by means, as it were, of a belt course. In other words, the continuous frieze may have served the same visual purpose in these buildings as the contemporary use of dark stone in the Propylaia, which established a uniform level above several staggered surfaces.

An extension of this function is found in the three remaining examples. The architect of the Hephaisteion and the Sounion Temple seems to have been particularly concerned with the pteroma in front of the pronaos. In his earlier building he extended the continuous frieze beyond the antae, to reach the outer colonnade, and linked it visually through sculptural decoration with the corresponding Doric frieze on the exterior. In the Sounion Temple he made the continuous carved frieze encircle the entire area of the front pteroma, thus extending it both above the pronaos columns and antae and behind the Doric frieze of façade and side returns. The space thus delimited was smaller than in the Hephaisteion, but visually more coherent when seen from the interior.[5] Bassai represents a step further

[1] That the simile is not farfetched may be shown by an ancient Greek name for frieze: *tainia*, therefore a fillet.

[2] Note that the Older Parthenon (ca. 485) had an Ionic molding as toichobate (as shown by the extant anta base) and may therefore have been meant to carry an Ionic frieze. But the Older Parthenon also had prostyle porches. The frieze of the Peisistratid Temple remains an unproven, if highly plausible, assumption, which I fully accept.

[3] Note nonetheless that the Parthenon architect placed the entire naos—prostyle porches, parthenon proper, and cella—on a raised platform concentric to the stylobate, thus emphasizing the unity of the inner building, that is, the very same structure bound together by the continuous frieze.

[4] A Doric frieze encircled the hexastyle amphiprostyle Temple of the Athenians in Delos, ca. 425-417, which may have been planned by the same architect as the Nike Temple. An Archaic example of the same plan, also in the Doric order, occurs at Tegea in the Temple of Artemis Knakeatis: K. A. Rhomaios, *ArchEph* 1952, 1-32. See also E. Dyggve, *Lindos* 3:1 (Copenhagen 1960) 145 for the plans of a number of amphiprostyle temples, but, to my knowledge, the Athenian solution does not occur elsewhere.

[5] There is evidence to show that the Temple of Ares, by the Hephaisteion architect, was also carried across the antae to the peristyle at the East end,

in this use of the continuous frieze—though here, revolutionary, in the interior—since the sculptured band runs over the engaged Ionic columns of the lateral spur walls as well as over the projecting doorway on the North and the single Corinthian column standing between diagonal spur walls on the South side of the cella. Thus the entire usable floor space of the naos is defined, as it were, at a higher level and the disparate elements of engaged capitals, projecting jambs, and free-standing column are held together by the figured ribbon.[6] This specific form of spatial experimentation seems limited to the Fifth century and perhaps even to Athenian circles; later periods use the continuous frieze in different manners—more regularly but less imaginatively. In contrast to carved metopes and pediments, however, the sculptured frieze occurs rather frequently during the Fourth and the Hellenistic centuries, presumably also because a new building phase began in Asia Minor, which was geographically attuned to this form of architectural decoration.

To what an extent was the architect responsible for the decision to introduce a continuous carved frieze into his buildings? For the Hephaisteion master it was a matter of some concern, since he aligned his foundations accordingly and had therefore decided his plan from the very beginning.[7] Can we therefore assume that these are architectural experiments which do not require the planning contribution of a master sculptor? Certainly in the Hephaisteion the arrangement of the figures in the East frieze corresponds so well to the alignment of the supports below that sculpture and architecture are insolubly linked together; however, the process may correspond to that of writing lyrics for a tune, which occurs in chronological sequence but produces unified results. In the Parthenon it has been argued that Pheidias must have been the mastermind behind the whole, and Stillwell has shown that the arrangement of the figures on this frieze corresponds to the alignment of the peristyle columns, so that major scenes were selected, as it were, by the exterior frame for the viewer at ground level looking up at a slant. Granted that the arrangement results in the effect thus calculated, to what extent could such perspective highlighting have been planned beforehand by either sculptor or architect or even presumably by both of them together?[8]

---

but we cannot be sure that it was sculptured: M. H. McAllister, *Hesperia* 28 (1959) 32-33. A comparable experiment of using a frieze, though Doric, to line an area may have occurred in the so-called Great Temple of Apollo at Delos, presumably erected around 475-450 up to frieze height, but finished much later: on the inner wall faces of pronaos and opisthodomos ran a Doric entablature (*GdD*, 84). It has been suggested (e.g., Berve and Gruben, 393) that the Hephaisteion East frieze continued visually around the other three sides of the front pteroma as a smooth band painted blue; the color would have provided some connection all around. The Hephaisteion also had a frieze over the opisthodomos, presumably for symmetry, but this balancing element was omitted at Sounion. The difference in size between the entablature of the façades and that of the porches seems to have troubled the Greek architects, who adopted a variety of solutions, cf. J. J. Coulton, *JHS* 95 (1975) 13-24.

[6] A similar effect may have been intended in the Telesterion at Eleusis if G. E. Mylonas is correct in translating *diazoma* as a Doric frieze that ran around the interior columns defining the central space: *Eleusis and the Eleusinian Mysteries* (Princeton 1961) 118-19.

[7] Note also that the Hephaisteion has an Ionic toichobate, which may imply the planning of a continuous Ionic, *not* of a Doric, frieze from the start, regardless of the time of its actual execution. The Temple at Bassai has the antae of *both* porches aligned with a peristyle column, but a Doric frieze with carved metopes runs above them instead of a continuous Ionic band. Only the ceiling arrangement must have emphasized the area of the two front pteromata as a unit.

[8] H. Lauter has addressed himself to this problem in discussing the Korai (Karyatids) of the Erechtheion: *AntP* 16 (1976) 37-39 and passim. He believes that the planner of the building and the planner of its sculptural ornament were usually two different individuals; the architect would have estab-

Coulton has recently argued that architecture, at least during the Classical period, was not a profession which one embraced in order to make a living, given the inevitably sporadic nature of the commissions, and that ancient architects may have been by and large cultured and even wealthy men who supervised the erection of a building as a sort of liturgy to their city or state. The same would not be true of sculptors, who were more consistently active, and Pheidias himself is known to have attended to other tasks while the Parthenon was being built. In utilizing a frieze with prostyle porches the Parthenon architect may have simply followed Akropolis precedents—yet he seems to have been a Peloponnesian, therefore someone called in for the task because of special ability. These questions are at present unanswerable, but these are relevant issues that should be explored if we are to determine the greater or lesser originality of each contribution and the role played by masters and patrons within a building program.

THE PARTHENON FRIEZE

Brommer, in completing his monumental trilogy, has provided once again the most thorough documentation on this Parthenonian feature and both he and Robertson have already given impetus to various studies on the frieze. New theories have recently been proposed and others will no doubt appear in the near future, sparked by the exceptional photographic presentation of Brommer's work. We shall here confine our comments mainly to stylistic and compositional features of importance for the broader understanding of Fifth century sculpture, but subject matter is of primary concern and should be broached first.

There is general agreement that the relief depicts the Panathenaic procession, and only the specific occasion is debated. Three possibilities have so far been considered: (1) that the frieze portrays a generic Panathenaia, so that no date could be pinned to it, but all quadrennial celebrations of the festival would be adequately symbolized by it; (2) that it is a mythological rendering of the event, the institution of the procession itself at the time of Kekrops and Erechtheus/Erichthonios; (3) that it is the Panathenaia just before Marathon and the participants are the hoplites of Athens who will turn into heroes by virtue of their imminent death on the battlefield. In all three cases the key feature is the presentation of the peplos to the cult statue of Athena, a scene depicted on the East side, almost, but not quite, on the axis of the great doorway. As for the time sequence and location of the event, it is usually accepted that the West side shows preparation and incipient movement, while

---

lished which type of decoration to have, where and of what size, but the detailed design would have been the work of a specialist. Such specialist, however, would only have provided models, possibly in small scale, and the execution, including intermediate steps at full scale, would have been left to other sculptors.

In support of Stillwell's theory it can be argued that regulae and guttae over the two porches of the Parthenon gave some idea of the alignment of the columns and therefore of the stretches of frieze that would be framed by the peristyle, but such aid would be missing for the long sides. Art historians assure me, however, that such planning is not im-

probable nor overcomplicated. If indeed specific—and complete—portions of the figured frieze were singled out for viewing by the architectural frame, the decision seems all the more dependent on the architect in that the sculptor, when free to use his imagination, treated the pediments as penetrable. This pictorialism is in open contrast to the spatial definition of the frieze. In general, moreover, vase painters and sculptors tend to prefer a vanishing composition to the defined and complete pictures created by architects.

On the roles of Iktinos and Kallikrates see J. Mc-Credie, in *Studies von Blanckenhagen*, 69-73.

the East witnesses the arrival of the procession on the Akropolis; the gods are seated either there, invisibly, or on Olympos; and the visitor to the Akropolis would proceed with the sculptured horsemen and the chariots and the musicians and the sacrificial animals, in a regular crescendo up to the climax of the final scene to be revealed to him as he reached the East façade.[9] Therefore, the frieze would have, not the thematic unity of a bird's-eye view over events occurring simultaneously in one place, but the filmstrip development that can shift location as it records movement.

If this conception is correct, it is in contrast with the narrative approach of the metopes, particularly those of the North side. Moreover, regardless of whether the Ilioupersis involves a similar time sequence, the direction of the metopal scenes demands a reading from left to right, therefore from East to West, as shown by the movement of the figures. Finally, if the last three metopes (N 29-32) show the gods at rest after the event, as it has been suggested, we would definitely have there the end of the series, not the beginning, but —what is even more important—we would also have a gathering of deities away from what seems the focus of the program, which places all Olympians, on the frieze, the pediment, and the metopes, within the East side. Either another identification has to be found for the figures of the last North metopes, or we must admit that the planning of the sculptural program is not as rigorous as it has been suggested.[10] And even new identifications could not reconcile the difference in direction between metopal sequence and frieze.

As for the meaning of the frieze, theory 3 presents the difficulty that not a single element within the composition makes a clear allusion to Marathon; the presence of the full Olympian assembly, while surprising for a ceremony in honor of Athena alone, as Boardman has correctly remarked, is yet not enough to trigger a mental association with the heroization of the Marathonomachoi, especially since the latter were not yet dead at the time of the festival. Moreover, if the frieze of the Peisistratid Temple depicted a similar procession and gathering, no new meaning seems likely for this second version on the Parthenon.

Theory 2, the projection of the events into the mythological past, largely stems from the fact that we are reluctant to view the representation as "human" and contemporary for Fifth century Athenians. Brommer has argued that other friezes from the Archaic period had already depicted human beings outside of a mythological context and so there is no need to reject this possibility for the Parthenon frieze; yet his examples consist largely of chariot scenes or cavalcades, without narrative content, where the human element serves as an accessory. Even the banquet on the Assos frieze could easily be mythological (Herakles and Eurytos?), framed as it is by mythological scenes. On the other hand, whatever mythological interpretation has been suggested for the Parthenon frieze has failed to convince.

Theory 1 is not without its difficulties. Common objections are the omission or the

---

[9] This description is not meant to imply an actual increase in the movement of the procession as it approaches the East side; in fact, Brommer's diagram clearly shows that the rapid motion of horsemen and chariots occupies more than half the length of the long sides, but the composition then slows down and becomes truly solemn when it turns the corners. The sacrificial animals are restless, but in general, the mood is somber and there is no gaiety in the human beings, an impression heightened by the fact that, perhaps for compositional reasons, attendants and riders often incline their heads downwards.

For a penetrating description of the Parthenon frieze in musical terms see Dohrn, 16.

[10] Note however that Brommer, *Fries*, 146, speaks only of *emphasis* on the East side, not of an absolute rule of divine concentration.

modification of elements known to belong within the Panathenaic procession, the excessive number of horsemen which cannot be explained purely on aesthetic or historical grounds, and the relative obscurity of the central scene. I would add the surprising presence of all the gods stressed by Boardman, and the often repeated fact that the festival, though the most important to take place on the Akropolis, was directed toward a different temple and a different cult image, not toward the Parthenon itself. Even the argument that our ancient sources on the Panathenaic procession are late and therefore may reflect a different arrangement from that of the time of Perikles is weakened by the fact that the Athenian allies should have been included in a Fifth century depiction. It seems also remarkable that Athena should appear so relatively inconspicuous at her own festival; granted that missing attributes might once have made her identification obvious, she is still sharing a common mode of seat and clothing with the other deities, while only Zeus is singled out by his throne. I would be tempted to suggest that no specific ceremony is meant, but only a general display of religiosity by the Athenians toward all their gods, thus resulting in a procession with all the main elements of a festival but the specific features of none. Yet an abstract rendering of *pietas* seems a symbolic concept much more in keeping with Roman than with Greek practices, which tended toward the concrete. In addition, the central scene would remain unexplained; even if we visualize it as a standard ritual before a celebration, its location lends it an importance that belies the theory. It is troublesome, however, that the cloth being folded is not identified more specifically, either by its woven Gigantomachy or by other ornaments. At present only the selvage marks the edges of the cloth, thus implying its heaviness.[11]

I also find it difficult to accept that the ten male figures closest to the gods are the Eponymous Heroes. Supposedly six of them (figures 18-23) are on the left and four (figures 43-46) are on the right of the central scene, and this asymmetrical division has been considered significant for their identification, together with their different age renderings. On the basis of the division by slabs, however, some scholars prefer to identify figures 18-19 as marshals, while adding figures 47-48 to the Heroes. This very uncertainty implies that no great difference is noticeable between obvious mortals and the presumed heroes, who in fact are not shown significantly taller than the attested marshals (e.g., 49) or even the women themselves (e.g., those on slab III).[12] Both beardless and bearded marshals are

[11] M. Robertson suggests to me that the woven Gigantomachy on the peplos may have been rendered in paint, but no traces of it can now be detected on the carving.

In a lecture at Bryn Mawr College (Nov. 3, 1978) to be published in her forthcoming book, *The Festivals of Attica*, Erika Simon has given a very convincing explanation of the Panathenaic festival on the frieze: the two streams of the procession would correspond to the sacrifices at the two altars, one for Athena Polias and Pandrosos and the other for Athena Parthenos; the two empty stools are being set up for the invisible deities, Pandrosos and Kourotrophos, corresponding to the chthonic aspects of an Athena strongly connected with vegetation and fertility. The gods are participating in Athena's festival in the same way in which she partakes of other deities' celebrations. The thematic link is strong: the East Pediment shows that Birth of Athena which is being commemorated through the Panathenaia; the goddess's birthday present is that peplos which depicts the Gigantomachy also shown on the East metopes. Other difficult details, such as the male hydrophoroi, are explained by Simon as victors in the torch race with their prize hydriai. The debate over the Parthenon frieze is likey to remain open for years to come; it should be stressed, however, that not all gestures and renderings carry ritual connotations. Some motifs may have been selected solely for artistic rather than for symbolic reasons.

[12] Some of the "Heroes" (e.g., 43, 46) could be considered taller, were they to stand upright, since they are leaning on their staffs. However some of

attested throughout the frieze, and therefore the problem cannot be solved on the basis of age alone; costumes are also standard and easily paralleled. Since several of the figures in question are leaning on staffs, the entire group should perhaps be visualized as citizens who did not participate in the procession or who have already arrived and are chatting among themselves in small clusters while waiting for the rest of the cortege; their human unawareness of the gods would be easier to understand, and at the same time it would emphasize that the latter are invisible to mortal eyes.

Besides the difficulty of distinguishing between men and heroes, there is some difficulty in recognizing the gods themselves. Although a satisfactory identification has been worked out and is generally accepted, it should be admitted that characterizing traits are kept to a minimum and that iconography is different from traditional. The short hair of the gods, their relative youth, their uniform attire, the similarity even among the goddesses, are puzzling and misleading. Only Hera and Zeus are clearly marked by their gestures and status symbols.[13] An attempt has been made to correlate the deities on the frieze with specific cults of the Akropolis and Athens, but such systematic precision seems superfluous. Because of the gods' presence, the Parthenon frieze has been compared to a gigantic votive relief with the traditional difference in scale typical of such dedication, but this feature is introduced so subtly that the viewer is hardly aware of the greater size of the seated divinities. The juxtaposition of deities and common men *in architectural sculpture* remains unprecedented and, perhaps, still largely unexplained. The processional character of the composition is, at present knowledge, also very rare if not unique.

Style

The slabs of the frieze were in position by 438 and presumably the East and West sides had already been carved.[14] North and South may have been carved in situ because the re-

---

them stand straight (e.g., 18, 20) and therefore compare fairly with the mortals. Only an aesthetic principle of isocephaly seems to have prevailed in the composition, as contrasted with the undoubtedly larger scale of the seated gods.

Other possible arguments for a superhuman identification of the figures have been sought in the language of gestures. Thus figure 47 would be the marshal of the women on slab III, shown beckoning to them across the expanse of the invisible gods (and of the central scene?), while the alleged heroes, by turning their backs to their neighbors, would suggest their isolation from the world of men. Yet such poses are interspersed throughout the frieze and occur equally among mortals (e.g., 47-48); I believe that in this case the rendering was used simply to suggest spatial arrangement, with the men forming a semicircle or a group, rather than being paratactically aligned. In addition, the above interpretation would assign only one marshal (47)— and far from the immediate vicinity—to the women coming from the left, while three (48, 49, and 52) would be heading those coming from the right. Per-

haps a more balanced arrangement can be postulated.

[13] A third characterization may be that of Hephaistos: although his head is weathered, one can still distinguish flamelike curls radiating from his face and virtually engraved against the background, an appropriate rendering for the smith god. His lameness may be suggested by the peculiar shortening of his right thigh, but this trait may also be read as poor carving. I find it peculiar that the staff meant to convey his limping is so short as to fit under the god's armpit *in a sitting position*. Either a cane or a crutch, to be effective, should be taller. Kron (214 and n. 1033) has suggested that identification may have been simplified by added inscriptions, but the parallels she cites occur at moderate height or on other architectural members, where none have been noticed for the Parthenon.

[14] Brommer (180) points out that the order of the slabs on the West side could be shifted without altering the composition, since each slab is conceived as a self-contained unit, which speaks in favor of workshop carving. Harrison, in her review of Brom-

lief disregards, more than overlaps, the joints. In any case, the time span involved is limited and it is unlikely that work on the relief may have continued after 432, as one scholar has surmised. The slabs of the East side are unusually long and it has been suggested that they were quarried to specific lengths to accommodate the subjects. This may be so, but certainly architectural requirements were satisfied as well, with the large blocks working almost as cantilevers over the columns and their returns. The technical necessity to carve on the short faces of the long blocks, as visible at the corners, has also ensured a compositional desideratum: that each side begin and end with a quiet, single standing figure, as if to give a frame to the subject in motion within and a moment of rest to the eye.

Stylistically, we notice the same variety already mentioned in the other architectural sculptures, and the earliest date of the East frieze may be confirmed by a few carving details. Within the high quality of the whole there are several awkward renderings: for instance, the inability of the divinities to cross their legs properly. This is particularly obvious in the case of Demeter, whose legs appear in between Dionysos', and whose feet are difficult to reconcile with the position of her thighs.[15] Because of this peculiar arrangement, the front right leg of Dionysos' stool has also been carved differently from the others. On the laps of the seated gods the mantles are often rendered in a confusing way, without a proper modeling pattern to the folds, so that garments look mussed rather than gathered. Here too there is a difference between, for instance, the peplos and cloak arrangement of Demeter and the simpler and seemingly lighter peplos of Athena. The latter is treated with long continuous folds and carved to a relatively shallow depth, while Demeter's costume is rilled with dark disconnected channels alternating with thoroughly flat areas. The result makes her drapery look opaque, hiding the body underneath, while Athena's legs are revealed and emphasized. Yet even her carver had problems with profile breasts (her left, farther breast seems awkwardly close to the center of her chest) and with folds touching the seat. Especially on the seated deities of the left hemicycle (E IV) eye folds abound and texture is still doughy.

Difference in costume corresponds to difference in treatment. The processioning, stately women of the left side of the East frieze (E II-III) wear sleeved chitons under their himatia and peploi, occasionally with short cloaks over their backs; on the opposite half, the women on E VII-VIII have only the short cloaks and peploi or are so muffled in their voluminous mantles that they reveal little of the costume underneath. The peplos can be rendered with unusually short apoptygma or with surprisingly low kolpos. Note, on E VIII:57, that the himation is worn with a short triangular overfold over the left shoulder, forming a very wide omega fold in general correspondence to the upper arm beneath.

---

mer (*AJA* 83 [1979] 489-91), suggests that the frieze was entirely sculptured in situ, the East and West sides giving the masters a chance to become accustomed to the requirements of the task before tackling the long sides.

[15] M. Robertson, in commenting on this rendering (*Studies von Blanckenhagen*, 77) sees it rather as expressing a link between deities, equally meaningful whether the male figure is identified as Dionysos or, as he prefers, as Herakles. That "pervasive allusions to marriage, family life, and child rearing occur throughout the assembly of the gods on the east frieze" has been argued by Ira S. Mark in a paper delivered to the Meeting of the College Art Association in January 1978. In the same paper Mark maintained that the winged figure behind Hera on the frieze is Nike and not Iris, as often suggested; she would be there as symbolic of "the victory of marital union as seen in the archetype, the sacred marriage of Zeus and Hera" (quotations from the printed "Paper Abstracts").

This folding of the mantle occurs primarily in the Fourth century, and it is surprising to see it anticipated here. In general, the Parthenon frieze introduces clothing arrangements and poses that find no equivalent in three-dimensional sculpture until much later. For instance, Ares' pose, holding his knee (a pictorial motif which appears earlier in vase painting, though very awkwardly), is translated in the round by the Ares Ludovisi; W XII:22 almost anticipates the Apoxyomenos in its un-Classical covering of the central part of the torso; the sandal binders of the West frieze turn into the late Classical / Hellenistic "Jason," and the cross-legged poses of several standing figures on both East and West sides will delight sculptors a hundred years later. On the other hand many Polykleitan stances within the frieze are presumably echoes of contemporary bronze monuments (e.g., W V:9, N XLII:131), though musculature differs, especially kneecaps and Iliac crests (fig. 43).

One can assume that the anticipatory poses stem from the greater freedom allowed to sculptors of relief, especially relief so low as to belong almost with painting and drawing. This technical affinity is clear in the way in which a drilled channel contours the figures, separating limbs from their background, especially when the latter is part of the torso itself (e.g., E VI, Brommer, pl. 173), or sinking them into the plane of the drapery (e.g., S XLI:108). One visualizes outline sketches on the prepared slabs, which the individual carvers follow with their drills and chisels. Other revealing details are the pictorial, if sporadic, elements of the background in almost minimal relief and visibility: the ghostly eye of a horse within the circle of a human arm on N XLII, or the rider's hand on the same slab, almost disembodied and difficult to connect with the partly hidden head of figure 130. Hands and fingers are given unusual prominence: they bend and curve with all the delicacy of paintings, at times in slightly mannered gestures, at times in impossible foreshortening (e.g., N XLI:129 left hand; N XLII:133 right hand; S XXV:62 right hand, 63 right hand; fig. 44; and Brommer, pl. 145:1). Equal difficulty was met with the cow on S XL (fig. 45), which almost recalls Egyptian relief both in the frontal view of its horns and the modulation of the very low relief of its surface. Here, as often elsewhere, engraved lines mark wrinkles and folds of flesh, both on animals and humans.

Another pictorial detail may be the tendency to show limbs muffled in garments and hands disappearing under cloth. Already in the metopes a centaur's hoof was hidden under the garment of the woman in his grasp (S 10). On the frieze, among the many examples, note the right hand of W XVI:30 (better preserved in the cast, Brommer, pl. 46:1), that of N X:43, of Eros on East VI and, surprisingly, the left arm of Hermes on East IV. Does his pose have a special (chthonic) meaning? Several youths on the South side, leading the sacrificial animals, stretch their mantle forward with the gesture of the so-called Aspasia / Sosandra but with less artistic effects (S XLII:119, 122; S XLIII:127, Brommer, pl. 159:1). That the motif should appear repeatedly within a few slabs suggests that a single master drew them (rather than an overall designer for the entire frieze?). One may imagine that the pose was feasible only when the mantled figure was seen in profile from its right, and indeed a partial attempt to convey the same draping is made on N II:3 where, and perhaps because, the cow covers most of his torso. But this is insufficient explanation for the absence of the motif elsewhere on the frieze, given the freedom with which figures turn and interact within the main processional direction. This repetition of patterns among neighboring figures is also obvious, for instance, in the outline of the right legs on all three hydrophoroi of N VI or the women's bent legs on both sides of the East frieze.

Granted that rhythm is desirable and indeed achieved through such parallel outlines, the compositional principle of a single designer per stretch remains valid. Certainly the master was keenly aware of its frieze as architectural sculpture, since he deeply scored the skirts of his processioning women as if to imitate the fluting of the columns beneath.

As in the metopes, composition can be excellent and execution poor. The deeply carved folds of the mantle covering the lower face of a cow leader on N II are too horizontal to model the forms underneath and produce a flattening effect.[16] The legs of the charioteer sharply reigning in his horses on N XII form an impossible continuation to his upper torso; the peculiar drapery of N XVII:58 hides left arm and right leg like a conjuring trick. By and large, clothes are shown as thick and heavy, at times leathery; but a few examples of ribbon drapery also exist, and not just on women's garments. Note, for instance, the long flowing chiton of the apobates on N XVI* and the chitoniskos of the warrior on N XVII. Selvage is prominent everywhere, some of it rendered with such long and closely spaced strokes that it looks like a fringe or a special border rather than a wavy edge (fig. 45). A few instances of press folds occur: a peculiar attention to the creases apparent on a cloth that has been folded for a long time. In one example (S XLI:110) the single line appears in conjunction with a striation in the marble and may have been used, as Brommer suggests, to dissimulate the fault; but this trait has also been noticed in the Athena of the West Pediment. A common mannerism consists in turning up the hem of a garment, usually at the ankle (e.g., N IV:11-12; N X:40-42) but also at the slit in the chitoniskos (e.g., N XXXI:96-97).

Costumes present extreme variety, and only a single figure is shown entirely nude: the young groom W III:6. Given the fact that all other boys appearing on the frieze carry some mantle, either theirs or their master's, I wonder whether this figure too was originally meant to have clothing, perhaps on his farther arm. It is certainly remarkable, given the propensity for nakedness in Classical art, that even the most revealed bodies on the frieze should have some indication of clothing, however scanty, and this "prudery" must have iconographic meaning, especially in comparison with the predominantly naked Lapiths of the South metopes. Since the draped grooms show that nakedness cannot be taken as a sign of youth on the frieze, should we assume that clothing distinguished human from heroic or legendary characters?

On the other hand, partial nakedness is cleverly utilized not only to provide accents of color (or rather, lack of it against the polychromy of massed drapery and horses) but also to suggest the beginning of a row of riders abreast, or a moment of pause in the movement. Such pauses are also created by reversals in direction or by frontal poses, which are very frequent as well as, surprisingly, frontal faces. By contrast, no figure is shown entirely from the back, and the closest approximation to it, a rider on N XXXVIII (figure 118) remains unique. The frontal or three-quarter faces are usually quite successful, considering their difficulty in two-dimensional rendering and their rarity in vase painting. The frontal poses, however, can be awkward, often showing a dichotomy between the upper and lower

[16] Note the incongruity of a scene that depicts seminude figures next to the youth entirely muffled in his mantle, with complete disregard of climate, especially since the Panathenaia took place at the height of summer. This comment applies to all the various renderings of costume in the frieze. It could be argued that the leader of the animals protects his mouth against the dust raised by the cattle, as one can see in the Mediterranean area even today; but this rationalization should take second place to artistic selection for variety's sake.

body. These facing figures appear flat against the background, or with very little penetration into it, even in the case of the peculiar leaping warrior of W XIV (figure 27), whose precarious position over islands of rock recalls a slab of the Ilissos frieze.

A study of the Parthenon rocks has suggested that various locations in Athens and Olympos are meant by their presence. Yet their occurrence looks so clearly conditioned by the requirements of pose and action that the explanation seems unnecessary. Rocks sprout whenever a warrior has to tie his sandal, or a knight has to restrain his horse, or a groom has to hold back a cow. They are, so to speak, props in a bare landscape, with no three-dimensionality and no topographical value. The background itself is largely treated as impenetrable and, when men and animals appear as if occupying several planes, the effect is achieved purely through overlapping and layering, but without appreciable difference in the depth of the shallow carving.

A few final comments on anatomy and facial features: The typical Parthenonian "rosebud mouth" is actually created by a three-sectioned line. The upper lip has a pronounced central dip with a descending slash at either side, echoed by the lower lip and stopped at the corners by a drill hole. Thus many faces look slightly pouting because their mouths are downturned.[17] There is a great variety in the rendering of the eyes; some have the buttonhole effect of the Severe style, others show a clear overlap of the upper lid at the outer corner; in profile, they all appear wide open and triangular, some even deeply set. Ears are small, even excessively (e.g. Artemis'). Foreheads are low and sometimes creased. Hairstyles are highly varied and even old-fashioned among the men (note especially the braids of N X:41) while surprisingly short and fashionable among the gods. Some faces are lined as if from old age, not only among the elders but even, once, on a charioteer (N XVII:56). Bodies are muscular and great interest is shown in the rendering of arms and digitations. Some mature torsos show the protrusion of the sternum already noticed in the Poseidon of the West Pediment, others have an extended rib cage and horizontal accents at the waist. The young rider of W II (figure 2) gives the impression that loose skin twists on his taut stomach: an effect caused by diagonal wrinkles, which recall similar patterns on the Lapith of metope S 30. In some standing figures the stomach is suggested as rounded and protruding by the wrapping of the mantle (e.g., the hydrophoroi, N VI, fig. 46), but the standard figure is lean and athletic, with slim hips.

We cannot leave the Parthenon frieze without mentioning the horses, but these incredible animals have been so often discussed that there is no need to expand on them here. They are too small in proportion to the men, too lively in relation to the space, too patterned to be naturalistic, and too acrobatic to look real. Yet they remain one of the most successful artistic deceits of Greek sculpture.

OTHER FRIEZES

Only brief comments can be made about most of the remaining friezes, but their chronological sequence is important in documenting the evolution of Fifth century styles. The earliest seems to be the frieze on the Temple of Poseidon at Sounion, generally placed

[17] Since this rendering does not seem to occur on the preserved heads from the metopes, it may have been adopted to suggest more three-dimensionality in relief figures, or perhaps it represents instead a master's mannerism or even a definite stylistic feature.

around 444-440, although both a higher (ca. 449) and a lower date (ca. 420) have been suggested. A similar uncertainty prevails about the Hephaisteion friezes, which oscillate between ca. 450 and "at least twenty, and possibly fifty, years" later. The Ilissos frieze has traditionally been placed shortly after 449, but a later date has at times been suggested and has recently been convincingly argued both on architectural and stylistic grounds; the monument can therefore be almost contemporary with the Nike Temple frieze, in the 420s, with the Akropolis building probably slightly later than its "twin" near the river. The Erechtheion frieze is the single example that we can date on absolute evidence, since its building accounts testify to its carving between 409 and 406. The Bassai frieze must certainly be later than 425, the date now accepted for the inception of the temple itself, but how much later is still a matter of dispute and can only be argued on stylistic grounds; it is undoubtedly later, however, than all previously mentioned examples.

From the above list it is clear that fairly reliable dates exist only for the second half of the chronological span under review; we should therefore begin with the Sounion and the Hephaisteion friezes, which might possibly be earlier.

The Sounion Frieze

This frieze ran along all four interior walls of the front pteroma, and it seems to have depicted three subjects: a Centauromachy over the pronaos, a Gigantomachy on the opposite wall (that is, behind the Doric frieze of the East façade), and the Deeds of Theseus on the two side walls, between the first and third lateral column of the peristyle. This varied narrative is of interest in that no visual interruption occurred between subjects, and even the division by side was not strong enough to prevent their being read in a sequence. Also of interest is the relationship between the temple deity and the myths chosen for the frieze. The Gigantomachy may be explained on the grounds that Poseidon participated in the battle and even had a specific role within it—his unwitting creation of the island of Nisyros. The Deeds of Theseus and the Centauromachy may allude to the fact that the hero was believed to be Poseidon's son. It should be noted, however, that both the Centauromachy and the Deeds of Theseus occur also on the Athenian Temple by the same architect, which should alert us to the dangers of identifying temples through the subject matter of their sculptural decoration.[18]

The slabs of the Sounion frieze are in a very poor state of preservation, so that both style and, to some extent, composition are now virtually unreadable. A recent attempt to increase our knowledge through pieces preserved in museum storerooms has provided more legible fragments, but in the case of sculptures without stated provenience now in the Athens National Museum, attribution to the Sounion frieze must remain tentative. Basically, there are only two fragments on which we can safely comment: a naked male torso in violent motion and the upper body of a figure wearing a peplos which, though in

[18] A frieze with the Deeds of Theseus has also been recognized on a Delian building that does have stronger claims to a connection with Theseus, whether or not the structure should be identified as the Keraton, containing the altar of horns around which Theseus danced the crane dance after his victorious departure from Crete. The technique of the building is said to be clearly Athenian and, according to an inscription, work was already advanced by 345/4 (GdD, 98, no. 42; G. Roux, BCH 103 [1979] 109-35, esp. 123 n. 53). According to Marcadé, the sculptor of this Delian frieze treated his subject matter as a series of metopal duels: Au Musée de Delos (Paris 1969) 47-49.

Athens, is attested to be from Sounion. Two more fragments are probable: the lower part of a woman, which retains traces of a horse's forelegs against her body; and a centaur preserved only from just below the nose to the level of the first abdominal division. On this limited basis one can only say that the male torso shows the same mannerism of breath intake visible in some Parthenon figures, especially torso H from the West and, to some extent, also H from the East Pediment, although the Sounion build is leaner. The female legs show drapery with softer ridges, less sharp than the Parthenon pedimental renderings, but a comparison with the seated deities on the East frieze yields closer parallels. The poorly preserved slabs still show the outlines of lively compositions which, in the Centauromachy, include the episode of Kaineus and possibly Artemis' intervention in her chariot, two motifs later repeated in the Bassai frieze. If dating on so few and uncertain elements is valid, the Sounion frieze could well belong around 430. The style of the single figure definitely coming from one of the pediments may allow an even lower chronology, ca. 420.

The Hephaisteion Friezes

These occupy the entablature over the East and West porches. On the West, the decorated band runs from anta to anta and shows a Centauromachy from which women are absent; the East frieze stretches from South to North peristyle, thus spanning the passageways between outer colonnade and antae, and its subject matter is still unclear. It is usually assumed to represent the fight between Theseus and the Pallantids for the possession of Athens, but some discrepancy between the center episode and the rest of the action is difficult to explain. A Deed of Theseus would be appropriate if seen in correlation with the metopal decoration, and Theseus appears in the Centauromachy of the West side, thus connecting the two friezes as well. On the other hand, this emphasis on the Attic hero cannot be explained solely on the grounds of Athena's patronage, nor is a connection with Hephaistos obvious.[19] The identification of the temple itself is problematic, as previously mentioned, and it seems best not to try to force a meaning upon the iconography on the basis of cult, or vice versa. It should rather be admitted, as pointed out by Robertson, that many Fifth century friezes remain obscure, not just when fragmentary but even, as in this case, when preserved in their entirety. This obscurity may mean a change in preference from more popular to more unusual myths, but it also suggests that characterization is relative and based on few identifiable attributes. One wonders how clear such scenes would have been to contemporary Greeks and even whether some ambiguity might have been intentional, if the primary purpose of the sculpture was as architectural decoration.

The East Hephaisteion Frieze As already noted, this (figs. 47-52) is composed with remarkable attention to the underlying architecture. Thus the seated deities occur directly

[19] This point has recently been stressed by E. B. Harrison in her paper delivered at the London International Congress in 1978 (*Final Programme*, 65). She finds more "Hephaistos iconography in the Parthenon" than in the temple we call the Hephaisteion. Harrison has also suggested different identi- fications for the gods of the East frieze, and would date both East and West compositions between the Parthenon frieze and that of the Nike Temple. See also her discussion of gestures in *Studies von Blanck-enhagen*, 91-98, especially 94-95.

above the antae, the fallen warriors arch over the columns, and the fighting scenes fill the remaining areas in correspondence with empty space below. There is also a progression in narrative, with relatively quiet scenes marking the beginning and the end of the composition and the most violent action taking place in the center. Position therefore singles out the most important episode as well as personage, who is further characterized by his falling mantle and heroic pose as the typical "hero in distress" (fig. 51). It is perhaps incongruous that heavy fighting should take place so close to the seated deities that part of a warrior's shield disappears behind the first god on slab 5, but this excessive proximity may have been meant to convey that the divine spectators, as on the Parthenon frieze, are invisible to mortal eyes. Since their role is passive, the story cannot involve a god, but why are boulders being used only by the central figures?[20] The Pallantids were not true giants and were, furthermore, fifty in number: they should all have used the same weapons. Moreover, would Theseus' companions have taken prisoners (fig. 48)?[21] It is also impossible to distinguish parties on the basis of attire, since nude warriors occur apparently on both sides and we cannot tell whether the dead are friends or foes. An unusual motif is represented by the single archer stringing his bow (slab 6:29).

Stylistically, the East frieze has been acutely analyzed by Morgan and only few points need repeating here. The most remarkable feature is the freedom of bodies in space, with many back views, torsion, and strong foreshortening. The relief is so high that limbs and other parts of the figures are undercut or carved entirely in the round, yet the position of the sculpture on the building corresponds to that of the Parthenon frieze, which was executed in very low relief.[22] Perhaps greater visibility of the Hephaisteion frieze was possible from below the hill, yet Agora buildings must have impeded the view to a great extent and distance must have blurred compositional lines. The figures are widely spaced, however, either for greater clarity or as a consequence of their technique, and it is interesting that such foreshortening should be combined with less pictorialism and greater sculptural plasticity in approach. The advance over the Parthenon frieze is clearest in the positions of the seated gods which appear more three-dimensional and steeped in space. Motion lines are well controlled, especially in the fluttering skirt of warrior 2 on slab 1 (fig. 47); on figures 10 and 12 the undulating hems of the chitoniskoi convey twirling action. Bodies are rendered as lean and muscular, with greatest emphasis placed on epigastric arch and rib cage forming a strong caesura at waist level (figs. 48, 52). One fighter (slab 4:17 fig. 52) shows the same loose skin over the stomach area that appears on

[20] Harrison has pointed out that the boulders are only being pushed away by the human figures, not actually thrown. It should therefore be assumed that such rain of stones comes from the gods themselves. Harrison also sees Zeus' intervention in the striken pose of one of the Pallantids who clutches his neck as if hit by a thunderbolt, while his stomach muscles show the electric shock. A hole for a metal attachment may indicate the position of Zeus' weapon.

[21] None is implied in Plutarch's account (*Life of Theseus* 13), not even the betraying herald Leos, who seems to have acted voluntarily. The taking of prisoners is a relatively rare scene in Greek friezes,

and it seems surprising to find it on a Tarentine vase, though with different context: H. Sichtermann, *Griechische Vasen in Unteritalien* (Tübingen 1966) pl. 53. Some influence of the Hephaisteion friezes may be apparent in South Italian art. Cf. also a figure on the West frieze of the Nike Temple (fig. 58, block *a*) and, much later, a pirate on the Lysikrates Monument frieze, A. Stewart, *Skopas of Paros* (Park Ridge, N.J., 1977) pl. 51c.

[22] Rather than stressing the height of the Hephaisteion frieze, it is probably more correct to stress the unusually low carving of the Parthenon frieze, which remains virtually unparalleled until Roman times.

some Parthenon figures (the Lapith in metope S 30, the horseman on the frieze, W II:2). The arrangement of drapery on figures 21 and 26 recalls the figure on fragment *p* from the Nike Temple frieze. Violence and liveliness correspond to the approach on the Hephaisteion metopes.

The West Hephaisteion Frieze Its Centauromachy makes a slightly different impression, possibly because the equine bodies of the centaurs introduce oblique or horizontal masses contrasting with the more slender lines of the human figures. But while in the Parthenon metopes this horseback position seemed to give the centaurs the upper hand in the fight, in the Hephaisteion frieze roles are more evenly divided and the winners are not readily apparent. One centaur (W 2:5) is shown on its back, in a rolled-horse position that required from the sculptor a real tour de force in the twisting of the human torso; another centaur (W 4:19) is being stabbed in the chest in a composition reminiscent of the Olympia pediment and which will reoccur on the Bassai frieze; a third monster (W 3:15) may not yet have been wounded but is being seriously threatened by his kneeling opponent. Conversely, no human beings are shown dead, though Kaineus is being pounded into the ground (W 2:9) and two more Lapiths (W 1:1; W 4:18) are in grave danger.

Compositionally, spacing is again generous and foreshortening is employed, although with more restraint than on the East side. Rear views are limited to two centaurs (W 2:6; W 3:13), but penetration into the background is suggested in other ways, through diagonal poses. In addition, a considerable amount of landscape is introduced by means of an uneven ground line, which alternates with the architrave fascia in forming a stage for the actors.[23] There is another peculiarity which, to my knowledge, occurs in no other frieze: this West sculptured band extends between two antae, as it were: that is, the composition is framed by two piers in low relief, each surmounted by a squarish "capital" which continues as a flat fascia across the side pteroma spanning the passageway to the peristyle. On the sculptured frieze itself, between the "capitals," runs a low molding once decorated in paint, comparable to the normal fascia of Doric metopes. This projecting band appears also at the top of the East frieze, which, however, has no pillar frame since the relief slabs extend beyond the porch proper. The resulting effect is that of a spacious overhead to the figures, because the molding itself is overlapped by them but never to the level of the horizontal cornice. This arrangement corresponds to the normal Ionic placing of a frieze between two moldings, but the square capitals and piers at the ends of the West frieze interrupt the flow and almost suggest an architectural setting for the action, although the nearest figures stand clear of the frame. Perhaps the sculptor was trying to emphasize the shorter length of the West frieze and its definite termination (as contrasted with a possible extension around the cella) by means of these abstract brackets.[24]

It has often been noted that the first group of man and centaur on slab 1 is compositionally very close to Parthenon metope S 4, and other parallels have been drawn with the Akropolis panels. In addition, the Kaineus episode, which does not occur on the Parthenon,

---

[23] But note that Kaineus seems to sink into the architrave, with an illusionism comparable to that of the Parthenon East Pediment. By contrast, the same episode on the Bassai frieze is provided with a rising ground line into which the warrior disappears as if in a crater.

[24] Conversely, because of their presence, he did not need to use quiet figures at the ends of the composition, as he had done for the East frieze, which lacked the architectural projecting frame.

is compositionally self-contained as befits a metope. It is incorrect, however, to analyze the West frieze as if it were a sequence of duels susceptible of inclusion into a Doric frame. The entire scene has instead been conceived in continuous motion, with a major division in the center, to be sure, but also with a definite linking of action and reaction within the two halves. On slab 1, for instance, we begin with a true duel, but we then see a Lapith (3) lend a hand to a companion (4) who has brought down a centaur (5) but is being threatened in turn by a galloping monster coming to the rescue (6). Thus 3 and 6 cross glances, as it were, over the central core of 4 and 5. Yet the action is not spent within the foursome because warrior 7 tries to stop the galloping centaur from behind. The Kaineus episode has a closed, pyramidal structure, but here, too, warrior 11 (Theseus himself) comes to the rescue, properly emphasized by his relative isolation and traveler's hat. I find it intriguing that Theseus should have been connected with Kaineus, since the fate of the invulnerable warrior is sealed and not even Theseus could save him; it seems therefore as if the frieze master spent all his identifying elements in one place, wasting, as it were, his main hero in a situation where he can reap no success. It has been properly stressed that Theseus appears in the Harmodios pose, the equivalent of a definite attribute, which ensures identification.

The right half of the frieze is more weakly conceived: it consists of four duels grouped by twos through the centaurs' directions, with a secondary axis in the center formed by an isolated warrior (16) and some compositional, if monotonous, unity provided by the parallel animal bodies. In contrast, the left half of the West frieze seems more original and fluid.[25]

Stylistically, note the attempt to show limbs enveloped in drapery: the left arm of warrior 1 using his chlamys like a shield, and Theseus' mantle, which seems to cover part of his left arm and chest, though weathering blurs definitions. Human bodies are again lean and nervous; centaurs are long-waisted and humpbacked, all seemingly short-haired and with beards linked to the chest by small bridges of stone left uncut for further support. Faces are now badly weathered but close-ups show wide open eyes with sharp lids, comparable to Parthenonian renderings.[26] Drapery flies and curls against the background but is used to convey motion and is not a filling device.

Can the Hephaisteion friezes be considered later than the Parthenon frieze? Given the different technique and approach, it is perhaps methodologically improper to correlate the two; in addition, the heavy weathering of the Hephaisteion sculptures makes analysis uncertain. It does seem definite that influences move from the Akropolis down to the Agora, and it is difficult to visualize the Hephaisteion style as earlier than the Parthenon's. A date in the late 430s or shortly afterwards should not be wide of the mark.

The Ilissos Frieze

If a redating of its slabs has been convincingly argued, the same cannot be said of its cult identification and subject matter. Our understanding is hampered by the fragmentary

[25] Taken together, however, the two halves of the frieze balance each other and provide a good visual equilibrium.

[26] A head of a warrior in the Boston Museum of Fine Arts seems of the right scale and style to belong to the Hephaisteion, but it has proved impossible to join to the preserved torsos. See M. B. Comstock and C. C. Vermeule, *Sculpture in Stone* (Boston Museum of Fine Arts, 1976) no. 33, pp. 26-27; K. Stähler, *Boreas* 2 (1979) 185-88 (Ares Temple).

nature of the evidence, with few slabs surviving from a frieze which may have imitated the Nike Temple also in having a different topic on each side. After the Parthenon precedent it is perhaps natural to expect that external continuous friezes should have unity of content as well, but this had not been the practice before and the Parthenon may stand out once again as the exception. What can be said is that compositions seem more pictorial than in the Hephaisteion, with wider spacing and elements of landscape which go beyond the indication of an uneven ground line or the sudden appearance of a rocky elevation to serve as a seat. Though this formula is still used, it is better integrated with the narrative and the blank background, so that one man seems to be leaping across a chasm and others sit on true undulations of the terrain against which their belongings rest at different levels.

Scenes of violence are suggested by women being lifted by men (fig. 53) or being pulled away from the support they grasp, mysterious as the support itself may be in its interpretation (fig. 54). Renderings are three-dimensional and seated figures cross their legs in what may be the earliest instance of this pose in architectural sculpture.[27] Proportions are slender and lean, but all fine details are lost because of heavy weathering; thus drapery patterns cannot be properly analyzed except in general lines. It is significant that folds gather in between the thighs, while cloth stretches smoothly over limbs and stomach and grooves outline breasts, thus suggesting a transparency usually associated with the style of the 420s. The fluttering end of one mantle streams across the background, but with moderation. Tension folds occur both on seated and standing figures, but by and large simplicity prevails. The Parthenon richness is gone and emphasis is placed on bodily forms and volumes. In male anatomy strong indentations at the waist recall similar mannerisms in the Parthenon and the Hephaisteion.

Perhaps the most significant fact about the Ilissos frieze is that it was copied in Roman times (fig. 55); since so little of the sculpture from the temple remains, it is remarkable that such copies could nonetheless be recognized, and in Ephesos, therefore at considerable distance. The Ilissos frieze provides the first positive evidence that architectural sculpture in relief was not just imitated but copied, yet no such replicas have been found for the Parthenon frieze, albeit more extensively preserved. Perhaps the relative distance of the two friezes from the observer may have affected their copying. That one of the copies did not retain the same mythological content of the original can be surmised but not proved; nor can we, in any event, ascertain the meaning of the scene in either monument. To add to the problem, the identity of the deity to whom the Ilissos Temple belonged remains uncertain.

The Nike Temple Frieze

Virtually entirely preserved, plausibly restored to its original sequence and positively connected with an identifiable cult, the Nike Temple frieze (figs. 56-60) is also fairly closely dated around 420,[28] but the subject matter of its scenes remains in dispute. Here

[27] A presumably earlier instance occurs on a difficult monument: the so-called Ludovisi Throne (the nude flute-playing girl on one of the short sides, *Severe Style* fig. 71).

[28] Inscriptional evidence alluding to a cult statue

and a priestess can give a date for the temple between 427 and 423, and this is the period usually preferred in American publications. German scholars opt for a lower chronology and want to set the beginning of building activities not long before the

the main controversy is whether specific historical battles are depicted or whether such glorification of more or less contemporary events would have been hubristic and therefore an unlikely subject for architectural sculpture. The proponents of the first theory identify the battles of Marathon (490 B.C.) on the South, of Plataia (479 B.C.) on the North, and of Megara (458 B.C.) on the West, with a gathering of gods in honor of Athena Nike on the East side. The proponents of the second theory believe that generic victories are shown, with Persian opponents depicted on the South side to allude in general to famous Athenian enemies, without pinpointing locale and time. Finally, a few scholars have attempted to connect the friezes with mythological events, but have found no following.[29]

It would be important to determine which of the two main positions is correct. In favor of the first it has been pointed out that paintings in stoas are known to have portrayed Marathon and other historical battles (Mantineia and perhaps Oinoe); that Marathon, by the time of the Nike Temple, had already become part of Athens' glorious past and the Marathon casualties were worshiped as heroes (Paus. 1.32.4); and that to distinguish between media or even types of buildings is an unwarranted if not specious discrimination, since stoas were part of religious complexes and housed war trophies of the kind often dedicated in temples. The proponents of the second theory do in fact make such distinction, and there is an element of truth in the surmise that what is proper in a medium may not be appropriate in another, especially since the paintings in the Stoa Poikile may have been panels rather than murals insolubly connected with the structure.

T. Hölscher has examined this question in more general terms, as part of the concept of historicity in the Greeks; he sees special significance in the fact that portraiture began during the Fifth century, a fact which speaks for a heightened sense of human dignity, but he supports the second position, which may be preferable against this wider theoretical background. The question should be raised once again about the possible historic value of the Trojan War to the Greeks or of the Deeds of King Theseus to the Athenians; yet these subjects are unquestionably identifiable in architectural sculpture and on religious buildings. There is, however, some difference between events which were still within living memory of the older generations and others which were strictly part of the epic patrimony of the country. Hölscher makes the point that nakedness, or at least token armor, does not imply heroization but serves to concentrate attention on the vitality of the participants—which is ultimately responsible for the victory—rather than on their equipment. This explanation seems perhaps too subtle, and the unrealistic attire of the fighters

Peace of Nikias. H. Lauter (*AntP* 16 [1976] 44 and n. 120) considers the frieze one of the last elements of the building, more or less contemporary with the Erechtheion Karyatids or at least with their planning phase. But for the higher date of both frieze and balustrade see H. Jung, *JdI* 91 (1976) 124 and n. 113. For a review of the entire epigraphical evidence, see C. A. Picón, *AJA* 82 (1978) 73-76.

[29] An intermediate position, favored by M. Robertson (348-49) would consider depiction of the Persian wars suitable for a temple decoration, which would raise them to the semimythological/semihistorical level of the Trojan War. However, fights of Greeks against contemporary Greeks would still be excluded without additional and explicit evidence. Robertson speaks of the wars in which "kings Codrus and Erechtheus fell," and the tradition behind Euripides' *Erechtheus* has the Athenian killed by Poseidon's trident while erecting a trophy. It would be tempting to connect the trophy on the West side with this particular story, but not enough evidence is available: and this specific feature is not even mentioned by Ch. Kardara, who first suggested the purely mythological interpretation, naming Erechtheus and Eumolpos and Thracian (rather than Persian) troops: *EphArch* 1961, 65-158, esp. 84-92.

may have been meant to support a generic identification, whereas complete nudity might have entirely removed the action from the human sphere.[30] One could assume here the same undifferentiated portrayal advocated above for the Parthenon frieze, but it seems at least sure that different allusions were made by each side of the Nike frieze, since diversity was introduced in costumes (Persians appear only on the South side), manner of fighting (no cavalry is shown on the West side), and perhaps even outcome.[31]

That the East side shows an assembly of gods is beyond dispute, even if individual deities are hard to label; it is tempting to assume, given the small size of the building, that they play here the same role as on the Parthenon frieze, forming the culmination, as it were, of the three battle scenes as the forces ultimately responsible for the sorts of victory.[32] Their static, often frontal poses punctuated by wide empty spaces correlate well with the underlying architecture, and the ridged skirts of the many peplophoroi recall the fluting of the Ionic columns below.[33]

Stylistically, the Nike Temple frieze is very important because many of its motifs occur later in other and widely scattered contexts. Since its relatively small height and difficult visibility of three of its sides make this imitation and popularity surprising, perhaps the frieze itself may have borrowed its imagery from an earlier and famous monument more accessible for later inspiration. It seems actually quite possible that the shield of the Athena Parthenos may have been the ultimate source for some of these thematic conventions, especially that of the wounded comrade being helped from the field of battle.[34] Other major motifs are: (1) the hair-pulling scene, with the victim down on his knees, which seems attested already on the Parthenon metopes; (2) the stumbling horse with his endangered rider; and (3) the warrior in three-quarter view from behind peering above his shield.[35] Many of these traits are repeated in the friezes at Gjölbaschi-Trysa, but by far the most popular there is the swirling skirt, which occurs with variations on

[30] Note that fighting scenes in non-Greek or East Greek territory (where historical tendencies prevailed and human nudity was considered disgraceful) tend to show the warriors more heavily clothed. E. Harrison has conveniently provided photographic comparisons of related scenes on the Nike frieze and at Gjölbaschi-Trysa: *AJA* 76 (1972) pls. 74, 77, 78.

[31] E. Pemberton, *AJA* 76 (1972) 304, suggests that the West side shows not so much an even battle as an annihilation, but I am not sure I see this point.

[32] Pemberton, who supports a scene of homage to Athena Nike, assumes that the goddess stands alone between the two centrally seated gods, thus occupying the focus of the entire frieze; yet she correctly numbers the sequence to show that two, not one personage, occupy the center span: thus Athena was not alone in being spotlighted, unless the smaller figure close to Zeus is a Nike. Another theory maintains that this second personage is Theseus and that the scene represents his introduction to Olympos; this is however an unattested version of Theseus' story.

[33] Note in fact that the seated figures are placed consistently over the intercolumniations, in a re-

versal of the arrangement used on the East frieze of the Hephaisteion. It has been suggested that a Fourth century "Tribune" (?) in Phoenician Sidon but carved in Greek style recalls the East frieze of the Nike temple: *BCH* 100 (1976) 656-74.

[34] This motif is quite different from that of carrying a dead comrade away from the battlefield, which occurs as early as the Late Geometric period. For a list of examples see K. Fittschen, *Untersuchungen zum Beginn der Sagendarstellungen bei den Griechen* (Berlin 1969) 179-81.

[35] Note also the similarity to the Harmodios/Theseus of the Hephaisteion West frieze, the "hero in distress" convention of the slipping mantle, and the gesturing general, which also occurs on the Hephaisteion frieze. All of these motifs and their iconographic implications have been discussed by E. Harrison in support of her identification of the Battle of Marathon on the South side. J. C. Carter has now compared a figure falling backward and propping himself on his left arm with a fallen giant on a coffer from the Temple of Athena at Priene: *Studies von Blanckenhagen*, 141 n. 6, 149 n. 42.

the Nike frieze but is almost ubiquitous on the Lycian monument. Its first appearance, to my knowledge, is on the Hephaisteion frieze and includes the mannerism of the slightly upturned hem forming a wavelet.[36]

Among the motifs listed above, that of the stumbling horse (2) deserves special attention, since it occurs both on the Alexander Sarcophagus and on the Alexander mosaic; the presence of the historical ruler on these monuments has therefore suggested that they both reflect an actual episode of his Asiatic campaigns. If, however, one traces the theme back to the Nike frieze through the Nereid Monument, the Bassai frieze, and even some South Italian vases, the scene appears rather as a plausible thematic motif to be added for variety's sake to any battle employing cavalry. Its introduction into the sculptural repertoire may in fact have been prompted by the frequency of such occurrences in real life, but without any specific meaning attached to it.

Different styles appear on the four sides of the Nike Temple—so much so that Blümel had once thought some years had intervened in the completion of the sculptural decoration. This position is no longer held, but it may underscore the variety of renderings. We shall here concentrate on those common points that are helpful to determine the progress of Fifth century styles. The most obvious and most important is the flamboyant drapery.

On all four sides, but especially on the West, mantles fly and fill the wide spaces between the figures. Folds run evenly in S-curves with flat valleys in between and an occasional "double-track" rendering, which is typical of the late Fifth century and continues into the Fourth. On the South side, especially on block *l*, the drapery swirls in free-form patterns, while on the North some mantles almost encircle the entire body in great sweeping curves. Even the quieter East side has one running figure holding a flying scarf behind her as if it were fluttering in two directions at once (block *o*:22).

For the most part, drapery seems opaque and thick-ridged, but in between the ridges it clings flatly to the body in many points, thus modeling it emphatically.[37] Folds consistently cross thighs and curve around stomachs, either dipping or merging between the legs, and tend to form continuous catenaries above the chest, resulting in somewhat linear patterns. There is more variety on the East side, where "Aphrodite" (3), with her raised foot and cobwebby mantle, forms the perfect rehearsal for the Sandalbinder of the Nike Parapet. All peplophoroi emphatically differentiate between weight and free leg, the latter clearly shown by clinging drapery that catches at the ankle; one deity (19) increases her similarity to the Erechtheion Karyatids by stretching out her back mantle with her right hand.[38]

Despite their seeming isolation, there is variety and contact among the individual East figures. The first (1) holds a winged Eros by the hand; three women (4-6) are linked by their moving pose; a male leaning on his staff while crossing his ankles (11) seems in conversation with his female neighbor; two women stand close together in an embrace (20-21), while a seated lady (23) nonetheless forms a group with her standing and

---

[36] Compare, for instance, the Hephaisteion East 3:10 and the Nike frieze West *k*:17. For the swirling skirt, see Hephaisteion East 1:2.

[37] Thus the male sex of the Orientals on the South frieze is clearly shown and prevents a spontaneous identification of the scene as an Amazonomachy.

Many Persians are also bearded.

[38] This motif seems to have occurred also on the base of the Parthenos, as attested by the Pergamon replica and the Del Drago relief (Leipen, figs. 64, 66).

agitated companions (22; 24). The whole sequence is punctuated by four seated figures symmetrically spaced.

On the other three sides, poses are much more lively, as befits combat scenes. Many warriors are seen from the back or in daring overlap, as in the duel on West *l* (22-23). Ground lines are uneven, and one fallen body (West 5) is partly hidden behind the rocky outcrop onto which two fighters step (4, 6). The most pictorial scene occurs on the South side, where a rearing horse in almost frontal view has thrown his rider, who tries to save himself by reaching for the ground with his right arm (block *l*).[39] The naked warriors show a lean anatomy with pronounced hip muscles and some indentation at the waist, but without the emphasis of the Hephaisteion friezes; legs are often spread wide apart in lunging and squatting poses. Shields and other elements of the composition are frequently foreshortened, and space penetration is remarkable, especially in such a small compass. Painted details and metal additions must also have played an important part within the whole.

As a final comment, note that the Nike Temple battles work effectively as architectural friezes, flowing across the entire band with a rippling outline that recalls relief decoration on a molding and must have been quite visible in its general pattern even from afar, against the blue background. The wide spacing of the figures as well as the relatively strong undercutting and consequent shadow may have been motivated by this need for distant visibility.

The Erechtheion Frieze

Of all Fifth century friezes this is the most difficult to evaluate, although it is also the most precisely dated (409-406). An unusual technique was adopted for it, in that each figure was carved separately in white marble and then fastened against a continuous background of blue Eleusinian limestone (figs. 61-64). This method is attested for statue bases but was never used again for architectural purposes, perhaps because it was considered unsuitable. There are several statuary traits in the Erechtheion: not only this peculiar continuous frieze but also the use of Karyatids as support and even the parapet on which they stand, which resembles a tall orthostat base like that of the Athena Promachos nearby.

Because the frieze height is proportional to column height, the blue band in the entablature of the cella proper is slightly narrower than that around the North porch, therefore the relative provenience of the single figures can sometimes be determined on the basis of their size; no such clues exist for their sequence or their subject matter. In the First century A.C. damage to the building required that the entire West frieze of the cella be replaced, and some extant pieces have been identified as being of Roman workmanship despite their close imitation of Fifth century style. We have already discussed the questions of artistic conception and originality which the Erechtheion frieze and its many

---

[39] Another important pictorial detail is the elusive "trophy" on the background of the West frieze, which has prompted Pemberton's identification as the Battle of Megara. The lower part of the supposed tree trunk could only have been finished in paint, perhaps to suggest recession behind the fallen warrior. Its outline is too angular to represent a human being, but I am not entirely convinced that it does in fact represent a trophy, although I can provide no substitute explanation.

carvers raise (ch. 1) and in particular whether this handicraft approach is indicative of the position enjoyed by architectural sculpture among the arts. Here we shall concentrate on style. As for composition, nothing can be said except that groups exist, carved in one piece, and must have provided the only possible overlapping. The extant figures show no weapons or violent poses of any sort; the subject matter must have been relatively quiet. Given the many cults of the temple, one wonders whether the depiction of a single myth was attempted for the entire cella frieze or at least for the North porch, or whether a series of divinities and heroes were shown in juxtaposition. A Roman replacement piece represents a seated figure with an omphalos on his lap, who should be Apollo; he is the only identifiable image. Two women in an embrace could be Demeter and Kore; children and young boys remain anonymous.

A recent study of the Erechtheion sculptures has identified at least seven masters with their carving peculiarities, but differences are here less obvious than among the sculptors of the Nike Balustrade. Concentrating on renderings in general, the most important development, I believe, is the different approach to texture and transparency. Ribbon drapery and the lively concave folds of some Parthenon sculptures, with their overlay of oblique incision, are completely absent. Here transparent drapery clings flat within a minimum of folds; incision, where present, functions almost as a gradation in planes, running parallel to some of the low and smooth ridges which originate from anatomical protrusions. By and large, the body asserts itself under the cloth, which only color would once have made noticeable in places. A new detail is the rendering of rolls of flesh, both in seated and standing figures, which ripple under the garment thus making its transparency obvious. Even the navel is indicated regardless of its covering (fig. 62). Textural contrast is toned down. Drapery almost returns to the limp doughiness of the Severe style, but with greater roundness of folds, deeper and darker channels, and less even spacing of them. Indeed, folds are now gathered in key positions only, either to suggest the articulation of the body beneath or to convey the behavior of cloth per se; thus, in places patterns are highly logical and in others totally irrational. Most significant is the formula to suggest the knee in profile, with one long curve coming down along the thigh and a shorter one rising above the calf, meeting back to back at the joint to form a triangle. Limbs are shown in almost Hellenistic isolation, with long sweeping folds contouring them: thighs, calves, breasts, even stomachs. Ankles catch hems and turn them over or produce sweeping tension folds; seats are used as compression points for drapery, which is then made to radiate in parallel lines as it falls free again. "Knee wings," S-curves, and folds between the thighs are still used to convey motion, as well as the uncovered breast and leg. One figure shows the cobwebby mantle already noted in the Nike frieze, another has a surprising loop over her raised thigh, which recalls the akroterial figure in the Louvre. Drill channels abound and selvage seems not to be rendered at all.

THE BASSAI FRIEZE

This controversial monument is here included despite the fact that it probably dates after 400 B.C. and that the solution to some of its problems must await definitive publication of its architectural frame. Yet two considerations make it important for our purposes: (1) this frieze best exemplifies the latest developments of Fifth century traits and their transformation into the style of the next phase, albeit in the Peloponnese rather than in Attica; and, (2) in the variety of its renderings and the many instances of quotations from earlier monuments, this frieze may confirm our initial theory that such architectural sculpture was primarily intended to serve an architectural function and could therefore be carved almost piecemeal, as it were, without a previous model by a master mind. In this position I am sharply at variance with the most recent publication of the Bassai frieze, which sees its style as coherent and attributes it to a single master, Paionios, around 420-415, after the Olympia Nike. To my mind, differences in the renderings cannot be solely attributed to the various carvers of an original design but betray disunity of conception and artistic approach.

Two subjects are represented on an uneven number of slabs: twelve show an Amazonomachy in which Herakles participates, eleven a Centauromachy, which includes women at an idol and Kaineus. The arrangement within the interior of the temple recalls the sequence around the front pteroma at Sounion, with a comparable juxtaposition of different myths. Perhaps because of its inside location and its relatively short distance from the viewer, the Bassai frieze is much more crowded than all other architectural examples, with too much action to preserve distinct outlines. In addition, the non-Attic bodies are heavy, almost squat (although a few slim warriors appear).[40] Some women have rolls of flesh on neck and stomach, big breasts and swollen nipples.[41] Faces are wide and eyes smaller, in most cases no longer bulging but concave, in a typical Fourth century mannerism. And these massive human figures are carved in a very high relief, in places even entirely in the round, so that the effect is somewhat overwhelming and the background virtually disappears from view amidst the swirling garments. This massiveness of forms and emphasis on flamboyant drapery indicate a late style.[42]

Great variety occurs in the rendering of cloth, which can be deeply undercut or almost flat, virtually engraved so that only paint would once have made it apparent. Since such low relief can occur side by side with highly articulated drapery, one could suppose that the former was employed to suggest recession in space, yet systematic analysis does not confirm the theory. Many details, however, are successfully foreshortened, especially shields, which are often utilized to convey penetration into the background. Several figures are seen from the rear; one slab in particular (BM 533) suggests an almost circular composition by setting a facing Amazon on a rising ground line while her opponent is carved with his back to the viewer, standing on a lower level, and the leg of a second Greek crosses in front of hers. More daring but less successful is the scene with the dead centaur lying face down on the ground (BM 527).

Drapery is so flamboyant that it moves in all directions, off the body, regardless of the pattern of flight, and often curves upon itself, filling with air like a sail. At times it swirls in great curves around some figures, even forming haloes around heads, but without the

---

[40] Some male bodies seem to be built in two sections, but the effect is different from that observed in the Parthenon and the Hephaisteion, since the articulation seems independent from the expansion of the rib cage.

[41] Note also the peculiar renderings of the knuckles in several hands; others are instead simplified and in one case have truncated fingers.

[42] Additional late traits may also be the violent gestures, which seem directed to the viewer and, together with the pathetic content, almost beg for a sympathetic response—an approach totally different in conception from the aloofness of much Classical architectural sculpture, especially the cameolike Parthenon frieze.

unifying action such renderings have on the Nike frieze, because here no empty background is readily apparent.[43] In addition, while the mantles of the Nike frieze streamed more or less horizontally, here lines tend to curve downwards as in Dexileos' stele. Some ridges bend with nicks as if they were lead pipes; others turn upon themselves, showing their hollow interiors at the ends; omega and binocular folds abound. Over the human forms garments behave differently, often being almost carved into the flesh, although an occasional edge or an overfold fly out from the body as if windblown. Transparency is not pursued in itself, although some limbs are outlined by dark channels and some breasts by engraved lines. There are various ways of rendering skirts between the thighs: some dip down deeply with looping patterns and oval designs that have completely lost their original function of modeling folds and have turned into abstract decoration;[44] some skirts have tubular S-shaped folds running vertically from waist to hem; still others employ stretch folds with an ugly, flattening effect that seems to hamper motion, although the skirt itself is wide enough to form swirls and folds at the rear. These stretch folds occur to some extent on a few seated figures of the Parthenon Pediments, but the device at Bassai has been pushed to aesthetic extremes.

Other borrowed motifs include a split-axis composition (Herakles and an Amazon), which has been compared with the central action of the Parthenon West Pediment. The Hephaisteion may have suggested the scene of the Lapith stabbing a centaur in the chest; at Bassai, however, the action has been made more complex, because the monster, in turn, bites the man in the neck while jumping over a dead companion and kicking his hooves against the shield of a second warrior.[45] A similar schema, but confined to the two protagonists, appears on a Neo-Attic marble vase in Madrid, which is thought to reproduce the Centauromachy on the sandals of the Athena Parthenos. If this surmise is correct, it would increase the eclecticism of the Bassai frieze. Other standard motifs include the hair-pulling scene, the wounded comrade being helped (fig. 65), the warrior peering above his shield, the stumbling horse, and even the swirling motion of an Amazon being lifted by her ankle, which recalls the upside-down poses of one Parthenon metope and some of those on the Hephaisteion.

As a final technical detail that may support a Fourth century date, note the drill work in the beard of a centaur (BM 525): it recalls the similar rendering on the seated Asklepios in a relief from Epidauros.

OTHER MONUMENTS

The preceding survey has discussed strictly architectural friezes, in more or less "canonical" position within entablatures. Other friezelike compositions, both in terms of relative size and length, are those that adorned the armrests of Zeus' throne at Olympia

[43] One exception to this rule is slab BM 536, which differs from all others in having considerable overhead above the figures, relatively wide spacing and visible background, a minimum of flamboyant drapery in its upper half, and rather slender bodies for both warriors and Amazons.

[44] A similar decorative approach can be surmised in the rendering of some centaurs; note the pattern-

ing of ribs and muscles of the monster on BM 521. By and large, centaurs are all very muscular, with humped backs and even one case of residual mane.

[45] Hofkes-Brukker (*Bassai-Fries*, 51 and n. 28) believes that no intentional action is meant against the left-hand warrior, who is only accidentally too close to the centaur's hooves; yet, for a horse, that is definitely a kicking, not a jumping pose.

and the bases of some major cult statues of the Fifth century.[46] We know about them mostly from literary descriptions or through Neo-Attic reliefs, which are bound to distort or change individual traits and arrangements; they shall be discussed together with the cult statues themselves, which are similarly known to us largely through Roman copies. One more monument requires immediate consideration despite its architecturally ambiguous nature: the Nike Balustrade (figs. 66-81).

Insofar as the relief slabs ran above the solid walls of the Akropolis bastion, their visual effect could not have been much different from that of an entablature frieze on a nonperipteral temple. Yet proportions are different, since the parapet had a practical function that required a certain height;[47] a metal grille above the slabs also dispelled the architectural illusion. But the sequence is conceived as if the balustrade were indeed a frieze, with a series of Nikai erecting trophies, facing Athena and, as attested by two fragmentary examples, leading bulls to sacrifice. Athena occurs three times, once per side, almost as if in a Roman continuous frieze; but since the observer would have seen only one stretch of the balustrade at a time, the repetition would not have been apparent; each side was planned as if it were an architectural unit.[48]

The original study of the balustrade suggested that the reliefs extended only to the level of the temple façade and were carved by six masters. Later arrangements in the Akropolis museum have changed the position of some fragments and the length of the balustrade has been questioned: it might have stretched beyond the temple itself, almost to the Mycenaean wall. There is no doubt that hands changed according to the number of figures and not to the number of joints, as exemplified by the work of Master A and Master B side by side within the same slab; this method of parcelling out figures to carvers according to number and not to composition may suggest that no major master was involved in the execution of the balustrade, yet the beauty of the sculptures has always encouraged scholars to believe the opposite. The names of Paionios (Master B) and Kallimachos (Master E) have been proposed, and Despinis, on the basis of his true knowledge of Agorakritos, has equated him with Master A; but no confirmation is available from the sources, and the example of the Erechtheion frieze may disprove the notion. Since a virtual study for the Sandalbinder by Master E occurs on the East frieze of the Nike Temple, the same hands might have been involved in both,[49] and no great span of time could have

[46] The high-relief figures from the Agora once attributed to the Temple of Ares or to its altar are still virtually unpublished except for occasional mentions in other contexts. Since their original purpose is still undetermined, they are here included in the Appendix to this chapter.

[47] But note a surprising coincidence: according to some publications, the balustrade slabs and the Parthenon frieze have identical height, 1.06 m.

[48] Carpenter (*The Sculpture of the Nike Temple Parapet* [Cambridge, Mass., 1929] 77), has compared the compositional scheme of the balustrade to the Parthenon frieze; he has described the short East spur by the stairway as purely episodic in character and therefore similar to the Parthenon West side; North and South sides are meant as *pendants* on both monuments, while the fourth side (the West for the parapet) sees the culmination of the action around a central axis. The repeated presence of Athena on three sides of the balustrade, to my mind, weakens the comparison and betrays a different conception.

That the observer's viewpoint was carefully considered is shown also by the fact that the best preserved Nike from the East stretch is represented mounting a step, which was once flush with the top level of the real stairway; her action would have seemed to mimic that of the visitor (Carpenter, *Parapet*, 11).

[49] Despinis assumes that both the Nike temple frieze and the balustrade were designed by Agorakritos, although only in part executed (or "caressed") by him.

elapsed between the completion of the architectural and the inception of the free-standing frieze, given the danger for visitors to the bastion. If the Nike Temple was completed by 423, the balustrade could have been made as early as 421 or at least between 421 and 415, as suggested by those who try to connect sculptural activity with historical events. On stylistic grounds, other scholars have consistently preferred a lower date for the balustrade, within the last decade of the Fifth century. Perhaps the years around 410 are not wide of the mark, since there is no need to interpret the victories of the balustrade as a definite allusion to contemporary events. The cult of Athena Nike was very old on the Akropolis and would have required that type of subject even in time of defeat; moreover, practical rather than commemorative reasons required the erection of the parapet. Allusions must therefore be generic rather than specific, although one reading would see the trophies as appropriate for a naval, a hoplite, and a Persian victory (fig. 80).

The Nike Balustrade was carved in relatively low relief, despite its full exposure to the light and its rather lofty position. Stylistically it provides the best possible evidence for the contemporaneity of different approaches. Almost all renderings appear side by side, from engraved ribbon drapery (figs. 73-75) to flamboyant swirling costumes (figs. 70-71), from extreme transparency obtained through the clinging surfaces (figs. 77-78) to opaque ridges that hide the body beneath. The carving has been carefully analyzed; few comments are here necessary. Note, first of all, the presence of "Parthenonian" thin drapery (figs. 66-67) obtained through a belaboring of primary folds and the use of incision (Master A). In the more flamboyant renderings, note the omega folds or the binocular effect (fig. 72), and the sanguisuga curve at the ankle of the famous Nike by Master B which, like the uplifted overfold, seems dependent on a private puff of wind from below (fig. 70). These irrational deviations from the general movement of folds, especially those which upraise portions of the costume, are a trait of the late Fifth century spilling into the Fourth. The fan of folds at the edge of a seat already noted in the Erechtheion frieze is here repeated (fig. 74), as well as the double-curve pattern at the knee bend (fig. 77) and the use of a single ridge-and-groove to outline a portion of the body. The slipped-strap device is used in the Sandalbinder to obtain a single source of lines branching downward toward the hips,[50] to be counterbalanced by the ever deepening catenaries of the mantle, with an almost pendular effect. Tension folds between the breasts are a forecast of a similar rendering on the Bassai frieze. The deviation of apoptygma folds to convey a raised hip finds a counterpart in the Erechtheion Karyatids.

As a final comment, note that at least two slabs of the Nike parapet were adapted by Neo-Attic sculptors into different but recognizable scenes.

SUMMARY

In review, the Parthenon frieze seems unique both in technique and composition, although perhaps not in its architectural function; the Nike Balustrade may provide a distant parallel, while the Nike Temple and the East frieze of the Hephaisteion seem to have at least imitated its concept of divine assembly. Stylistically, friezes seem to cover the entire range and period under consideration, with no major gaps in time. Drapery patterns are

[50] The motif of a single source for branching folds forming a triangular pattern may also have originated in one of the Amazons on the shield of Athena Parthenos.

seen to change, from numerous but relatively logical, to fewer but more mannered and livelier. The two currents first noted on the Parthenon, toward either the modeling or the motion line, seem to merge as time goes on, to diverge again into extremes of transparency or flamboyance. Linear devices that were introduced with specific utilitarian purposes turn into mannerisms as the sculptors learn to express the volume of bodies through actual modeling or foreshortening. Perhaps the most significant development exemplified by the series of friezes is the progressive penetration of figures into the background and their relative freedom of movement into space. Connected with this complexity of renderings may be the use of the empty background, which serves to isolate the figures and make them intelligible at a distance.

The Parthenon frieze does not seem to have greatly influenced later monuments in terms of specific motifs, although drapery fashions that occur there for the first time find wide application in *free-standing statues*; the same is true for some three-dimensional poses. On the contrary, all other friezes prove to be veritable samplers of motifs that are consistently repeated in later reliefs. Their diffusion can be understood when no great geographical or chronological distance intervene, but is harder to explain in the case of imitations in non-Greek territory several generations later. Manner and reasons for this transmission deserve specific consideration. Another important aspect of Fifth century friezes is their relative ambiguity, which prevents us from identifying their subjects with any assurance. Pausanias, who so meticulously describes statue bases and paintings, leaves friezes entirely out of his account, perhaps because they were not associated with the "big names." That without his help we are unable to understand the scenes represented is a point of some concern, possibly reflecting shifts in the cultural outlooks of the times. If, moreover, our surmise is correct, the lack of attribution to great masters underlines once again the relative unimportance of architectural decoration as sculpture per se.

Despite all possible reservations about the importance of architectural sculpture and the role played in it by major masters, this detailed review of proven Fifth century works should now be helpful in assessing other Fifth century originals, both in the round and in relief, in the following chapters.

APPENDIX 4

1. *Relief figures from the area of the Temple of Ares, Athens.* These numerous fragments from a high relief have not yet been officially published, but they deserve mention here because they have occasionally been cited in the literature as belonging to the entablature frieze of the Temple of Ares. Other possible suggestions have attributed them to the altar or to the base for the cult statue in the Temple of Ares (for the latter, see Delivorrias, 97-98, and *Kernos,* [Festschrift Bakalakis, Thessaloniki 1972] 24-34, esp. 31-32). The most recent theory (E. B. Harrison, *AJA* 81 [1977] 424 and nn. 88-89) is that the reliefs may have formed a parapet surrounding a terrace and the altar of Hephaistos, which was later damaged and reused in connection with the Temple of Ares, where the fragments were found. With a calculated height of ca. 0.85-0.90m, this Pentelic frieze would form a good parallel for the Nike Balustrade, which may therefore no longer be unique. Harrison has anticipated her conclusions that the scene represented the Birth of Pandora, a narrative subject contrasting with the more general allusions of the Nike Balustrade, but all discussion must await the forthcoming publication of the evidence.

At present, stylistic description and illustration are available for the seven fragmentary female figures that Harrison has presented in connection with her analysis of Alkamenes' sculptures for the Hephaisteion (*AJA* 81 [1977] 165-66, figs. 20-25; see also the head S 1978, figs. 34-35, and four others, p. 279, figs. 18-21). Among these, the best known is the peplophoros closely comparable to the Prokne-and-Itys and which has been previously mentioned in connection with that group (Agora S 870, Harrison, fig. 25; H. Knell, *AntP* 17 [1978] 9-19). An earlier study has also established a comparison between the head at present on the Prokne and another frieze fragment, head S 1494 (B. Freyer, *JdI* 77 [1962] 218, fig. 5; but see Harrison, *Gnomon* 52 [1980] 71-72).

Among the other figures, note the occurrence of at least one belted peplos worn with a long himation; S 679 (Harrison, fig. 20) which has most convincingly been compared to the Velletri Athena. S 676 (Harrison, Fig. 23) wears a belted chiton with very short overfold forming multiple omega folds in stepped pattern.

The frieze has been generally dated around 420, and its connection with Alkamenes' style (or perhaps just that of his workshop) is usually considered assured. Note that the Temple of Ares has the same plan as the Hephaisteion, including the alignment of the East antae.

BIBLIOGRAPHY 4

FOR PAGE 73

On friezes and their distribution in the Archaic
    period see *Archaic Style*, ch. 9; for the develop-
    ment of the Greek frieze in general see
    Hesperia 35 (1966) 188-204. On Iktinos' in-
    volvement at Bassai and on the role of Kal-
    likrates as contractor see J. R. McCredie, in
    Studies von Blanckenhagen, 69-73; for the
    chronology of the Bassai frieze see bibl. for
    ch. 2.

FOR PAGE 75

For the single Corinthian column at Bassai I fol-
    low the theories of F. Cooper, of imminent
    publication.
Architecture of the Hephaisteion: see, e.g., Dins-
    moor, 179-82; *Agora* 14, 140-49.
Stillwell: R. Stillwell, *Hesperia* 38 (1969) 231-41.

FOR PAGE 76

Coulton: J. J. Coulton, *Ancient Greek Architects
    at Work* (Ithaca, N.Y., 1977) ch. 1.
Parthenon frieze: the best illustrated monograph
    is Brommer, *Fries*; see review, *AJA* 83 (1979)
    489-91, with important corrections and sugges-
    tions (E. B. Harrison). A lucid and brief ac-
    count with (incomplete) photographic com-
    mentary: M. Robertson and A. Frantz, *The
    Parthenon Frieze* (Oxford 1975). Some recent
    articles on the frieze will be mentioned infra;
    note S. I. Rotroff, *AJA* 81 (1977) 379-82; M.
    Brouskari, in *Festschrift Brommer*, 65. Mytho-
    logical context of the Panathenaia: Ch. Kar-
    dara, *ArchEph* 1961, 61-158.
Panathenaia before Marathon: J. Boardman, in
    Festschrift Brommer, 39-49.

FOR PAGE 77

Parthenon North metopes 29-32: the theory of
    the gods at rest in M. Bieber, review of Brom-
    mer, *Metopen*, in *AJA* 72 (1968) 394-97.
The interpretation of a *Dios Boule* has been re-
    cently suggested by E. Simon, *JdI* 90 (1975)
    109-11.
Brommer's argument against theory 2: *Fries*,
    152-53; cf. also pp. 263-70 with tabulated ex-
    planations on the central scene.

FOR PAGE 78

The most extensive discussion of the Eponymous
    Heroes in general is by Kron, who attempts
    (pp. 202-14) the identification of the various
    figures on the Parthenon frieze. Her theories
    are discussed and different identifications are
    proposed by E. B. Harrison, *Greek Numismat-
    ics and Archaeology: Essays in Honor of Mar-
    garet Thompson* (Wetteren, Belgium, 1979)
    71-85; she gives iconographic and symbolic
    reasons for her suggestions. For a division
    based on the arrangement of the slabs, see
    Robertson and Frantz, captions to slabs IV-
    VIII. See also F. Eckstein, *Stele* (Athens 1980)
    607-13.

FOR PAGE 79

The iconography of men leaning on staffs has
    been recently traced by M. A. Zagdoun, *FdD*
    4:6 (1977) 2-15, with bibliography.
A recent discussion of the gods on the frieze,
    proposing to identify Herakles in the so-called
    Dionysos, is by M. Robertson, in *Studies von
    Blanckenhagen*, 75-78.
Correlation of deities and cults: E. G. Pemberton,
    AJA 80 (1976) 112-24.
Comparison with votive reliefs: J. H. Kroll, in
    AJA 83 (1979) 349-52.

FOR PAGE 80

East slabs quarried to specifications: Ashmole,
    Architect and Sculptor, 126-27.

FOR PAGE 81

Polykleitan poses on the frieze: cf. T. Lorenz,
    Polyklet (Wiesbaden 1972) 52. "Aspasia/
    Sosandra": *Severe Style*, figs. 105-108.

FOR PAGE 82

Fringelike selvage: cf. Brommer, *Fries*, pl. 155.
Press folds: cf., e.g., Brommer, *Fries*, pl. 101.
Awkward frontal poses: cf., e.g., Brommer, *Fries*,
    pl. 8 (W 1).

FOR PAGE 83

The various dates for the temple at Sounion are
    discussed by A. Delivorrias, *AthMitt* 84 (1969)
    127-42, especially p. 138 n. 54. This is the basic
    article on the friezes.

BIBLIOGRAPHY 4

FOR PAGE 84

Hephaisteion friezes: the quotation is from Morgan, "Friezes," 232; the entire article discusses the sculptures.

Ilissos frieze: traditional dating and new chronology are discussed by C. A. Picón, *AJA* 82 (1978) 47-48; in agreement is now A. Krug, *AntP* 18 (1979) 7-21.

The latest discussion of the Erechtheion frieze is P. N. Boulter, *AntP* 10 (1970) 7-28.

Bassai frieze: for a recent publication with ample photographic commentary see *Bassai-Fries*; a book by F. Cooper on the whole architecture of the building and its predecessors is forthcoming.

FOR PAGE 85

On the Hephaisteion friezes, beside the bibliography for ch. 2:26, see also H. A. Thompson, *AJA* 66 (1962) 339-47; S. von Bockelberg, *AntP* 18 (1979) 23-50.

In discussing the Ilissos frieze, Picón makes comments on most of other contemporary friezes.

The comment by Robertson is on p. 349.

FOR PAGE 86

Hero in distress: the iconography is discussed by B. Shefton, *Hesperia* 31 (1962) 356-60, there called "the himation motif."

FOR PAGE 87

Fragment *p* from the Nike Temple frieze: C. Blümel, *JdI* 65-66 (1950-51) 45, fig. 8.

FOR PAGE 88

For close-ups of faces on the Hephaisteion friezes see Koch.

A date in the 430s or shortly afterwards is also supported by W. Fuchs, *Die Skulptur der Griechen* (Munich 1969) 440-41.

Ilissos frieze: style and composition are analyzed by Picón (bibl. for p. 84). See there also for the Roman copies.

FOR PAGE 89

Nike Temple frieze: the main article is by C. Blümel, *JdI* 65-66 (1950-51) 135-65. For recent additions, changes, and interpretations see E. B. Harrison, *AJA* 74 (1970) 317-23; id., *AJA* 76 (1972) 195-97; id., *AJA* 76 (1972) 353-78; E. G. Pemberton, *AJA* 76 (1972) 303-10.

Cf. also Hölscher, *Historienbilder*, 91-98, for a discussion of the historical meaning of the friezes. A fragment from the frieze is in Boston: see Comstock and Vermeule, no. 34, p. 27.

FOR PAGE 91

For a discussion of the Shield of Athena Parthenos and its bibliography see ch. 7.

FOR PAGE 92

On the motif of the stumbling horse and its historical context see L. Giuliani, *AntK* 20 (1977) 26-42, especially p. 33, with the theory that the imagery goes back to the Amazonomachy on the Throne of Zeus at Olympia.

For examples of the Nike frieze drapery see, e.g., Blümel, *JdI* 65-66, p. 163, fig. 25; Harrison, *AJA* 76 (1972) pl. 46:3.

The similarity with the Erechtheion Karyatids has also been noted by Lauter, *AntP* 16 (1976) 44.

FOR PAGE 93

Erechtheion frieze: Most recent discussion of hands and style, with the addition of several new fragments, including some from the Agora: P. N. Boulter, *AntP* 10 (1970) 7-25. The fragment in Cambridge is published and illustrated in L. Budde and R. Nicholls, *A Catalogue of the Greek and Roman Sculpture in the Fitzwilliam Museum* (Cambridge 1964) no. 26, pl. 6. See also Brouskari, 152-56. For a chronological discussion, besides Boulter, see also B. Vierneisel-Schlörb, in *Festschrift für Gerhard Kleiner* (Tübingen 1976) 63-66 and footnotes.

On the stylistic difference between the Karyatids and the frieze see H. Lauter, *AntP* 16 (1976) 40-42.

FOR PAGE 94

For some Hellenistic "parallels" cf., e.g., Boulter, pl. 18b, with a statue from Magnesia in Berlin (R. Horn, *Stehende Weibliche Gewandstatuen in der Hellenistischen Plastik, RömMitt EH* 2, 1931, pl. 38:3); a figure with cobwebby mantle, Boulter, pl. 3, with the Isis from Delos, Horn, pl. 29:1. The Erechtheion figure with a loop on the thigh is Boulter, pl. 1.

Bassai frieze: the most complete illustration of the frieze slabs is *Bassai-Fries*, with up-to-date bibliography.

102

FOR PAGE 97

Nike Balustrade: The main stylistic discussion remains R. Carpenter, *The Sculpture of the Nike Temple Parapet* (Cambridge, Mass., 1929). Cf. also Brouskari, 156-63.

FOR PAGE 98

For the dating of the balustrade see Boulter, in her discussion of the relationship with the Erechtheion frieze; also Vierneisel-Schlörb, in *Festschrift Kleiner*, 63. H. Jung, *JdI* 91 (1976) 119-20 and n. 113, compares the balustrade with the Erechtheion Karyatids and considers them contemporary.

For the interpretation of the trophies see R. Carpenter, *AJA* 33 (1929) 467-83; E. G. Pemberton, *AJA* 76 (1972) 304 n. 13.

For Neo-Attic reliefs see Fuchs, *Vorbilder*, 6-20; also Bieber, *Ancient Copies*, 30-32, pl. 9.

CHAPTER 5

Greek Originals: Sculpture in the Round

AFTER the wealth of architectural sculpture reviewed in the previous three chapters, the relative dearth of free-standing originals from the Fifth century comes as an anticlimax. Moreover, in recent studies some of the statues normally considered to be Greek works have been questioned as possible Roman copies, others have been redated to later periods, and pieces thought to be free-standing have occasionally been attributed to pediments or other architectural complexes. Indeed, some of our best dated evidence for Fifth century statues comes from the Erechtheion Karyatids, which are intrinsically architectural and therefore subject to specific aesthetic rules that make them somewhat atypical for contemporary sculpture in the round.

To be sure, there are many pieces scattered through the various museums which can certainly claim to be Greek originals; yet their fragmentary state or relative insignificance preclude extensive discussion in this context. In recent years attention has been called to groups of Greek statuettes having the same provenience; they seem to have been dedications at a sanctuary in imitation of its cult statue(s) but they are all relatively small and cannot be considered copies in the standard sense of the word. Yet neither are they *bona fide* originals, since they derive their stylistic schema from an earlier prototype, and should rather be studied for their iconographic significance in connection with cult statues. Other important marble originals are in fact cult statues, and others have been plausibly connected with major masters, so that they require separate discussion.

Particularly poor is our information on Fifth century male figures, which are almost exclusively preserved in Roman copies. The relatively numerous bronzes from the Severe period find few counterparts in this later phase. The most important is probably a life-size but highly fragmentary statue recovered from a shipwreck in the Straits of Messina; its facial features are so remarkably veristic that a much later date might have been suspected, were it not for the fairly close dating of the rest of the cargo from the same ship. Two more life-size statues found in shallow waters at Riace Marina in Calabria have been attributed to the Fifth century, but they have not yet been published after cleaning, and preliminary photographs suggest that they may be Classicizing rather than truly Classical. The same is true for the large bronze head supposedly from Beneventum (but actually from Herculaneum) in the Louvre, which is now generally accepted as being a work of the late First century B.C.; it will be discussed in another context. A small bronze head from Cyrene can rank as portraiture and deserves separate treatment under that heading. Still smaller bronzes rank as statuettes and are therefore not included in our survey; yet, were we to describe the most significant figurines, in view of the gaps in our evidence, we would still be struggling with chronology. For instance, a particularly important "Polykleitan" bronze statuette in the Louvre is included in Lullies and Hirmer as a Fifth century original, but it has recently been redated by Zanker to Tiberian-Claudian times and labeled a copy, while a case could also be made for its being a Classicistic creation, since it once had wings on its head.

In our discussion we shall therefore concentrate on only a few major monuments that seem particularly representative of the various stylistic trends during the Fifth century. But it is relevant to ask why so few original monuments have survived. Literary sources and extant statue bases indicate that most of the works created during the period under review were in bronze or other precious material and were therefore particularly subject to destruction in later times. In addition, since Classical sculpture was highly appreciated by later connoisseurs of Greek art, whether Hellenistic rulers or Roman citizens and emperors, statues from that period were more frequently "collected" than Archaic or Hellenistic monuments. Finally, art as such was limited to votive offerings in sanctuaries or to public monuments erected by the state, and sculpture was not yet used for private enjoyment or for the adornment of villas and public places; a relatively small number of monuments was produced, in contrast with Hellenistic and Roman practices.

GREEK ORIGINALS IN MARBLE

The Erechtheion Karyatids

Although this name is commonly used to define the maidens of the South porch (figs. 82-83), the contemporary building accounts refer to them exclusively as *korai*, and it has recently been argued that the term *Karyatid* should be reserved for another type of anthropomorphic support, with raised hand. Nonetheless the term is currently understood to refer to any female figure used in place of a column and will be used here with this meaning. Who the Erechtheion *korai* are is a moot question, and the point is still being debated. That they are the Arrephoroi seems improbable, since these were girls seven years old or slightly older; but all other suggestions are equally uncertain. To my mind they are simply Karyatids, that is, architectural supports, of particular richness and beauty but anonymous, like other forms of architectural decoration.

As statues, the Erechtheion Karyatids have been recently discussed and described in detail by H. Lauter, who has carefully pointed out the many differences from kore to kore.[1]

[1] Lauter refers to the statues with letters of the alphabet, from A to F, and his nomenclature will be followed here. Kore A is the first on the West side of the porch, next to the wall and behind Kore B, at the South West corner of the parapet, facing the Parthenon. Kore F occupies the position corresponding to Kore A, on the opposite side, near the small entrance opened into the balustrade. The shift in weight occurs on either side of the central axis of the porch, between Korai C and D, which therefore exemplify all others. The main differences among the korai are observable in the way in which the folds are arranged between the breasts and over the hip, in the length of the overfold, in the treatment of the mantle over the back, and in the arrangement of the hair, which is fastened at different levels over the nape or twisted in different locks. It is interest-

ing that the Karyatid with the most artificial treatment of the rear mantle (Kore D) should also have the most naturalistic rendering of the hair mass, while the Karyatid with the most elaborate mantle (Kore C) combines it with a very artificial hair pattern. The apparent uniformity of the Karyatids in frontal view is countered by their very obvious difference from the rear.

For all his close analysis, Lauter did not observe one detail that has now been pointed out by Brommer, *AA* 1979, 161-62, fig. 1. On the back of Kore E, to her left, and on the lower layer of her mantle, in a smooth area in between curving folds, a small rectangular boss has been left. This is not a puntello, and Brommer compares it to one on the North door of the Erechtheion (left jamb). He interprets it as a form of superstition, requiring that a building

These differences are probably due to the various hands who carved the figures after two possible prototypes provided by a single master; Lauter has ventured the suggestion that the master was Agorakritos, while the sculptor who actually executed Kore C may have been connected with Alkamenes' workshop, since this figure is different from all others in details that resemble instead the Prokne and Itys. We shall here be concerned solely with stylistic details without trying to point out what may be typical of a specific sculptor or to summarize Lauter's observations.

The Erechtheion Karyatids can be approximately dated to the period between 421 and 409; the lower limit is provided by the building accounts of that year, which indicate that the statues had already been carved, while the upper limit is based on the general assumption that the temple itself was started at the time of the Peace of Nikias. A closer approximation places the Karyatids around 415 and certainly not later than the Sicilian disaster of 413, which is usually considered responsible for the interruption of building activities. That an interruption occurred is beyond doubt, but historical reasons for artistic events are often doubtful; nonetheless, stylistic analysis confirms a 420-415 date for the Karyatids, once their specific function is taken into account.

The massiveness and four-sideness of the figures have often been noted, together with the fact that the shift in balance is not reflected in their shoulders, which remain level (fig. 83). Yet what is surprising is not this relative immobility, but the fact that the sculptor was at all willing to give his figures what could be termed a temporary pose instead of a more static stance with weight evenly distributed on both feet. The difference between free leg and weight leg and the concomitant pronounced shift of the hip on the side of the supporting leg are contemporary stylistic traits; yet the foot of the bent leg does not trail but is thrust slightly forward. Archaic Karyatids were also carved with one foot forward, albeit with rigid knees, presumably in conformity with the standard posture for Archaic free-standing figures, and it may be that the Erechtheion master wanted to reflect the same tradition, though converting it as much as possible into Fifth century stylistic idiom.[2] Certainly he took care that the deeply fluted portion of the skirt which covers the weight leg appeared always toward the outer side of the central axis, so that a columnlike effect would be apparent at the edges of the porch.

Fifth century traits are the quasi-transparent clinging of the peplos over the breasts, which appear clearly defined beneath the drapery; the catch of the material at the ankle of the forward foot with the concomitant long curving folds; and especially the pattern of reversed curves at the side of the bent knee (fig. 82). This motif, which can be noted on figures from the Erechtheion frieze and the Nike Balustrade, is not apparent on the

should never be completely finished, and since no similar practice has been noticed for sculpture so far, he takes this feature as a sign that the Erechtheion Karyatids were probably considered integral parts of the temple, quite different from true free-standing statues. This assumption seems correct; it is likely, however, that the boss may have served as a reference point for what must have been a form of copying the basic dimensions and outlines of a model six times, although no true pointing machine was involved.

In August 1979, the Erechtheion Korai were re-moved from their outdoor position on the Akropolis and housed in the museum, while modern replacements have now been set up in the porch.

[2] To be sure, the stance with a free leg forward is attested for the Fifth century, and is sometimes called "Attic," in contrast to the stance with a trailing foot, which is considered Peloponnesian or Polykleitan. But the Athena Parthenos has the free foot behind, or at least not forward of the other, and we would have expected the Karyatids to copy this pose, given their strict connection, both visual and topographical, with the Parthenon.

Parthenon frieze, and should be no earlier than ca. 425. A comparison between the processioning women of the Parthenon East frieze and the Erechtheion Karyatids is significant in terms of stylistic development.

Resemblances are obvious: the Parthenon figures are also peplophoroi, and some of them hold phialai, which we know to have been held also by the Karyatids through their more completely preserved Roman copies. The bent leg of the relief figures shows them in motion, rather than static, yet note that architectural intent was probably present in correlating the fluting of their skirts with the underlying columns. As for the differences, the Parthenon women wear the peplos with a lower kolpos that does not curve markedly to emphasize the roundness of stomach and hips; the overfold is either long and smooth or significantly shorter and lined by straight pleats; no major steep folds stem from the bent knee to the ground; finally, some of the women wear a chiton as an undergarment. The Karyatids have a more pronounced curve to their shorter kolpos, which dips lower on the side of the free leg; their longer overfold runs more or less parallel to the kolpos, though on a straighter line, but its folds tend to emphasize the salience of the breasts and especially the tilt of the hip by their deviation and catch on the side of the weight leg; in the skirt at least one or several folds run along the shin of the bent leg. In neither monument, however, does the skirt show a distortion of the straight lines over the weight leg at the point where it meets the foot, a trait that will instead be prominent in Fourth century peplophoroi.[3]

If the Karyatids represent the stylistic advances of the late Fifth century in the richness of their folds and the modeling quality of their clinging drapery, nevertheless they show some archaizing traits besides the level shoulders and the forward foot. Note in particular their long locks falling over the chest. To be sure, they serve the practical function of strengthening the neck and bridging the relative gap between head and shoulders: given the architectural purpose of the statues, the narrowing of the figure at the neck would have conveyed visual, if not technical, fragility. However, the spiral form of the locks is definitely Archaistic, and the total coiffure is in contrast to current hairstyles;[4] long tresses over the

[3] Note also that the vertical folds of the skirt run uninterrupted to the ground, even in close proximity of the curves created by the forward foot. In Roman copies of the Erechtheion Karyatids a flat triangular area stretches like a sail between the last vertical and the first curving fold, bridging the transition. This rendering (which is perhaps incipient in Kore D, Lauter, pl. 32) appears in later monuments, both Greek originals and Roman copies, and may be a chronological feature, probably determined by the increased interest in clinging, transparent drapery.

[4] Note in particular the braids encircling the head which, however, cannot be paralleled in extant Archaic sculpture and do not seem to become fashionable until the Fourth century. Such coiffures may nonetheless have been added in metal to wooden figures: see *Archaic Style*, 316 n. 15 and *Hesperia* 46 (1977) 322. The whole hairstyle of the Karyatids recalls metal renderings, especially in the waves over the temples (which differ from statue to statue and are of two basic kinds) and on the nape, and indeed even the braids are attested in *male* bronzes of the Severe period. Only a few of the Parthenon peplophoroi on the East frieze have long tresses over their backs and none, as far as I can see, wears locks falling over the front. Since there is a remote possibility that Karyatid supports had already been employed on the Archaic Akropolis (*Archaic Style*, 108-109 n. 31, 204-205 n. 24), the Erechtheion Korai may imitate a local prototype in stone.

Note also the vertical braid over the forehead: it is best preserved on Karyatid C and missing entirely on A, unclear on the others because of their weathered state—another instance of the variations among figures. This great crown of braids might have been added to increase the mass of the head and ease the transition to the capital proper, or it might have been an elegant replacement for the twisted pad that women use when carrying weights on their heads; certainly the central braid served the practical purpose of cushioning the head against the load. In at least one Karyatid (Kore D), however, a cloth pad is suggested plastically under the echinos.

I was convinced that the Karyatids' hairstyle was totally artificial and impossible in nature, but Carol

back appear on cult statues, but they too betray some Archaizing intent, while forward locks are typical of Archaic korai. Fifth century female figures are usually shown with hair gathered in a chignon or otherwise supported to leave the nape free, and other arrangements seem always to convey either specific status or antiquity. In the Karyatids the Erechtheion sculptor might have meant to suggest not only venerability but probably even a statuelike quality to soften the incongruity of a human figure supporting an entablature, light as that of the Erechtheion porch might have appeared. That the mantle held aside by the left hand is also an Archaizing trait may be disputed, since peplophoroi on the Nike Temple frieze and elsewhere are shown in the same pose; yet antiquarian touches may be argued in all cases and certainly the association with Archaic korai holding their skirts aside would have come spontaneously to mind in viewing the porch maidens.[5]

Should the heavy, full face of the Karyatids be attributed to their functions or does it reflect contemporary style? The latter seems the correct supposition in view of other preserved examples. Eyes are large and almost bulging, mouths straight and wide, chins pronounced and articulated by a definite indentation beneath the lower lip; Venus rings appear on the neck. This type of face is confirmed for the Fifth century by "Prokne" and what remains of the Nemesis of Rhamnous and Paionios' Nike (cf. fig. 85).[6]

The Nike of Paionios

This is probably one of the best known Classical monuments (fig. 84); yet it bears reviewing in this context because it clearly exemplifies the coexistence of diverse stylistic currents. At first glance, no other work could seem farther in spirit from the Erechtheion Karyatids; yet the Nike can be dated precisely to the same period, since the occasion for its erection was the Battle of Sphakteria in 425 and the statue itself must have been carved within the next few years. Upon further analysis, moreover, the same formal language can be detected on both monuments and the difference explained in terms of function and narrative.

Whereas the Karyatids are columnar and mostly static in appearance, the Nike is lively and caught in actual flight, as indicated by her tilted pose with a bird crossing under her feet. Whereas the Karyatids' drapery is opaque and sober, the Nike's is flamboyant in excess and totally transparent where it clings to the body. We have the impression that her vigorous body is entirely revealed, while the Karyatids appear matronly modest under their

---

Solomon, of the University of Pittsburgh, showed me that she could reproduce it with her own long hair.

[5] This motif might have been introduced to animate the fall of folds of the short back mantle; yet little advantage is by and large taken of this opportunity, and all Karyatids except C display an almost foldless and undisturbed back panel in the upper layer of their overfolded cloak. Only the lower layer is pulled forward by the left hand, thereby creating long curving lines along one side. Kore C has the most elaborate mantle, entirely covered with angular folds, while Kore D reveals an unexpected calligraphy of thin and metallic catenaries over both lay-

ers of her cloak, in full contrast with the plasticity of her front. Note that the shift in stance is not operative for the arm position: all Karyatids hold their mantle aside with their left and a phiale with their right hand, presumably because libations could only be poured on the proper side.

[6] Lauter (p. 23 n. 62) has suggested that the fullness of Kore C's face may also convey her youthful age, but no great difference marks her rendering from that of the other Karyatids in this respect.

H. Knell, in discussing the Prokne (*AnP* 17 [1978] 9-19 esp. n. 9) states that the head does not belong to the statue; however, it can still be compared for purposes of style and date.

covering. Yet both monuments depict the same garment: a peplos pinned over both shoulders and belted under the overfold of the Karyatids, and over it on the Nike.[7] The left pin of the latter has unfastened, so that the material, in falling, has revealed her breast; but note how Paionios has avoided the total exposure of the body on that side by pretending that the garment still holds up in the back, perhaps kept in position by the wing, which is set high over the shoulder, as if growing from the point where a peplos is usually fastened.[8] We shall now try to single out the formal elements that link the Nike to the Erechtheion Karyatids; for simplicity's sake we shall refer to the latter as if they were a single statue, since the differences among them are a matter of detail.

(1) *The stance.* Both figures have one leg forward and one behind. To be sure, neither of the Nike's feet supports the weight of her body, but her total pose has been skillfully analyzed by Borbein and Hölscher as an example of contrapposto, which is emphasized by the garment's arrangement and by the different position of the wings. In the Nike the contrast between upper and lower body is strengthened by the position of her arms, while the Karyatid keeps her shoulders level; nonetheless the tilt at the waist is suggested in both: in the Nike by the slanting overfold, in the Karyatid by the dipping kolpos. In brief, both bodies show uneven but balanced weight distribution according to the same chiastic principles.

(2) *The modeling drapery.* Folds are used to contour elements of the body in order to suggest their profile; in the Nike this procedure acquires a calligraphic effect over the stomach area, which is almost treated like an ovolo molding, but the same principle is at work in the Karyatid through the curving of the kolpos and the catenaries between the breasts. In the latter, a catch in the apoptygma and a deviation in the course of the folds suggest the tilt of the hip in the same way in which the curving hem over the right foot suggests the Nike's ankle.

[7] Hölscher and other authors call it a chiton, but selvage is preserved at the hem on the Nike's right side and the drapery looks heavier where it leaves the body. It is more difficult to explain how the costume allows the uncovering of the left leg, since the opening is on the right. It has been argued that the garment consists of two equal panels held together by the belt and the single pin on the right shoulder, and thus free to open on both sides (P. Wolters, quoted by G. Treu, *Olympia* 3 [Berlin 1897] 185). It is obvious, however, that the skirt of the peplos has been rendered as lifted above the left leg and tucked under the belt on that side, presumably to allow greater freedom of movement. A comparable arrangement, with a shorter garment, can be seen for instance on the so-called Mattei Amazon (M. Weber, *JdI* 91 [1976] 56-62). The motif on the Nike is now obscured by the fact that the edges of some folds have broken off.

[8] This is how I understand the stretch of material under the Nike's left armpit, with its many curving lines rippling concentrically away from the breast. The obvious edge that crosses diagonally from the right shoulder to slightly above the belt I interpret as the unpinned material folding over, so that the line below the left breast would not be a true edge but a double thickness of material. A comparable rendering more clearly expressed can be seen on the so-called Lansdowne Amazon (Weber, *JdI* 91 [1976] 30-46), while similar stages of the motif appear on a figure from the Erechtheion frieze (Boulter, pl. 1, Athens Akr. 2825, pp. 8-9, with comparison to Paionios' Nike) and on a fragmentary akroterial figure from the Delphic Tholos, which also recalls the Olympia Nike (Schlörb, in *Festschrift für G. Kleiner* [Tübingen 1976], p. 83, pl. 14:2; *BCH* 76 [1952] fig. 22, p. 465). Lullies (commentary to pl. 178) gives, however, a different explanation: "The front section of the garment falls diagonally across the upper part of the body in a curve from the right shoulder to the left hip; the back section is drawn forward under the left arm." We could, in final hypothesis, have here an example of artistic license or a misunderstanding of the costume; obviously the sculptor did not want to leave the Nike's left side exposed, and he increased the length of the garment (which, were it a real peplos, would be too long for normal wear) in order to convey motion and flight.

(3) *Transparency.* In both statues the effect is achieved by making the drapery cling flat to the body in between folds, as for instance over the breasts, which are clearly modeled, as it were, *behind* the ridges. A second method is employed in both figures: drapery over the leg is basically smooth but occasional low and flat ridges either cross it (thus modeling the form at the same time, as in the Nike) or run along it, curving at key points to suggest articulation. Note that essentially the same dichotomy apparent in the Nike's costume, when on or off the body, occurs in the Karyatid in the contrasting treatment of the garment over each leg. Other points of similarity between the figures are also the full forms of the body, its proportions and, as far as we can judge from the remains and the alleged Roman replicas of the Nike's face, the facial features (fig. 85).

It has been claimed that Paionios' Nike is a basically frontal composition that loses impact from other viewpoints, and the observation is reinforced by a glance at the restored cast, in which the shell-like mantle provides an effective back curtain that partly envelops also the sides. Hölscher has stressed the virtuoso quality of such carving and the risk involved in pushing the marble practically to its breaking point. In this respect the Nike is very different from the Erechtheion Karyatids, but these features are, if not dictated, at least motivated by the nature of the statue and its allegorical message. The flying effect is conveyed not only through the inflated mantle and the windblown peplos, which almost adheres to it, but also by the sweeping curve of the overfold, which looks as if lifted by air from below: a motif very popular at the end of the Fifth century. Other details of greatest development in later years are the incised line that curves above the right breast and the smaller ridges grouped by twos, in a forecast of the "train tracks" so typical of the turn of the century. The style of the Bassai frieze has been compared with that of Paionios' Nike and many similarities do in fact exist, but the architectural monument lacks the stylistic coherence of the Olympia figure and certainly uses drapery in a later and more excessive formula. The Nike has also been connected with the work of Master B on the Nike Balustrade in Athens, and the comparison seems closer, although the famous Victory restraining a bull has little plasticity in her body forms and only the flamboyance of her folds recalls the Olympia statue. On the other hand, the drapery formula of divergent lines linked by catenaries occurs to a much greater extent in the Sandalbinder, which is carved with more emphasis on anatomical volumes. We therefore see Paionios' Nike as incorporating several stylistic traits which, at least on the balustrade, correspond to different carving hands. This in itself is not as surprising as the fact that the balustrade masters were probably from Athens while Paionios was from Mende; the obvious conclusion is either that style(s) ignore regional boundaries or that Athens has the artistic lead at this time.

One final comment on wings. In the depiction of Nikai much ground has been covered since the first Archaic attempts. In the early figures wings were small and inorganically connected with the body, almost like two appendages fastened, metaphorically and technically, onto the figure's back without affecting its front view. In addition, their relative smallness and the fact that the body was shown in the running pose made the wings almost a dispensable accessory for the flight. The one major example of a Nike from the Severe period, the statue from Paros, has lost her wings and therefore their relative size cannot be gauged; however, her legs are slightly bent and do not seem to support her weight, so that her wings must have played a greater role in the composition. Her peplos, as far as can be noticed in its present state, was pinned normally, if incongruously, as if unhampered by the wings. More plausibly, in Figure N ("Iris") on the Parthenon West Pediment, the chitoniskos was shown as tied by a cord between the wings, which would have appeared to emerge from the enlarged side openings.

It may have been the desire to present a coherent form of clothing, together with the need for more organic and plausible means of flight, which prompted a change in rendering the wings: instead of being attached in the area of the shoulder blades, they were made to originate from the top of the shoulders near the neck and almost to the collar bones. This is the rendering in Paionios' Nike as well as in several Victories on the Nike Balustrade, where the form may be partially determined by the need to make the wings visible on relief figures in frontal poses. On the balustrade, however, we find the additional detail of the wing interfering, as it were, with the Nike's clothing (fig. 79), perhaps as a further hint to the organic reality of the appendages: a motif that is repeated in one of the Epidauros akroteria in the Fourth century.[9] Yet other Victories of the end of the Fifth century seem not to have this forward placement of the wings, nor do we find it consistently in later examples. Perhaps the motif originated with Paionios' Nike and might have been partly prompted by the static needs of the daring pose; aesthetic reasons may also have been at work, given the high positioning of the statue on its unusual triangular pillar[10] and the spectator's viewpoint from below, whence the wings would appear to frame the face with an interesting juxtaposition of human and "animal" elements.

OTHER FIFTH CENTURY ORIGINALS: RIBBON DRAPERY[11]

The Agora Aphrodite

Closer to the flamboyance of Paionios' Nike, yet different in her treatment of drapery, is an over-life-sized figure in the Agora Museum, which has been recomposed from many fragments after being extracted from the Late Roman fortification tower into which it had been built in antiquity. Despite her damaged and headless condition, the statue is most impressive and deserves an important position among Fifth century originals. It represents a woman standing with her weight on her right leg, the left trailing behind and to the side in what appears like a momentary pose, which Harrison, in her sensitive publication of the piece, defines as swaying. The upper part of the figure is covered by a long-sleeved chiton with short overfold, which the wind blows up over the right breast; around the hips and thighs swings a heavy mantle, surging like a wave to rest on the bent left arm. The bravura with which the tip of this garment was carved free of the body and supporting arm equals that of Paionios.

[9] This point is made by E. B. Harrison in her unpublished manuscript on the Classical sculpture from the Agora, but in a different context.

[10] It has been suggested that Paionios invented this form of support specifically for his Nike, and certainly its wedgelike shape increases the apparent instability and weightlessness of the statue's pose. Allusions to tripod supports, and therefore to victory, are also obvious. Yet it seems that the Olympia Nike had originally been planned for a square pillar that was subsequently altered, presumably by Paionios: Hölscher, "Die Nike," 76 n. 16. See also his comments on pp. 18-84, 91, and K. Herrmann, *JdI*

87 (1972) 232-57. For the tripod allusion see Borbein, *JdI* 88 (1973) 165-73, esp. 169.

[11] Carpenter's definition (*Greek Sculpture*, p. 151) does not quite correspond to mine in that he envisages the "ribbons" running contiguously to cover the torso, so that the nude is smothered rather than modeled. I would extend the term to include widely spaced ribbons, with flat stretches of transparent drapery in between, as long as the folds are not single-ridged. Hiller, p. 54, repeats Carpenter's definition and considers the rendering an innovation since the Nike Balustrade.

What imparts to the statue its peculiar swaying effect is a skillful combination of opposites, both in stance and in drapery lines. The pose is basically chiastic, but the out-thrust position of the right hip is emphatically stressed by the deviation of the chiton's folds in the same direction, while the tight wrapping of the himation along the entire right side allows the eye to continue a sinuous descent from breast to ankle. On the other hand, this rightward movement is counterbalanced by the fluttering mantle, which looks as if it had just been flung over the left arm. Its mass partially fills the great void produced by the raised shoulder (though this portion of the statue is almost entirely restored) in conjunction with the free leg, since the left knee not only bends but moves inwards, while ankle and foot swing outwards. Here again, the edge of the mantle, crossing back over the left thigh and lying in waves between the knees, calls attention to the position of the free leg, since its diagonal hem continues the oblique line of the shin. This detail is now partly obscured by the fragmentary condition of the surface, but one can still appreciate the wedge pattern of folds and limb echoing the figure's indented contour on her left side. The mantle swag over the bent arm and the out-thrust foot thus form the two balancing ends of a V-line that seems to penetrate deeply into the composition: the effect is successful because the wide space between the feet is filled by the stabilizing verticals of the full skirt.

The chiton gives an impression of extreme transparency: nipples and navel are fully revealed and the median line can be detected above the rounded abdomen. Not only is the cloth treated as if wet: its folds lie flat between sharp edges, like ribbons applied onto an alien surface; here and there the undercutting is stronger and the fold rises with metallic thinness, contouring the body beneath; in places the opposite approach prevails and a thin line is engraved onto the surface, either along a "ribbon" or within the flat spaces in between. The mantle acts as a foil to the chiton, its folds thicker and smoother but separated by deep and narrow valleys of irregular course. Although the cloth is gathered at the top in many-layered thickness, it does not form the twisted roll so typical of Fourth century or Hellenistic sculpture, but lies almost without appreciable volume, except where it curves out slightly under the impact of the emerging torso.

This type of drapery finds many parallels in various figures of the Nike Balustrade, as the initial publication points out. Indeed, a good visual comparison is provided in the same article by the juxtaposition of the Agora "Aphrodite" and Figure N from the parapet.[12]

There is less virtuoso handling in the Victory, and the drill has been used too facilely between fingers and mantle folds, but the rendering of the chiton is close enough to suggest chronological proximity as well. To my eyes the statue in the round seems slightly later, although perhaps it is only better. Harrison compares her to the work of the balustrade's Master A, Despinis agrees and places her among the creations of Agorakritos' circle. One suggestion, that the Aphrodite is Roman work, seems unfounded.

The Barberini Suppliant

That this type of drapery exists in undoubted marble originals should be of help in determining the true nature of a much debated piece, the so-called Barberini Suppliant in the Louvre (figs. 86-88). This most enigmatic statue has never been properly identified despite innumerable attempts; it is also uncertain whether it is a Greek original or an excellent copy

[12] The identification of the Agora statue as Aphrodite is made on the basis of the voluptuous appearance of the figure.

(either Roman or even more or less contemporary with the prototype) from a bronze; finally, it has been suggested that the piece is pedimental because of its narrow compositional depth and its medium, and in fact the figure could easily fit toward the corner of a gable, perhaps in an Underworld scene like that discussed in Appendix 3. However, this supposition may be weakened by the fact that replicas of it exist, which would be improbable in the case of inaccessible architectural sculpture, unless removed from its setting and therefore from its meaningful narrative context. Equally doubtful is the interpretation of the figure as a grave monument, in keeping with the somewhat sorrowful expression; a pathetic type of funerary sculpture would be unprecedented within the Fifth century and could not explain the popularity implied by the reproductions.

Identification usually rests on two details: the single bare foot and the peculiar platform on which the figure reclines; since the latter is generally taken to be an altar, the woman could be seeking asylum, hence the nickname. The low shape of the structure has also been seen as an indication that it was meant for chthonic sacrifices, whereby identification as a person about to be sacrificed (Iphigeneia) could be defended. But no certainty exists that an altar was really implied: a chest is an equally possible interpretation, or even a step. The slightly romantic expression of the face could be considered a copyist's contribution if the piece is, as I believe, a Roman reproduction. As for the sandal, the initial suggestion by Visconti, that the figure represents Dido, would have explained the feature according to Vergil's description of her death, but a Roman content is unlikely for a work in undoubtedly Greek style. All the major heroines of antiquity (Alkmene, Penelope, Kallisto) as well as semidivine personages (an Erinys, or even Ariadne, as per the original label) have at some point been suggested. The most recent hypothesis, that the figure represents Danae, finds supporting iconographic parallels only for the sitting position, but the most distinctive feature of the Danae type, the stretching out of the garment over the lap to receive the Golden Rain, is missing in the sculpture. It is easier to refute previous theories than to produce new ones. I am struck, however, by the many traits that recall Aphrodite: the slipping sleeve uncovering (with restraint) the youthful breast and the pose so reminiscent of the reclining goddess M on the Parthenon East Pediment.

Connection with the Parthenon may also be argued on the basis of drapery style. The Suppliant's mantle rises and sinks over and around the thighs with continuous, logical ridges, which model the forms underneath and recall the seated divinities (E-F, fig. 22) of the East Pediment. There are the same tension folds originating from the bent knee and the catch at the ankle where the material folds over. Texture is treated in comparable ways, although the Barberini Suppliant shows no selvage. Further similarities can be found in the head, despite the relative scarcity of the Parthenonian parallels in the round. In the Suppliant the semicircular wavelets that characterize the strands over the temples appear at a stage intermediate between the so-called Laborde Head, which has often been attributed to the Akropolis temple, and the Nike of Paionios. A date shortly after the completion of the pedimental sculpture, between 430 and 425, would therefore seem appropriate for the statue in the Louvre. But is it truly a Greek original or only a copy?

For all its excellent carving, I believe that the statue in Paris is a Roman replica. In favor of a bronze prototype speaks not so much the ribbon drapery, which, as we have seen, is actually typical of stone works and relies on skillful handling of the chisel, but rather the rendering of the eyes. Such sharp eyelids are not common in Fifth century marble sculpture, and the recessed position of the eyeballs suggests insertions in a different medium.[13] Karouzou has advanced the possibility that the Louvre piece may indeed be a copy of a metal statue and still be dated just after the original creation; recent research has in fact shown that such more or less contemporary copying did take place during the Fifth century, specifically for dedicatory purposes. It would be difficult, however, to advocate votive imitation in the case of as large a statue as the Barberini Suppliant. Moreover, certain traits in the Louvre statue speak in favor of an Augustan or slightly later date: the shape of the eyes at the outer corners (especially when seen in profile) and the slightly pathetic expression conveyed by their position; the calligraphic arrangement of the hair waves on either side of the central part; the harshness of the lips.

The Barberini statue has been included in this chapter, rather than being discussed later with the other Roman copies, because the figure retains its head and therefore provides further evidence for its chronological assessment. A complete sequence of ribbon drapery can then be established, from its first tentative appearance on the Parthenon metopes (ca. 440) to the pediments (ca. 435) to the Barberini Suppliant (ca. 430-425) to some figures from the Nike Balustrade (ca. 420-413) to the Agora Aphrodite (ca. 415-410). Toward the end of the Fifth and the beginning of the Fourth century the ribbon style seems to disappear, or at least to be supplanted by ever-more transparent renderings with fewer "ribbons" virtually incised into the flesh. Perhaps the akroterial figure from the Agora, which is sometimes attributed to the Hephaisteion but should belong to the 380s, can serve as representative of the trend in later times. Some of the free-standing figures from the Nereid Monument in Xanthos continue the same development.

THE "QUIET STYLE" OF CA. 420

This definition stems from a recent analysis by E. B. Harrison in connection with the cult statues of the Hephaisteion.[14] It is based on some Roman replicas as well as on original Greek reliefs, and it is difficult to find a proper representative among extant statues in the round. The closest is perhaps a female statuette in Athens, Akr. 1310 (figs. 89, 90), broken just below the hips but with head preserved. It portrays a young girl in chiastic pose, with lowered right shoulder and slightly out-thrust hip; over a peplos she wears a mantle, which encircles her hips and is draped around her left shoulder with the tip pulled back along the upper arm. The figure has been usually dated around 420, although at least one author prefers a date in the early Fourth century. The piece may possibly fall under the category of almost contemporary copies made within Classical times without thorough mechanical reproduction, and this impression is reinforced by the fact that several other works known only through Roman copies show similar drapery patterns. In the specific case of the Akropolis girl, the general schema of her costume is close to that of the Velletri Athena (fig. 115), even to the detail of a tip of the kolpos overlying the rounded edge of the himation over the right hip. The pose is reversed, however. Despinis has suggested that the Akropolis statuette may have been made in Agorakritos' workshop.

Typical traits of style are: the opaque texture of the cloth, with little differentiation

[13] To be sure, Fourth century sculptors gave their statues a melting gaze by making the eyeballs slightly concave rather than convex. However, this rendering was combined with narrower eye sockets and the lids did not project so far as to overshadow the eye itself.

[14] Note, however, that Harrison does not name the style but only cites its characteristics; neither does she identify as such the temple standing on Kolonos Agoraios, which we have been calling the Hephaisteion.

between peplos and mantle; the V-pattern of the neckline repeated by the folds between the breasts; the contrast between straight and curved linear patterns, especially clear in the area of the stomach; the even rhythm in the spacing of valleys and ridges, which gives an impression of quiet despite the obvious richness of the garments.

Harrison has emphasized that this style is transitional between the Parthenon and the Erechtheion friezes as a definite phase marking the period around 420; she has also stressed that works in this style reveal "the first real invasion of Polykleitan influence into Attic art." I prefer to see this stylistic manifestation as just one among a variety of others, and would accept Polykleitan influence earlier, in Parthenonian times, although not perhaps quite as forcefully. Concomitant with this distinctive manner I would see the flamboyant style of the Nike of Paionios, with its transparency, and the ribbon style discussed above. As the Fifth century progresses, I see the last two trends developing to excesses, with drapery becoming more and more subordinate to the volume of the body underneath and therefore resulting in sheer decoration; the "quiet style" continues in sporadic form and can even be found in some Fourth century works, where, however, poses and different spiritual content betray the later date.

While a complete review of the various drapery styles and their chronological development during the Fifth century can only be attempted after relief work and, to some extent, Roman copies have been taken into account, it is perhaps appropriate at this point to raise again the question of whether such variations in stylistic fashions can be attributed to individual masters. Harrison, for instance, suggests that the "quiet style" was developed by Alkamenes and occurs specifically in works by him or connected with his workshop; Despinis seems to favor the circle of Agorakritos. If such theories are accepted, we would have to return to a conception of distinctive artistic personalities capable of influencing the sculptural development of their times. But if such trends were contemporary, no single style entirely eliminating others or, conversely, being entirely free from traits proper of another stylistic current, then perhaps the conception of "anonymous" workshops is closer to the mark. By this term I mean the group of carvers assigned to a specific project but not necessarily dominated by a single master. Without denying the presence of a planning mind responsible for composition and perhaps three-dimensional models of some sort, the definition eliminates the concept of genius implicit even in the Renaissance *bottega* and becomes closer to that of the *fabbrica*, especially of medieval times. Rather than speaking of Pheidias' or Alkamenes' style, descriptive terms such as Parthenonian or quiet style should be used to reflect the choral composition of the works and the possible coexistence of trends. In the architectural sphere a major project like the Parthenon required the use of so many hands that more than one workshop, and therefore more than one style, were employed; a smaller project like that of the Ilissos Temple could be more confined, and therefore a distinctive and unparalleled style could develop, which explains our difficulty in coming to a proper chronological assessment. In all cases, crossovers and stylistic overlappings were possible, as is dramatically demonstrated in the Nike Balustrade, where some of the traits of the quiet style itself are present.

Beyond the questions of authorship and chronology there remains also that of diffusion. In discussing the various styles through Greek originals we have used examples almost entirely confined to Athens; the two exceptions—the Nike of Paionios and the Barberini Suppliant—are anomalous, in that the former was set up in an international sanctuary and we know nothing about her maker's sphere of action, while the latter is a Roman copy which provides no indication as to the setting of the original. A systematic review of Greek territory provides little information, however, on Fifth century sculpture in the round outside of Attica. Thessaly, which has yielded some Severe and some Fourth century pieces, registers a gap for the fifty years under revision. Boeotia is represented primarily by grave stelai. The same is largely true of the Cyclades: some male torsos in Delos may still be Severe, and the one with the Polykleitan pose is too fragmentary for specific analysis; I know of no female figures from the period. Somewhat the same conditions apply to the Peloponnese as a whole, and even the female head from the Argive Heraion has generally been connected with the sculptural decoration of the temple. Asia Minor seems equally sterile and so, to some extent, is Magna Graecia.[15] It seems worthwhile then to mention two small pieces that may suggest the spread of Attic influence abroad and the relative omnipresence of certain stylistic currents.

The first, under-life-size, is a female figure in Parian marble from Tarquinia now in Berlin. Her Etruscan findspot suggests a provenience from South Italy, perhaps Tarentum. The youthful lady, probably Aphrodite, wears a belted chiton with buttoned sleeves and a himation that covers her head and wraps around her hips. She supports her weight on her right leg while her left elbow leans on an Archaistic idol with high headdress. Her left leg is held slightly forward with knee partially bent, but her feet are kept clearly apart, so that no torsion is implied by the pose, which remains fully frontal. Despite the fact that both the figure's hands are restored, their original position is certain: the right held a tip of the mantle covering the head,[16] while the left was outstretched, holding some object. The general pose is comparable to that of the Leaning Aphrodite often attributed to Alkamenes, of which the best known, if not the only, replica is in Naples; but there the goddess appears leaning on a plain pier, her mantle falls closer to her head and neck and, most important, her left leg is forward of the right so that the feet are virtually aligned on the vertical, thus imparting some torsion to the pose.[17] Yet an undeniable similarity exists between the statue in Naples and that in Berlin, especially in how the kolpos overlaps the mantle over the right hip, a mannerism which recalls both the Velletri Athena and the Akropolis statuette.

[15] J. Marcadé, *Au Musée de Delos* (Paris 1969) 43-46, specifically comments on the remarkable lack of sculpture from the Classical period, during the Athenian patronage. Large-scale monuments of some importance seem to have resumed on the island only after the middle of the Fourth century. The only Fifth century piece that he mentions is a fragmentary draped figure leaning against a tree trunk on which a snake climbs, of difficult identification, which may perhaps represent Athena Hygieia. Similar comments are made for Samos by H. Kyrieleis, *AthMitt* 93 (1978) 179: neither originals nor copies of Classical works have been found at the Heraion, with the possible exception of an athletic torso and a male head, of debated chronology (see Appendix 8). Even the recent publication of the finds from Olympia, P. C. Bol, *Grossplastik aus Bronze in Olympia* (*OlForsch* 9, 1978) 34-38, has very little to offer for the period 450-400. Original statues in terra cotta of considerable size (much larger than statuettes) have been found in the Sanctuary of Demeter at Akrokorinth, and their publication by N. Bookidis is forthcoming in the *Corinth* series; at present see *Hesperia* 41 (1972) 317 (25-30 statues estimated) pl. 63.

[16] Although both sections of the mantle on either side of the head are restored, the arrangement of the drapery over the statue's back clearly shows that the restoration is correct in its general lines.

[17] It may be that a Fifth century type of drapery was combined with a more three-dimensional pose in later periods. To be sure, leaning poses are attested both in the Nike Balustrade and the Erechtheion frieze, but relief motifs always seem to precede comparable renderings in the round, often by considerable time.

Like these two pieces, the Aphrodite in Berlin is a representative of the quiet style. Although a thinner chiton, rather than the heavier peplos, covers her body, little or no transparency is suggested by the rendering of the drapery, which bends in rhythmical folds over the belt at the waist. That the figure may be slightly later than 420, or at least that her style might be contaminated by other currents, is shown, however, by the engraved semicircle which outlines the top of the right breast, and by the parallel tracks which descend from the nipples. Other stylistic traits of note are the segmented neckline and the tension folds over the right leg, as well as the contrast between curved and straight lines provided by the different patterns of chiton and himation. A certain harshness in the use of the drill and the superficial rendering of the back could suggest that this piece too is a Roman copy rather than a Greek original adaptation or replica, but these traits are more probably the result of function and of a degree of provincialism or relative importance, since the statuette is not a pretentious work.[18]

The second work (fig. 91), also small, is undoubtedly a Greek dedication, presumably to Artemis, found in 1911 in Sorrento during repairs to a water main and now in the local museum. The fragmentary votive inscription has been variously dated: originally attributed to the Hellenistic period, it was later placed toward the end of the Fifth or the beginning of the Fourth century. What remains of the statue is a headless,[19] armless figure wearing a belted peplos and a himation and seated sidesaddle on a long-necked but headless animal, presumably a hind. The tip of the mantle, which falls along the animal's neck, as well as the swag crossing the left thigh, recall Archaic renderings in their zigzag edges strongly undercut, a trait that Harrison has noted in the quiet style. However, the increased transparency of the treatment, here extended also to the mantle, and the strong volume of the bodily forms underneath lend a touch of flamboyancy to the piece, which makes it a quieter forerunner of the Formia Nereids. The back of the piece has a rough finish, and it has been suggested that the dedication stood in some kind of chapel or family shrine. The weight of the goddess over the hind was partly supported by a tree-like projection under the animal's belly, apparently growing in from an irregular base line. This pictorial detail imparts an almost *à-jour* relief effect to the sculpture in its present fragmentary state and may be a typical South Italian touch.

MALE FIGURES AND OTHER TYPES

Literary sources and extant bases make it clear that the male statues were created primarily in bronze, and this fact explains their almost total disappearance. Our main example of Fifth century anatomy in marble remains the Peiraeus Youth (fig. 92), which probably served a funerary purpose. As far as we can tell, no particular restrictions attached

[18] The same kind of rear surface treatment appears on other Greek originals, for instance the Grimani statuettes in Venice (*AntP* 11) and the Peiraeus Maiden published by S. Karouzou, *AthMitt* 82 (1967) 158-69, pls. 85-86—Athens Nat. Mus. 176, to be discussed in ch. 8.

[19] The head seems to have been added separately, in a technique that some authors consider typically South Italian. Since the animal also is headless, it is impossible to tell whether the work depicts Artemis on a hind or rather Aphrodite on a goat, after a well-established iconographic type of the goddess (Aphrodite Pandemos). The long garment worn by our figure, while not compelling, would seem more appropriate for Aphrodite than for Artemis.

to media, such that, for instance, all grave monuments had to be in marble, all votive offerings in bronze, or all cult images in terracotta.[20] On the contrary, we have clear examples of cult statues in a variety of media, and dedications could certainly range from terracottas to bronzes. The only possible reservation could be made for funerary images, which may have been exclusively in stone. To be sure, the popular form of tomb marker during the Fifth century seems to have been the relief stele, but a few individual statues remain, presumably depicting the deceased in heroic (or youthful) nudity, almost as if continuing the Archaic tradition of the funerary kouros. These figures are usually smaller than life-size and not of very high quality, in definite contrast with contemporary gravestones, which in the late Fifth century are still rare enough to be individual pieces of excellent workmanship and composition.

The Peiraeus Youth has been considered funerary largely on the basis of its size and the "withdrawn" expression of his face, so that other purposes cannot be entirely excluded. The youth stands in chiastic balance, his weight resting on the right leg, the left shoulder raised in correspondence with the bent knee. Since both legs are missing from below the knees, it is impossible to tell how far the left foot trailed, and the left arm is broken off just below the biceps, so that its action cannot be ascertained. The right arm is entirely preserved down to the empty hand, and the position of the fingers suggests than an object was once held along the body, perhaps a strigil or a slightly larger, sticklike object.[21] It has been mentioned that a certain hesitancy exists in the rhythm of the pose, with the movement apparent in the legs decreasing in the upper torso, and the delicate modeling of the body as well as some of the facial traits may place the statue in the early Fourth century. On the other hand, the massiveness of the face and the semicircular pattern of the curls seem to me more in keeping with a date ca. 420-410.

The main points of interest in the statue are its pose and the rendering of its anatomy. The head appears slightly misplaced over the uneven shoulders, facing straight ahead despite the tension in the large neck. This is perhaps the disturbing element in the composition as contrasted with the Polykleitan stance. There may also be too much discrepancy between the left and the right pectoral, the former appearing as if under a strain which the corresponding arm position does not justify. Anatomically, the emphasis on youthful forms has softened all patterns, so that the epigastric arch is not noticeable and the groin does not form a strong balancing accent below the hips. These muscles are faintly indicated in frontal view, yet they appear quite distinct in outline, so that a certain contrast exists between the silhouette and the surface of the total figure. Finally, two superimposed lines in the pubic area are finely engraved, like wrinkles, while little depth is given to the navel.[22] The total effect is linear and colorless. The strong patterning of the hair locks contrasts with the anatomical rendering, and the schematic treatment of the ear confirms

[20] This type of distinction has been advocated for Etruscan sculpture, but it is questionable.

[21] Another suggestion, that it held a vessel, is based on a comparison with a servant boy in a Funerary Banquet relief (Kraiker), but this reconstruction seems unlikely, because the statue did not belong to a larger (narrative) context.

[22] Note that similar engraved lines mark the joints of the fingers and the fleshly portions of the right hand; they are obviously a device to convey youthfulness through pudginess. J. Frel, *Les sculpteurs attique anonymes 430-300* (Universita Karlova, Prague 1969) p. 10 n. 8 and p. 11, considers the statue within the Parian tradition and assigns it to his "Sculptor of Ampharete."

that this is a work of no great artistic merit and of conflicting approaches. The asymmetry in the face would seem to demand a greater torsion in the pose, almost as if a model for a figure in motion had been used for, or ineptly transformed into, a quietly facing figure.

A second male statuette (fig. 93) was found in 1890 within the Temple of Themis at Rhamnous and is preserved together with its pillar bearing the votive inscription; its function is therefore beyond doubt. The youth was dedicated by Lysikleides son of Epandrides, presumably around 420, as style and epigraphy suggest. He stands frontally, supporting his weight on the left leg, the right bent and to one side. His right arm is raised level with the shoulder and bends upward at the elbow, but the hand is missing and it is impossible to reconstruct its original position.[23] The left arm is lowered along the side and bent slightly forward at the elbow, but is broken at the wrist and we are therefore missing the attribute, possibly a phiale, which the hand once held. A mantle rests on the left shoulder, crosses the back of the figure and curves to the front just below the right hip, where it begins to climb toward the right armpit; a triangular overfold creates the appearance of an apron in front of the body.

Despite the dating, which should be approximately contemporary, the Rhamnous Youth is stylistically different from both the Peiraeus Boy and the Maiden Akr. 1310 (figs. 89, 90), yet this latter and the Rhamnous figure have been associated with Agorakritos' workshop. In contrast with the male statue, the Rhamnous Youth shows clear anatomical markings: a well-articulated epigastric arch and a prominent hip muscle, which overlaps the thigh with a deep indentation. Also the Rhamnous Youth faces straight ahead, but his shoulders are level and therefore the ambiguous effect of the Peiraeus Boy is avoided. His mouth is smaller in proportion to the face and recalls some figures from the Parthenon frieze; yet his hair is reminiscent of Severe coiffures.

The contrast with the Akropolis maiden is best expressed in the treatment of the garment. Whereas the female costume was uniformly rendered as thick and opaque, the boy's himation clings to the body with such emphasis as to appear transparent; in the area of the right thigh, overfold and mantle look as if they form a single and diaphanous layer. The radiating pattern of folds so typical of the quiet style occurs only below the triangular "apron" and contrasts with the independent and more irregular design of the overfold. Ridges are almost metal-sharp and the deep valleys in between are narrow and follow the contours of the limbs, so that the bent right leg is outlined by shadow almost in its entirety. The heavy fall of the mantle folds on the left side reaches the base and provides a needed support for the ankles as the compositional equivalent of a strut or tree trunk, but the artifice is apparent and brings a certain stiffness to the whole. This too is not a superior statue but a rather modest if competent and pleasing work.

Two marble statuettes, both belonging to the period around 420, are meager harvest for the whole line of Fifth century male figures. Pausanias, for instance, tells us of the great votive monuments erected by the Spartans (10.9.7ff.) and by the Athenians (10.10.1) at Delphi which comprised well over thirty and thirteen figures, respectively, all as large or larger than life-size, yet they have all disappeared without trace. So have the thirty-five boys and their trainer and the flute-player made in bronze for Sicilian Messane by

---

[23] This gesture would be understandable in a divine or regal figure, but is somewhat unusual in a youth. Perhaps the hand was simply empty and raised in salutation or prayer, like that of the youth on the so-called Cat Stele discussed in ch. 6.

Kalon of Elis at Olympia around 430. Also the many athletes who set up images at the sanctuary are recorded—if at all—only through Roman copies, and even the wounded or fighting warriors on the Athenian Akropolis can no longer be visualized and stylistically examined. Certainly the male body lent itself to a variety of active poses and narrative representations, although descriptions of the Delphic monuments and the remains of their bases suggest that paratactic display of quietly standing figures was common also for bronze statuary despite the potential of the medium. A special paratactic alignment was that of the bronze Eponymous Heroes in the Athenian Agora, which seem to have stood on a tall base surrounded by a stone balustrade where special announcements were set up as if on a bulletin board. Since allusions to the group exist as early as the late Fifth century, the statues must have been made around or at least by that date, although the present position of their base, opposite the Metroon, is probably due to a relocation in the Fourth century B.C. It has been suggested that the East frieze of the Parthenon gives us an echo of these ten statues in the male figures standing before the seated gods, but the poses are too pictorial and three-dimensional to fit the linear arrangement demanded by the Agora foundations. Some of the Eponymoi must have been depicted as young, but some as elderly men partially draped. Since this type is not known through contemporary Attic originals in the round,[24] at least a remote hint of their appearance may be supplied by the bronze statue (figs. 94, 95) found in 1969 in the Straits of Messina (Porticello) as part of a wreck, which is dated by its cargo to the late Fifth or early Fourth century B.C.

Although the ship was excavated with scientific methods, the first spectacular finds were made by illegal divers interested solely in personal profit, so that it is highly probable but not absolutely proven that the two bronze figures seized in fragments by the Italian police originally came from the same wreck.[25] They are undergoing cleaning and restoration and only preliminary notices and photographs have been published, on which the following comments are based. There were two life-size male figures, one naked and probably youthful, another (which concerns us here) semidraped and elderly, with head entirely preserved. A squarish tenon on the right side of the neck shows that the head was cast separately and connected to the body by the tongue-and-groove system. Parts of the hair (for instance, over the nape) were cast solid and added later, so that some are now lost, but features under them appear complete, such as the right ear. The man has a striking physiognomy: a high, prominent forehead with receding hairline suggesting baldness; rather deep-set and relatively small eye cavities, the inserted material still preserved in one of them; an aquiline nose dipping sharply over the voluminous mustache, which hides the lips almost entirely—an unusual feature. Finally, the man has a surprisingly long beard. The total effect is that of an individual, a philosopher type,[26] such as one would expect from the Fourth century or even the Hellenistic period. How can this head be reconciled with the date of the wreck?

I believe that the stylistic traits of greatest importance support a chronology around 450

[24] This is all the more surprising since we have definite evidence that statues which once stood in the Athenian Agora could be and were copied. E. B. Harrison (*Agora* 11, 132-33) has suggested, however, that some of the prytany herms in the Fifth century may have copied the heroic bearded heads of the Eponymous Heroes. Cf. Kron, 231 n. 1126.

[25] An isolated piece of bronze drapery was actually recovered in situ on the wreck, so there is every reason to believe that the sequestered fragments have the same provenience.

[26] The relative smallness of the eyes could perhaps suggest a blind Homer.

or only slightly later. The hair patterns are linear, for instance, volume and plasticity being obtained through the layering of the strands rather than by means of the plastic shape of the strands themselves or through the total mass. A view of the head from above reveals an unusually realistic detail: the combing of loose waves of hair across the bald pate, but even this feature is obtained through linear, not through plastic, means. The impression of age is increased by the peculiar horizontal accent formed by the temples, the eyes and the bridge of the nose, almost like a gash which sets out the bulging forehead as if it were a shelf; but there is otherwise little modeling of the facial structure and certainly no prominent cheekbones. The distinctive shape of the nose may look portraitlike, but it can also be found on the centaur of Parthenon metope S 1. Finally, the total outline of the face is relatively contained, and only the long and tapering beard removes it from the series of cubic structures from the Severe period. The fragment of drapery, presumably part of a himation or a short chlamys over a shoulder, shows parallel ridges and grooves in keeping with the suggested date, but too little is preserved for diagnostic purposes. However, the statue must have been an impressive work, and it is remarkable that the total cargo of the wreck, with its lead ingots and scrap metal, implies that also the figured bronzes were to be recycled. That relatively new statues of artistic value should deserve such treatment adds one more problem to those of their origin and style. They could have been made in Magna Graecia, as perhaps suggested by the unusual realism of the bearded head, but the location of the wreck per se gives no assurance as to their provenience, as confirmed by the variety of amphoras found together with the bronzes.

SUMMARY

A brief review of our evidence on Greek originals from the Fifth century has to take into account some of the statue bases and the literary sources. The types of monuments being set up varied a great deal. Male and female figures usually occurred within a narrative or mythological context, or they were votive offerings imitating a cult image. Very few funerary statues in the round seem to have existed. Seated figures seem particularly scarce: they may have belonged to the last two categories, if they were not pedimental, which is always a difficult point to establish. The later Fifth century in general sets the fashion for historical, commemorative monuments erected at the expenses of the state, or occasionally by private victorious individuals, in their own city or more often at the major sanctuaries of Delphi and Olympia. Such monuments were often allegorical, like the Nike of Paionios, but the human form was not necessarily predominant, as shown by the bronze chariot on the Akropolis with which the Athenians commemorated a victory over Boeotians and Chalkidians in 506 (Paus. 1.28.2). Since fragments of its dedicatory inscription seem to date from the mid-Fifth century, we learn that such monuments could be erected considerably later than the event.[27] Political implications may also have been present in the large bronze Trojan Horse dedicated by a certain Chairedemos and made by Strongylion shortly before 415, which Pausanias describes as having Greek warriors

[27] In this particular case the possibility exists that the late inscription goes with a replacement monument, since fragments from the original Archaic base remain and suggest that the initial dedication might have been destroyed by the Persians; see R. Meiggs and C. Lewis, *A Selection of Greek Historical Inscriptions* (Oxford 1969) 28-29, no. 15.

inside, peeping out of it. The sides of its large marble base on the Akropolis show traces of the wheels, which clearly characterized the horse as a contraption and may have given Pausanias the idea that it was in fact a siege engine (1.23.8). Another Trojan Horse was dedicated by the Argives at Delphi after a victory over the Spartans in 414—a clear case of the same subject used by different people with different meaning (Paus. 10.9.12). A large bronze bull was erected for unknown reasons by the Council of the Areopagos near the West steps of the Parthenon, presumably as an immortal version of the beast of sacrifice. None of these monuments can at present be fully visualized.[28] We must conclude that our picture of Fifth century sculpture in the round is precariously limited and that judgment based on the extant originals is bound to be seriously slanted.

[28] Other statues of bulls are known through the literary sources: even if we leave open the question of authorship for Myron's cow, there was a large bull dedicated by the Korkyrans at Delphi, of which part of the inscribed base remains. A relative visualization is offered by the silver bull recently reconstructed at Delphi: P. Amandry, *Etudes Delphiques* (*BCH* suppl. 4, 1977) 273-93. It was approximately 2.30m long and 1.25m high, built over a wooden armature and an intermediate layer, perhaps of wax or plaster. Its style seems Ionic, probably Archaic, and it may have been one of Kroisos' dedications to the sanctuary.

APPENDIX 5

1. *Demeter in Eleusis, inv. no. 64* (fig. 96). This over-life-sized marble statue, headless and with lower arms broken off and missing, has always been considered a Demeter of the late Fifth century B.C. (see, e.g., BrBr 536). The identification rests on the findspot, the garment (a peplos belted over the overfold and a shoulder mantle), and the rather matronly appearance. The raised left arm might once have held a scepter, thus characterizing the elder, rather than the younger, of the two Eleusinian goddesses. In addition, because of the alleged resemblance of the statue to the figures from the base of the Nemesis at Rhamnous, the Eleusis figure has traditionally been given to Agorakritos. Despinis (p. 186), after his identification of the original fragments of the Nemesis, has suggested that the Eleusis piece is indeed closely related to the style of that master, but is probably by a member of his workshop (one of his closest and earliest pupils) rather than by the Parian sculptor himself.

In her review of representations of Demeter and Kore, A. Peschlow-Bindokat has included the Eleusis statue as one of the only two sculptures in the round known from the Fifth century (*JdI* 87 [1972] 60-157, esp. 127-32, Cat. S.1 on p. 156). She admits, however, that no other depiction of Demeter wearing a belted peplos in this fashion is known. This costume is more typical of Athena or other younger women. The original effect of the Eleusis statue, with a mantle reaching to the ground near the right foot, would probably have been more matronly than at present, with that garment largely broken.

It is worth noting that a comparison has been made between the Eleusis torso and a statuette of Athena, Akr. 3027: E. Raftopoulou, *BCH* 90 (1966) 68 n. 3 and fig. 16 on p. 67. Although only drapery patterns are being compared, the two sculptures seem quite close both in pose and style; the Akropolis statuette differs in having a diagonal aegis crossing her breast and in lacking the himation, but another (life-sized) statue of Athena considered a variant of the same type includes also the mantle: C. Praschnicker in *Antike Plastik* (Festschrift W. Amelung, Berlin and Leipzig 1928) 176-81, figs. 1-4; E. Berger, *AntK* 10 (1967) 85, n. 8, pl. 24:8. Both figures of Athena are reconstructed as leaning on a shield, in analogy with an Attic relief of 409 B.C. (Praschnicker, 178, fig. 5). However, the high position of the left shoulder, at least in the statuette, could allow a restoration with a spear. Perhaps a similar attribute should be visualized for the Eleusis torso, which would therefore be a variant of the same Athena type with the elimination of the aegis but the retention of the mantle. Spear, perhaps a helmeted head, and the very manner of wearing the peplos would have been more than adequate characterization (cf. *Severe Style* 29 n. 1). Certainly some doubt should remain as to the traditional identification as Demeter. In addition, the peculiar plan of the Telesterion at Eleusis may also speak against the use of an image of the goddess in a centralized position.

Not entirely compelling either is the comparison of the Eleusis torso with the figures from the Nemesis base, although a proper discussion must await the official publication of the latter. Good photographs of some fragments published by K. Schefold (*R. Boehringer: Eine Freundesgabe* [Tübingen 1957] 556-63, figs. 9-27) seem to show a different treatment of the tubular folds, which do not fork into parallel ridges as consistently as they do in the "Demeter," while transparency is obtained through different devices. It has been noted that the back of the Eleusis statue is somewhat perfunctorily carved and a certain harshness in the general treatment may suggest that we have a good copy rather than a true Fifth century original.

2. *Bronze female head from the Agora, B 31.* Found in a well abandoned in the Third century B.C. behind the Stoa of Zeus, this almost half-life-sized original has grooves cut along its hairline and on either side of the neck for the insertion of gold plates, allegedly over a backing of silver. In his detailed publication of the piece H. A. Thompson advanced the theory, now generally accepted, that the head belonged to a Nike because of the narrow portion of chest visible below the neck and meant for insertion into a draped body. He argued that the highly pointed V-shape of the exposed flesh demanded a garment worn

123

unusually close against the neck, such as would occur if wings pushed up the cloth. He therefore associated the head with the "Golden Nikai" mentioned in treasurers' accounts as repositories of the public gold, and explained the elaborate plating system as a technique conditioned by the need to remove and replace the gold as needed; he further correlated the plating channels, some of which had been carefully filled with bronze, with historical events causing in turn the stripping and the regilding of the head. (*HSCP* suppl. 1 [1940] 183-210; for the initial account of the find see T. L. Shear, *Hesperia* 2 [1933] 519-27; more recent summaries in *Agora* 14, 190-91, *Agora Guide*, 253-55, where the head is dated ca. 420-415 B.C. For a detailed investigation of the Golden Nikai see D. B. Thompson, *Hesperia* 13 [1944] 173-209.)

The cylinder projecting atop the head and variously pierced both vertically and horizontally was immediately explained as the core for a *lampadion* coiffure, and the additional holes in its vicinity as fastening points for the cascading curls (Shear, figs. 8-9, pp. 523-24). H. A. Thompson, who gave a detailed description of the various drillings (*HSCP*, 183 n. 2, 184 n. 1; cf. his fig. 7) opted for a compact bun of hair and suggested a wreath, but not all holes are accounted for by this reconstruction. Most recently E. B. Harrison (*AJA* 81 [1977] 168 and figs. 32-33; 418-19 and figs. 2-3) has commented on the asymmetry and the difference in expression between the two halves of the face.

In 1971 the discovery of a fragmentary equestrian bronze statue from another Agora well provided a parallel for the technique of gilding plates rabbeted into grooves (T. L. Shear, Jr., *Hesperia* 42 [1973] 165-68, pl. 36). Yet it was pointed out that the channels cut through the composition with no regard for the design, presumably because the gold was not meant to be removed, as contrasted with the careful positioning of the channels in the bronze head. It is, nonetheless, legitimate to ask whether the difference may be due to the relative size of the two sculptures and their date, the equestrian figure (probably Demetrios Poliorketes) being approximately one century later than the female. Note also that in the latter, the right neck groove cut through an engraved curl escaping from the mass, a detail which could not have been reproduced in the plating. For a recent technical dis-

cussion see "The gilding of bronze statues in the Greek and Roman world," by W. A. Oddy, L. Borelli Vlad, and N. D. Meeks, in *The Horses of San Marco, Venice* (Olivetti, Milan 1979) 182-87.

Is the Agora head truly a Nike? The treasurers' accounts seem to convey a different picture of the Golden Nikai being dismantled and reassembled for weighing purposes, a procedure that could not easily be carried out on works gilded with the technique of the Agora head. Akroterial figures of Nikai in gilded bronze are mentioned in treasury accounts that have been associated with the Nike Temple (P. N. Boulter, *Hesperia* 38 [1969] 133-40), and perhaps the Agora figure adorned one of the roofs in the marketplace. Moreover, the narrow area of exposed chest, while in keeping with a winged figure, could also fit one with raised arms or with a short mantle draped over both shoulders (cf., e.g., Demeter on the East Parthenon frieze). The *lampadion* coiffure seems demanded by the course of the strands, which show no other termination, but the substantial size of the cylinder in proportion to the head, and the intricate system of holes may suggest that the figure was meant for suspension and that the specific hairstyle was selected to provide plausible cover for the support. Conversely, another object could have been fastened above the separately cast curls of the *lampadion*.

The head is important as a Fifth century original, confirming the practice of Venus rings and the strong outline of the female face popular around 420 B.C. If a Golden Nike, it may have been made by a jeweler rather than a sculptor, as D. B. Thompson suggests. Of the extant masters' names cited in the treasurers' accounts (Deinokrates, Timodemos, [. . .]atides) none is familiar from other sources.

3. *Marble head of a youth, AKr. 699.* This piece has frequently been connected with the Parthenon metopes, but its scale seems slightly too large for the Lapiths of the South metopes. Brommer, *Metopen*, 132, no. (34), rejects the attribution. Most authors agree, however, that the head should be assigned to the Parthenon workshop or to Pheidias' circle, approximately ca. 447-438 B.C.: see, most recently, Brouskari, 131, fig. 252. This work seems of better quality than most of the preserved heads from the South metopes; note in particular the well-defined lids and the subtle modeling around cheeks and

mouth. Many details were enhanced by paint. If the head belonged to a statue in the round, independent from any architectural context, its importance lies also in confirming the presence of Classical originals in marble on the Akropolis.

4 and 5. *Two marble heads of Athena in Taranto, Nat. Mus. inv. nos. 3883 and 3899.* The former, 0.37m high, is illustrated in R. R. Holloway, *Influences and Styles in the Late Archaic and Early Classical Greek Sculpture of Sicily and Magna Graecia* (Louvain 1975) 9 and bibliography on p. 51:7, figs. 63-64. The latter head, 0.32m high, is best seen in *Magna Graecia*, pls. 98-99. Both heads are helmeted, although in both the head cover is damaged and in the second at least parts of it were added separately.

Several holes for metal attachments have been interpreted as part of the helmet, fastenings for a wreath or traces of separately carved locks. Of interest in both heads is the delicate modeling of the facial features, especially around the mouth, and the elongated eyes with rounded inner corner dipping toward the nose, which are reminiscent of some pieces from Selinus. These two heads deserve special attention in view of the scarcity of marble sculpture in Taras. Although they retain traits of the Severe style, they should both be dated after the middle of the Fifth century. Since they were found within the city itself, it has been suggested that at least one of them belonged to a cult image.

FOR PAGE 104

Statue from Straits of Messina: see infra, p. 120.

Statues from Riace Marina: see ch. 9.

Bronze statuette in the Louvre: Zanker, no. 29, pp. 32-33, pl. 34:1, Lullies and Hirmer, fig. 183; S. Boucher, *BCH* 100 (1976) 95-102. See also App. 8:2.

FOR PAGE 105

Erechtheion Karyatids: The main publication is Lauter, which is entirely devoted to the subject; a companion volume, by E. Schmidt, deals with the copies (*AntP* 13 [1973]). See also Bieber, *Ancient Copies*, 29-30.

One more Roman copy of the Karyatids, which was found too recently to be included by E. Schmidt, is briefly mentioned in *Hesperia* 44 (1975) 22-23, nos. 26-27, pls. 7-8.

Meaning of term: the opinion is by H. Plommer, *JHS* 99 (1979) 97-102. On this subject see also H. Drerup, *MarbWinckProg* 1975/76, 11-14. A. Schmidt-Colinet, *Antike Stützfiguren* (Frankfurt 1977), is devoted entirely to the subject of Karyatids and Telamones.

On the meaning of Erechtheion Karyatids see, e.g., Kron, 87-88 (accepting Picard's theory that they form a baldacchino for the Kekropion).

FOR PAGE 106

On the Prokne and Itys see ch. 7.

FOR PAGE 107

For a discussion of Classical Peplophoroi, including the Erechtheion Karyatids and the Parthenon frieze, see H. Jung, *JdI* 91 (1976) 118-23.

On the central braid of the Karyatids see Lauter, p. 38, who argues for the presence of this trait on all of the Korai except A; however the rendering is unclear on the others.

FOR PAGE 108

For a close-up of the peplophoros on the Nike Temple East frieze see *AntP* 11 (1972) fig. 5 opposite p. 65.

Nike of Paionios: the best discussion, both in terms of style and of historical connections, is Hölscher "Die Nike"; interesting stylistic analysis also in Borbein, p. 168.

A historical discussion based on the inscription of the triangular pillar is in Meiggs and Lewis, *A Selection of Greek Historical Inscriptions* (Oxford 1969) 223-24, no. 74.

FOR PAGE 110

Despite its lofty positioning, the Nike may have been copied; a recent find from the Agora seems to give one more replica of the head type: *Hesperia* 40 (1971) 273 and pl. 58:1.

Nike of Paionios connected with Bassai frieze: Ch. Hofkes-Brukker, *BABesch* 42 (1967) 10-71, esp. 10-11, no. II; id., *Bassai-Fries*, 128-32.

Nike of Paionios connected with Nike Balustrade: R. Carpenter, *The Sculpture of the Nike Temple Parapet* (Cambridge, Mass., 1929) 29-31, 78.

Nike from Paros: *Severe Style*, figs. 56, 58.

FOR PAGE 111

Agora Aphrodite: Agora Museum S 1882; E. B. Harrison, *Hesperia* 29 (1960) 373-76, pl. 82; S. Adam, *Technique*, 15, 31, 126, pl. 15c; Despinis, 188, dated at the end of the Fifth century, from the circle of Agorakritos. The suggestion that the statue is a Roman copy is by H. von Heintze, *RömMitt* 72 (1965) 37 and n. 150. W. Fuchs, *Die Skulptur der Griechen* (Munich 1969) 209, attributes the figure to Kallimachos.

FOR PAGE 112

Barberini Suppliant: of the vast bibliography on this subject, note in particular J. Dörig, *JdI* 80 (1965) 143-66 (considered the Alkmene by Kalamis); P. Mingazzini, *AntK* 11 (1968) 53-54 (considered Iphigeneia); S. Karouzou, *AntK* 13 (1970) 34-47 (considered Danae). For a discussion of the head type see E. Herscher and B. S. Ridgway, *AJA* 75 (1971) 184-88, esp. 187. Good illustrations of details in Dörig, esp. figs. 4, 5 (contrast the latter with Carpenter, *Nike Parapet*, pl. 22a, opp. p. 53), 6, 7, 19, 21, 23, 39-40, 48, 53, 56, 58, 74, 88a,c,e, 89d, 92e,f.

FOR PAGE 114

Akroterial figure from the Agora: see ch. 3, p. 62 with bibl.

Definition of quiet style: E. B. Harrison, *AJA* 81 (1977) 164-66, 416.

Akr. 1310: dated to the Fourth century by Brouskari, 164 (ill.). The best photograph is in R. Kabus-Jahn, *AntP* 11 (1972) figs. 12-15, cf. p. 20. Despinis compares its head to some from the Nemesis base: p. 177 and nn. 353-56. See also F. Hiller, p. 54, and B. Schlörb, *Untersuchungen zur Bildhauergeneration nach Phidias* (Waldsasen/Bayern) 38 n. 33.

For a discussion of the Velletri Athena and the draping of the mantle, see chs. 7-8.

FOR PAGE 115

Style transitional between Parthenon and Erechtheion: E. B. Harrison, *AJA* 81 (1977) 416. The quotation is from pp. 164-65.

For a discussion of workshop versus masters see R. Bianchi Bandinelli, *Archeologia e Cultura* (Milan and Naples 1961) 46-65, enlarged version of a speech delivered on Jan. 22, 1957 and printed in *ArchCl* 9 (1957) 1-17.

FOR PAGE 116

Head from the Argive Heraion: see Delivorrias, 190-91, with bibliography. Illustration in Berve and Gruben, pl. 48.

Figure from Tarquinia: Blümel, *Berlin* no. 117 (K 6) pp. 98-99, figs. 192-95; S. Hiller, *AntK* 19 (1976) 30-40, esp. p. 34, pl. 7:3. Cf. a relief in the Vatican, Helbig⁴, no. 1001, p. 719, with Aphrodite leaning on a herm.

Leaning Aphrodite in Naples: Harrison, *AJA* 81 (1977) 276 and figs. 15-16 on p. 277; S. Hiller, *AntK* 19 (1976) 32-34, pl. 7:2. Single replica with veiled head.

FOR PAGE 117

"Artemis" in Sorrento: A. Levi, *NSc* 1924, 375, pl. 18; A. Rumpf, *RömMitt* 38/39 (1923-24) 475 (dated to the beginning of the Fourth century); *AA* 1926, 221-22 (end of the Fifth century; H. 0.82m).

On the Formia Nereids see, e.g., S. Lattimore, *The Marine Thiasos in Greek Sculpture* (Los Angeles 1976) 51 and bibliography in n. 26 on pp. 66-67.

Peiraeus Youth: Lullies and Hirmer, pl. 198 and its commentary; the main publication is by

W. Kraiker, *Die Antike* 14 (1938) 196-201 with 4 ills.; see also F. Hiller, 17, 42, pl. 5 and fig. 10; J. Frel, *Les Sculpteurs attiques anonymes* (Prague 1969) 10-11, no. 8. The hesitancy in the pose and a Fourth century date are suggested by Lullies.

FOR PAGE 119

For the connection between asymmetrical facial features and motion in the pose see L. A. Schneider, *Asymmetrie griechischer Köpfe vom 5. Jh. bis zum Hellenismus* (Wiesbaden 1973).

Rhamnous Youth, Athens Nat. Mus. 199, H. 0.92. Attributed to Agorakritos' workshop by Despinis, pp. 174-75, probably by a student. S. Karouzou, *AthMitt* 82 (1967) 160, pl. 89, compared to the Kore from Peiraeus.

On the monuments erected at Delphi see the discussion by Hölscher, "Die Nike," 77-78.

FOR PAGE 120

On the Eponymous Heroes in the Agora, cf. bibliography for ch. 4:78; the study of the original location of the monument on the basis of recent excavational evidence is by T. L. Shear, Jr., *Hesperia* 39 (1970) 145-222; cf. also Travlos, *Pictorial Dictionary*, 210-12; R. E. Wycherley, *The Stones of Athens* (Princeton 1977) 52-53; Kron, 228-36, does not accept the identification of the earlier base because she considers it too small.

Fifth century allusions to the Agora group: Aristophanes, *Clouds*, 207.

Bronze statue from the Straits of Messina (Porticello wreck) now in the Reggio Museum: *JHS—AR* 23 (1977) 63, fig. 30; D. I. Owen, *Antike Welt* 4 (1973) 3-10; id., *Archaeology* 24 (1971) 118-29; id., *Magna Graecia* VI/9-10 (1971) 6-8. G. Foti, *Calabria Turismo* 6:18 (1973) 9-15. On the material from the wreck see also C. J. Eiseman, *AJA* 79 (1975) 374-75, and id., *JNautArch* 2 (1973) 13-23.

FOR PAGE 121

Bronze chariot of Chalkidian Victory: Meiggs and Lewis, *A Selection of Greek Historical Inscriptions* (Oxford 1969) 28-29, no. 15.

Trojan Horse by Strongylion: cf. Hölscher, "Die Nike," 80; F. W. Hamdorf, *Stele* (Athens 1980) 231-35.

Chapter 6

Greek Originals: Reliefs

Aside from architectural sculpture, which has already been discussed, and decorated statue bases, which require separate treatment, Greek reliefs can be grouped under three headings: figured gravestones, votive plaques, and the carved *en-têtes* of decrees with symbolic figures representing the parties involved. All three kinds were meant to be set up at about eye level and therefore required no elaborate perspective arrangement and little depth. Yet this low-relief technique is not an immediate consequence of the function or of the setting, since Fourth century stelai could be carved in a very high relief and ultimately with figures almost in the round; we should therefore consider the relatively low projection of most Fifth century carvings as largely a matter of choice. In comparison with later production moreover, Fifth century works seem more individualistic, less mass-produced, and by and large of better artistic quality, although inferior or indifferent examples are also extant. Athens, as usual, has provided the most abundant documentation for the period, but relief work seems to be the one form of sculpture to have survived from other areas of the Greek world (except perhaps the Peloponnesos) in sufficient quantity to allow some understanding of stylistic trends and regional preferences. Reliefs provide a latitude that we sadly lack for evaluating sculpture in the round.

Of the three above-mentioned types, the last is an Attic practice, although "copies" were set up in other areas under Athenian political influence. These record reliefs (*Urkundenreliefs*) used to be considered potentially very useful for a general chronology of Attic sculpture, since they accompany texts dated by archonship years. It has now become increasingly obvious that their usefulness is relative, for two main reasons. First, the figured panel was conceived as subsidiary to the main purpose of the stele, the inscription, and could be carved with a minimum of competence. Second, the figures usually reproduced specific cult images as symbols of the cities involved, and therefore imitated earlier works; the archonship under which the decree was passed represents only a *terminus ante quem*. In addition, the integration of some archons' names, and by extension the specific years of certain decrees, are debatable issues and very different suggestions have been made. Finally, the geographical limitations of the type further diminish its general importance. We shall therefore mention record reliefs only incidentally.

Iconographically, the division of reliefs into three groups may be somewhat specious. If the divinities heading historical inscriptions are seen as tutelary deities under whose patronage the decree was placed, there is little to distinguish record reliefs from votive offerings. In turn, gravestones straddle a thin line between human respect and heroizing honors, so that a case could be made for considering a tombstone as a votive relief of sorts. The distinction is perhaps of greater importance for iconographic than for stylistic purposes and can be disregarded in this context. Yet, while record reliefs are a Fifth century

128

innovation, votive and funerary stelai have a long tradition, both in Attica and elsewhere within the Greek world, with the two types occasionally influencing each other both in format and content. This is a major topic and it would be fruitless to attempt here a summary history of such reliefs, but a few basic points may be stated.

Votive reliefs may have started earlier than figured gravestones, if the Seventh century seated lady on a stele from Paros does indeed represent a divinity rather than a deceased. But it ought to be emphasized that reliefs from the islands and the East Greek world (perhaps also from Sparta) during the Archaic and Severe periods can seldom be assigned with certainty to either category, since often interaction among humans or between human and animal figures imparts to the scene an everyday quality quite different from the splendid isolation of the deceased on Sixth century Attic funerary stelai. Even single figures, seated and holding attributes, can hardly be classified as either divine or mortal, and in general it can only be said that non-Attic Archaic reliefs present more iconographic variety than the Athenian series. It was generally held that the Ionic world preferred un-figured grave markers and that the introduction of the human figure on Ionic gravestones occurred only toward the end of the Sixth century under Attic influence. In recent years, however, more examples of figured tombstones have been found in Asia Minor and the islands, so that our current theories probably need revision. A monumental corpus of East Greek grave stelai has just been completed, forming a useful counterpart to the important, if outdated, collection of Attic gravestones. Other studies have attempted similar compendia for different regions; for instance, Thessaly and Boeotia. We still need a comprehensive treatment of votive reliefs, although occasional monographs and articles on single pieces have been published.

Within the funerary sphere, the total picture presents considerable gaps. Athens, for still obscure reasons that cannot be limited to a hypothetical antiluxury decree, seems to have stopped producing elaborate stone monuments from ca. 490 to ca. 430. During this time, however, white-ground lekythoi continue to represent mourners near tall stelai, and we may assume that the monuments were made of more perishable material or in a labile technique, and thus have not survived in recognizable shape. Another theory assumes that it was only the first casualties of the Peloponnesian War which gave the impetus for the resumption of funerary sculpture in Athens, the first being perhaps a most impressive state monument meant to exalt the value of self-sacrifice for the city. At any rate, figured gravestones resumed around that date in a different, wider format possibly influenced by that of votive reliefs, and continued until the end of the Fourth century in ever-greater size and complexity. Next to the stelai, sculptured stone vases and other funerary monuments with relief decoration were made, obviously by the same workshops that produced the gravestones and probably also the votive reliefs. On this assumption, attempts have been made to recognize hands and masters, much along the lines of J. D. Beazley's pioneer work on Attic vase painters. Although such efforts are made easier by the large number of monuments extant from the Fourth century, some Fifth century groupings could also be established. The rest of the Greek world is more sporadically represented, and only Lakonia, Thessaly, and Boeotia have produced true "series." Single examples, however, come from several of the islands and from the Asia Minor cities and colonies, although a distinct division between funerary and votive monuments is occasionally still difficult to establish. The Peloponnesos, as usual, is represented by a very limited sculptural selection, and the few grave stelai extant all seem under a certain amount of Attic influence—indeed, it seems fair to state that the latter is pervasive throughout the Greek world and that variations are largely limited to style and individual renderings.

No comparable gap is noticeable among Attic votive reliefs, but artistic life in Athens seems to quicken its pace after the inception of the great Akropolis program, so that the majority of extant monuments date after 450, with ever-increasing numbers in the following century. The introduction of the cult of Asklepios in 419/18 is important in this respect, since it opens the way to a series of healing scenes with characteristic iconography. In general, when gods and humans are confronted, the worshipers are shown on a considerably smaller scale than the divinities, thus attesting to the nature of the relief, but even in Attica some representations are problematic and not all figures can be identified with certainty. Votive reliefs elsewhere are less numerous and especially scarce in the major sanctuaries of Olympia and Delphi; when they occur, they honor minor divinities more frequently than the main gods of the sites and many appear the product of popular, almost primitive art. One is struck once again by the generally higher level of sculptural expression in Athens, even within the sphere of commercial and private rather than official monuments.

Given the great number of reliefs extant, we shall concentrate here on a few works significant for their peculiarities, whether stylistic or iconographic.

VOTIVE RELIEFS

Attic votive reliefs of the Fifth century occur in a variety of formats and compositions, but their stylistic development basically conforms to that attested for architectural sculpture and statuary in the round. They can be narrative or mythological in content, or show a gathering of divinities in more or less paratactic arrangement, with or without worshipers; they can belong to the so-called Funerary Banquet type, where the hero reclines on a couch surrounded by his wife and his belongings, often with an attendant or more; they can portray the dedicant in a pose of victory or, rarely, in the thick of action; finally, but seldom, they depict a sacrifice. Frames coincide with the plain edge of the slab, sometimes completed by simple moldings; a pedimental crown may top a wide stele and piers may delimit the field at the sides, or the top edge may simulate a tiled roof, but such elaborate contours are exceptional.[1] By and large, the shallow depth of the carving requires little framing and the frequent top molding seems a carry-over from architectural sculpture, a tectonic need for spatial definition. Often the slab tapers upward, perhaps for one of those optical refinements that are hard to explain in practical terms.

Although evolutionary changes are difficult to trace and exceptional renderings are

[1] No totally convincing explanation has been found for such architectural quotations. It is improbable that the dedicant meant to suggest the house of the god—a sort of abbreviated shrine—since pedimented tops occur also above mythological action-scenes and on grave stelai. Moreover, the idea of the apparition within a temple is negated in those cases where antefixes clearly indicate the side portion of a roof. Perhaps the obvious answer is that the top molding is understood as physical protection for the slab, and therefore as a covering which, by similarity, can take the place of the traditional covering for a shrine or house, and therefore also its appearance. Once a rooflike top is adopted, it is an easy step to supply piers or columns as lateral frames. On the other hand, as often the case in the ambiguous world of religious art, some more specific symbolism should not be entirely excluded.

frequent, it is generally correct to state that scenes tend to become more complex and the numbers of worshipers to increase the closer they are to the Fourth century. Concomitantly, the relief becomes higher and the frame, when present, more elaborate. A similar development can be traced for gravestones.

In Athens, the deity most often portrayed is Athena, but Herakles also occurs. Asklepios and his healing family are popular, though yielding to Amphiaraos at Oropos. Eleusis has produced several votives to Demeter and Kore; Artemis occurs frequently at Brauron, especially in that hunting capacity which finds greater currency in iconography than in cult. Local heroes are also important, as well as river gods, Pan, and the nymphs: an understandable choice for a form of art which caters to private beliefs and popular, rather than official, cults.

Two of the best known Attic reliefs fall in this category: the so-called Xenokrateia relief (fig. 97) and the double relief (amphiglyphon) showing Echelos kidnapping Iasile on the one side (fig. 98),[2] and a gathering of divinities on the other. The monuments have been extensively discussed and often illustrated. They were found in the same place, near the old mouth of the Kephissos River in New Phaleron, and it has been suggested that they were set up in the family shrine of the Echelidai. They have been recognized as approximately contemporary products of the same workshop, and Frel has drawn up a list of carvings that he attributes to the Xenokrateia Sculptor, as well as others by masters belonging to the same artistic circle. Striking resemblances do in fact exist between the two Phaleron reliefs showing divine gatherings; the more active scene on the amphiglyphon is given by Frel to another hand.

The Xenokrateia relief can be connected with a pedestal carrying the dedicatory inscription to the river god Kephissos. The other gods shown on the relief are there mentioned collectively, so that much speculation has gone into their identification. Only Apollo, sitting on an imaginative tripodlike throne,[3] and Acheloos, with his human face and taurine body, can be definitely recognized. Xenokrateia herself appears in the foreground, much smaller than the divinities; in front of her, her child reaches up to a male figure with no distinctive attributes, whose right foot is raised on an elevation. He is also shorter than the standing deities, a difference that cannot be purely a consequence of the bending pose. A reduction in scale for the foreground figures would also be contrary to any possible perspective intent. He has been called Kephissos by some scholars, a priest of the sanctuary by others.

Be that as it may, the taller background figures are certainly gods, and only the stiff goddess with polos at the extreme right may represent the idol rather than the divinity

[2] The names of the protagonists are inscribed on the upper molding, but the reading is uncertain, and some scholars prefer Basile; see M. Guarducci, in *Phoros, Tribute to B.C. Meritt* (Locust Valley, N.Y., 1974), 61.

[3] This throne is described in detail by Svoronos, *Das Athener Nationalmuseum* (Athens 1908) text, pp. 495-96, but later publications refer to it only briefly, and more recent literature calls it simply a tripod. Yet the sculptor has avoided the possible awkwardness of showing Apollo's legs draped over the side of the tripod bowl, and he has clearly established a horizontal seat-line, an armrest supported by a griffin and a coiling snake on each side of the "bowl," of which they represent the traditional handles, rearing up to join behind Apollo as the backrest of the throne. Under Apollo's feet the omphalos serves as footstool, flanked by the two eagles, one of which appears partly hidden by Xenokrateia's leg; the birds face in opposite directions, as demanded by the myth and as seen in traditional iconography. A proper description and a useful line drawing are given by A. Linfert, *AthMitt* 82 (1967) 149-57, drawing on p. 152.

herself. She may be Hekate Kourotrophos, therefore shown here in single rather than in triple form; it has in fact been suggested that all of the deities portrayed are concerned with the birth and care of children. Another, less likely, hypothesis identifies her as a nymph Kallirhoe.[4]

A surprising feature would be the double appearance of the Kephissos; according to one theory, the river god would be shown twice: in smaller scale, as object of the veneration of his devotees, and in larger scale, as member of the company of the gods, in the center of the composition and in a frontal pose meant to emphasize his importance as recipient of the dedication.[5] If this theory were sound, we would have a most unusual duplication of personages, a practice that is usually associated only with Roman continuous reliefs. Other explanations, however, seem more plausible.[6]

On the other hand, and without for a moment doubting the correct dating of the Xenokrateia relief within the Fifth century, it is useful to note other traits in its technique and composition that recall Roman imperial works: the introduction of occasional frontal figures in a largely profile arrangement; the use of lower relief to suggest distance and overlapping, almost to the extent of producing disembodied heads and unarticulated bodies;[7] the dichotomy between the upper and the lower parts of figures;[8] the conversational grouping of confronted personages. All these traits occur, to be sure, on the Parthenon frieze,[9] but the Xenokrateia relief, with its static quality, more monotonous pattern, shallow carving, and denser spacing, comes closer to the Ara Pacis or other Julio-Claudian monuments. The illusionistic effect produced by the rendering of Acheloos (a

---

[4] Kallirhoe's name appears on an inscribed stele which was found within the same sanctuary and which lists several divinities; this inscription has traditionally formed the basis for all identifications of the figures on the Xenokrateia relief.

[5] The frontal figure does not have fluvial horns—but neither does the foreground personage who is usually identified as the Kephissos because of his relationship to the worshipers. Interestingly enough, the Kephissos on the Echelos and Iasile amphiglyphon by the same master is shown horned and bearded, so we cannot assume that the fully humanized rendering of the Xenokrateia relief is dictated by the special beliefs of a private family cult or by the whim of the sculptor.

[6] Linfert has made a convincing case for Echelos, the ancestral hero of the Echelids and the god of the sanctuary. Margherita Guarducci, (*Phoros*, 57-66) favors the identification of a hornless Kephissos but considers the foreground figure with raised foot as anonymous priest of the river god. Her suggestion is based on a different reading of the dedicatory inscription which, in her opinion, contains no specific allusion to a teaching of Xenokrateia's son Xeniades by Kephissos, but only a general exhortation to worshipers. According to Guarducci, therefore, the divinities in the background are: Apollo, Artemis, Leto (a female, rather than a male, figure), Kephissos, Hestia (perhaps an echo of the Hestia by Pheidias on the base of the Zeus at Olympia), Rhapso (men-

tioned in the inscription, a healing nymph), two nymphs, Kallirhoe and Acheloos.

[7] It is hard to see or imagine the lower body of the goddess next to Apollo, and a third figure from the right, not counting Acheloos, has a perfunctory body.

[8] Note that the central male figure has crossed (?) feet in profile to left, as contrasted with a frontal upper torso.

[9] Linfert makes an interesting comparison between the Xenokrateia relief and the East frieze of the Parthenon, but he bases it on composition rather than on rendering. According to his interpretation of the inscription and his identification of the various figures, the central scene would be the focus of the whole ritual: the confrontation of the worshipers and Kephissos, with his acceptance of the child. The figures in the background would be divided between Olympians to the left and lesser gods to the right, with Hermes and Echelos marking a break in the rhythm to emphasize the action taking place in the foreground and acting as the mediators between Xenokrateia and the Kephissos. According to Linfert, the gods, from left to right, are: Apollo, Artemis, Hermes, Echelos, Eilethyia and Leto in conversation, two nymphs and the spring Kallirhoe next to her father, Acheloos. To me this last figure looks too "Karyatid-like" (as noted by S. Karouzou, *Catalogue*) to be a real presence; her polos would be iconographically more appropriate to Hekate.

protome rather than a total figure) is a standard convention rather than a conscious attempt.

Stylistically, the Xenokrateia relief should date around the time of the Nike Balustrade. The "Kephissos" bending toward the child recalls the Sandalbinder Nike or the comparable figure on the East frieze of the Nike Temple, but without achieving the dramatic effects of its prototype. The seated Apollo has the typical catch of drapery at the edge of the seat, with consequent outlining of the legs under the cloth. The third figure from the right, in lowest relief, conveys the bending of the right knee through the pattern of two opposing curves. Finally, garments cling in places as if wet, or in large oval patches, but without transparency. The total effect is rather opaque and sober, as in the quiet style. Paint must have added a certain amount of details and attributes to the scene.

The amphiglyphon of Echelos and Iasile shows similar traits but better carving; although equally reliant on paint for clarity and accuracy, it achieves more volume and greater transparency. The side with the divine gathering shows once again the river god Kephissos, but this time as a mature bearded man with horned head. The three women to the right, in affectionate contact, are probably nymphs, while a hero and Artemis have been identified at the extreme left. Yet the figure at this edge of the panel has ambiguous features: its hair is short, like an athlete's, and its breasts are not prominent enough to ensure a female identity. The costume is equally ambivalent: it recalls the chitoniskos with unfastened right strap usually worn by Amazons, but the cloth obviously continues under the ribbonlike pattern crossing the chest below the right breast, so that both shoulders are covered; that we have here no conventional strap for a quiver or a sword is shown by its course, from upper left to lower right rather than vice versa, as customary.[10] This personage is so close to the Hermes of the so-called Orpheus Relief (fig. 129)[11] that it seems the sculptor may have used an available cartoon without taking proper care to eliminate discrepancies and correct details. A pattern may have been employed also for the Hermes leading Echelos' quadriga in the kidnapping scene.[12] His flamboyant drapery is virtually engraved against the background, and his stance recalls dancing figures of satyrs on Red Figure vases or, in sculpture, the so-called Myronian Marsyas stealing after Athena's flutes. This question of patterns and their diffusion is quite complex and will be discussed later. On the amphiglyphon, Hermes' pose is made possible by the rising

[10] Walter, *ArchEph* 1937, 110 and n. 1, explains the costume as an undergarment fastened over both shoulders and a nebris-like belted upper garment draped so as to leave the right breast and shoulder free. A nebris, however, as for Artemis-Bendis, would have features identifying it as a skin, such as paws and tail; and a "nebris-like" garment is otherwise unknown. Walter also argues against identification as Hermes, supported by some scholars, on the basis of the hairstyle and the tripartite band, which he considers typically female. Cf. also Svoronos, 122. I agree that the personage is feminine.

[11] This important relief will be discussed in ch. 8, together with the problem of Roman copies.

[12] The scene itself is fairly typical, and a kidnapping by a youthful hero on a chariot occurs in several versions on the Lokroi pinakes. The Attic relief shows no indication of struggle, so Iasile must be a willing victim, as appropriate to the future mother of a long dynasty. In artistic terms, Iasile seems larger in scale than Echelos, although a glaring discrepancy is avoided through her bending pose; however, the hero's body is only partially shown, so that perspective regression is here more probable. A similar composition, although perhaps more flamboyant in style, occurs on a fragmentary relief in Chios, which preserves only the couple in the chariot, but which is particularly interesting for the distribution both of the motif and of the Attic style; it has in fact been compared to the Echelos and Iasile relief: see R. Kekule von Stradonitz, *BerlWinckProg* 65 (1905) 1-18, esp. pp. 15-16 and photograph on p. 15.

ground line, a landscape element unusual in kidnapping scenes. That some illusionistic effects were deliberately attempted is shown by the distortion of the wheel, the staggering of the horses, and their particular relationship to Hermes. Although sixteen equine legs are meticulously carved, only two of them touch the ground, giving the impression of a take-off rather than of an uphill gallop, for all the pains taken by the sculptor with the terrain, both in outline and texture.[13]

Landscape Reliefs

Perhaps the most surprising aspect of the votive reliefs, one that is not usually associated with Greek art, is the amount of landscape they depict. The many panels where figures stand on an even ground line against a smooth and neutral background—like actors on a stage—can be countered by the many where the action takes place on rocky terrain, against the opening of caves, with an occasional tree as part of the background;[14] in a few pieces the presence of registers creates an illusion of depth and space. In such cases the influence is not from architectural sculpture but probably from painting, not only for murals or for stage scenery, but also for votive pinakes, such as those with shutters mentioned in literary sources and others occasionally depicted within the context of larger reliefs. As already suggested for the Attic gravestones during the Severe period, we may be missing a whole series of votive stelai made in perishable material, as appropriate to the modest means of the worshipers. The rapid development of sculptural workshops at

[13] Such a rendering for horses becomes standard in the so-called apobates reliefs and continues well into the Fourth century, as attested by some votive reliefs from the Amphiaraion at Oropos, which follow almost the same pattern as the Echelos relief: B. Petrakos, *Ho Oropos kai to hieron tou Amphiaraou* (Athens 1968) pls. 38-39. See also the appendix to this chapter.

[14] An occasional tree, perhaps with specific identifying functions, appears also on some record reliefs: e.g., that commemorating a 405 B.C. treaty between Athens and Samos, set up in Athens in 403/2,—Kephisophōn Paianieus—Akr. 1333; or that with Athena and Erechtheus, in the Louvre, Ma 831, dated 409/8. A tree appears on a presumably mythological amphiglyphon with Athena on one side, Marsyas and Olympos (?) on the other, from the Academy: *BCH* 83 (1959) 581, figs. 15-16. An unusual tree in terms of texture and elaboration appears on a fragmentary relief from Delphi, presumably depicting Dionysos seated on a rock near which a large animal reclines. A pinax on a pedestal in the background identifies the scene as taking place within an open-air shrine. Cf. *FdD* 4:6 (1977) 23, number 4, fig. 15; dated to the last quarter of the Fifth century. As many as three trees appear on a votive relief to Herakles, together with the indication of a temple, three worshipers, and a bull. The plaque has been retouched and reworked, but it is undoubtedly an original of ca. 430; see G. Traversari, *Scul-*

ture del V°-IV° secolo A.C. del Museo Archeologico di Venezia (Venice 1973) no. 9, inv. no. 100; pp. 30-31.

It is perhaps legitimate to ask why such trees usually appear leafless. That leaves could be rendered in relief sculpture is shown by the tree on the Corfu Pediment (ca. 570) and the so-called Olive Tree Pediment from the Athenian Akropolis (ca. 550). In many cases the leaves were probably added in paint, but engraved outlines would have made them clearer, especially in low relief. Since the Delphi relief does not preserve the upper part of the tree, we cannot tell whether a more realistic foliage went with the naturalistic rendering of the trunk. In other instances the lack of leaves may be due to the general stylized rendering. Note, however, that a similarly barren tree appears in the Alexander Mosaic, despite its obviously pictorial nature. Can the bare tree be taken as some kind of symbolism? This would make sense in connection with a battlefield, but seems less pertinent in the case of votive reliefs.

For painted landscape elements on Attic votive reliefs (although mostly later than the Fifth century) see S. Karouzou, in *Studies von Blanckenhagen*, 111-16. For ground lines in the pediment of the Olympieion at Akragas see ch. 3, n. 5. G. B. Waywell's dissertation on landscape reliefs is in press.

the time of the great building program and the increased prosperity of the citizens may have prompted the translations of these offerings from wood and terra cotta into stone. One may also surmise that some votive reliefs were made in bronze, since at least one such has survived from the Hellenistic period in Delos, but pictorial elements are less likely to be derived from metal than from painted plaques.

The best known of these landscape reliefs from the Fifth century is the dedication by Pythodoros, son of Epizelos (fig. 99), in Eleusis. The dedicant, an historical figure, was strategos with Nikias in 414/3 and had participated in the peace treaty with Sparta in 421, probably as hipparchos. This military title can also be integrated in the fragmentary inscription accompanying the relief. The scene has been taken to depict an episode in that war in which Pythodoros commanded the cavalry and is therefore dated around 420, as a more or less private thank offering to the Eleusinian deities, perhaps for a safe escape from danger. The relatively small plaque is broken on both sides, but seems preserved to the original height.[15] It is impossible to tell whether the present division in two registers continued into the missing section, or whether the irregular ground line separating the upper from the lower scene served a topographical function within a more complex landscape—for instance, as a path winding upward against a mountain. Since faint lines in the background suggest distant hills, the latter hypothesis seems improbable. Yet even a linear arrangement in two registers manages to convey an impression of depth, with figures moving into space, or even of distance, with the higher level being implicitly farther from the viewer, as in a Polygnotan painting.

On both levels a fight is taking place between cavalry attacking from the right and foot soldiers fleeing in front of them or attempting to defend wounded comrades fallen on the ground. Similarities with the Nike Temple frieze are obvious, although the spacing of the figures is denser and their drapery quieter. The weathered surface and the relatively small size of the warriors preclude detailed comment, but the upright soldier in the lower register seems to have that sharp indentation at the waist which is typical of male anatomy in the Ilissos and the Hephaisteion friezes. Bodies are muscular and lean, with proportionately small heads; foreshortening is good and overlapping convincing. There is no indication as to which, if any, of the warriors is Pythodoros; victorious cavalry appear both above and below, and it is unlikely that the same man was depicted twice within the same panel, which should be read as a bird's-eye view of simultaneous events and interpreted as a generic battle scene. The rank of the dedicant mentioned by the inscription would have made it clear to the viewer that he belonged with a victorious party.[16]

Other reliefs where landscape is suggested by registers, though in less formal fashion,

---

[15] That the plaque continued at least for some distance to the left is shown by the hind leg of a horse appearing in the lower level, in motion to the left. Enough space to reconstruct the entire horse must therefore be allowed. Traces of a tenon on the bottom surface show that the relief once stood on a pillar and was therefore definitively votive, rather than architectural.

Some authors, e.g., Clairmont, *GRBS* 13 (1972) 55, date the relief between 413 and 410.

[16] It is usually suggested (Hölscher, *Historienbilder*, with additional bibliography) that Pythodoros is the rider in heavy armor fighting on the upper level, since a hipparchos would be at the head of his troops. But we cannot safely guess how much of the original scene is missing, and therefore whether the rider's position is as central as it appears in the present state. As for the double appearance of the same personage, the Xenokrateia relief provides a highly doubtful contemporary parallel, and even the theological explanations advanced for the divine Kephissos would not obtain for the human Pythodoros.

are fragmentary and less well known. One of the most intriguing—the so-called Lenormant or Trireme Relief—has recently been reconstructed by L. Beschi on the basis of scattered fragments in Athens, an old drawing and a fragmentary replica in Aquila, probably from Rome but of Greek date. The original fragments come from the Akropolis and represent rows of oarsmen within a boat. The scene, unusual in itself, becomes more remarkable when completed with a large figure of the hero Paralos seated on a rocky promontory overlooking the ship. The discrepancy in scale between the two sections of the scene is enormous and lends a flavor of popular art to the relief, although it has been suggested that it represents the sacred trireme *Paralos*, of historic importance in the events of the Peloponnesian War. The votive offering, to be dated at the end of the Fifth century, may therefore have had public character, which might explain why a replica was carved presumably at the same time.

Also copied during the Greek period and even adapted at a later time is a highly fragmentary and complex monument of the end of the century that is connected with the introduction of the cult of Asklepios into Athens by Telemachos in 420 B.C., and its reception by the poet Sophokles. A lengthy inscription was carved on a tall pillar under a figured heading; this, in turn, was topped by a rectangular block decorated on all four sides and forming a bracket on which a pinax was inserted with reliefs on both faces. The general arrangement is thus clear, but the figured scenes are so poorly preserved that no agreement has been reached as to their integration. It is certain, however, that the crowning pinax showed on one side a large door or gate with a pedimented roof; to the left of the gate a horizontal band suggests the upper edge of a precinct wall, beyond which appears the top of a leafless tree with a heron or a stork perched on its branches. It has been suggested that this is a propylon marking the entrance to the Pelargikon—the wall of the storks—on the Athenian Akropolis, near the Asklepieion. The positioning of the tree beyond the wall creates a spatial effect that recalls some motifs in Pompeian wall paintings of the Second Style, and this impression is heightened by the decoration of the bracket block, where a similar low parapet creates a horizontal division of the scene at midheight and separates the foreground figures from others (including some horses) represented as if behind the wall.[17] Throughout the decorated areas, whether on the pillar itself, the bracket block, or the pinax, large personages alternate with smaller, even diminutive figures, which appear at different levels with various attributes; they have been identified as other deities and descendants of Asklepios.

The Torlonia Relief. An elaborate landscape relief that obtains comparable effects without formal divisions into registers was found in Rome and has been therefore considered non-Attic and possibly South Italian (fig. 100). A recent interpretation explains it as a depiction of cults on the South slopes of the Akropolis and consequently ascribes it to Athens, but new topographical studies of the area may invalidate the theory.

The panel, now in the Torlonia collection in Rome, lacks its upper part; it was originally of considerable dimensions. In the foreground appears a hero with a hunting club walking his horse. He moves toward an altar or eschara next to which stands a male worshiper, clearly identified as such by his smaller size; the youthful hero is followed by his hunt-

---

[17] Beschi, *ASAtene* 45-46, n.s. 29-30 (1967-68) 416-17, rightly compares the horse protomes and the "windows" with the traditional paraphernalia of the Funerary Banquet reliefs.

ing dog. As a backdrop to this scene, at a higher level, two figures sit on rocky ledges, flanking a shrine that rises directly behind the hero with the horse. The naiskos consists of two columns between which appears the lower part of a draped figure, presumably a cult image. The break has removed the tops of the naiskos and the two seated figures, which are also obviously divine; the one on the right is clearly male, since his torso is bare and he wears only a himation wrapped around hips and legs; the figure on the left is female, since she wears a chiton under the mantle.

The image within the naiskos has been considered female by Beschi; he suggests that the relief was dedicated to the hero Hippolytos, who had a cult near the Asklepieion and was connected with Aphrodite Themis. Thus the seated male would be the healing god, as a topographical indication, while the seated female would be an epiphany of Aphrodite as contrasted with her cult image appearing within the shrine. It has however been objected that what remains of this statue shows it wearing only a himation, as appropriate to a male. It may then represent Asklepios or Hippolytos himself, who would appear in two forms, as an idol and as an apparition come to share the sacrifice of the offerer. If, however, this shrine is an Attic Heroon, it is unlikely to have contained a cult statue. Funerary shrines housing heroized images of the deceased are instead known from Magna Graecia, especially from Tarentum; thus the question of the provenience of the Torlonia relief should be reopened on iconographic grounds.

Stylistically, slight confirmation for a South Italian origin may be found in the treatment of the drapery of the seated man, which appears unusually transparent and linearly flamboyant, such as one would expect in Athens only at the very end of the Fifth century, while the general treatment of the total relief is reminiscent of the Parthenon frieze. In addition, the dog has virtually been carved into the rock, with little projection and volume of its own. Whether the landscape itself, perhaps more extensive than in any other Attic relief, could be considered as further evidence is debatable, since this, as all other traits, could be the result of a pictorial origin for the scene. But the human figures have a substance that contrasts with this theory; the youthful hero recalls the Doryphoros in his general chiastic pose, if not in his attire, and looms too large for his horse, which is small even by Parthenon standards. The traditional date of ca. 420 should be lowered to the end of the century, whether the relief is accepted as Attic or as South Italian.

Colossal Reliefs

The Torlonia relief, even in its present damaged state, is an ambitious monument of considerable size. Other fragmentary reliefs can be reconstructed with life-size figures, for instance the very fine piece from the Ilissos area with a seated and a standing goddess in affectionate embrace, which can be shown to be votive because its partially preserved inscription can be integrated "Demeter."[18]

While discussing the Herakleion at Thebes, Pausanias mentions (9.11.4) a colossal votive offering to Herakles and Athena made by Alkamenes and commissioned by Thrasy-

[18] Since gravestones usually depict human figures at natural scale, fragmentary reliefs could be interpreted as funerary rather than as votive by those who question the possibility of such large size for the latter category. Uncertain examples are, for instance, Akr. 1350 (Brouskari, 83 fig. 161, dated 480-470) and Akr. 1334 (Brouskari, 173 fig. 373, dated to the Fourth century). However, some pieces are certainly votive.

boulos and the other Athenian exiles when they were able to overthrow the dictatorship of the Thirty Tyrants in 403 and return to their city from Boeotia. The Greek text is uncertain and two different readings have been given: according to the first, the thanksgiving offering consisted of two colossal statues in a marble resembling Pentelic (or of Pentelic type); according to the second, it was a colossal relief (*typos*) in Pentelic marble. The supporters of the first interpretation stress the fact that colossal reliefs are rare, if not totally unknown, during the Classical period; yet, since a few of them are actually extant, the possibility remains open. This kind of monumental offering, because of its very scale, should rank in importance with sculpture in the round, and it raises interesting questions of setting and meaning.

One such panel, entirely preserved, has indeed given rise to much speculation on its date and purpose: the so-called Great Eleusinian Relief. Its votive nature has also been challenged because other replicas of it, to the same scale, were made in Roman times; it has therefore been suggested that the original served some specific cult purpose, perhaps in place of statuary in the round which could hardly have been placed properly within the Telesterion at Eleusis, a building quite different in ground plan from the standard Greek temple. Yet the same objection can be raised for the plaque, since no place in the building seems suitable for a "cult relief" meant as a focus of attention. The fact that some of the Roman replicas are in terracotta indicates a possible decorative function, perhaps to be explained by the mythological content of the scene; a more personal subject including a specific dedicator might not have been copied in later times, but the mere phenomenon of reproduction does not necessarily invest the original with sacred significance.[19]

The scene depicted is usually explained as Demeter and Kore giving Triptolemos the ears of wheat that symbolize the task of teaching their cultivation to the rest of humanity. Since the relief was found in Eleusis, and since torches and scepter are attributes appropriate to Demeter and Kore, not much doubt exists as to the identity of the female figures, although not all scholars agree that the Mother is the peplophoros facing the boy, while the Daughter is standing behind him. Difference in the coiffures, the relative youthfulness of one type of costume versus the other, the more or less matronly appearance of the bodies, have been argued to support either view, but the point seems relatively unimportant. More relevant is the fact that during the Fifth century Triptolemos is usually represented as a mature man seated in a winged chariot rather than as a standing boy, but other explanations of the scene have not been convincing. Were it not for the fact that the peculiar hairstyle of the youth, knotted over the forehead, clearly marks him

[19] The original Eleusinian relief was found reused in the pavement of the Chapel of St. Zacharias in Eleusis, ca. 100m to the East of the sacred precinct. The replicas consist of: (1) fragmentary slab in New York, presumably found in Rome, which has been restored with plaster casts of the missing portions taken from the Eleusinian relief; (2) marble foot supposedly found together with replica 1 but showing a different weight distribution; (3) fragmentary head from Corinth; (4) four fragments from at least two terracotta replicas of the Eleusinian relief, from the Villa of A. Voconius Pollio near Marino. Of the above, the head from Corinth (3) has been questioned as a true replica, on the grounds that other fragments from that site show similar technical traits and should belong to a single large monument of different composition. I believe the connection is one of workshop and not of monument.

The marble foot also in New York (2) had suggested to G.M.A. Richter the possibility that a matching but mirror-image relief had been set up as a pendant to replica 1 in the Roman period; she had further speculated that such an arrangement existed also in the Greek period and that therefore replica 2 corresponds to a Greek original of the same date as the Eleusinian Relief. This theory has not yet found further confirmation.

as an adolescent, it would be tempting to suggest that he is the dedicant, therefore a mortal shown on a reduced scale.

Another suggestion, however, could reconcile also this feature. Among the various officials of the Eleusinian mysteries, inscriptions mention the Hearth Initiates, young boys (occasionally also girls) who were at some period selected by the archon basileus and usually belonged to the wealthy and aristocratic families of the Kerykes and the Eumolpids, traditionally connected with the cult of Eleusis. The earliest mention of such office dates from 460 B.C., and some Roman statues of "Eleusinian attendants" perhaps reproduce originals of the Severe period. Such statues are characterized by a peculiar coiffure with a knot over the forehead; this is not identical with that of the youth on the Great Eleusinian Relief, but the general pattern of long strands brought forward over the temples is similar. The "Triptolemos" can be more closely compared to some Boeotian terracottas of the Severe period and even with a semidraped youth on the Parthenon frieze (fig. 43), so that the hairstyle need imply nothing more than adolescent fashions.[20] Nonetheless, the coincidence is striking, and the relatively early date of the Great Eleusinian Relief (contemporary with the Parthenon frieze, according to the latest theory) makes it a likely candidate for its being the votive relief by one of the wealthy families whose child had been selected for a recently established and greatly honored office at Eleusis. Commemorative statues of Hearth Initiates are well attested for the Hellenistic and Roman periods, and the popularity of the office in those times may explain the copying of the relief. Against this theory may stand the relative nakedness of the youth, as contrasted with the tunic worn by the preserved statues. The scene may then depict the actual institution of the office rather than the individual, with heroic nakedness introduced to remove the action from the contingent human sphere and to raise it to a higher, permanent level. In that case, Demeter would just be showing, not giving, the ears of wheat to the boy, as part of the apopteia,[21] while the ritual fillet or crown of the Hearth Initiate would be placed by Kore over the boy's head.

The last suggestion about Kore's gesture, previously advanced in other contexts, has recently been disputed by Schneider in his thorough publication of the Great Eleusinian Relief and its replicas. He maintains that the holes for metal attachments should not be explained as fastenings for a single object but for two: one for the youth's hair knot and the other for the deity's bracelet. He also illustrates a Boeotian skyphos with a standing and youthful (though not boyish) Triptolemos between Demeter and Kore which, if not identical, nonetheless provides a good parallel for our scene; this general connection with Boeotia, both in hair fashions and in iconography, allowed Schneider to make further stylistic comparisons and to assert that the Great Eleusinian Relief must have been carved by a Central Greek master under Athenian influence who, however, represented a mythological scene according to a local rather than to an Attic tradition. Schneider's stylistic

[20] Although more frequent on males, the rendering occurs also on female figures, for instance, the Iris of the East frieze of the Parthenon or, in the Hellenistic period, the Fanciulla d'Anzio. Perhaps this coiffure serves as the identifying attribute of an attendant, regardless of sex. The corkscrew curls of the statues in Rome are a Classicizing alteration of the Roman period: J. Raeder, *JdI* 93 (1978) 263-65.

[21] Theoretically, Demeter could be holding the myrtle staff proper to the boy's office, but Erika Simon has pointed out to me that the staff is usually shown as a very substantial object, which would be difficult to connect with the hand in the relief, and that Demeter is never shown with it, except for one dubious and late example.

comments are compelling. His attribution would at once explain that certain harshness and rigidity which many had noted in the carving and had attempted to justify on grounds of deliberate religious Archaizing, or of copying, or of early date. The sculptor may have relied on paint to make certain details clear, but there is a basic unevenness of rendering and some difficulty with foreshortening which results in the cascading toes of the goddesses looking almost like those in Assyrian reliefs. Schneider has also pointed out the peculiar arrangement of the garment on the deity with the torch: it does not conform to the position of the legs and hampers rather than helps in understanding the body beneath. This lack of volume to the figures, the subdued articulation of the stance, the variation between high and low relief, and the strict adherence of the figures to the contours of the field are non-Attic traits that speak convincingly for a Boeotian or, more generally, a Central Greek origin.[22]

Schneider implies that Triptolemos' pose, with right leg advanced and bent at the knee, also confirms Boeotian connections, since it finds a good parallel in the so-called Agathokles' stele from that area.[23] The stance is, however, widespread: it occurs also on the "Ionic" Nisyros stele and other East Greek as well as South Italian reliefs. Such a rendering seems rather to be the relief equivalent of the new experimentation with balance in statues in the round of the Severe period: an attempt to convey in outline the shift in weight of figures like the Blond or the Kritian Boy. Therefore, it would be a chronological rather than a regional trait, which then continued beyond the limits of the Severe period in areas of lingering styles not quickened by the rapid developments of the major sculptural centers. The pose with bent leg advanced rather than retracted and both feet flat on the ground is usually called "Attic" as contrasted with the "Argive" or "Polykleitan" raised heel and trailing bent leg; yet pure Attic works like the Athena Parthenos deviate from this rendering, which I would rather label Severe or Lingering Severe, as the case may be. The stance and its development within the Fifth century will be discussed in later chapters; here it is enough to add that it may have had a longer life in reliefs than in statuary in the round because it produced a more eloquent silhouette and avoided the difficulties of the "Polykleitan" pattern; some Classical occurrences may also be explained as attempts to convey movement rather than a stationary pose, as in the procession of the peplophoroi on the Parthenon East frieze.[24] Insofar as the "Triptolemos" of the Great Eleusinian Relief is definitely shown at rest within the Classical context, his "lingering Severe" pose may be considered an additional trait in favor of a Boeotian origin.

Proposed dates for the Great Eleusinian Relief have oscillated between 460 and 410, with Schneider lately opting for contemporaneity with the Parthenon frieze. The presence

---

[22] The acceptance of a Boeotian master as the carver of the Great Eleusinian Relief need not invalidate our suggestion that it represented the dedication of a Hearth Initiate, given the proximity of Eleusis to Boeotia and the independence of sculptors in accepting commissions.

[23] This comparison had already been made by Dohrn (pp. 40-48, esp. 42-44), who also pointed out the Ionic influence on the pose, but without suggesting a Boeotian master for the Eleusis relief; he attributed such echoes to hieratic Archaizing, and therefore dated the monument far too late.

[24] Note the interesting if very awkward solution of the so-called Mourning Athena Relief (*Severe Style*, fig. 69), where the retracted leg is almost impossible to reconcile with the frontal upper torso; but there the sculptor has managed to conceal the legs entirely under the fluted skirt, letting only the feet convey the pose. In contrast, some figures of the Parthenon frieze, which compare with the Eleusis boy either in pose or in the prominence and clarity of the buttocks in profile, usually cross the right leg over the left foot, e.g., West III, 6; East V, 35; North XLII, 134.

of selvage and the relatively short kolpos and overfold in the peplophoros could support this suggestion, but a slightly lower chronology might be advocated on grounds of provincialism. The flatness and harshness of folds and grooves in the peplos skirt are signs of quality and style rather than of date, since none of the Parthenon figures quite matches them in execution. In general, all non-Attic reliefs under Attic influence present similar problems of chronology, not simply because of a possible time lag in the transmission of motifs or stylistic traits, but also because of a certain conservatism inherent in "provincial" areas. Many works that in Attica would be dated within the Fifth century can in fact belong to the Fourth. The Augustan copyist who made the New York replica, besides altering some details, also changed the chiton of the second goddess to ribbon drapery, which does not appear in the original. As for the adaptation of the relief, also in New York, showing two goddesses around an altar (?), Schneider may be right in considering it a fake, but the same ribbon drapery has been developed a step further, and the himation clings with patterns and mannerisms typical of the late Fifth century. This stylistic coherence may indeed reflect a true prototype of around 400.[25]

Comparable to the Great Eleusinian Relief in its stylistic mixture and, to some extent, also in size is the votive relief (fig. 101) found in Mantineia, where it represents an unusual occurrence. The fragmentary slab shows the lower part of a palm tree flanked by a standing woman holding a peculiar object, which has been convincingly identified as a liver. Möbius has therefore proposed that the plaque depicts Diotima, the prophetess from Mantineia mentioned by Plato in the *Symposion*, although she has usually been considered a literary fiction. The presence of the palm tree would connect the priestess with the cult of Apollo. Möbius's theory has been generally accepted, together with his stylistic analysis, which ascribes the work to a Peloponnesian artist active in Athens and under the influence of Alkamenes around 410-400. As in the Eleusis Relief, we find here the same harshness of long vertical folds in the skirt of the peplos, the same silhouette-like definition of the advanced leg under the smoothed cloth, the same parallelism and closeness of the figure to the edge of the field. That the style is later is shown by the transparent effect of the upper part of the garment, the nicks and bends of some of the tubular folds, and the way in which long lines emphasize the bend of the knee and the catch at the ankle; yet the body is not properly thought out under the drapery and lacks the clear articulation typical of Attic renderings. Allusions to the style of the Bassai frieze seem justified and, together with the relative absence of gravestones and votive reliefs from the Peloponnesos, confirm the possibility of Attic influence, whether or not we can go so far as to pinpoint the sphere of the sculptor's activity within Alkamenes' workshop.

A more relevant question is whether the relief is truly votive or funerary. Möbius has pointed out the almost total absence of gravestones of this format from the Peloponnesos, and has also explained the raised right arm of Diotima as a gesture of prayer; this latter, however, can occur also within the context of a tomb monument, as several examples at-

---

[25] The "adaptation" looks more Attic than either the original or the copy of the Great Eleusinian Relief, and poses are certainly better foreshortened and thought out. The scale is smaller, however, than in the Eleusis original. Schneider has questioned the authenticity of the New York adaptation on the basis of the unusual treatment of its back, which is hollowed out in correspondence with the parts of greatest projection on the front, as in a terracotta plaque made from a mold. Some details of the round "altar" are also unattested elsewhere.

test. Even with the integration of the missing upper portion, the height of the plaque would remain within the range of Attic gravestones, always much larger than the average votive relief. An argument in favor of a dedicatory offer lies in the findspot of the Mantineia relief: between the South retaining wall of the theater and the back wall of a temple, therefore within the area of the Agora where an honorary monument is likely to have been set up. Literary sources, especially Pausanias, often refer to such tributes being erected in Peloponnesian market places, and at some sites hero cults and graves resided in the agora itself. On the other hand, marble slabs were often moved and reused in antiquity, so we cannot be sure that the original setting always corresponded to the findspot. A cavity for a tenon on the right short face of the Mantineia slab suggests that some kind of architectural frame may have been added to it, and this feature is more in keeping with a funerary than with a votive relief; since this hole could also be attributed to a secondary use, it cannot be taken as decisive evidence. The answer may lie somewhere in between the two positions: the stele could be funerary and honorary at the same time, in a mixture of meanings that is certainly attested for Sparta during the Archaic period and later. In either case, its size is impressive and its importance made greater by the lack of comparable local examples.

A similar situation occurs in Cyrene, a city whose founding hero ranked a tomb in the agora itself. From that area comes a fragmentary stele with a frontal warrior (fig. 102), which was not found during systematic, controlled excavations, so that hypotheses on its original setting remain tentative. The size is monumental and the rendering of the human figure recalls the Polykleitan Doryphoros, but the pose is inverted since the shoulder is raised on the side of the weight leg. Whether this arrangement was suggested by the three-quarter view demanded by the relief technique, or whether it represents a deliberate choice, it is now impossible to tell. However, the same stance has been employed for the foreground hoplite on the stele of Chairedemos and Lykeas from Salamis and for the warrior on the Megara stele in Worcester. This similarity has usually been taken as a sign that these two gravestones are by the same master, who might have exercised some influence on the Cyrene sculptor. Yet the pattern may be the only reasonable one in terms of high relief, since other monuments with no stylistic similarity also employ it, or reverse the schema when the figures face in the opposite direction; the weight leg thus adheres to the background, while the bent leg can be more freely articulated as if in the round.

A recent study has emphasized the superior quality of the Salamis stele versus the Cyrene relief, particularly in terms of composition: the position of the spear, the arm with the shield and the chlamys. In addition, the Polykleitan influence on the Salamis gravestone is underplayed in favor of a strong Attic component. Yet, in comparing the Cyrene relief with the funerary stele, it is obvious that the latter is indeed much more Polykleitan despite its alteration in the pose. In particular, Chairedemos' torso corresponds to the Polykleitan patterns as we know them through the replicas of the Doryphoros, with a strong epigastric arch continued down to the level of the iliac crests and counterbalanced by a comparable groin line. The Cyrene hoplite, instead, stresses the expansion of the rib cage and has that horizontal accent at waist level which we have noted in several Attic figures from architectural sculpture. It is now impossible to comment on the head type of the Cyrene relief, since it is missing, but certainly Chairedemos' head, in its proportions and general outlines, is closer to the Doryphoros' copies than to the Parthenon frieze. The gravestone is therefore a good example of Peloponnesian influence on Athenian workshops, while the Cyrene relief demonstrates the spread of Attic influence abroad, even in areas that should have had stronger artistic political ties with Asia Minor and the islands.

Excellent contrast is provided by the large relief in Samos (fig. 103), which has also been explained as votive by some and as funerary by others. That the latter hypothesis seems more probable, given the area where the relief was found, is of secondary importance to the stylistic and iconographic considerations, especially since both these aspects appear to be under Attic influence. But what a difference from the Cyrene relief! The naked youth on the right half of the Samian stele stands in a truly chiastic pose, weight leg against the background but corresponding to a lowered right arm stretched toward a seated figure now highly fragmentary. In his left arm the youth holds a square box, which obscures the central part of his torso and forces the shoulder up on the side of the free leg. The head, as so often in Fifth century figures, bends down, this time toward the seated person, who provides a natural lower focus. The youth is obviously athletic: note the strong shoulder muscles, the bulging arms, and the iliac crest; the trochanteric depression is clearly shown on the left (although rather too forward on the thigh, instead of on the buttock) and the calves are well developed. But the total effect is one of plumpness and softness, in typically Ionic fashion. The relief is relatively low, almost calligraphic in its contours; the youth's head is particularly cameolike in its definition, and the peculiar rendering of the eye, with its elongated upper lid, heavy and undercut, is strikingly different from the wide-open stare of the youths on the Parthenon frieze. The swirling curls of the hair are accented by drill holes and recall Severe coiffures but with a freedom possible only within the Classical period. Since the box hides the edge of the pectorals and the epigastric arch, no internal accent counterbalances the fluid outline, and the box itself is too pictorially rendered to create its own break; thus the general impression is graceful and delicate, and the youth, for all his broad shoulders and firmly planted leg, seems to sway rather than stand fast.[26]

What is Attic about the stele is not just the youth's pose but also the relationship between the standing and the seated figure. The latter has been interpreted as Hera or another female divinity, but a more plausible explanation identifies it as male because of the strong left arm holding a staff. The fillet floating in the background looks as if it could be connected with the staff, but no likely meaning for it comes to mind. The youth himself seems to be giving another fillet to the seated figure (and holds two more rolled inside his box); I wonder if the funerary interpretation of the scene is correct, since fillets usually adorn a grave, but they would not be handed directly to the deceased. Moreover, at least in Attic iconography, such square boxes are held by female attendants to matrons; perhaps the Ionic master adapted an Attic scene to a male context. Also under Attic influence is the rendering of the drapery, which confirms a date at the very end of the century. Folds are few, with sharp ridges merging occasionally into wide, flat sections, but their irregular course is alien to the more logical Attic art; a cobweb effect hints at transparency, but the nearer leg is revealed only in its basic contour, the farther almost not

[26] Perhaps this effect is partly created by the low relief, which has forced the sculptor to expand his figure over a broad surface, rather than carving it in depth, thus increasing its swing. However, both technique and foreshortening are a matter of choice, and a firmer stance could have been achieved with a strong profile pose.

at all. A truly Athenian master would have paid greater attention to the physical volumes in connection with such light drapery.[27]

It is quite difficult, instead, to point out what is non-Attic in a small votive relief found a few years ago on the island of Kos. It shows three girls dancing around an altar and moving to the left toward a much smaller worshiper, while the head of Pan peeps from a "cutout" at the upper left corner. A distich below the relief scene identifies it as a dedication to the Charites by Peithanor son of Charmios. The three dancers could easily be nymphs or even maenads and no specific attribute identifies them as the Graces. The sculptor has tried to differentiate them through their costume, since the first wears a sleeved chiton, the second a belted peplos with a long overfold, the third a chiton and a himation, but they are obviously sisters and very similar. Their drapery has the calligraphic elegance of the very end of the Fifth century, with folds that have turned into sheer pattern and decoration; even their flamboyance is less due to motion than to taste. The different garments seem to have uniform texture, which results in considerable transparency; under the "railroad tracks" of the folds the body is firmly modeled and properly articulated without the soft relaxation of the Samian youth. This is the style of some figures from the Nike Balustrade pushed one step further, of the Nike of Paionios rendered in two dimensions: note the "sanguisuga" at the right ankle of the third Grace, which has turned into a veritable sail, and the many nicks and bends in the tubular folds ending in omega patterns. This stylistic phase is not represented in original Attic reliefs, but it occurs in the many Neo-Attic replicas of the famous Maenad Reliefs. It is helpful to have this Koan panel show us that such mannered drapery is not an exaggeration or even an invention of the Neo-Attic copyists. Geographically, this relief brings us closer to the Nereids of the funerary monument in Xanthos.

GRAVESTONES

One work that has not yet been satisfactorily explained in terms of its nature—whether votive or funerary—and of its proper stylistic milieu is the famous Albani Relief (figs. 104, 105) in Rome depicting a dismounted rider ready to give the coup de grâce to a fallen opponent. The relief is exceptional for its very large size and format, quite unparalleled among grave stelai, as well as for its pictorial elements of landscape side by side with a plain background. It is therefore usually assumed that the slab was set up as part of a state monument (a *polyandrion*), perhaps connected with the Battle of Delion (424 B.C.) or, more probably, with the Archidamian War, and that the mountain and the river appearing at the extreme left edge provided topographical clues to make the historical encounter recognizable by the Athenian viewer. The relief was found in Rome, however, where it was probably brought during antiquity, and later repairs and reworking have obscured some of the original rendering. Thus, the river now appears to be part of the horse's tail, while the branch (?) above the mountain is, in its present state, incomprehensible. A still unpublished theory known through brief references in other publications suggests that the Albani slab was part of a triptych in front of which Perikles pronounced his famous funerary oration, and that it was this connection with the Thucydidean passage (2.22ff.)

[27] The contour of the farther leg may be suggested by the third ridge counting from the right, but that may also be another fold; in either case, the rendering is confusing.

which prompted the removal of the slab from Athens to Rome. Another view would limit the monument to a commemoration of a specific corps, rather than of all the war dead, and assumes that the cavalry, rather than the state, was responsible for setting up the relief, perhaps atop a relatively short list of casualties. Certainly the focus of the scene is on a rider, with no indication of other fighting troops, as in other state monuments, and therefore its scope seems more specific than general. Finally, it has even been questioned whether the carving is pure Attic in style or whether it has Ionic traits instead. One cannot begin to answer these questions, especially without direct examination of the monument, but a few details can be pointed out.

Similarities between the Parthenon frieze and the Albani Relief have been stressed more often than the differences,[28] but there are numerous variants in the renderings. For instance, the sharp line of the eyebrow typical of a Parthenonian face is softened and blurred in the relief: the rosebud mouth with its distinctive curves to the upper lip is changed to a straight pattern in the relief; ears have a different convolution, less plasticity than on the frieze; hair renderings seem shorter—or recut—and the fallen warrior has a peculiar profile, with a concave line from forehead to the tip of the nose. But these are details that could have been altered by reworking; in addition, so many hands worked on the Parthenon that no two renderings are exactly alike. More distinctive is the treatment of drapery: the peculiar transparency and "elastic" folds of the chlamys held up for protection by the fallen warrior, the lack of selvage throughout, and the somewhat confused system of folds over the stomach of the rider, which seem to conform neither to motion nor to modeling principles. The sculptor was probably trying to suggest that the horseman had just dismounted to face his opponent, hence the great billowing of his chlamys, which extends from left to right even behind the horse's head; this is, however, a pictorial foreshortening not to be found within the Parthenon range. Other points are puzzling: is the cavity behind the victim's head part of the rocky background or is it a recut or blurred indication of a petasos? What is warlike about the men's equipment, except perhaps the short sword once in the rider's hand? Yet attempts to read the scene as mythological have failed to convince. Perhaps a more meaningful question is whether a Fifth century state polyandrion or cenotaph would have received this format; there is evidence, instead, for votive reliefs of exceptional size, as already discussed. Could the Albani Relief have been set up as a private thank offering by a man of some status who had safely escaped from an ambush, perhaps by brigands, while traveling? The high quality and the size of the monument read, to our modern minds, as signs of importance and therefore of official commission, but these assumptions have already been debated in the case of the Great Eleusinian Relief, with a negative answer. Even the removal of the slab to Rome is not an implicit statement of public importance. Be that as it may, the date of the Albani Relief seems correctly fixed around 430-425.

Other monuments of approximately contemporary date are undoubtedly funerary, of

[28] Despinis, 189-90, notes, however, some dissimilarities; he attributes the Albani relief neither to Agorakritos nor to his immediate workshop, but stresses island-Ionic traits.

One similarity which has attracted less attention occurs in the Hephaisteion frieze: note the deep fold of flesh at the waist of the fallen Albani man and compare the bound prisoner on Hephaisteion East frieze slab 1 (fig. 48). Lullies (in Lullies and Hirmer, caption to pls. 180-81) points out the clockwise movement of the composition, which centers in the swirling folds on the stomach of the Albani rider and moves along his raised right arm, imparting to the relief charm and restlessness.

high quality and justly famous. The best is perhaps the so-called Cat Stele (fig. 106) from Aegina (*not* Salamis, as often stated), which continues an Ionic iconographic tradition of showing the deceased with a living attendant and with his pets.[29] For all its renown, however, some details of the slab are still unclear. One interpretation sees the youth as alive, having just removed his pet bird from its cage because of the threatening presence of a cat over a pillar. Another theory, perhaps preferable, suggests that the youth is shown as a ghost, invisible to his mourning servant; the "cat" over the pier would represent his tombstone,[30] in a peculiar revival of Archaic monuments crowned by sphinxes if not by felines; the pet bird would then be symbolic of the soul, or be an indication of the relatively young age of the deceased, whose gesture would be one of prayer or farewell. But what, then, is the peculiar object behind his hand? A bird cage would no longer be plausible, and nothing should be hanging over a grave. Perhaps the object is a lantern, again intended as symbolic, but parallels are hard to find; no bird cage, on the other hand, resembles it either. It is also unclear why the molding below the crowning fascia should stop just before the end of the slab, just behind the "lantern."

Stylistically, the Cat Stele is very close to the Parthenon frieze, certainly closer than the Albani Relief. Both deceased and servant have the rosebud mouth and the wide-open eyes of Parthenonian figures. The drapery is also similar, but at a more advanced stage, with sharper edges to its ridges, greater adherence over certain areas, and that motif of opposing curves used to indicate contrasting movement which occurs more frequently at the knee bend, but appears here over the right thigh. Note also the use of incisions at the right armpit, in contrast to the dimpled modeling of the left hand. For all its frontal pose, unusual in an Attic gravestone, the youth is shown with a three-quarter torso, as indicated by the narrower right half of his chest, so that the profile head does not look incongruous. His weight rested on his right leg, to which attention was probably drawn by means of the long diagonal fold cutting in between the thighs. Note that the floral border changes pattern at mid-stele: the lilies' petals are simpler and fewer to the left, while the central leaf of one palmette has been obliterated. This crowning ornament is highly unusual for an Attic funerary relief and recalls architectural patterns for temple simas.

As famous as the Cat Stele is the so-called Hegeso Relief (fig. 107), from the name of the deceased engraved on the architrave. The scene of the seated lady confronted by one or more women is attested in earlier Attic reliefs that may be votive or heroizing; it is certainly used for gravestones during the Severe period, outside of Attica, and it appears in the North of Greece (in the area of the Black Sea) earlier than in Athens, although in more linear form.[31] Athens picks up the schema and with the usual Attic flair for volume

[29] Lullies (captions to pl. 182) considers the sculptor of the stele an Ionian although active on the Parthenon. Despinis (p. 192, and footnotes 405 no. 4 and 462) agrees with an Ionic master but not Agorakritos; he finds the style close to but much later than the Parthenon. Although a servant appears also in the purely Attic Hegeso Stele, no explicit message of mourning is given in the scene. In the Cat Stele, instead, the young servant obviously does not see his master and seems to be standing attendance at his grave, with an emotional overtone atypical of Attic art in the late Fifth century.

[30] Note that the animal's head, now broken off, once faced forward, as suggested by the traces of the neck, rather than upward toward the bird, as would be required by the first interpretation.

A bird cage of somewhat similar shape occurs on a late Fifth century Attic pelike, known to me only through the illustration in the *Sale Catalogue of the Summa Gallery Inc.* (Beverly Hills, Cal.) December 1976, vol. 1: *Ancient Art*, no. 19.

[31] See for instance the Stele from Dioskouria (?) near the mouth of the Besletka River in Georgia: Pfuhl and Möbius, *Die Ostgriechischen Grabreliefs*

and depth changes it into a masterpiece. The relief of the Hegeso Stele is relatively shallow, yet by carving the backrest of the chair before the framing anta the sculptor has given this scene added depth and illusion. The veil so plastically rendered over Hegeso's left shoulder is barely engraved behind her face, to suggest distance. The same is true of the contour of her farther arm, that of the servant, and the lid of the jewel box. Under the massed drapery Hegeso's body is remarkably clear: both prominent breasts and the long, slender legs; it is not immediately noticeable that her right breast should not be seen entirely in profile, given the twist of the upper torso. Beneath that breast a chiton fold bends double in touching the mantle massed in her lap, a mannerism of the late Fifth century which will find great currency again in the Hellenistic period.[32] Hegeso, her drapery, and her seat are remarkable for their great accuracy in articulation: note how the mantle tip hangs on a straight vertical as demanded by its weight, how every rivet in the chair corresponds to the cross-piece behind. That this is not fortuitous can be shown by comparing other chairs on similar stelai, for instance one in New York of slightly later date. On the contrary, Hegeso's *klismos* could be, and has been, reproduced by a modern carpenter as a functional chair of great elegance.

The young maiden standing in front of Hegeso wears a long-sleeved costume of uncertain name.[33] It is obviously a household garment not meant for outdoors but resembles a tunic worn by citharodes and actors; it may therefore be of Oriental origin. Hegeso herself could be the wife or daughter of an ambassador (the Proxenos of the inscription, if this is a title rather than a first name) and may have known foreign places. What is interesting in the servant's costume is the sculptor's willingness to dispense with horizontal accents in favor of long sweeping folds from shoulder to knee. A subsidiary point of origin at the right breast produces a hint of catenaries, while a catch at the ankle builds a contrast between the oblique folds of the front and the steep vertical of the back drapery and marks the course of the bent leg. An equally straight fold between the legs suggests that the body weight is carried by the farther leg, a pose confirmed by the outline of the left hip. The circular composition formed by the continuous line of arms, box, heads, and glances centers in Hegeso's raised right hand as its focal point,[34] and it is not immediately

---

1 (Mainz 1977) no. 65, pl. 17, ca. 425. Note the complexity of the scene, including a child, which is unusual for Attica. A second example from the end of the Fifth century, is Pfuhl and Möbius, no. 63, pl. 16, from Mesembria. Despite strong Attic influence, the scenes have a touch of pathos (because of the presence of a child) that is absent from Athenian works. For an example shortly before 450 see the stele of a lady and a maid from the Molivoti peninsula on the Thracian coast near Komotini, Salonika Inv. 1251: H. Hiller, *Ionische Grabreliefs, der ersten Hälfte des 5. Jahrhunderts v. Chr.* (Tübingen, 1975) N 1, pl. 21.

[32] Note also that one of the folds hanging vertically behind her calf has a wide ridge interrupted half-way by a groove ending along a straight line —a stylistic trait found also on the Nike Balustrade and the Erechtheion frieze.

[33] J. Thimme, *AntK* 7 (1964) 16-29, discusses the costume of both figures in the context of the total meaning of the scene, which he considers an example of worship of the dead taking place at the grave, rather than an everyday scene of a mistress adorning herself before an outing which, in the viewer's mind, would imply her departure from this world. Thimme calls the maiden's dress a long-sleeved chiton and stresses that this type of garment is inappropriate for a slave girl, as the figure has usually been defined (see esp. pp. 19-21). I cannot agree entirely with Thimme's interpretation, but the true meaning of the scene need not affect a stylistic examination of the stele.

[34] The necklace (?) being lifted from the box was rendered in paint, presumably for ease in carving. J. Thimme would prefer a fillet, in keeping with his otherworldly interpretation of the scene.

apparent how much taller the lady would be than the maid, were she to stand up: her body crosses from one edge of the slab to the other. The architectural frame to the scene expands rather than confines the space, since the servant can lean against one anta, while the chair overlaps the other.

These two last reliefs are so well known and illustrated that they would have needed no comments.[35] However, they provide strong parallels for statues or individual renderings that have survived only in Roman copies. It is therefore important to note them in undoubted Greek originals, which will be mentioned again in later chapters. It is also useful to have these Attic works in mind when examining non-Attic grave reliefs.

Boeotian and Other Stelai

Once again, a review of all known monuments is impossible in this context, and other monographs have already attempted it. We shall here mention the originality of some pieces, especially the so-called Boeotian Rider Stelai, which start in the Archaic period and show a galloping horseman or occasionally the dismounted knight near his horse, a type unknown in Attica outside of a narrative context. Another unusual type of stele is closer to painting than to carving, since it is executed in dark limestone, against a roughened background, with the main figure rendered in outline and paint. Since the latter is now lost, the present appearance recalls modern rubbings of brass tombstones in medieval England. These peculiar Boeotian "reliefs" are an engraving technique known from Chios and other islands since the Sixth century, but they are obviously related to contemporary vase painting and seem short-lived: only seven are extant, four of them fragmentary, dating between 420 and 400.

Precise dates for more conventional grave reliefs are nonexistent and two recent studies come to different conclusions. It is difficult to decide what belongs to the Fifth and what to the Fourth century; certainly production quickens as the years progress. Only one stele can here be analyzed, to be contrasted with Attic renderings by which it is influenced: the so-called Polyxena Relief (fig. 108). The name is provided by an inscription carved in Boeotian script on the architrave of the architectural frame, within which the figure stands in fully frontal pose. This frontality is unusual in Attic funerary reliefs, and it could be surmised that Polyxena herself is treated as a divine apparition, since she is probably the priestess of the goddess whose idol she holds in her left hand; however, the pose occurs already in some Archaic Ionic gravestones, specifically for women, and also in other provincial Fifth century reliefs.

Perhaps as a result of this frontality, Polyxena appears heavy and squat, almost ill proportioned. She wears a peplos with overfold, which she has pulled over her head like a veil. The Running Niobid in Copenhagen (figs. 31, 32) does the same, but hers is a gesture of protection; in Polyxena the rendering is more surprising, even within a religious context.

---

[35] As already mentioned, Fifth century gravestones are much more original in themes and renderings than the more routine Fourth century production, and many would deserve individual attention. I should particularly like to point out a fragmentary stele from Salamis showing a young actor, presumably seated, gazing at a large theatrical mask, which he holds in his outstretched right hand: E. Tsirivakos, *Deltion* 29:1 (1974, published 1977) 88-94, and French summary on pp. 277-78, pls. 48-51. The carving has been dated to ca. 410 and assigned to the Parthenon tradition.

Unusual also is Polyxena's hairstyle, which has been described as a series of curls massed on either side of a central diadem; but the smooth mass with engraved wavy lines above the center of her forehead, if indeed a diadem, lacks proper depth and does not seem to encircle her head. Such Archaizing curls and the wide, heavy-jowled face over the thick neck are non-Attic features.

More in keeping with Athenian practices is the rendering of the transparent drapery, but here too the foreign version is apparent. The presumably woolen peplos is treated like a chiton and its transparency is excessive: it looks as if the sculptor drew the contour of her left side first, then added the drapery at some distance. The fold marking the axis of the figure depends from the stomach, yet it does not convey the volume of the body but flattens it. The whole system of folds seems symmetrically worked out around the points of greatest projection in a woman (the breasts and the rounded belly), in contrast with the diagonal lines, which suggest the weight shift toward the right leg, yet the anatomy is almost masculine, athletic.

The total rendering of the body lacks articulation; the weight leg is too hidden behind the drapery, the free leg is too prominent, and the cloth adhering to it has been turned into pure pattern. The pose is chiastic and "Polykleitan," but the shoulders are almost straight; the same stance is obvious in the statuette held by Polyxena, on which the bent leg appears even more disembodied. To judge from the remaining traces, the idol probably wore a polos and a veil, perhaps even some kind of apron or an object held in front of her chest.[36] In her lowered right hand Polyxena once held a metal object separately attached and now lost, possibly the key to the goddess's temple.

Thessalian grave reliefs are even more linear[37] and decorative; there are few of them for the Fifth century, some still Severe in style, others more influenced by Attic models but almost confused, as if patterns of folds had been adopted without complete understanding of the underlying principles. Frontal poses are fairly frequent and so are children and small figures. Spartan reliefs have such emphasis on engraved outlines and folds, are so peculiar in their poses—some of them conveying a pathos entirely alien from the collected figures of other gravestones—that no possible influence from Athens can be postulated.

SIDONIAN SARCOPHAGI

This last group of reliefs does not fall under any of the previously mentioned types and can only be treated incidentally. The four decorated caskets found within the Royal Nekropolis at Sidon, in Phoenicia, have received great publicity because they included the spectacular Alexander Sarcophagus, but only one other piece, the so-called Satrap Sarcophagus, has been as thoroughly published. The other two—the Lycian Sarcophagus and that

[36] Published descriptions of this statuette are incomplete: the figure deserves closer examination. E. B. Harrison suggests to me that Polyxena may not be fully grown. This observation could explain some of the awkward features noted above. It is also likely, Harrison believes, that the stele belongs well into the first quarter of the Fourth century.

[37] That linearity and patterning are not completely absent from Athenian works can be shown, for instance, by a votive relief with a horseman, Akr. 3360 (Brouskari, *Catalogue*, p. 181, fig. 360; J. Dörig, *AntK* Beiheft 9 [1973] 17, pl. 6:1). Here, however, the effect may be due partly to the weathering, partly to mediocre workmanship. It is certainly uncommon in the best Attic carvings, although in the Thessalian reliefs it seems independent of quality; see e.g., Biesantz, *Die thessalischen Grabreliefs* (Mainz 1965) K 29, pl. 4; K 21, pls. 5-6; K 22, pl. 7.

of the Mourning Women—have been well illustrated but still await proper treatment.[38] More recently the discovery of a relief "tribune" in Greek style has shown that the presence of the sarcophagi was not an isolated instance of Greek imports in that non-Greek area, although only for the Alexander Sarcophagus can a stylistic connection with a Greek center (Rhodes) be more or less established. The Satrap Sarcophagus has been discussed elsewhere as an example of Lingering Severe and need not be reconsidered here. The Lycian Sarcophagus may, strictly speaking, fall outside the scope of this book and date from the early Fourth century; but its Parthenonian inspiration is so frequently mentioned that a few comments may be added.

The nickname derives from the shape of the lid, like an upside-down boat, which is typical of Lycian monuments, both in rock-cut reliefs and in the round. This distinctive group of monuments has been enriched by several examples in recent years and has received a good deal of attention by French scholars. However, the Sidonian Sarcophagus seems to have borrowed from Lycia mainly the shape and, vaguely, the hunting theme: the specific rendering of the scenes, other mythological allusions, and the style of carving are entirely different from the Lycian monuments and definitely Greek. Of particular interest is the fact that the figures on all four sides of the casket stand on ground strips which form virtual islands above the architectural base moldings; one step beyond their present position and the centaurs, riders or animals would fall off their perch. It is unclear why the sculptor of the sarcophagus adopted such a rendering, unless he wanted to differentiate between the functional, plain fittings of the casket and the "realistic" scenes to be visualized as taking place within a natural landscape.

The Kaineus episode on one of the short sides is echoed at the opposite end by two rampant centaurs locked in combat. Both compositions are triangular in outline and in very high relief; the shield of Kaineus adds to the impression of depth, as in the Bassai or the Hephaisteion friezes. On the long sides, a lion being hunted by two quadrigas is balanced on the opposite face by a boar on which five riders converge. Looking at photographs of the scene, one is struck by the dense compositions. The lion seems almost an afterthought and is so crowded under the horses' legs that the attackers' spears could not possibly reach him. The horses seem unaware of the beast and their heads fan out according to the same pattern for both chariots. The boar is equally overwhelmed by the riders and one horseman twists in an almost ludicrous position to throw his now absent javelin. What no photograph can convey, however, is the excellence of the carving and the masterly treatment of the very high relief. Contrary to what occurs with the Parthenon metopes, here the overall design seems poor but the execution is superb. The subtle yet great modulation of the plastic surfaces can only be appreciated with direct inspection.

The pattern of folds is inspired by Attic prototypes: on the side of the boar hunt, note, for instance, the wavelet formed by the skirt of the rider at the extreme right and his billowing mantle with omega folds at its edge. The catenaries of his transparent costume bring out the roundness of his body underneath and recall Paionios' Nike. Yet everything is slightly more linear than one would expect on an Attic work: note especially the hair of the rider wearing a smooth cap. Perhaps the most non-Athenian feature of the whole boar-hunt scene are the horses, unusually smooth and stylized, with faceted heads on which

---

[38] I understand, however, that R. Fleischer and his   students are working on these two sarcophagi.

markings look as if applied externally. Among the superb details, note the head of the second rider from the right: a bearded man (partly hidden by the overlapping horse of his companion) whose intense gaze is emphasized by his deeply set mouth.

On the side of the lion hunt, the long-sleeved costumes of the spearmen are not Greek, but the long skirts of the charioteers, with their sweeping S-curves, are traditionally Greek: they are not likely to be Amazons, as sometimes stated. Perspective effects are obtained by slanting the chariot wheels, varying the height of the relief (the farther arm of the central hunter is a mere contour line) and virtually eliminating the bodies, so that the expressive heads appear thrust forward into space. Coiffures look windblown with speed,[39] foreheads have Parthenonian creases and mouths are slightly parted, with drill holes at the corners.

SUMMARY

A survey of original Greek reliefs seems to demonstrate once more the pervading influence of Attic styles and compositions, even in non-Greek territory. Outlying areas usually emphasize linear patterns at the expense of volume and therefore their renderings can often be easily distinguished from Athenian works. Votive reliefs include some major monuments, both in dimensions and execution, and the same is true for some grave reliefs, but both categories, and especially the former, can comprise mediocre pieces. The amount of landscape and background details among votive reliefs is in contrast with the relative plainness of architectural or even funerary sculpture, and is probably more directly conditioned by contemporary monumental painting. However, stylistic trends in the treatment of drapery or of facial features seem to conform to the general development of sculpture in the round. Hands have been recognized in some of these reliefs, and workshop connections have been postulated, but no major master can be surely linked with the production of these reliefs, despite their occasional excellence.

That some votive panels were set up in more than one replica seems to confirm the possibility of contemporary copying; the need for such duplication should probably be sought in official rather than private purposes. Some of these replicas were found in Italy, yet their duplicates are known to have stood in Athens. This fact may suggest that even votive reliefs were taken from Greece, but whether in ancient or in more recent times is impossible to tell. Undoubted Roman copies of some major reliefs do exist, however, as well as possible variants, yet the mere fact of having a Roman copy of a Greek relief is no assurance that the original was votive rather than funerary in nature.

In general, gravestones outside of Attica show more complex scenes with some emotional content even when under obvious influence from Athens, where grave stelai seem to carry a less explicit message of mourning. Yet similarity of motifs among reliefs coming from widespread geographical areas seems to indicate that (Attic ?) pattern books of some kind were available and that even Athenian workshops could adapt and modify some of their own standard renderings. In brief, relief sculpture at the level of private commissions seems more akin to vase painting (or rather to commercial production) than to architectural sculpture, although the latter may have provided some of the patterns and have used some in its turn.

[39] Compare the similarity of this trait, and of the general pattern, in an Apobates relief from the Am- phiaraion at Oropos, Petrakos (supra, n. 13) pl. 39.

1. *Votive relief to Helios in Kansas City.* This piece in the William Rockhill Nelson Gallery of the Atkins Museum of Fine Arts (Inv. no. 45:32/7) is of particular interest because of its provenience: for a long time it was immured in the Castello Giusso at Vico Equense, south of Sorrento where the relief may originally have stood. Attention to it in its new location has recently been called by K. Stähler, *Boreas* 1 (1978) 103-12, who mentions earlier bibliography. He identifies the charioteer as Helios, despite previous suggestions of a female divinity; the astral connection is made clear by the plastically rendered waves, from which the chariot wheel emerges and on which the horses gallop. That the animals are not winged may be a local trait rather than an argument against the identification.

The general typology is that of the many Fifth century charioteer reliefs investigated by G. B. Waywell, *BSA* 62 (1967) 19-26, esp. 23-25. According to him, this form of dedication, in special vogue from the second half of the Fifth into the Fourth century, consists of: (a) abduction scenes, (b) apobates scenes, and (c) *solo* charioteers, presumably victors in Panhellenic or local races. A fourth category of divine apparitions should be added. The Kansas City relief displays the usual indication of speed through flying drapery, but the scarflike mantle rising high to the level of the god's head is an exaggeration typical of the end of the Fifth century. Stähler stresses Attic influence but points out Magna Graecian features, such as the lack of a terminal element, either monument or human figure, providing a static frame to the composition. The Kansas City relief may date around 400 or even shortly after.

2. *Stele of Krito and Timarista from Kamiros (Rhodes)* (fig. 109). There are several notable features in this gravestone. The rounded top with projecting molding is unusual, although popular in the late Hellenistic and Roman periods, and only one other Classical example comes readily to mind: the stele of a young girl from Liatani, Boeotia, Richter, *MMA Catalogue*, 50, no. 74, pl. 60b, dated ca. 440. In the Rhodian stele the names engraved above the figures belong epigraphically to ca. 380, yet style and findspot of the relief suggest a date no later than the last decade of the Fifth century, before the synoikismos of Rhodes in 408. The slab was meant for insertion into a base which, as suggested by Robertson (pp. 369-70), probably carried the original and fuller epitaph. In this case, the lettering below the molding could have been added a few decades later, perhaps at the time when damage demanded the recutting and repair noticed by Frel around the head of Krito (*AAA* 3 [1970] 367-71; *AAA* 5 [1972] 75, no. 4, and 77 with good photographic detail in fig. 5. I agree that the rough surface is *not* intended for the addition of a stucco coiffure). Although the roughly cut lower end of the slab would have been only partially visible when set up, the sloping ground under Krito's feet is an intentional element of landscape and may support Frel's contention that the younger figure is the deceased, as contrasted with the general view that Timarista, with her matronly aspect and her veil, should be the commemorated dead. In favor of this second position, however, note that the peplos belted over the overfold is unusual for humans and, in Attic circles, was almost an attribute of Athena. Timarista's right hand, moreover, held an object once rendered in paint; in the most recent publication of the stele it is called a fillet: E. Pfuhl and H. Möbius, *Die ostgriechischen Grabreliefs* 1 (Mainz 1977) 22-23, no. 46, pl. 12, with previous bibliography. See also P. M. Fraser, *Rhodian Funerary Monuments* (Oxford 1977) 9 and n. 23 on pp. 89-90.

Although Rhodes has recently yielded a series of later gravestones with two women embracing (Pfuhl and Möbius, nos. 722-25), the stele of Krito and Timarista is heavily influenced by Attic works. Frel (*AAA* 1970) has attributed other pieces to the same hand: a fragmentary stele from Marion, Cyprus, and the Kos relief with dancing Charites (supra, p. 144). The Rhodian gravestone should date ca. 410.

3. *Stele of Eupheros, Athens Kerameikos Museum P 797* (fig. 110). This gravestone is datable not only on stylistic grounds but also on the contents of a grave found in close proximity, south of the Sacred Way in the Kerameikos. The burial was that of a boy approximately fifteen years old. Next to it another grave was marked

by a plain stele inscribed "Lissos," and it has been surmised that they served for two brothers who probably died in the same epidemics that plagued Athens in 430-427. The vases found in Eupheros' tomb are said to belong to the last quarter of the Fifth century, yet the stele is placed "at the latest" around 426, presumably because of the historical connection: B. Schlörb-Vierneisel, *AthMitt* 79 (1964) 85-104, and esp. 90-92 (grave), 93-95 (stele), 101-104 (relief). Both Schlörb-Vierneisel and J. Frel (*AAA* 3 [1970] 367-71) detect in the relief a certain academic quality and old-fashioned character, perhaps because the general format and the isolation of the deceased recall Archaic Attic gravestones; but they disagree in attribution. Frel suggests that the slab had been used before, since the relief panel is sunk into sides already bordered by anathyrosis. To this secondary use may also be ascribed the cursory treatment of the hair. The pediment and the solid area between the akroteria were decorated with painted elements, of which traces are still discernible. Of interest is the obvious athletic allusion of the strigil (two such implements, in bronze, were found within the grave), the "Parthenonian" silhouette with inclined head and bent leg forward, and the drapery marked by oval patches that adhere to the flesh in between ridges. The stele has been mentioned by E. B. Harrison as an example of the Quiet Style (*AJA* 81 [1977] 416 n. 37), and a date around 420 should not be excluded, despite the tempting historical connection with the plague, since it is still compatible with the tomb contents.

4. *Ekphora relief, Athens Kerameikos Museum P 779.* This fragment has been interpreted as a funeral scene: the carrying of wooden coffins, by phyle, of the war casualties, as described by Thucydides, 2.34. The two men sitting in the cart, both apparently of mature age, have been identified as tribal elders, although another suggestion would see in them the eponymous heroes of the various phylai, since undoubtedly other carts would have appeared in the missing part of the slab. For discussion see K. Gebauer, *AA* 1942, col. 255 and fig. 28 on cols. 247-48; R. Stupperich, *Staatsbegräbnis und Privatgrabmal im Klassischen Athen* (Münster 1977) 16 and n. 4, Cat. no. 278. The Kerameikos relief has been dated to the end of the Fifth century; because of its low height, it could have appropriately crowned a casualty list, perhaps for the Peloponnesian War.

It could also have decorated a *polyandrion* erected at public expenses for the same event. Although only one such relief can be definitely shown to have belonged to a state monument (Athens Nat. Mus. 2744, for the dead of the Battle of Corinth, 394 B.C.), the Kerameikos fragment compares favorably with it in dimensions, and the existence of decorated polyandria is usually assumed on the basis of "quotations" on other gravestones. See recently Stupperich, 4-26, and Ch. Clairmont, *GRBS* 13 (1972) 49-58, especially 56-57 and n. 4 on p. 53, which lists "combat reliefs" comprising more than a single soldier. For the type of early wheel on the Kerameikos relief, see L. Beschi, *ASAtene* 47-48, n.s. 31-32 (1969-70) 92-93.

5. *Fragmentary record relief (?) from Ephesos.* The broken slab, carved in very low relief, preserves a female figure, from neck to knees, holding hands with an almost entirely missing man wrapped in a mantle and leaning on a stick. The piece has been published by V. M. Strocka, *ÖJh* 49 (1968/71) 41-49, who considers the marble local and the style Ionic, yet inspired by Attic works. Although the format of the panel when whole, with the two figures standing close together, is dissimilar from the wide rectangles typical of Attic record reliefs, Strocka has suggested that this was the function of the Ephesian carving, since its style dates it to the last decade of the Fifth century; yet it was considered important enough to be transferred to the Third century city where it was found. The figures, according to his interpretation, would represent Artemis holding a bow and shaking hands with Androklos, the founder of Ephesos. This interpretation, however, is largely based on the "bow," which would definitely identify the female figure as the goddess; its rendering is unclear and the long peplos belted over the overfold does not provide adequate support for the theory. Of special interest, nonetheless, is the use of an Attic formula translated into local style: note how the Ionic master has downplayed the volume of the overfold and of the peplos in general, but without conveying the effect of transparency. For the statement that record reliefs could occur in non-Attic territories see Strocka, 47 and n. 22. If this Ephesian example has been correctly identified, Artemis would stand for the temple and Androklos for the city proper, stressing the independence of the two.

6. *Amphiglyphon from Brauron (Athens Nat.*

Mus. 4468 ?). The inv. number is mentioned by G. Kokula in her Munich Dissertation, *Marmorlutrophoren* (Köln 1974) 4 and n. 9, pl. 1:1-2; it does not correspond, however, to Karouzou, *Catalogue*, 29, where the number refers to a metope from Megara. The amphiglyphon is, to my knowledge, unpublished: it is interesting because it may represent the earliest representation of both a loutrophoros and a lekythos on a stele, shortly after the middle of the Fifth century. Marble versions in the round seem to appear shortly afterwards, around 430 B.C. The marble loutrophoroi, in their two basic forms (with two or with three handles) have been collected by Kokula, who has also included representations on stelai. The lekythoi are discussed by B. Schmaltz, *Untersuchungen zu den attischen Marmorlekythen* (Berlin 1970). Both types of vessels, a stone translation of the terracotta shapes current in the Classical period, were used as tomb markers and were often decorated both with painted ornaments and with relief scenes comparable to the gravestones of their time. Schmaltz has pointed out, however (p. 116), that on relief lekythoi warriors predominate and the women are shown in iconographic formulas quite different from those on contemporary stelai. Kokula has suggested that the two-handled loutrophoroi stood over the graves of unmarried men, while the three-handled version (hydriai) marked the burial of women. However, while a man's celibacy was noted well into his maturity,

only young maidens were commemorated by vessels connected with marital rites, presumably because a man could be expected to marry until relatively late in his life, while for a woman who had reached her twenties the likelihood of marriage was minimal (p. 187). The greatest popularity of both forms occurred during the Fourth century, particularly in Attica; a few examples have been found in territories under Athenian political control, but some must have been made solely because of artistic influence.

7. *Fragmentary stele from Apollonia, Cyrenaica.* It deserves mention because of its uncommon representation and its provenience from an area that did not favor gravestones. It has been published by J. Ph. McAleer, *A Catalogue of Sculpture from Apollonia* (*Libya Antiqua*, suppl. 6, Tripoli 1979) 78-81, no. 73, pl. 30.1. It retains the lower part of a female figure in front of a deep chest under which stands a vessel (probably an exaleiptron). The woman holds the lid of the chest open, whether to place or to remove an object is unclear. The scene can be compared with a well-known Lokrian pinax or, more remotely, with the Grottaferrata stele. Like the former, the Cyrenaican relief may allude to wedding rituals, perhaps because the deceased had died unmarried. It has been dated within the last third of the Fifth century and it would seem to be another example of widespread Athenian influence on both sculptural style and customs, if not a direct Athenian import.

FOR PAGE 128

No comprehensive work on Greek reliefs has yet appeared. Votive reliefs have been briefly treated by Hausmann. G. Neumann, *Probleme des griechischen Weihreliefs* (Tübingen 1979) appeared too late to be consulted, but includes many of the monuments treated here. A corpus of Attic votive reliefs (*Corpus I, Attic Votive Reliefs of the 6th and 5th centuries B.C.* [Athens 1977]) by E. Mitropoulou, is incomplete and inaccurate, although it provides some useful photographs.

There is a much larger bibliography on funerary reliefs, of which only the most recent can here be mentioned: P. M. Fraser, *Rhodian Funerary Monuments* (Oxford 1977) deals with some Classical pieces (esp. pp. 8-11), and E. Pfuhl and H. Möbius, *Die ostgriechischen Grabreliefs* 1 (Mainz 1977) includes 101 items of pre-Classical and Classical date. J. Frel has attempted to define sculptural hands and workshops, which may have produced both funerary and votive reliefs in Athens: *Les Sculpteurs attiques anonymes 430-300* (Prague 1969), and, with B. M. Kingsley, *GRBS* 11 (1970) 197-218. Frel has also published several other articles on the subject in various periodicals.

On record reliefs, the basic work remains R. Binnebössel, *Studien zu den attischen Urkundenreliefs*, 1932; for criticism see J. Marcadé, *RA* 1941, 217-18, or P. Bernard, *BCH* 85 (1961) 470. An interesting attempt to utilize record reliefs can be found in Dohrn; his low chronology is open to debate.

FOR PAGE 129

For Archaic reliefs, both votive and funerary, see *Archaic Style*, ch. 6.

Thessalian funerary reliefs: H. Biesantz, *Die thessalischen Grabreliefs, Studien zur nordgriechischen Kunst* (Mainz 1965); Boeotian reliefs: W. Schild-Xenidou, *Boiotische Grabund Weihreliefs archaischer und klassischer Zeit* (Munich 1972).

Theory of antiluxury decree and disappearance of Attic gravestones between 490-430; see, e.g., Ch. W. Clairmont, *Gravestone and Epigram* (Mainz 1970) 41-45.

This theory is doubted by, e.g., D. Bradeen in *Phoros, Tribute to B. D. Meritt* (Locust Valley, N.Y., 1974) 30-31. Cf. also R. Stupperich, *Staatsbegräbnis und Privatgrabmal im klassischen Athen* (Münster 1977) 18 and n. 4, also 85-87 and nn.

FOR PAGE 130

For a discussion of Peloponnesian stelai see H. Möbius, *JdI* 49 (1934) 45-60, and the updated reprint in *Studia Varia* (ed. W. Schiering, Wiesbaden 1967) 33-46.

On scarcity of votive reliefs in major sanctuaries see, e.g., M. A. Zagdoun, *FdD* 4:6 (1977) 23.

Funerary Banquet (*Totenmahlreliefs*): for the type and general catalogue see R. N. Thönges-Stringaris, *AthMitt* 80 (1965) 1-99; for the type in Fifth century Asia Minor see J. J. Dentzer, *RA* 1969, 195-224; for the type in Fifth century Attica, see J. M. Dentzer, *BCH* 94 (1970) 67-90. A book by B. Fehr, *Orientalische und griechische Gelage* (Bonn 1971) deals also with the origins of the iconography and renderings in the round. Some of the reliefs from the Amphiaraion are illustrated by B. Ch. Petrakos, *Ho Oropos kai to Hieron tou Amphiaraou* (Athens 1968).

FOR PAGE 131

For representations of Demeter and Kore on Fifth century reliefs see A. Peschlow-Bindokat, *JdI* 87 (1972) 109-27.

Some of the Brauron reliefs are illustrated by P. Themelis, *Brauron, Guide to the Site and Museum* (Athens 1971); see also J. Kontis, *Deltion* 22 (1967) pls. 103-105.

Xenokrateia relief, Athens Nat. Mus. 2756; name derived from inscription on pedestal associated with sculpture.

The most recent discussion of both the inscription and the representation is by M. Guarducci in *Phoros, Tribute to B. D. Meritt* (Locust Valley, N.Y., 1974) 57-66; for a different interpretation see A. Linfert, *AthMitt* 82 (1967) 149-57. For workshop attributions see Frel, *Sculpteurs attiques anonymes*, no. 66, pp. 19-20.

Amphiglyphon of Echelos and Iasile: Athens Nat. Mus. 1783. The basic publication of the finds from the sanctuary of the Echelidai is

O. Walter, *ArchEph* 1937, 97-119. See also Guarducci, and Linfert; Frel, no. 65 (attributed to master of Xenokrateia relief); the kidnapping scene is no. 41, attributed to the Dion sculptor, pp. 16-17.

For the theory that the foreground male figure represents the Kephissos see, e.g., Linfert; he is called a priest by Guarducci.

FOR PAGE 132

Hekate Kourotrophos: suggested by M. Ervin, *Platon* 1 (1959) 146-59, esp. 148 with discussion of all inscriptions and identification of the female figures. The same identification is supported by S. Karouzou, *JHS* 92 (1972) 68 and n. 26; *AthMitt* 89 (1974)159; see also Schuchhardt, *Alkamenes*, 28 n. 46 and fig. 27 on p. 29. Both Guarducci and Linfert identify the figure as Kallirhoe.

Double appearance of Kephissos: advocated by Walter (pp. 106-107) and Hausmann (p. 63).

Acheloos: see the discussion of the river god on votive reliefs by H. P. Isler, *Acheloos* (Bern 1970) 29-43, esp. p. 30; the discussion includes the Xenokrateia relief and the amphiglyphon of Echelos and Iasile.

FOR PAGE 134

Pinakes depicted within other reliefs are listed in *FdD* 4:6 (1977) 26 and n. 4.

FOR PAGE 135

For the bronze pinax from Delos and its marble pillar, as well as for the matching stone pillar with cutting for a similar bronze panel now lost, see Hausmann, figs. 52-53 on pp. 86-87, text on p. 82.

Pythodoros relief, Eleusis Mus. 51. The historical connections are discussed by A. Andrewes and D. M. Lewis, *JHS* 77 (1957) 177-80, esp. p. 178; Ch. Clairmont, *GRBS* 13 (1972) 49-58, esp. p. 55. Hölscher, *Historienbilder*, 99-101, doubts the historical connection except for the choragic victory of 415/4, see his n. 504 with previous bibl. and n. 507. The ancient source is Thuc. 6.105.2; 5.19 and 24. A thorough stylistic analysis of the relief is yet to be done.

Other landscape reliefs have been put together from many fragments by L. Beschi, *ASAtene* 47-48, n.s. 31-32 (1969-70) 85-132, esp. fig. 6 on p. 96, fig. 8 on p. 99. The Paralos relief is discussed on pp. 117-32, a reconstruction appears on p. 127, fig. 24. Cf. Brouskari, Akr. 1339, pp. 176-77, fig. 379.

FOR PAGE 136

Telemachos Monument: L. Beschi, *ASAtene* 45-46, n.s. 29-30 (1967-68) 381-436; E. Mitropoulou, *A New Interpretation of the Telemachos Monument* (Athens 1975).

Torlonia relief: Dohrn, 31-32 (dimensions given as H. 0.40, W. 0.67, to be reconstructed to almost double the present height.

For a reconstructed drawing see H. Kenner, *ÖJh* 47 (1964/65) fig. 32 on p. 46, discussion on pp. 44-47 in terms of theatrical landscape. For an interpretation in terms of Attic topography see L. Beschi, *ASAtene* 45-46, n.s. 29-30 (1967-68) 511-36, esp. 515-17. A different interpretation of the area around the Asklepieion on the South Slope of the Akropolis is presented by S. Walker, *BSA* 74 (1979) 243-57, esp. 247-48.

FOR PAGE 137

Relief with Demeter and Kore from the Ilissos area, Athens Nat. Mus. 3572: Ch. Karouzos, *AthMitt* 54 (1929) 1-5 pl. 1; S. Karouzou, *Catalogue*, 60: pres. H. 1.15, pres. W. 0.53.

Colossal work by Alkamenes: considered statues by Schuchhardt, *Alkamenes*, p. 8; considered relief by Dohrn, p. 15.

FOR PAGE 138

Great Eleusinian Relief: L. Schneider, *AntP* 12 (1973) 103-24, is the most complete discussion of the monument and its replicas or adaptations, with bibliography. See also *JdI* 87 (1972) 110 and no. R 4 in list of Fifth century reliefs.

FOR PAGE 139

The officials of the Eleusinian Mysteries and their costumes are discussed by K. Clinton, *The Sacred Officials of the Eleusinian Mysteries* (*TAPS* 64:3, 1974) esp. pp. 98-108, 113, for the Hearth Initiates. For a typical statue cf. *Severe Style*, fig. 112.

FOR PAGE 140

Nisyros stele: *Severe Style*, fig. 61.

Attic stance: see also ch. 7:178, ch. 9:239. For a discussion see, e.g., L. Beschi in *Sculture Greche e Romane di Cirene* (Padua 1959) 110; Dohrn, 54-55; F. Hiller, 11-19.

FOR PAGE 141

Mantineia relief ("Diotima"), Athens Nat. Mus. 226, said to be in Pentelic marble, pres. H. 1.48 (woman's head and top of palm tree missing).

Both lateral edges are preserved. The identification of the figure with Diotima was made by H. Möbius, *JdI* 49 (1934) 45-60, reprinted in *Studia Varia* (ed. W. Schiering [Wiesbaden 1967]) 33-46. On the historicity of Diotima see, e.g., *OCD*, s.v.; for the opposite opinion see, e.g., *EAA*, s.v. Robertson, 384, ascribed the relief to Kephisodotos.

FOR PAGE 142

Cyrene stele: Paribeni, *Catalogo*, no. 51, p. 36, pls. 50, 53; L. Beschi, *Sculture Greche e Romane*, 93-145 (reconstructed H. 1.80); see also bibliography for stele of Chairedemos and Lykeas.

The Megara stele and the Chairedemos/Lykeas gravestone are discussed by R. Vasić, *AntK* 19 (1976) 24-29. He believes them superior to the Cyrene relief. Frel, *Sculpteurs attiques anonymes*, 23 section ii, groups of the Salamis and the Megara stele; T. Lorenz, *Polyklet* (Wiesbaden 1972) 51, groups all three (including the Cyrene relief) and gives them to a sculptor influenced by the Ares Borghese master.

FOR PAGE 143

Samos relief: the latest discussion is in E. Pfuhl and H. Möbius, *Die ostgriechischen Grabreliefs* 1, no. 54, p. 25, pl. 14; the votive hypothesis is suggested by W. H. Schuchhardt, in *Essays in Memory of K. Lehmann* (Locust Valley, N.Y., 1964) 293-99; the most important article is by P. Zanker, *AntK* 9 (1966) 16-20; cf. his n. 4 for a list of other funerary monuments from the same area.

FOR PAGE 144

Relief from Kos: the latest reference is in F. T. Van Straten, *BABesch* 51 (1976) 1-38, esp. p. 1 and n. 1 with previous bibliography; *AAA* 3 (1970) 250, 369.

The Maenad Reliefs are discussed in ch. 8.

Albani Relief: Hölscher, *Historienbilder*, 109-110; Despinis, 189-90; Fuchs in Helbig⁴, no. 3252; R. Stupperich, *Staatsbegräbnis und Privatgrabmal*, 18-19 with nn., Cat. no. 546 on p. 183; Robertson, 368-69, mentions tentatively a possible connection with a cavalry encounter in 408 B.C. The theory of the triptych and Perikles' funerary oration is by Fuchs; cf. also Ch. Clairmont, *Gravestone and Epigram* (Mainz 1970) 43; contrast D. H. Bradeen, in *Phoros, Tribute to B. D. Meritt*, 30 n. 10, who stresses the lack of evidence for decorated state monuments during the Fifth century.

FOR PAGE 145

For the theory of a cavalry monument see Hölscher; for a comparison with the Parthenon frieze see, e.g., Dohrn, 18-20.

FOR PAGE 146

Cat Stele, Athens Nat. Mus. 715, found on Aegina in 1829; G. Welter, *AA* 1938, cols. 531-34, explains why the relief was wrongly thought to come from Salamis, and mentions a comparable stele from the same workshop, Athens Nat. Mus. 1385. A recent discussion appears in Robertson, 367-68. A good technical analysis is given by Adam, *Technique*, 110-13. For the youth's gesture see G. Neumann, *Gesten und Gebärden in der griechischen Kunst* (Berlin 1965) 46. For the floral border see H. Möbius, *Die Ornamente der griechischen Grabstelen* 2nd ed. (Munich 1968) 106. For architectural comparisons see, e.g., the sima from the Argive Heraion, Berve and Gruben, pl. 86b.

Hegeso stele: Robertson, 370, mentions that there are probably archaeological grounds for dating it after a reorganization of the cemetery in 394/3; a similar attempt had been made by Dohrn, who devoted a lengthy discussion to the piece, pp. 96-114 (p. 113: "hardly datable before 390").

FOR PAGE 147

Stele in New York, Metropolitan Museum; G.M.A. Richter, *Catalogue*, no. 77, pp. 51-52, dated at the turn of the century.

Cf. also the Boeotian stele of Diodora from Thespiae, Schild-Xenidou, no. 23, last quarter of the Fifth century.

FOR PAGE 148

On the Boeotian stelai related to painting see Schild-Xenidou, 176-78 (her catalogue K 43-48); cf. also A. Kalogeropoulou, *AAA* 1 (1968) 92-96.

Polyxena Relief: Blümel, *Berlin*, no. 6, pp. 17-18 fig. 12 (K 26); Schild-Xenidou, no. 32, dated toward the end of the Fifth century.

For the Running Niobid in Copenhagen see ch. 3.

FOR PAGE 150

"Tribune" from Sidon: E. Will, *BCH* 100 (1976) 565-74. The upper frieze recalls that of the Temple of Athena Nike (East side), the charioteers on the short sides are after the

Maussolleion. The date given is in the mid-Fourth century.

For the Lycian Sarcophagus see Lullies and Hirmer, figs. 193-97.

On Lycian sarcophagi in general see, e.g., P. Demargne, *FdX* 5 (Paris 1974); on their general themes, P. Demargne, *CRAI* 1973, 262-69.

For a recent attempt to change the traditional sequence of the Sidonian sarcophagi, and for extensive comments on the Lycian Sarcophagus (dated to ca. 400), see H. Gabelmann, *AA* 1979, 163-77. The identification of the lion hunters as Amazons is mentioned, e.g., by Lullies; Gabelmann, p. 166, speaks of ephebes.

CHAPTER 7

The Great Masters

OUR information on the Great Masters is largely derived from literary sources of the Roman period, and it is legitimate to raise the question whether our conception of the major Greek sculptors is not colored by a possible bias in our authorities, or at least by the fact that we seek information from these treatises which, because of their very nature, classify the material by masters. To be sure, some Fifth century sculptors were already famous in the Hellenistic period, long before Roman Imperial times, but many of the accounts about them are anecdotal rather than historical in nature, and in some cases have been shown to be not only inaccurate but definitely wrong. We are much more concerned with the fame of the masters during their own lifetimes, and more specifically with the status of such sculptors and their workshops. Our review of Greek original reliefs has shown that many of them could be of exceptionally high quality and that a few could reach considerable size; yet, except for Pausanias' controversial mention that Alkamenes made a colossal votive relief, no extant work has yet been successfully connected with a so-called major master. An examination of Greek architectural sculpture has also suggested that much of it can be considered a choral enterprise by anonymous carvers, even if working under the direction of a master coordinator, who need not have been a sculptor himself. Finally, the question has been raised whether a sculptor acquired notoriety in the ancient world not so much because of the beauty of his creations but because of their intrinsic importance. In other words, was Pheidias famous because of his distinctive artistic style or because he had made the Athena Parthenos and the Olympian Zeus? Was he known in later times as the planner of the architectural decoration of the Parthenon (indeed, a fact mentioned only by Plutarch) or as the maker of precious cult statues *qua* cult statues?

To be sure, this proposition could result in a vicious circle: how are we to determine whether the project made the sculptor famous or whether it was assigned to him because of his established reputation? Successful completion of a major task is bound to produce bigger and better commissions, but public works in Athens were a state enterprise that some people were asked, or undertook, to coordinate as a form of service to their city—or for strong personal political reasons. In the Fifth century, art, especially monumental sculpture, was still intended to be purely religious or civic and was not yet used for private consumption or edification. This kind of mentality is less likely to place emphasis on individual styles and masters, even if they existed. Although Perikles, more than Pheidias, was acknowledged as the mastermind behind the planning of the Akropolis program, we know of his involvement in it largely through Plutarch's *Life of Perikles*, an obviously eulogistic and probably exaggerated account. This source has been recently criticized both in terms of Fifth century epigraphic evidence and democratic institutions, and it is likely that neither Perikles' nor Pheidias' role in the Parthenon was as important as stated by Plutarch. No major master's name has been connected with the Hephaisteion, the Nike Temple, or the Erechtheion by Greek or Roman sources, except for mentions of cult images or other paraphernalia within the buildings. We should distinguish, moreover, between information derived from contemporary inscriptions and information gleaned from literary accounts, between Pausanias, who lists as he sees and learns with a minimum of personal screening, and Pliny, who intentionally selects and emphasizes. Yet even Pliny is no Roman Vasari, and perhaps no Latin writer would, or could, have compiled a biography of Pheidias or of Polykleitos. Certainly none was written during the Fifth century.[1]

However, the later fame of a master may rest upon many imponderables. Some sculptors are known to have written treatises on their theories (or their technique?), and their names may thus have survived through the ages more on philosophical than on purely artistic grounds. Others may have achieved a degree of immortality through the subject matter of their works, which appealed to the particular needs of the Romans to decorate their amphitheaters and villas. Still others may owe their reputation to the fact that their statues stood in Delphi or in Olympia, the two major sanctuaries of antiquity. Finally, some may have been known not through their own work but through the anecdotes or the writings connected with the works themselves. For instance, Strongylion is mentioned by Pliny (*HN* 34.82) because Brutus of Philippi fell in love with his statue of a youth and his Amazon was carried around in the retinue of the emperor Nero. As for Myron, his most famous creation in antiquity was not his Diskobolos but his cow, probably because of the many epigrams and *beaux mots* which had been written about it in Hellenistic times; yet the realism these verses so highly praise seems rather improbable for Myron's time, both as an achievement and as a goal.

At the present state of our knowledge, many sculptors listed by the ancient sources remain totally unknown, even when cited as pupils of Polykleitos and Pheidias, while many important works exist that cannot be associated with specific masters. Moreover, the Roman writers often give us contradictory information on the makers of certain statues, and obviously proper evidence was lacking even in their own days, with some well-known names attracting a flurry of attributions, regardless of chronology and plausibility. A thorough analysis of this problem goes beyond the scope of this book, and personal skepticism on attributions prevents me from attempting some of my own. Therefore, I shall discuss what is positively known about Fifth century masters from a specific point of view: the fact that most, if not all of them, can be connected with cult statues,[2] while others are

[1] Although Thucydides and even Herodotos may have had some antiquarian interests, biographies of artists and art-history texts in our sense of the word are unlikely within the Fifth century. That some may have been written during the Hellenistic period is suggested by F. Preisshofen, *JdI* 89 (1974) 50-69, but by that time anecdotes were taken as facts. For a different point of view see Hölscher, "Die Nike," 92-98.

[2] From the iconographic point of view it is interesting to note that not all twelve Olympians were represented by Fifth century statues, whether cult images or votive offerings. Even deities that occurred frequently on reliefs are not known from comparable types in the round; this is particularly true of Artemis, who was, however, highly venerated in Athens and Attica. I wonder if any relationship might exist between the presence of ancient xoana and therefore the absence of "new" cult images, or, conversely, the creation of new statuary types in connection with the establishment of new cults. It is certainly intriguing that several statues in the round of Artemis should be known for the Fourth century, almost as if old images had to be replaced by that time. The forthcoming *Iconographic Lexicon of Classical Mythology* (LIMC) should be particularly helpful for a

cited as the makers of portraits, a genre that was hardly approached before the Classical period. Both categories (cult statues and portraits) include a few original pieces, but we shall now be squarely confronted with the problem of assessing Roman copies.

THE MAKERS OF CULT STATUES

Pheidias

Without a doubt this is the name that tradition and modern scholarship have presented as the greatest Fifth century master, yet the Roman writers praised especially his ability to lend dignity and impressiveness to his divine figures, rather than naturalism or originality in his art. He was born into a family of artisans and initially trained as a painter; his brother or nephew Panainos was a painter and Pheidias sought his help at Olympia. Likewise he employed the engraver Mys in Athens, perhaps as a result of his own background. Universal agreement exists about attributing to Pheidias the Olympia Zeus and the Athena Parthenos. The long controversy over the correct chronological relationship between the two statues should have been brought to an end by the finds at Olympia, which to my mind convincingly demonstrate the priority of the Akropolis image; thus, a whole set of ancient sources which refer to Pheidias' death in Athens can be discarded as anecdotal. That there was trouble, largely political, is probable, however; it also confirms the hypothesis that Pheidias left Athens to accept the commission at Olympia shortly after finishing the Athena in 438, most likely before the completion of the Parthenon in 432. He died at Olympia and his successors were given some kind of priestly title with the task of oiling the statue to prevent the ivory from cracking. In later times the Zeus was considered one of the Seven Wonders of the World.

Given the priority of the Athena, she should be discussed first. She is known from a great number of copies, in a variety of sizes, media, and techniques, most of them ranking as religious souvenirs. Information on the statue and its many details has been conveniently and scholarly collected on the occasion of a small-scale reproduction attempted by the Royal Ontario Museum in Toronto in the 1960s. The need to translate theory into three-dimensional form forced Neda Leipen to take position on many controversial points, and she has published the evidence for her decisions together with a good photographic commentary. We can therefore confine our remarks to specific problems of personal interest.

We are still ill-informed about the chryselephantine technique, but certainly the preciousness of the material was partly meant as expression of divinity; actual remains of gold and ivory statues have been found at Delphi from the Archaic period, and the practice seems to have started in East Greek territory, where ivory working had a long history. Yet the gold of the Parthenos was removable and was indeed taken away and turned into gold coinage in 295 B.C. That it was replaced, and probably in the original form, is shown by all later accounts, including Pausanias' elaborate description, and by the Roman copies, so that a detailed wooden armature must be postulated, on which the gold could again be modeled and hung to replace what had been melted down. In this respect the

study of "popularity" in sculpture according to periods and deities. For useful comments on statues of

Zeus at Olympia and their masters see R. Wünsche, *JdI* 94 (1979) 107-11.

molds from the Zeus at Olympia do not help our understanding, partly because they have not yet been properly published and explained, partly because the technique employed on that statue might not have made provision for the removal of the metal parts.

That a major statue can be disassembled need not affect its artistic conception and execution, but if the underlying core was the primary carrier of the style—in other words, if the statue was so completely carved in wood that the gold could be replaced purely as a form of revetment—did the finished product correspond to a wooden image rather than, for instance, to a marble or a bronze sculpture? Since only the flesh parts of the figure were in ivory—a rather thin veneer at that scale—and most of the statue was covered by the gold, this is a legitimate question. From what the copies tell us, however, no great difference can be noticed, and certainly carving skills in the Fifth century could obtain whatever effect was desired. The only "technical" feature seems to be the long fold, which stems from the bent left knee and runs vertically down to the ground, in contrast with the more oblique course of the leg itself. In the marble replicas this fold serves as a veritable strut or tree trunk to reinforce the ankle, yet the wide skirt alone should have been adequate to prevent breakage in marble, so we cannot assume that the rendering was introduced by the marble copyist for the specific needs of his medium. Replicas of the Parthenos are too consistent, moreover, for this to have been an arbitrary modification, as contrasted with the supports introduced by copyists in reproducing other famous works, which vary greatly in their shape and position. This fold may have been demanded by the chryselephantine technique, but it is difficult to see why a wooden statue (even if overlaid with gold) would have needed it. Certainly such an enormous figure could not stand without proper armature, and the big pole attested by the hole in the floor could have been no more than the spinal cord for the statue, to be supplemented by an adequate system of branching rods and ribs.[3] The skirt fold will therefore be considered purely as an element of style.

When the Parthenon pediments required considerable repair during Antonine times, it is legitimate to assume that some damage may have occurred to the cult statue itself. As Damophon of Messene, in the Hellenistic period, was commissioned to repair the Olympian Zeus, similarly some artist must have been employed to repair the Athena, but we have no specific information about it. It is probable, however, that this activity around the Parthenon attracted renewed attention to the statue or increased its accessibility, thus provoking a flurry of replicas, since so many of them seem to date from Antonine times. There may have been more than one major fire in the Parthenon history, and a recent architectural

[3] Such an armature would have allowed the positioning of the Nike on the Athena's hand without need for a supporting column underneath. The arguments for or against such a support have been endless, and no conclusive proof can be found. The problem has been well summarized by N. Leipen, who added such a column in her Toronto model and gave it the first known Corinthian capital of antiquity, with gold leaves. On purely subjective grounds I would prefer an original without the column, like the Delian Apollo, who held the three Graces on his hand, or the Apollo Philesios at Didyma, who balanced a hind without additional help. The cantilever principle, so well employed for the pedimental sculpture of the Parthenon and even architecturally for the entablature of the Propylaia, would have been used to keep the Nike in equilibrium. It has been suggested that a Corinthian capital connected with the Parthenos would have had symbolic value as well and could easily have launched the type, but in this case it is difficult to see why no Corinthian column should have appeared in Athens until approximately a hundred years later. Note that the column capital of the Varvakeion replica is not as unusual as often stated; a comparable shape appears already in the Sixth century, over the heads of the Siphnian Karyatids at Delphi.

study suggests that the well-known replacement of the base, and therefore of the statue itself (?), may have occurred as late as the Fourth-Fifth century A.C. Be that as it may, it is perhaps safe to state that Pheidias' opus underwent several repairs and probably complete replacement within its existence as a pagan cult image. Its end is not known, but it can be no later than the conversion of the Parthenon into a Christian church during the Fifth century A.C.

Was the Athena Parthenos a true cult statue? Some scholars have maintained that she was only an artistic way of displaying the public treasure, or perhaps even a way of keeping the communal gold under the citizens' eye, since the removal of any amount would have left a gap in the statue and been immediately obvious.[4] On the other hand, the Athena and her paraphernalia begin to appear in the temple inventories only after the Gorgoneion was stolen from the shield during the Peloponnesian War. It seems improbable, moreover, that such an elaborate temple and image were erected solely as a glorified treasury and votive offering. Certainly the Athena seems to stand at the beginning of a long line of divine statues made of similar materials, yet their cult nature has never been questioned. Of all the many chryselephantine images listed by the ancient sources, not one has come down to us in a convincing copy; in particular, the very Zeus of Olympia, by the same master of the Athena and much more famous in antiquity because of its location, is thoroughly lost to us: we know only some details of its throne. That this situation is not the result of a religious taboo is shown by the fact that the cult statute of Nemesis at Rhamnous has recently been recovered in the original, thus allowing the recognition of many replicas. Nor can the size of the chryselephantine colossi have created difficulties for the copyist, since the Athena Parthenos herself was enormous, yet abundantly copied. Accessibility was no problem, as many of the Athena replicas are only approximate and simplified versions, if nothing else because of the reduction in scale. The Olympian Zeus was also imitated in the Fourth century by the statue of Asklepios at Epidauros,[5] and it may have been reproduced more or less faithfully at Cyrene in Roman times, just as the Athena Parthenos was duplicated in the cult images at Priene and perhaps at Aphrodisias and Notion. It is perhaps simpler to admit that we cannot today establish what made a statue

[4] This theory had met with some favor because a comparable parallel had been assumed in the bronze head of a female figure from the Agora, with grooves for the insertion of gold and silver plating. This piece had been interpreted as one of the Golden Nikai mentioned by the Athenian accounts (D. B. Thompson, *Hesperia* 13 [1944] 173-209; *Agora* 14, 190-91, here Appendix 5:2). However, a recent find from a Hellenistic context—fragments of an equestrian bronze statue probably of Demetrios Poliorketes—has shown that the method of gilding adopted for this honorary piece was the same and that therefore we are confronted with a purely technical trait in both cases: *Hesperia* 42 (1973) 165-68, pl. 36. Note in addition that the Athena Parthenos represented a relatively minimal portion of the treasure of the Delian League, according to Thucyidides' account (*Hist.* 2.13), even after the expenses for the temple itself had been met. On the ultimate provenience of the Parthenos' gold see S. Eddy, *AJA* 81 (1977) 107-11.

[5] Note that even a *bona fide* artist, Thrasymedes of Paros, when commissioned to make this cult image, imitated a previous work rather than producing his own creation. To be sure, he may have introduced stylistic changes in the drapery in keeping with his own times, which might have escaped the Roman traveler confronted with a basically similar type, a bearded, venerable man seated on a throne. Nonetheless, it is quite conceivable that Thrasymedes considered his imitation a virtue rather than a fault, in contrast with our conception of artistic personalities. A late source (Athenagoras, *Leg. pro Christ.* 17.4) affirms that the Epidauros Asklepios was by Pheidias—a typical example of how erroneous attributions could be made in antiquity on grounds of technique and general appearance; cf. *AJA* 70 (1966) 217 and n. 4.

a good subject for copies, since fame and artistry alone are certainly not sufficient motivations. In this context, note that the Athena Promachos, a definite landmark on the Akropolis and a virtual sister of the Parthenos, was not copied at all, as far as we know, by those sculptors who made so many reproductions of her chryselephantine sibling.

The Athena Parthenos was so big that its size is difficult for us to visualize. It is simpler to understand that the Nike standing on her hand (with or without the help of the support) was approximately six feet, a size we can easily conceive. I wonder whether Pheidias might have intended to provide a human-reference scale in setting the Nike near the Athena (although even that height would have been heroic for a female figure in Fifth century Greece), to enhance the grandeur of the goddess. But even the Nike, at that level, would have seemed smaller to the awed viewer. The awe would have been increased by the semidarkness of the temple, the indirect light provided by the reflecting pool, with its dancing glitter sufficient to highlight but not to reveal the entire statue. The water basin, if it really existed (and I believe it did), for all its shallowness effectively prevented visitors from moving close to the Athena. Seen from a considerable distance, in somber light, armed and flanked by a powerful snake, the goddess must have seemed forbidding. It has actually been suggested that the story of Pandora narrated on the statue base might have added to the feeling that the gods were, if not positively hostile, at least aloof or indifferent to mankind; yet perhaps only a few philosophical spirits in Athens could have received such a message. The majority of the citizens might have gloried in the size and richness of the statue or in the thought that such a formidable goddess was their patron. But would they have looked at it as a work of art?

The decoration of the statue certainly made its impact on contemporary artists. The technique of the base, which probably consisted of gilded figures attached against a background,[6] inspired other pedestals for cult images, and the very frieze of the Erechtheion. The Amazonomachy reliefs on the outer side of the shield provided themes for contemporary architectural friezes, including those of the Hephaisteion and Nike Temple, as well as for many Neo-Attic reliefs of later date; these Roman decorative copies may also have included excerpts from the base and the Centauromachy depicted on the soles of the Athena's sandals. The Gigantomachy engraved (or inlaid)[7] inside the shield may have influenced only some vase painters, but we are in a difficult position to judge, with much of the evidence missing. It has been suggested that the greater or lesser popularity of the replicas depended to some extent on the visibility of the original; the shield, the sandals, and the base, being more or less at eye level, would have become well known and therefore easily recognizable even if reproduced out of context. Yet only the bottom part of the shield, at best, would have been level with the viewer (as shown by the scale model in

---

[6] Another possibility, which E. B. Harrison tells me she favors, is that the decoration of the base consisted of carved marble reliefs: G. P. Stevens, *Hesperia* 24 (1955) 257 and 260. A. Delivorrias, in *Kernos* (Festschrift Bakalakis [Thessaloniki 1972]) 24-34, has suggested that bases for marble cult statues carried marble reliefs, while bases for bronze cult statues followed the Erechtheion-frieze technique of having marble figures carved separately and attached to a background of a different color; he bases his conclusion on a fragmentary figure of Athena that seems made for attachment to a background and which he would therefore assign to the base for a cult image in bronze.

[7] The metal-inlay technique, known since Mycenaean times, can produce very colorful results comparable to painting. A striking example from the Roman period is a swag of bronze drapery from an imperial statue that stood in Volubilis; for color photographs see Ch. Boube-Picót, *Les Bronzes Antiques du Maroc*, 1, *La Statuaire* (Rabat 1969) pls. 17 and 37.

Toronto), and the base was visible only across the reflecting pool. It is more likely that these parts were reproduced because sketches or models for them existed and because their narrative content incorporated some innovations in form and iconography that appealed to contemporary taste, especially the shield. These compositions may, however, have been closer in nature to painting than to sculpture.

The evidence for the arrangement of the base is scanty, although its length must have made it comparable to a small frieze. Indeed, whatever remains on the base of the Pergamon Athena replica (of Hellenistic date) recalls the East frieze of the Nike Temple. Helios rising on his chariot and Selene sitting on her mule have been recognized in the sketchy rendering of the so-called Athena Lenormant replica and are appropriate enough links with the East Parthenon Pediment, and perhaps even East and North metopes, to be plausible.[8] The Neo-Attic Del Drago relief shows Poseidon with one foot raised on a rock, in a pose familiar from the West frieze; but the lovely Amphitrite looks too close to the Fourth century Artemis of Gabii to be completely genuine, and a critical review of the problem has recently suggested that this and other evidence for the Parthenos' base include later material. Note, however, the several goddesses lifting their mantles behind them in Fifth century votive or record reliefs; these have been identified as Demeter or Kore, but obviously the gesture is appropriate to other figures, since the so-called Frejus Aphrodite (figs. 126-27) displays it. The pose may well have found its earliest sculptural expression in the "bride" of the Olympia East Pediment, but it became popular in Parthenonian circles, as shown not only by the statue base but also by Figure L of the East Pediment. A seated Athena from the Nike Balustrade is depicted in the same action. Other personages of the Parthenos' base are restored on almost pure speculation, although the theory that Pandora herself looked like a stiff idol is probably correct.

Even less can be said about the Centauromachy on the sandals, although a marble vase in Madrid may reproduce some scenes. One more possibility, which has not usually been considered, is that the groups of Herakles and a centaur on the helmet of the so-called Pasquino (the Menelaos supporting the dead Patroklos) may derive from the same source. The shoes themselves were, according to Pollux, "Tyrrhenian": a sign of Etruscan contacts with Classical Athens that we might tend to underestimate.

By and large, the most famous composition was the Amazonomachy on the shield. Its motifs appear on so many later monuments that we can plausibly assume many drawings were made and circulated widely, either directly or in the form of metalwork and vase paintings shipped to Magna Graecia. Various attempts at recovering the original arrangement of the figures have been made, with differing results and, once again, complete agreement is impossible. It is likely, however, that certain basic types occurred here for the first time: the warrior helping a wounded comrade; the warrior peering from behind his shield or otherwise hiding his face (the so-called Perikles);[9] figures seen from the back as if twirl-

---

[8] Helios and Selene may also have framed the Gigantomachy on the interior of the Parthenos' shield and are described as part of the Birth of Aphrodite scene on the base of the Olympia Zeus. It has been suggested that this interest in celestial phenomena may have originated in Perikles' intellectual circle, on the basis of Anaxagoras' philosophical thought; the statesman may have passed his interest on to the sculptor, or may have suggested the theme. However, Anaxagoras' theories were purely materialistic, whereas these sculptural personifications seem connected with a literary or a pictorial tradition.

[9] A somewhat similar rendering had already appeared, however, on the North frieze of the Siphnian Treasury.

ing in space; and the pose of the warrior on his knee for a back wound, which is echoed by the Stumbling Niobid in the Terme. The hair-pulling motif here finds the form of a figure being overtaken and held by its hair, a rendering that may have appeared also on the metopes. The "heroic diagonal" introduced with the Tyrannicides becomes more and more emphatic. One more figure, an Amazon falling headlong from a height, as indicated by her flowing hair and bent knees, seems surprisingly to come from a non-Greek repertoire: from Assyrian reliefs of city sieges, in turn recalling Egyptian scenes of fortresses under attack. The motif occurs again and again in Lycia during the Fourth century, in semihistorical reliefs probably under Oriental inspiration even if of Greek execution, but the Parthenos' shield may already have drawn from such sources in Attic territory. Yet note that only the lunate shield (*pelta*) characterizes the Amazons as Easterners. Their attire and helmets are Greek, and one has again the impression that no great confrontation of East and West is meant but purely a mythological episode connected with an Attic hero.

The falling Amazon's schema reinforces the suggestion of the diagonal poses that some landscape was included in the scene. The Toronto reconstruction introduces some Polygnotan rocks and hillocks, while some Neo-Attic reliefs show the ashlar walls of the Akropolis in the background. Yet a recent study maintains that the battle depicted could not have taken place on the citadel and that the figures, with their appliqué technique, could not have conveyed an impression of space in the original, nor could they have been derived from pictorial models. I should like to see the Amazon falling headlong off the Akropolis wall, in conformity with the Oriental prototypes. The amount of landscape attested by (admittedly later) Fifth century votive reliefs confirms that such rendering was entirely possible at the time, despite the fact that architectural sculpture did not utilize it, except perhaps for the Ilissos frieze.[10]

Three more monuments should be added to Leipen's list, two of them rather unexpected. One is a large fragmentary sarcophagus from Aphrodisias, which has received only preliminary mentions; despite the relative popularity of Amazonomachies on Roman sarcophagi, this is the first casket to show unmistakable derivation from the Parthenos' shield; some of its figure types are well attested, but others may be new. The second piece is a relief fragment with a mounted Amazon fighting a warrior on foot; if this Neo-Attic work belongs with the same series from the Peiraeus inspired by the shield (Second century A.C.), we would have an indication that cavalry was also used in the fighting, and this evidence could effectively eliminate the Akropolis as the battlefield. On the other hand, the West metopes of the Parthenon included horsemen, and it may even be that this relief draws its subject from yet another monument.[11] The third example, from Cyrene, is a Gorgoneion retaining

[10] E. B. Harrison has anticipated me in this conclusion and has worked out a topographical system of walls and gates, which she will publish in a forthcoming article. Some of her views, presented in a lecture in Basel, are summarized in *AntK* 21 (1978) 114. Harrison suggests that the composition contained allusions to both Marathon and the events of 480 B.C. The shield as a whole would represent the city as a whole, while the Amazons were depicted assaulting the Akropolis and scaling its walls. Additional support may be found in the depiction of walls on a large volute krater by the Niobid Painter from Spina. This vase has now been published by P. E. Arias in *Forschungen und Funde, Festschrift B. Neutsch* (Innsbruck 1980) 51-55. See also the summary printed in the Congress's *Final Programme*, p. 79.

[11] This relief is known to me only through the mention by C. C. Vermeule, *Greek Sculpture and Roman Taste* (Ann Arbor 1977) p. 12 and fig. 10. The caption states that it came "from the waters around Peiraeus harbor," and the pitted surface confirms the claim. The framing molding could correspond to some of the Peiraeus slabs depicting the

traces of figures at its periphery, which has only recently been recognized as a replica of the famous shield.[12]

Nothing more can be said about the style of the original sculptures, since only schemata can be safely derived from Roman replicas. What can we say about the Athena herself? Limiting comments to the overall pattern, we may describe the statue as stylistically in keeping with its decade (447-438), though with a greater stiffness, determined perhaps not so much by size or technique as by religious conservatism and therefore by function. Archaistic traits may be noted, as in the Erechtheion Karyatids, in the long locks over the chest. Could they remotely reflect a metal coiffure on the venerable wooden idol? The pose, with one knee bent, does not really produce a trailing leg and the feet are roughly aligned, again like the Karyatids, but this stance seems directly derived from Severe renderings experimenting with balance. The belted overfold is typical of Athena, but its almost straight lower edge and the limited curve of the kolpos over the belt are early traits, which do not yet convey the roundness of the body beneath. By contrast, the figures of both pediments and frieze show much greater use of modeling lines, and the tectonics of their bodies are not so much conditioned by the articulation of their garments—rather, the opposite is true. In the Athena Parthenos, perhaps because of its great height overall, the emphasis has been placed on strong horizontal accents at modulated intervals: the shoulder line, the lower edge of the aegis, the belt (with a minimum of curve), the hem of the apoptygma, and finally that of the peplos. This last, longest stretch from hem to hem is briefly interrupted by a minor accent produced by the bent knee. The total effect seems heavy, though majestic; only the right profile gives an impression of cascading folds, where the edges of the peplos meet, in a richness contrasting with the austere simplicity of the front.

Other Works by Pheidias

These can only be discussed briefly. The Zeus of Olympia is the second best-attested statue, and its authorship is not in dispute but, as already mentioned, its appearance can only be conceived in general terms, through the literary descriptions. His long locks are attested by the account that some were stolen for their value, but we need not visualize the lengthy corkscrew curls of Archaistic herms, which may not appear before Roman times.

More concrete evidence comes from the molds found near the workshop of Pheidias at Olympia, but they are relatively small for a statue of that colossal size. Some are for the Zeus itself; others, on a much smaller scale, show the groups of folds branching off the buttons of a chiton's sleeve and must belong to the Nike on Zeus' hand. Here too is the familiar

---

Amazonomachy of the shield. However, it seems unlikely that figures on horseback would have appeared on the latter, and the style of the two figures may even be somewhat later than the Fifth century. Vermeule writes in general terms of the relief as connected with the Parthenon metopes and Athena's shield but does not make a definite attribution. The relief was in the Cranbrook School, Broomfield Hills, Michigan, and seems now to have been sold to Japan (E. B. Harrison, review of Vermeule, *Archae-

ology 32 [1979] 68-69).

[12] A recent suggestion would recognize an Amazon from the shield on a fragmentary relief from Sardis: N. H. Ramage in G.M.A. Hanfmann and N. H. Ramage, *Sculpture from Sardis: The Finds through 1975* (Cambridge, Mass., 1978) no. 188, fig. 338, pp. 83 and 137-38. The Sardian sculpture has been dated to the First century B.C., and it may be a Hellenistic adaptation rather than a true replica, since no specific figure on the shield is cited as parallel.

dispute over whether a column stood under the hand or whether the armrest of the throne provided adequate support. I tend to favor the second suggestion. The molds, in terracotta, have raised borders all around that have not yet been properly explained in terms of a chryselephantine statue; perhaps gold was poured in a molten state, or gold sheet was hammered into the mold and the part over the border was rabetted into grooves cut into the wooden core, but even this does not seem a good solution. That the molds may have had to withstand some pressure is shown by the fact that larger pieces had metal reinforcements in the back. The great contribution made by the molds has been to show that the style of the folds should come after the Parthenos, and this has been confirmed by other objects found in the same deposit, including the famous mug with Pheidias' name scratched on its bottom.

Slightly more indication exists for some of the decoration on the throne of Zeus. More explicitly than with the Birth of Pandora, the myths represented show a streak of cruelty toward man. Fink, in his discussion of the subject, has suggested that Pheidias attempted to show both sides of the god's nature, and certainly the huge statue itself, crammed within the narrow compass of a cell that was not originally built for its bulk, must have created an awesome and aloof impression, even more so than the Athena. The armrests of the throne terminated in sphinxes devouring Theban youths, and some highly fragmentary groups in black marble found in Ephesos have been thought to imitate the ebony originals. The sphinxes are very feminine, both in their animal and in their human aspect, with Fifth century heads and no trace of Archaizing. A large marble disc in the British Museum has long been recognized as a Neo-Attic adaptation of a continuous frieze, presumably a long strip of ivory inlays along the arms of Zeus' throne; figures excerpted from the repertoire of the disc occur also in decorative reliefs of different format, and a vase in Leningrad has been recognized by Brian Shefton as sketching the Niobids' arrangement on the seat, thus making their position secure.[13] Once again, it is the subsidiary decoration that receives the attention of the copyist or the contemporaries, and the reasons must be comparable to those obtaining for the Athena. On the evidence of the replicas, the composition included Apollo and Artemis shooting down the sons and daughters of Niobe, respectively. The helping-comrade motif reoccurred, as well as the figure wounded in the back, as on the Parthenos' shield; the arched corpse is comparable to those on the East frieze of the Hephaisteion. Flying drapery filled intervals and a certain amount of landscape was probably included; the closest overall parallel seems to be with the Ilissos frieze. Finally, one more detail of the throne has recently been pointed out: a kneeling Nike near the leg, as it appears on coins of Elis, and which may survive in almost life-size replicas in Naples, Detroit, and Stockholm.

[13] This Red Figure vase, not yet published, is mentioned by M. Robertson, 319 and n. 66 on p. 672. A relief from Modena (G. V. Gentili, *BdA* 59 [1974] 101-105 and figs. 1-2 on p. 103) has added one more group to the composition: a young girl seeking refuge near a bearded man seated on a rock, presumably Amphion. An attempted reconstruction on the basis of the new Modena piece would mix male and female Niobids, instead of separating them strictly by sex. Yet other figures seem to have been added to a Niobid frieze from Isthmia, of which some fragments have been recovered within the Temple of Poseidon, others from the Byzantine fortress: see *Hesperia* 22 (1953) 191, pl. 58f; *Hesperia* 24 (1955) 129-31, pl. 50a-b; *AJA* 72 (1968) 269, pl. 91:17. According to the last report, the relief may date from the Hadrianic period. For an entirely different rendering of the myth, presumably dating around mid-Fifth century, from Cyrene, see *EAA*, s.v. Cirene, p. 671 and fig. 912 on p. 683: an altar of Artemis.

The Athena Promachos on the Akropolis was of bronze and shown with upright spear,[14] in a quiet pose rather than the striding combat that is the traditional iconography of the type. Its base was plain and has been partly recovered, including a Roman repair to the crowning molding. The Promachos was not a cult image but a votive offering from the spoils of Marathon, yet she may have been almost a preliminary model for the Parthenos: perhaps this explains why copyists preferred to reproduce the gold and ivory statue, or perhaps we are unable to distinguish one type from the other in the later replicas. The shield was engraved on the outside with a Centauromachy by Mys (who supposedly also engraved other decoration on the statue), and Pausanias' comment (1.28.2) that it was ultimately designed by the painter Parrhasios may be an anecdote grown with time to add fame to fame, or simply a reflection of the pictorialism in the representation. According to the building accounts, the bronze statue may have taken nine years to build, from 465 to 456, and would therefore technically fall within the Severe period. Some scholars have wanted to identify the Promachos in the so-called Athena Medici type (fig. 111), known through many replicas usually of over-life-size. But stylistically this Athena is more advanced than the Parthenos, and although the Promachos had no religious restrictions imposed on its iconography, not being in a temple, it would probably not have been more developed than the Parthenon sculptures themselves.

Conversely, a recent study of the Athena Medici has suggested that, since so many replicas of the type are in the akrolithic technique, the original must have been similarly made or else be a chryselephantine statue. Through an examination of the literary sources, the study concludes that the Medici Athena reproduces either the akrolithic Athena Areia made by Pheidias for Plataia or the gold and ivory Athena which Kolotes made for Elis. The problem here is twofold: to determine the true position of the Medici type and to establish the value of the ancient sources. In fact, Kolotes' authorship is mentioned by Pliny (*HN* 35.54) but Pausanias (6.26.3) gives that Athena to Pheidias, since it is unlikely that two different chryselephantine statues of the same goddess existed in the same town. Kolotes was one of Pheidias' helpers at Olympia, so either statement is plausible, and it may easily be that the maker of the more famous Zeus was later credited with all the works of his collaborators in that unusual technique. Two more chryselephantine statues are in fact given to Pheidias by Pausanias: the Aphrodite Ourania in Elis (6.25.1) and the Athena at Pellene in Achaia (7.27.2), which was supposedly earlier than the Parthenos and the Plataian akrolith. It seems surprising that Pheidias should have been asked to make a chryselephantine image for a relatively obscure town in Achaia *before* the Athena Parthenos had started a fashion, as it were, for cult statues in that technique. It is more likely that unfounded attributions were made in later times by the local "guides" to increase interest in their holdings. The Plataian akrolith sounds somewhat more plausible and almost a preliminary for the Athena Parthenos, since it was made of wood overlaid with

[14] This is suggested by the fact that the sun reflected on it was visible to sailors coming from the direction of Sounion—since this is the likely interpretation of Pausanias' rather cryptic words (1.28.2). The epithet of the statue is not assured, however, since Pausanias does not immediately identify the Athena as Promachos, and the type, as known from the Sixth century and the Panathenaic amphoras, depicts a striding and threatening figure in combat position. On the type see H. Herdejürgen, *AntK* 12 (1969) 102-10, with previous bibliography. For possible echoes of the Pheidian Promachos in a statue in New York and in the Athena of the Niobid Painter krater see E. B. Harrison, *ArtB* 54 (1972) 390-402, esp. p. 396 and figs. 15-20.

gold except for the flesh parts, which were in Pentelic marble. Its connection with the spoils from Marathon adds to the picture of a relatively young sculptor being asked to produce various votive offerings related with the great event, and moving to bigger and better commissions. However, Pheidias also made a large group of bronze statues from the spoils of the same battle, this time at Delphi: they represented Apollo, Athena, Miltiades, and the Eponymous Heroes of the Attic Tribes; it was therefore a group of at least ten figures and was probably commissioned by Kimon in an effort to rehabilitate his father, Miltiades. Even if workshop attendants and pupils collaborated on such monuments, the schedule seems tight, and should include around 451 the bronze Athena Lemnia, an almost definite attribution, as a dedication on the Akropolis, presumably by the Athenian Kleruchoi to the island. Perhaps at Delphi Pheidias was himself only an apprentice, whose later reputation overshadowed that of the workshop's owner. I am inclined to accept as Pheidian only the Delphic monument (whole or in parts), the Athena for Plataia, the Athena Promachos, the Athena Lemnia, the Athena Parthenos, and the Olympia Zeus, in that approximate order. This list makes Pheidias a bronze caster and a sculptor in the chryselephantine technique, which probably involved some of the same experience in metal working. Most of the other monuments attributed to Pheidias by the various sources I would consider questionable accretions to his oeuvre. Pheidias' role in the Parthenon project seems to me far more limited than usually envisioned, a position that has now been convincingly argued by Himmelmann on other grounds.[15]

As for the second part of the problem, where does the Athena Medici belong stylistically? The so-called akrolithic technique of the Roman replicas seems to me an uncertain basis on which to rest conclusions. First of all, some of the parts reproduced in marble (those covered by the chiton) could have been of gilded wood in the original, unless we assume an outlay of ivory greater than in the Parthenos. The copy in Saloniki, with its wooden *core*, is likely to have employed a structural device to lighten the weight, save marble, and allow assemblage of separate marble parts, rather than to imitate an akrolithic or chryselephantine original.[16] Finally, the peculiar type of the Athena, with one leg covered by a thin chiton emerging from the heavy folds of the peplos skirt, seems mannered and artificial: a form of exhibitionism unexpected from a cult statue in any technique. Since textural differentiation between chiton and peplos could have been rendered in the same medium even in an akrolith, there is no reason to suppose that the arrangement reflects an exploitation of the akrolithic or the chryselephantine technique for its contrasting effects. The general type could be Parthenonian, especially in the richness of the folds over the left side, but such style could easily be recreated in Roman times and I wonder whether to consider the Medici Athena a Greek or (tentatively) a Roman invention in Greek Classical idiom.[17]

One last comment about the Athena Lemnia, so beautiful as to be nicknamed *morphe* in antiquity. Furtwängler identified the type in the so-called Dresden Athena with diagonal

---

[15] If the trial of Pheidias is indeed to be dated to 438/7, the sculptor's participation in the carving of the Parthenon pediments would be effectively precluded: see G. Donnay, *AntCl* 37 (1968) 19-36.

[16] Copying involves only the outer surface of a statue and is not concerned with its *thickness*, be it marble, ivory, bronze, or gilded wood. A chiton rendered in marble for color contrast brings to mind

Roman statues made of different-colored stones, or even in marble and bronze, rather than a Greek akrolith with only its fleshy parts of stone.

[17] That the Saloniki replica of the type may have been used as a stock body for a portrait of Julia Domna is no indication, however, against a cult function of the original, since the same use was made of replicas of the Nemesis by Agorakritos.

aegis, which he completed with the head in Bologna (fig. 112).[18] This latter, by itself, had been variously interpreted as male or female, but the controversy was abandoned after Furtwängler's identification, which won great favor, with only isolated voices raised in disagreement. The beautiful Bologna head may have been considered transformed by the hand of the copyist to the point that its Fifth century traits have been virtually obliterated, but I find it hard to believe that a work antedating the Athena Parthenos could have had such tapering chin, delicate cheeks, and realistic hair welling up under the fillet.[19] The romantic expression could have been added by the Roman carver, but the basic proportions of face and head should have remained the same, and they are not only different from the heavy face of the Athena Parthenos, but also from any Parthenonian head, whether from the pediments or the frieze.[20] The closest parallel to the Bologna head is a replica of the Polykleitan Diadoumenos, a fact that could confirm a Fifth century date for the former while increasing the complexities of stylistic assessment. However, that particular replica of the athlete is the least Polykleitan of all, with obvious modifications by the copyist; other replicas show a more typical configuration of jaw and cheeks, considerably closer to the pattern of the Doryphoros. Since all Polykleitan works are known only through later copies, it seems arbitrary to decide which rendering is more truly faithful to the original and then to use this conclusion to support or deny the Pheidian claim of another work. I am more inclined to believe in the extant original works reviewed in the previous chapters, which are consistent in showing heavy facial features regardless of their workshop affiliations. The refined oval of the Bologna head must therefore be out of context within the Fifth century.[21] The piece is probably a Classicizing creation of surpassing beauty.

Agorakritos

According to Pliny (*HN* 36.17), Pheidias allowed some of his own works to be signed by Agorakritos of Paros to promote his youthful and handsome pupil to whom he was at-

[18] The pertinence of head and body types is allegedly assured by one other complete replica of lesser quality, also in Dresden and originally from the same Chigi collection in Rome as the headless statue integrated by Furtwängler with a cast of the Bologna head. Aside from possible representations on gems and reliefs, and a few heads of reduced scale and doubtful connection, very few replicas of the head are extant: one, extensively integrated, is placed over an alien body, two others may not reflect the same original. It is worth repeating a frequently voiced criticism: that the Bologna head seems too small in proportion to the Dresden body.

[19] It could be argued that the Lemnia portrayed the goddess considerably younger than the Parthenos, but even this rejuvenating process is hardly in keeping with Fifth century tendencies; there is, moreover, no reason for the Lemnians to have wanted an adolescent Athena.

[20] It is irrelevant, in this context, whether Pheidias' hand should be recognized in any of the architectural sculptures from the Parthenon. Suffice it to note that there is a definite female head type, ba-

sically derived from modes of the Severe period, which emphasizes a U-line for the chin and which continues at least as late as the last quarter of the Fifth century. Remarkable similarity exists among various heads, some of them Greek originals, which can be attributed to different masters: Paionios' Nike, Alkamenes' Prokne, Agorakritos' Nemesis, and the Erechtheion Karyatids.

[21] I am not as sure about the body type, the so-called Dresden Athena. Except for the unusual diagonal aegis, its drapery pattern is in keeping with a date around 450, but it is surprising that no hint of weight shift should be given, after Olympia, and probably even after the Promachos. Nothing in the type assures us that it is the Lemnia, and the ancient sources are not detailed enough to allow further speculation. No argument can be made on the basis of fame: the Lemnia was very well known in antiquity, yet basically only two replicas of the Dresden type are extant. However, the same consideration applies to the Athena Promachos and the Olympia Zeus.

tached. If we disregard the romantic overtones of a later source, the information reveals that some confusion between Pheidias' creations and those of his workshop existed already in antiquity, At least two statues, the Nemesis of Rhamnous and the cult image of the Athenian Metroon in the Agora, are attributed to Agorakritos by Pliny, to Pheidias by Pausanias—the Nemesis, in either author, within the context of an anecdote that sounds rather improbable, given what we know of local cults and historical circumstances. A fragmentary head of the cult image had been found at Rhamnous in 1812, but a recent feat of investigation and reconstruction by G. Despinis has brought to light many fragments belonging to the body and has allowed the identification of many Roman replicas (figs. 113, 114). At once we have gained an idea of an undoubted cult image, the remains of what may be the only original cult statue preserved, a glimpse into the style of Agorakritos and the knowledge that temple images could be closely copied, since the Roman replicas are not all approximations, like those of the Athena Parthenos, but some are accurate reproductions of good quality and heroic scale. All this may lead us to attribute a disproportionate importance to Agorakritos who, in fact, is mentioned very seldom by the literary sources (basically, only by Pliny and Pausanias) and, it seems, largely because of his connection with Pheidias.

Significantly, Agorakritos is only cited as having made cult statues (one in marble, two in bronze, and one in an unspecified medium, probably stone), not for collaborating on the Parthenon. But he was a Parian and may have been called to Athens to work on the Akropolis at the time when the great building project required help from abroad. On the other hand, Athens had a tradition of island artists coming in during the Archaic period, and Agorakritos need be no more than a casual immigrant later enlisted by the Parthenon workshop. Certainly Paros, with its marble quarries, maintained a tradition of stone carving that should have made it a logical source for sculptors even when Pentelic was the marble employed for the project. Agorakritos may therefore have expended most of his activity on the Parthenon sculptures, hence the few attributions. Despinis has tried to reconstruct his career and sees his influence, or at least that of his workshop, in the Nike Temple frieze and Balustrade; thus the pupil might not have followed the master to Olympia, presumably being still detained by the Parthenon project. We must then assume that his fame did not reach Pheidian proportions (or that architectural sculpture did not), since Agorakritos' name is not officially connected with the Nike Temple or other works, and the styles of the Nike Balustrade are much less coordinated than those of the Parthenon.

From the fragments of the original Nemesis, suitably in Parian marble, Agorakritos appears as a sculptor fond of incision—not necessarily a stone technique—which he runs *alongside* folds or in the valleys between folds; he may also start a pattern as a groove and continue it as a ridge. His folds and incisions are never straight but always wavy; he is fond of "wet drapery," which appears adhering to the body in patches rimmed by sharp edges.[22] The Roman replicas of the Nemesis show a peculiar trait verified by the original fragments: the folds of the apoptygma, at the hem, look like tubing from which the chiton's folds emerge, bending over the belt at the waist in a distinctive manner. The general appearance

[22] An earlier phase of this rendering can perhaps be recognized on the Olympia sculptures, in particular some from the East pediment, although obviously the cloth appears much thicker and more opaque.

of the statue is "Pheidian" in stance and drapery, although the goddess wears chiton and himation. What is left of the original face has heavy proportions, wavelets of hair above the temples and massive braids hanging over the shoulders in the back, like the Karyatids: perhaps an old-fashioned hairstyle in keeping with its cult purpose. The entire statue, in its adornment and attributes, is full of mythical symbols and allusions, including the base. Despinis dates the statue to ca. 430, the fragmentary figures from the relief base to ca. 423, the akroterion (see ch. 3) to ca. 420-410. The temple, by the Hephaisteion architect, was never finished and one wonders about the discrepancy in time between statue and base.

This latter has not yet been fully published, but its subject matter is known through Pausanias: Helen being brought before Nemesis by Leda in the presence of the Dioskouroi and some of the Homeric heroes. The figures were carved directly on the slabs, not attached separately, despite Dohrn's statement, but the relief was so high that some pieces appear almost in the round. Robertson comments on the predilection for the *femme fatale* shown by the bases of Fifth century cult statues, but a case could also be made for miraculous births: Pandora (Athena Parthenos) from a statue, Aphrodite (Olympia Zeus) from the sea, Helen (Rhamnous Nemesis) from an egg (even if only as an allusion), and, we may add, Erichthonios (Athena and Hephaistos) from the Earth. These, however, are all myths connected with the main divinities, which make good narrative, and can provide enough figures to fill friezelike spaces on bases of uncommon length for colossal statues. From the head fragment and head-to-body proportions of the figures from the base, the original Nemesis has been reconstructed as 3.50m tall.

Other works and attributions remain within the realm of speculation. Of those mentioned by the literary sources, there is ambiguity over the Mother of the Gods, and Despinis' identification of the Roman copy in Levadhia is not entirely convincing. More compelling is the equation of the Dresden Zeus-type with the Zeus/Hades for Koroneia, together with Athena Itonia.[23] Patches of wet drapery on the Zeus recall the Nemesis and can be seen in an original work—the Cat Stele—which some (but not Despinis) associate with Agorakritos himself. The Athena Hope-Farnese, suggested by Despinis as the Itonia, makes a good composition together with the Dresden Zeus type, but looks rather Fourth century to me, while the Zeus should precede the Nemesis by approximately ten years, as also seen by Despinis.

Purely stylistic attributions should be safer but are hardly more convincing. That some figures from the Parthenon program had already been credited to the Parian sculptor by previous scholars need be no more than a coincidence, since nothing was known of Agorakritos' drapery style prior to Despinis' discovery, and the Cat Stele is an ambiguous link by Despinis' own reckoning. One Greek original which tradition had repeatedly associated with Agorakritos, a peplos-wearing Demeter in Eleusis, is rejected by Despinis as not good enough for the master (See Appendix 5:1). As J. M. Cook has stated, "Much of this needs rather special pleading because of the difficulty of distinguishing between individual style and the general movement of the times."

Was Agorakritos a major sculptor *in the eyes of his contemporaries*, or did his name come down to us purely because of its association with cult statues and a possible anecdotal relationship with Pheidias?

[23] On both the Cybele and the Zeus/Hades see   also ch. 8.

Alkamenes

Somewhat the same situation occurs with this other attested pupil of Pheidias. He was an Athenian, either by birth or by acquired citizenship, since some late sources call him Lemnian, therefore from an island under Athenian kleruchy during the Fifth century. Pausanias mentions that Alkamenes worked on the West pediment of the Temple of Zeus at Olympia, and if any credence should be placed on his comment, then the sculptor can only have repaired or replaced some preexisting statues, in imitation of a Severe style no longer current in his own time. His other dated works are—presumably—the two bronze cult statues of Athena and Hephaistos for the Hephaisteion, which building accounts place between 421 and 415,[24] and a colossal votive offering for Thrasyboulos after 403 (here briefly mentioned in ch. 6), which may have been one of his last creations.

As a pupil of Pheidias, Alkamenes is certain to have contributed to the Parthenon sculptures, and his hand has been recognized in the models for the Erechtheion Karyatids and related statues. In the literary sources, however, he is only mentioned for divine images, except for the group of Prokne and Itys on the Akropolis which, Pausanias says, was dedicated by an Alkamenes. It has usually been taken for granted that the dedicator was also the maker of the monument, though in marble as contrasted with his known preference for bronze.[25] Pausanias also gives to Alkamenes a chryselephantine Dionysos for the temple near the theater in Athens, but recent study of the building foundations has revealed that the structure dates from the mid-Fourth century. Alkamenes' creation may have preceded the erection of the temple; whether it actually stood elsewhere even in Pausanias' time is not clear from the text, but if it was the cult image for the Fourth century building, it may have been made by a different sculptor and later associated with the Pheidian circle on the basis of its material. Attempts to recognize it in Roman copies have not met with general agreement.

At least two of Alkamenes' works were probably Archaizing: the Hermes Propylaios and the three-bodied Hekate Epipyrgidia, which have received renewed attention in recent scholarly publications.[26] It seems clear that both types were echoed in many later

[24] Although this attribution is a matter of common assumption, it is good to be reminded (as Morgan, "Pediments," does in Appendix 4) that the argument rests on tenuous evidence: Cicero (*Nat. D.* 1.30) and Valerius Maximus (8.11) mention a statue of Vulcan by Alkamenes in Athens; Pausanias (1.14.6) in describing a temple of Hephaistos in Athens comments that he was not surprised to find Athena standing beside the smith god because he knew the story about Erichthonios. It has therefore been deduced that *both* these statues were by Alkamenes. Representations of Hephaistos are relatively rare, and thus some credence may be lent to the theory, but in Athens the god held a prominent place and it would be strange that only one image of him could be found in the city. Regardless of attribution, however, the building accounts mention the expenditures for the years 421/0 to 416/5 as recorded by the Epistatai of the two statues for the Hephaisteion, so that two such images must have

existed, even if we are not sure about the location of the temple and the name of the sculptor is not given by the official inscriptions. The question has been thoroughly reviewed recently by E. B. Harrison: *AJA* 81 (1977) 137-45 and especially n. 15 on p. 139. On the iconography of the god, including Alkamenes' statue, see F. Brommer, *Hephaistos: Der Schmiedegott in der antiken Kunst* (Mainz 1978) esp. ch. 7, pp. 75-90.

[25] Note, however, that Pliny, *HN* 36.15-16, mentions Alkamenes among the sculptors in marble.

[26] W. Fuchs (*Boreas* 1 [1978] 32-35) has now suggested that neither the Hekate nor the Hermes were truly Archaizing, but rather had strong affinities with the Severe style. He bases his assertion on a fragmentary sculpture from Hadrian's Villa at Tivoli, retaining the bodies of two peplophoroi in a triangular arrangement with a missing third figure. I wonder, however, whether this is a true copy of a Classical original; the arrangement of folds over

variants, both of Greek and Roman times, perhaps because the peculiar mixture of Classical and Archaic traits appealed to the decorative sense of the latter and the religious conservatism of both. Certainly both divinities lent themselves to an unusual form of representation, in almost pillarlike form, because of their peculiar divine nature; but it is legitimate to ask whether the inclination to Archaize was typical of Alkamenes and whether other cult statues by him had similar traits. The famous Aphrodite in the Gardens has also been considered an Archaizing statue on the basis of Pausanias' account,[27] but different interpretations of the passage are possible. Though said to be the most important of Alkamenes' works, it has not been securely identified and speculation seems fruitless at this point. Of the two types most frequently mentioned in this context, the leaning Aphrodite in Naples is chronologically appropriate in the general schema of its drapery, though surprising for the position of its legs. The other type (figs. 126, 127), the so-called Aphrodite of Frejus (but truly from the neighborhood of Naples), has been found in terracotta versions that include a tree, thus recalling the epithet of Alkamenes' statue, but the rendering seems removed from our conception of the sculptor's style, which is largely based on the Prokne and Itys.[28]

This group has been found on the Athenian Akropolis and a fragmentary head has been joined to it, with relative plausibility. Scholars are divided on whether the group is an original or a Roman copy: the official publication in *Antike Plastik* opts for the first alternative, but Schuchhardt's monograph on Alkamenes, posthumously published, favors the second. A sensitive technical analysis by Sheila Adam supports the first position and throws light on the dramatic conception of the group. What has been considered a flaw in the composition—the fact that the child seems carved out of the mother's thigh— acquires poignant meaning when it is seen as the normal reaction of a child who senses danger and hides within his mother's skirts, only to find that she is the source of the

---

the bent leg indeed recalls the Athena Parthenos, but the long diagonal ridge going from left shoulder to right ankle seems a mannerism of a later period, as well as the shallow catenary from breast to breast. Perhaps the piece is a Roman creation recasting a Greek composition into a different (earlier) style for the sake of originality, like the Esquiline Venus and Stephanos' athlete, and is therefore Severizing rather than Severe.

[27] Loredana Capuis, *Alkamenes* (Florence 1968) 25-26, assumes from Pausanias (1.19.2) that the Aphrodite by Alkamenes was hermlike and therefore Archaizing. But would Lucian then have selected her hands for his Panthea? Moreover, Pausanias seems to refer to two statues, one within and one without the temple, and only the latter is hermlike. Capuis's discussion of these objections is not convincing.

[28] One more type has been introduced into the discussion by A. Delivorrias, *AntP* 8 (1968) 19-31. He published a fragmentary female torso from Daphni, Athens Nat. Mus. 1604, approximately life-size, and considered it the cult statue of the sanctuary of Aphrodite known to have existed at the site. Given the position of the arms (the left raised

so high that the neckline slips down the right shoulder) and the possible parallel of a relief also from Daphni showing the goddess leaning against a tree, Delivorrias assumes that also the torso in the National Museum represented Aphrodite in that position. He further assumes that the Daphni statue was a replica of the famous Aphrodite in the Gardens by Alkamenes, a theory repeated by S. Karouzou, *Catalogue*, 96-97. Delivorrias himself, however, points out the appropriateness of a tree as a symbol of Aphrodite, a goddess connected with vegetation and rebirth; even if the support of the Daphni torso were indeed a branch, as plausible, we have no assurance that this was the schema of Alkamenes' statue, since different types are now known to have been given a tree as support in replicas. The Daphni torso represents, however, an interesting original of ca. 420, even if it throws only tenuous light on Alkamenes' work; the transparent rendering of its drapery seems in contrast with whatever else is usually attributed to that master.

For a seated type also occasionally identified as the Aphrodite in the Gardens see ch. 9.

threat.[29] The tragic irony of the situation would not have escaped the Athenians familiar with this Attic drama. The left arm of the woman raised toward the face would have spelled indecision and grief, in a gesture long established within the sign-language vocabulary of Greek sculpture and which reoccurs in Medea faced with a similar dilemma.[30] A tragedy by Sophokles entitled *Tereus* is known only through fragments but seems to have been performed before or around 431 and the representation may have inspired the dedication by the sculptor. Stylistically, the group could fit easily within that period, since the drapery is heavy and opaque without the transparency around the breasts that we find in the Erechtheion Karyatids and with a certain monotony of catenaries in the overfold, which do not react to the strong swinging of the left hip.[31]

Those who consider the group a Roman replica may ascribe such rendering to the copyist, together with the monotony of the folds over the back which, however, is not unlike the patterns on the Karyatids. To be sure, the Erechtheion Korai were not easily seen from the back, while the Prokne and Itys stood free, on the path between the Propylaia and the East façade of the Parthenon, to judge from Pausanias' account. Yet they may have had their backs toward a precinct wall, and even the Fourth century Eirene and Ploutos have a perfunctory treatment of their rear (albeit enhanced by the Roman copyist), yet we know that they stood freely in the Agora. With the focus of the monument clearly set on the front, the back view may have been of relative importance even if exposed.

Whether original or copy (and I tend toward the first possibility), the monument gives us an idea of Alkamenes' style: monumental, solemn, quiet, with heavy drapery. How the master might have developed in later years has been recently suggested by E. B. Harrison in her attempt to reconstruct the Hephaistos and the Athena Hephaistia, the bronze works of 421-415. Here we can only speculate from undoubted Roman copies, since the metal has long been lost. The god has been recognized in a marble torso in Athens, a herm in the Vatican, and various reproductions on lamps and reliefs, all of them too different to give us more than the general lines of the workman type, without any assurance that we are dealing with a famous original.[32] Indeed one may speculate whether the Vatican herm could be a Classicizing creation or a head of Odysseus; in addition, if one accepts Harrison's identification of the Velletri Athena as the Hephaistia, it is surprising that the goddess should be copied so frequently as contrasted with the very few and disparate replicas of her partner in cult.[33]

The Velletri Athena (fig. 115) fits within the range of the Quiet Style and, because she wears her aegis turned toward the back rather than protecting her chest, she may also fit with the myth of Erichthonios: the goddess would have moved her fierce covering out of

[29] Even in its present fragmentary state the child's body shows a great deal of torsion and perhaps its almost relieflike rendering may have been dictated by the sculptor's inability to deal with such a pose in three dimensions or by the pictorial origin of the motif.

[30] The pose may appear also on one of the Parthenon metopes, South 19.

[31] Adam suggests that Sophokles' play was performed in 413 and dates the sculptural group around 415; E. B. Harrison, *AJA* 81 (1977) 421, prefers a date around 440 on stylistic grounds; the official publication of the work, in *AntP* 17, favors ca. 430-420. The 431 date for the *Tereus* is given by Schuchhardt, *Alkamenes*, 17 and n. 14.

[32] One can at least note that the typology is quite different from the Hephaistos as he appears on the Parthenon East frieze and, perhaps, on the East frieze of the Hephaisteion.

[33] A more traditional candidate for the Hephaistia is the Athena Cherchel-Ostia; see, most recently, W. Fuchs, *Boreas* 1 (1978) p. 34, n. 13 and pls. 7-8. To my mind, however, this type could date as late as the Fourth century.

the way to pick up the child. The statue had usually been attributed to Kresilas on the basis of a vague resemblance with the portrait of Perikles by that sculptor, but Harrison makes a case for Alkamenes. I find that too little is known of either master to accept either identification, except for the fact that the style and period could be appropriate for both. Comparisons between the Velletri Athena and original Greek works in smaller scale, both in relief and in the round, as proposed by Harrison, are compelling and establish as authentic a whole series of traits that could have been easily imputed to the whim of the Roman copyist. Note, for instance, how the kolpos of the belted overfold dips low over the right hip, overlapping the roll of the mantle, and how the overfold itself, below the belt, bends over and is pushed up and under in colliding with the mantle, forming a pattern of collapsing folds similar to layered dough. The Velletri Athena has a braided mass of hair falling over her back, which compares well with the Rhamnous Nemesis and the Erechtheion Karyatids and cannot therefore be considered an Archaizing trait typical of Alkamenes; in this feature, too, the statue is a distinctive product of its time. Whether she is truly the Hephaistia is almost irrelevant, compared with the great achievement of having the type firmly established as going back to a late Fifth century original.

Harrison's conception of the group, with a very elaborate "anthemon" between the two deities, is based on the building accounts, which specify the use of a surprising amount of tin and copper, presumably for this floral element. Its appearance is conjectural, however.[34] Equally hypothetical is the reconstruction of the base for the two cult images. The Neo-Attic relief with the Birth of Erichthonios is probably correctly derived from the central scene,[35] but the other figures are taken randomly, if plausibly, from the vast repertoire of Neo-Attic reliefs. Some of them, to my mind, come from too long an iconographic tradition of dancing nymphs and Graces to have been specifically made for the Hephaisteion base; that they may have been adapted for it is possible but not provable. If, however, the other statue bases (for the Athena Parthenos, the Zeus, the Nemesis) can be taken as an indication, their scenes were novel enough to establish, rather than to adapt, iconography, even if new poses and types were still within limits of the accepted and the recognizable. The Birth of Erichthonios, an unusual myth, would seem to fall within the same category.

[34] The building accounts speak of the anthemon "below the shield," and Harrison has reconstructed this element with the Medusa Rondanini as its device. This famous Gorgoneion, best known through the replica in Munich, has been variously attributed to Pheidias or to Kresilas, but J. D. Belson, in *AJA* 84 (1980) 373-78, argues that the iconography places the creation of the Medusa not earlier than the Fourth century; a tentative suggestion is also made that the Rondanini type may have adorned the gilded bronze aegis which Antiochos IV hung on the South wall of the Athenian Akropolis. The Medusa would therefore be one more example of Hellenistic Classicizing trends.

[35] Since the Neo-Attic relief with this central scene, in the Vatican, is of large scale, Harrison rejects the base at present in the Hephaisteion as being the original support for the cult images, and uses both the scale of the Velletri Athena and of the conjectured *anthemon* to reconstruct a group too large to fit within the Hephaisteion. This may be so, but Neo-Attic reliefs are notorious for altering the scale and format of their prototypes, so that caution is required in assessing the dimensions of a total reconstruction (both statues and base) founded largely on Roman copies. Even the Velletri Athena exists in a variety of formats, from over- to well under-life size. However, Professor Harrison has pointed out to me that there are basically only two distinct groups: (1) copies at the scale of the original and so all the same scale with each other, and (2) copies of reduced scale with no common scale between them. These two classes also exist in Neo-Attic reliefs and it is important to make the distinction. Only for types where the original was too big to copy full-size does an undifferentiated variety of formats exist.

One more divine image is attributed to Alkamenes by the ancient sources: that of Ares in the Athenian Temple. Since images of this god are rare, the attractive Ares Borghese, known through numerous Roman copies, has usually been given to the Athenian sculptor, but the attribution remains only plausible, not certain. If the Prokne and Itys is the only monument that can definitely be connected with Alkamenes, it offers no grounds for comparison with a standing male nude. The Ares Borghese, which was favored by Roman emperors as a stock body for their portrait, was also used together with female statues which, as Aphrodite, served as stock body for the emperor's consort; but this is not a strong enough basis to suggest that the Ares was originally part of a group. More compelling is the criticism that the type is not frontal, as one would expect from a cult image. The god stands in an almost diagonal pose, head inclined and glance to the ground, therefore without rapport with potential worshipers. It has been argued that this aloofness conveys the restless and unfriendly nature of the god of war, but this may be specious modern reasoning. The statue is impressive, Polykleitan in its articulation of the torso, yet without chiasmos in the level shoulders and the weight distribution. The free leg (the right) is advanced diagonally, and the head turns in the same direction, so that a long line could be traced from helmet tip to toes.[36] This pose seems the logical development of the so-called Attic stance, which by the Severe period had transformed the forward leg of the Archaic kouroi into a bent free leg in front of the body, foot flat on the ground. The raised heel and trailing leg of "Polykleitan" statues made the alternate ("Attic") pose seem too static, so that movement was added by thrusting the forward free leg to the side, thus imparting an oblique direction to the torso. The next step, to be achieved by the late Fourth century, is represented by the pose of the Apoxyomenos, torsional and with weight in unstable balance between both legs; or by that of the Herakles Farnese, with the free leg so far forward that the feet are virtually aligned.

The face of the Ares Borghese (in the Louvre replica) has a touch of romanticism perhaps attributable to the copyist, but the large eyes have a rising lower lid, which becomes a standard trait of the Fourth century and produces a melting gaze. The dripping hair at the temples is unusual in any period (an allusion to the god's Thracian origin and fashions?). A firm attribution seems impossible, although the original should date from the end of the Fifth century.

On the basis of the Prokne, and of the relief figures from the area of the Temple of Ares, Alkamenes has been credited with a solemn, dignified style, almost the epitome of Classical modes, and many other works have been connected with him. Certainty is lacking in all cases.

THE MAKERS OF PORTRAITS

According to the ancient sources, within his group of bronze statues at Delphi Pheidias included not only mythological heroes but also a figure of Miltiades, a truly historical personage. The sculptor might have known the general and have attempted to convey his features. The work has not been recognized among the Roman replicas and, being at Delphi, it might not have been copied in antiquity. It is also doubtful, however, that it was a true portrait.

[36] Somewhat the same pose occurs in the so-called Naukydes' Diskobolos, which is usually dated to the early Fourth century, even if it does not belong to Polykleitos' school.

Portraiture is nonetheless one of the important phenomena of the Fifth century. The statues of the Tyrannicides erected in the Agora in 477 may have stood in splendid isolation for several decades, but had opened the way to the concept of contemporary individuals' being immortalized in heroic form. The dead and fighters of Marathon had been granted heroic honors and had achieved immortality in people's minds as well as in great murals by Polygnotos and other painters. Politics were increasingly dominated by individuals, and confrontation with the foreign enemy had engendered a sense of history, which found its best contemporary expressions in Herodotos and his work, as well as in some theatrical plays.

For all this background, portraiture might not have found fertile soil in Athens had it not also been for influence from abroad. In the East the traditional devotion to individual rulers had long been expressed through portraiture on coins, and the attempt to reproduce specific features and distinctive facial traits may also have originated in that region. The mainland of Greece probably continued to produce character portraits, rather than true representations of individuals, but the conception of specific likenesses was introduced through the foreign contacts. It may be significant that in Athens the early portrait statues were set up as dedications by the individuals themselves, long before the practice of honorary statues was resumed by the state; at the same time, in Persia or in East Greece portraits of Greek statesmen were erected at public expense.

That the Severe period in Greece knew true portraiture has been claimed on the basis of the remarkably individualistic herm of Themistokles from Ostia. Although some scholars have always insisted that the portrait dated from later centuries, they usually affirmed it on the grounds that such realistic features were impossible around 460. E. B. Harrison has recently argued on grounds of style that the Ostia herm has a Fourth century face, with the receding cheeks and good profile views typical of that period, to which a Severe hairstyle has been added to lend an earlier appearance. She has, nonetheless, suggested that a true contemporary portrait of Themistokles existed, and has recognized it in the so-called Pausanias, whose intricate beard arrangement she attributes to Persian fashions. When Themistokles' memory was rehabilitated in the Fourth century, a proper "democratic" hairstyle was considered preferable, thus giving origin to the Ostia herm type. The stylistic analysis of the latter seems convincing, while acceptance of the "Pausanias" as a Severe portrait erected in Oriental territory would confirm the precedence of that area in this genre.

Both the Pausanias and the Ostia Themistokles are known only through Roman copies. Original portraits of the Fifth century can hardly have survived, especially since the Greek conception demanded a complete statue rather than a herm. One possible exception is the small bronze head from Cyrene (figs. 116-118), which has been considered a portrait of Arkesilas IV, one of the kings of that North African city, made around 440 (by Amphion of Knossos?). Once again, the presence of an absolute ruler would explain the individualism of the head and the interest in portraiture, while the impulse may have come from Egypt or Persia, even if execution is purely Greek. Yet the Cyrene head can be compared to some of the bearded men on the Parthenon East frieze, and its claim to rank as portraiture is due not so much to marked physiognomic traits as to the Royal diadem encircling the head. Within the kingly type the head is what we would expect from the Fifth century. What is remarkable is rather the smaller-than-life-size. To make a human being on a larger scale

179

might equate him with the immortals and therefore be considered a legitimate act of heroization; but no reasonable explanation can be found for a reduced scale, except perhaps that of convenience. Portraiture on coins and gems may have paved the way to acceptance of three-dimensional likenesses in small dimensions.

The bronze "philosopher" (figs. 94, 95) recovered from the Porticello wreck in the Straits of Messina, in natural size, may be a second example of original portraiture, perhaps also originating from North Africa or, as a second possibility, in Magna Graecia itself, a land of tyrants and strong individual rulers where portraiture could have been at home. From mainland Greece no original portrait is known. The literary sources mention several, which have anecdotal character and deserve little credence. The story that Pheidias included his and Perikles' portrait on the shield of the Athena Parthenos has been shown to be no earlier than the Hellenistic period, when such action could have been not only possible but also plausible. That Pheidias at Olympia made a statue of Pantarkes, a youth with whom he was in love, is probably a similar late invention of the local guides, accepted by Pausanias as in keeping with his own times, but both the athletic subject and the intent of portraiture seem alien to Pheidias' oeuvre. Pliny mentions (*HN* 34.88) that Nikeratos "represented Alkibiades and his mother Demarate performing a sacrifice by the light of torches," a description that brings to mind a painting rather than a sculptural group; nothing definite is otherwise known about the master, and his date within the Fifth century is set only through that of his more famous subject.

Kresilas

One master whose name is more than a mention in the literary sources is Kresilas of Kydonia, in Crete, who made statues of the "Olympian Perikles" and his father, Xanthippos, which Pausanias saw on the Athenian Akropolis, perhaps as personal dedications of either the individuals involved or of a private citizen after Perikles' death. While the statesman's father remains unrecognized or was not copied in Roman times, the portrait of Perikles has come down to us in Roman herms, the best known of which are those in the Vatican and in Berlin. Since no other sculptor is known to have made portraits of Perikles (although many are known to have existed), it has usually been assumed that these herms reproduce the head of Kresilas' statue. This may be a logical assumption, but it should be kept in mind that, had a likeness of Perikles not come down to the Romans, they would probably have invented one by the First century A.C., as they are likely to have created the portrait of Aspasia at that time (see ch. 9).

The Perikles of the Roman herms is, however, fully in keeping with what we expect from a Fifth century portrait. The statesman is represented as a warrior, and we know that Perikles, self-conscious about the peculiar shape of his head, tried to disguise it under a helmet, without nonetheless being able to escape the jokes of the playwrights. In fact, the herms show a surprising mass of hair through the eye cavities of the Corinthian helmet, though none should be visible at that level within a helmet pushed back above the forehead. Other distinctive features are not easy to single out. The eyes are large, the lids and eyebrows sharp as befits a bronze original. The beard hugs cheeks that betray prominent zygomatic bones, but the impression of age varies from replica to replica, that in the British Museum looking more romantic than the impassive one in the Vatican, that in Berlin more colorful. Beyond these comments I would hesitate to go. Whether Kresilas' style can be adequately gauged through this one work known solely from Roman copies is open to serious doubt.

To be sure, many other attributions to the master have been suggested, including the Velletri Athena, which Harrison has lately given to Alkamenes and which she therefore discusses in contrast to the Perikles. Kresilas is also known to have made a Demeter for Hermione. From the literary sources the Cretan sculptor seems to have been interested in unusual subjects with a certain realistic content: a wounded Amazon and a man collapsing because of his wounds, the *volneratus deficiens* (Pliny, *HN* 34.74-75). The question of the Ephesian Amazon is complex and involves other sculptors, including Pheidias and Polykleitos. I personally believe that the so-called Capitoline type may have been made by Kresilas, or at least within the Fifth century, and that it and a companion piece may have spurred the creation of similar types in later periods; but the issue is controversial and important criticism has been raised against my suggestion. Usually the so-called Lansdowne Amazon is attributed to Kresilas, while the Capitoline type is given to Polykleitos, but even these two positions can be reversed. In any case, a certain relationship between the two types is undeniable and some explanation for it should be found, if mine is not accepted.

Another major piece recently attributed to Kresilas is the so-called Protesilaos (figs. 119-122), known through a helmeted replica in New York and a headless one in London. This is an interesting composition in that the stance with one leg bent and one free has been exploited to throw the weight of the body back on the bent knee, in a reversal of the Polykleitan tradition. Like the Ares Borghese, the Protesilaos forms one continuous slanting line from head to toes, but the effect is entirely different: not a stationary but a highly precarious pose which will be momentarily shifted. Frel has noticed that the statue in New York shows a gash wound under the right armpit and has therefore suggested that the warrior is Kresilas' *volneratus*. This theory has started a controversy, since the replica in London could be taken for a Poseidon. The issue is complicated by the fact that the two statues do not correspond in all details: the large head and heavy drapery of the New York replica are more in keeping with a relatively early date, perhaps around 440, while the more lively folds of the British Museum copy compare well with the style of the late 430s. A bronze statuette of a wounded warrior (Amazon ?) from Bavai, which has equally been associated with Kresilas' *volneratus*, is entirely different in pose and general appearance, but there is some question as to its composition, not to mention its authenticity. I like Frel's explanation of the pose and the consequent dating of the "Protesilaos" in New York, but I would not presume to assess Kresilas' style on such a debatable basis. Finally, not even mentions in literary sources can be invoked for assigning to Kresilas the superb Diomedes, another favorite attribution of our handbooks. (See Appendix 7.2.)

SUMMARY

The picture emerging from this brief review of major masters is unsatisfactory at best. Although for Pheidias we would seem to have the original sculptures from the Parthenon, we cannot tell how much—if at all—the master contributed to their conception and execution. On the basis of all the other works, known only through Roman replicas, we must admit that we know very little about Pheidias' style. For both Agorakritos and Alkamenes we have more concrete evidence through original works and, were we to judge from the Nemesis and the Prokne respectively, we would have to accept that the two pupils of Pheidias had differing and distinctive styles. How much of this difference is attributable to chronological development and iconography, and how much to artistic personalities, is open to question. Were it established that Agorakritos stands for the "transparent drapery" on the Parthenon and that Alkamenes is responsible for the "heavy drapery" there, we would still not know to what an extent these renderings were part of the stylistic currents of the time, witness the subsequent difficulty in distinguishing Pheidias' oeuvre from his pupils' not only today but, apparently, also in antiquity. Attributions to the two masters not supported by literary sources remain subjective and open to disagreement. Kresilas appears even dimmer as an artistic personality, despite his unusual interest in realism and portraiture.

Perhaps the safest statement which can be made is that the masters of the Fifth century produced many cult images, often of colossal size and frequently in precious materials; these divine images may have established their reputations, especially since Pausanias listed them as a matter of course in his account. Undoubtedly, however, spurious works came to be attributed to the more familiar names through the years, probably out of ignorance as much as by intent. Other works listed by the literary sources, especially by Pliny, do not even command the credence of the local information given to Pausanias, since many of the statues mentioned had been moved to Rome or, in any case, away from their original settings. The anecdotal character of some of these works makes their authorship doubtful. Portraiture was probably created in the Fifth century, even on the Greek mainland, but we have few originals on which to base our comments. Without advocating a position of extreme skepticism, it would seem best to judge Classical sculptures on the basis of their iconography and style rather than by attributions to individual masters and in illustration of the literary sources.

1. *The Asklepios Giustini*. The type takes its name from a headless replica now in the Conservatori Museum, once in the Giustini Collection, while the head type is usually represented by a replica in Berlin. Both these pieces are illustrated in the most recent discussion of the matter by L. Beschi, *ASAtene* 47-48, n.s. 31-32 (1969-70) 101-107, figs. 13-14 on pp. 110-11. Previous opinions suggested that the type reflected the cult image in the Athenian sanctuary of Asklepios, after the cult was introduced to the city in 420 B.C. Such a statue, in gold and ivory, was stated by Pausanias (1.20.2) to have been made by Alkamenes. On the assumption that the sharpness of the rendering in several of the replicas truly reflected a chryselephantine original, and to reconcile some of the Peloponnesian stylistic traits that had been pointed out in the Giustini type, H. Heiderich (*Asklepios* [Diss. Freiburg 1966] 17-35) suggested that the original was by Kolotes and was the cult statue of the Asklepieion at Kyllene in Elis. Earlier, F. Poulsen (*ActArch* 8 [1937] 133) had opted for a Classicizing creation, while H. von Steuben (Helbig⁴, no. 1774) favored a Fourth century date to conform with the revised chronology of the second Temple of Dionysos in Athens. A major point in the discussion on chronology and location of the original is the similarity of the type with representations of the god in votive reliefs. Beschi reviews this material and suggests that a bronze original of ca. 370 lies behind the Giustini type. He would accept a Peloponnesian stylistic tradition and a location of the statue in Athens, probably as a votive offering rather than as a cult image in a period when the Asklepieion from private foundation became public property.

To some extent, the geometric patterns created by the himation folds on the Giustini type recall the Severe "Aspasia-Sosandra" type. But the material clings to the body, revealing the underlying anatomy as if transparent. The elongated and slender proportions, particularly of the legs, support a Fourth century chronology. Rather than a truly Classicizing work, the Asklepios Giustini could be considered a case of lingering Classical style.

2. *Diomedes Cumae/Munich*. Known only from three major replicas and the cast of a lost one in bust form (Dresden), this impressive figure has been identified as Diomedes with the Palladion because of the strongly contracted muscle of the (broken) left arm and the impression of action conveyed by the sharply turned head and the bent left leg held at a considerable distance from the right. Furtwängler attributed the original to Kresilas on the strength of resemblance between the Diomedes' head and those of the Velletri Athena, the Capitoline Amazon, the Perikles, and the Medusa Rondanini. Of all these works, the last is probably a Classicizing rendering that does not belong to the Fifth century; the Capitoline Amazon has been variously given to Kresilas or to Polykleitos; the portrait of Perikles is only tentatively assigned to the Cretan master, since many statues of the statesman existed in Athens, most of them helmeted; finally the Velletri Athena has recently been attributed to Alkamenes. Note further that no extant ancient source speaks of a Diomedes by Kresilas. The connection with the master must therefore remain doubtful (cf. M. Weber, *JdI* 91 [1976] 95-96).

The statue itself is best known through the replica from Cumae (now in Naples), which does not include the sword strap but retains the shoulder chlamys. The body rendering is quite close to that of the Doryphoros (cf. Hiller, pl. 3:4-5a), but the differences have been carefully analyzed by T. Lorenz, *Polyklet* (Wiesbaden 1972) 49. W.-H. Schuchhardt (*AntP* 1 [1962] 36-37) stresses the Polykleitan nature of the hair pattern (see his figs. 1-2 and pls. 28-29, esp. 29c, for the Dresden cast). The face, with its strong chin, highly placed mouth, and peculiar hairline above the creased forehead, recalls Severe works, specifically the Myronian Diskobolos Lancellotti. It has been said to express the pathos of the action, but this may be a subjective impression. The youthful beard is unusual, unless other statues had it rendered in paint; it may be closer to Roman rendering of the late Flavian, Trajanic, and Hadrianic periods. It occurs, in sparser form, on the head from Sperlonga, which has been attributed to a Theft-of-the-Palladion group in the grotto: see *AntP* 14 (1974) 38-40 and pls. 37-

40 on the Sperlonga fragments (B. Conticello) and 95-103 on the Roman replicas (B. Andreae). The subject is depicted on Attic Red Figure vases (F. Brommer, *Vasenlisten zur griechischen Heldensage*, 3rd ed. [Marburg 1973] 425), but sculptural representations are supposed to begin with a "famous creation by Kresilas" (see, e.g., Andreae, and *EAA*, s.v. Diomede [L. Rocchetti]).

The subject seems to have been popular with the inhabitants of the Tyrrhenian coast, since the best replica of the "Kresilas' Diomedes" was found at Cumae, and Sperlonga included the episode in its monumental repertoire. In addition, several Roman emperors had their portraits added to the Fifth century body type: see, e.g., H. G. Niemeyer, *Studien zur statuarischen Darstellung der römischen Kaiser* (Monumenta Artis Romanae 7, Berlin 1968) 54-59 and 108, no. 100, pl. 36 (Augustus from Otricoli in the Vatican, ca. 2 B.C.), no. 101, pl. 37:1 (Hadrian from Carthage in Tunis). It should be stressed, however, that the reconstruction of the "Kresilas' Diomedes" with the Palladion is tentative, since not even the more complete statue from the Grotto of the Sybil in Cumae retains the all-important idol in the left hand. [For a new replica recently found in Perge see *AJA* 84 (1980) 509.]

3. *The Kassel Apollo.* This type is named after the best replica in the Kassel Museum, but the most recent study (E. Schmidt, *AntP* 5, 1966) lists a total of two complete statues, five torsos, thirteen heads, and three statuettes. The Apollo (or rather its bronze prototype) has been attributed to Myron, Pythagoras, Kalamis, Kallimachos, Hegias, and especially Pheidias. Pausanias (1.24.8) mentions a bronze Apollo "opposite the temple" (i.e., the Parthenon), which was called Parnopios because it had freed the Athenians from the locusts, but its attribution to Pheidias seems a matter of hearsay (*legousi*). The other major identification of the type would see in it the Apollo Alexikakos by Kalamis, which Pausanias (1.3.4) saw in front of the Temple of Apollo Patroos; he was told that the epithet was acquired when the god stopped the plague in Athens during the Peloponnesian War, though the statement has been disputed on the basis of Kalamis' general chronology. Of the replicas of the Kassel type, only one torso and one head were found, not far from each other, in Athens, near the Olympieion, and seem to be of Ha-

drianic date. Schmidt, who has studied all replicas specifically from the point of view of their Roman chronology, suggests that a special interest in this type originated under Hadrian.

The composition has been hailed as the first epiphany of a divine figure portrayed in arrested motion, bow in one hand and laurel branch in the other (Karouzos). There is in fact a certain momentary aspect to the stance, which is perhaps caused by the strong slant in the hips and the pronounced turn of the head away from the bent leg, almost anticipating the movement in the Belvedere Apollo. The statue retains nonetheless several traits of Severe style, for instance the even alignment of the shoulders and the "dry" rendering of the groin-hip line, which contrasts with the "Classical" expanded ribcage. More specifically, the head, with its cubic structure and its braided hairstyle, seems more in keeping with a Severe than with a Fifth century date, which should definitely apply were this Apollo a replica of the Alexikakos.

The coiffure of the type is troublesome. Although it generally recalls that of the Erechtheion Karyatids, the braids do not encircle the head, as in the female figures, nor can the spiral locks be considered their unplaited termination. Thus the braids end abruptly without running under the mass of shorter locks that project over the temples. I know of no parallels for this arrangement, and although a Classical dating cannot rest solely on the coherence of a rendering, the illogical nature of the hairstyle should be noted. One replica of the body, in the Capitoline (Schmidt, pl. 16), has been completed with a head of the Tiber Apollo type, which may be a skillful restoration but nonetheless seems to agree with the terminations of long locks loose over the back of the torso. It is perhaps significant that a single head (in the Clemen collection, Schmidt, pls. 23-24) undoubtedly reproduces the Kassel Apollo but has the same mass of loose curls over the nape. It may suggest that there was some contamination between the Kassel and the Tiber types and that the two were the products of the same (Roman) ateliers. Except for the greater development of the upper torso and the different inclination of the head, the two types are indeed comparable and had been attributed to the same master by at least one scholar (E. Buschor; cf. J. Dörig, *JdI* 80 [1965] 232 and n. 410). J. Raeder

(*JdI* 93 [1978] 265-66) has recently suggested that spiral curls in paratactic arrangement are a Classicizing formula of Hadrianic/Antonine sculptors, but he accepts the Kassel Apollo as a genuinely Classical example. The lack of true parallels for the coiffure and the definite difference with Fifth century representations of Apollo in relief (e.g., the Parthenon East frieze, the Hephaisteion East frieze, some of the votive reliefs) may indicate that the Kassel Apollo is a Roman creation or, at best, a Classical work with a Roman hairstyle. For a presumed Hellenistic variant see J. Inan, *Roman Sculpture in Side* (Ankara 1975) 29-31, no. 4, pl. 12.

4. *The Pitcairn Nike with aegis in Philadelphia* (figs. 123, 124). This life-size statue, on loan to the University Museum (L-65-1), has been extensively discussed only by R. Carpenter in the collection of studies in honor of G. P. Oikonomos (*ArchEph* 1953-54, 41-55). Noting the strange differences in the form of attachment of head, arms, wings and feet, as well as the presence of red pigment on the drapery, Carpenter suggested that the statue copied a chryselephantine original: arms and feet would have been added in alabaster, and the head in stucco to simulate ivory, while the drapery was gilded and the wings were of gilded wood. The Philadelphia Nike comes from Cyrene, where a reproduction of the Olympia Zeus by Pheidias had been set up in Roman times; however, Carpenter argued that pose and style seemed more appropriate for the Victory on the hand of the Athena Parthenos. This position has been neither challenged nor generally accepted. Leipen (p. 35) underplays the differences between the Philadelphia statue and the Nike on the hand of the Varvakeion statuette, such as the lack of the rolled mantle around the waist and the addition of the aegis. Her reconstruction for the Ontario Museum, however, does not greatly resemble the Pitcairn Nike and seems closer to the Berlin statues, which are traditionally considered replicas of the Pheidian statue in Athens (see, e.g., Leipen, fig. 78). Today one further argument can be added to Carpenter's reluctance in associating the Philadelphia Nike with the Olympia Zeus: the molds recovered from the workshop area give indication of a chiton sleeve that is too small to belong to the Zeus and must therefore belong to the Victory on his hand (see G. Heiderich, *Asklepios* [Diss. Freiburg 1966] 30-

35, esp. 31-32, with attribution of the Olympia Nike to Kolotes). The bare arms of the Pitcairn statue are further proof that it could not have duplicated the Olympia Nike. On the other hand, the Berlin Nikai wear a sleeved garment, but they correspond neither to the Varvakeion replica nor to the Philadelphia Nike. The question of their "Pheidian" style is complex and their present appearance is more Roman than Greek. However, in common with the Pitcairn Nike they have the pose with both knees slightly bent, as if alighting. A similar rendering occurs on the large terracotta statues of Roman date found in 1956 in a well south of the Odeion of Herodes Atticus (cf. Travlos, *Pictorial Dictionary*, 364 fig. 468; Brouskari, 85, nos. 6476, 6476a), but these seem Severizing rather than Classical and, despite their findspot, cannot be used in connection with the Parthenos.

The connection of the Philadelphia Nike is perhaps equally tenuous. Stylistically, the statue should belong around 440-430, as surmised by Carpenter; its chronological position would have been clearer when the undercut edge of the overfold was still intact, forming a virtually straight line across the thighs. The exposed belt and the wide arch of the shallow kolpos are also in keeping with this date. The drapery of this marble figure has been given texture by a series of "short irregular strokes" which Carpenter (p. 51) considers "a familiar device of the copyists to reproduce the coldwork engraving of a metal prototype." However, they also appear on some supposed Greek marble originals, such as the "Nikeso" from Priene and the Fanciulla d'Anzio, but on none of the extant original bronzes. This texturing could be purely a chronological trait alien to the Fifth century and proper to later periods, yet this surmise need not affect the dating of the Nike, where the rendering may indeed have been added by the copyist. Certainly the drapery of the Philadelphia statue gives no hint of the transparency or nudity so typical of these flying figures after 425.

More suprising is the presence of the aegis on a Nike: were it not for the unsupporting legs, it would be tempting to suggest that the original was an Athena later transformed into a Victory by the addition of wings. Note, however, that such a type of winged and flying Minerva is known from the Roman world, although inspired by Classical types with transparent drapery: cf. specifically a statue from Bulla Regia with aegis and belted peplos, on which the wings were added in bronze: L. Savignoni, *Ausonia* 5 (1910) fig. 18 on p. 92. The Philadelphia Nike wears her aegis backward, as in the Velletri Athena, a trait which here could have no connection with the Birth of Erichthonios.

For another Nike type presumably from the late Fifth century see J. Inan, 43-47, no. 9, pl. 21; the Victory wears a peplos which she holds spread out with both hands while the material clings to the legs; a replica of the same type exists at Antioch in Pisidia. The prototype may be Roman, however.

5. *So-called Cherchel Demeter type*. It is mostly known through three replicas, one in Berlin and two from Cherchel (ancient Iol/Caesarea), Algeria. The figure has been considered a Demeter, and the presence of two identical images on the same spot has been explained in terms of the African cult of the Cereres, although there is no evidence that the statues were found in a religious context. The Berlin replica comes from Rome. An iconographic study of Demeter and Kore (A. Peschlow-Bindokat, *JdI* 87 [1972] 129-30) has stressed the uncertainty of the identification: Hera, Hestia, Leto, or Aphrodite are other possibilities. In the most extensive discussion of the type in recent years, J. Dörig (*JdI* 80 [1965] 241-53) has advocated that it reproduces the Aphrodite by Kalamis on the Athenian Akropolis, probably to be identified with the Sosandra. If this connection is accepted, the original could be dated around 450, on the evidence of the inscribed base from the Akropolis. The Cherchel type is usually placed in the 440s.

The Berlin replica has been given a chiton under the peplos (visible as buttoned sleeves on the upper arms), and her total appearance seems stylistically more advanced than the Cherchel replicas, which are usually considered the best. These two seem more Severe in many of their traits, and the total effect is somewhat eclectic. In particular, the density of the cloth, the sparse folds of the apoptygma, the monotonous effect of the catenaries echoing the neckline, and the uncertain modeling effect of the crossing folds in front contrast with the wide proportions of the figure, the rich and low kolpos, the clinging of the apoptygma over the stomach, and the elaboration of the short mantle over head and shoulders. The bent leg creates a peculiar triangular pattern on the proper left side, and

the strong fold descending from the knee seems unjustified, since the leg is forward rather than to the side. In some of these features the Cherchel statues resembles the so-called Müller Peplophoros (*Severe Style*, 133, fig. 167), which has been defined as a pastiche or an eclectic work. The rectangular panel of the apoptygma defined by the vertical folds descending from the breasts and the catenary between them, with two ridges crossing in the center, can be found in two of the bronze "dancers" from Herculaneum (*Severe Style*, figs. 170-71, extreme right), which are now recognized as Roman creations in Severe style.

The head of the type is known from the Berlin replica and one of the two from Cherchel (the second was completed with a cast of the head of the first statue). Again, the Berlin version is somewhat different, but both heads retain the undulating pattern of curls framing the forehead on either side of a pronounced central part. The effect of an "ogival canopy" is exaggerated on the Cherchel head, and the elaborate waves over the temples are fuller than traditional Fifth century renderings. The hairstyle recalls that of the so-called Lysimache (see ch. 9, p. 231, fig. 146) which at least K. Schefold considers Classicizing: *Die Bildnisse der antiken Dichter, Redner und Denker* (Basel 1943) 200, comments for p. 35. Note moreover that Dörig's attribution of the original to Kalamis was made on the basis of the similarity between the head of the Demeter and that of the Tiber Apollo, a replica of which also comes from Cherchel, which I consider a Roman creation.

One previous opinion is that the Cherchel statues are adaptations by a Roman sculptor from two different prototypes: P. Wuilleumier, *Musée d'Alger*, suppl. 47-48, as quoted by M. Leglay, *La Sculpture Antique du Musée Stéphan Gsell* (Algiers 1957) 10-13. More generally, the type is considered Pheidian and the standard comparison is with the peplophoros of the Great Eleusinian Relief or the Diotima (see ch. 6). Since the Berlin replica is stylistically more advanced and therefore less contradictory than the Cherchel statues, it is perhaps unnecessary to conclude that the type is a Roman creation in Classical style. The sculptor of the Algerian replicas should rather be held responsible for Severizing his work. The question deserves further attention.

6. *Peplophoros from Pergamon, Berlin Muse-*

um P 23. Ever since its discovery in the area of the Pergamon Library, this headless statue has been recognized as closely related to the Prokne and Itys, but the degree of relationship has been debated. The original publication (F. Winter, *AvP* 7 [Berlin 1908] 25-33, esp. 30-32, no. 23, pls. 6-7) considered it a copy of a work by the master who had made the Prokne; later publications stressed instead its character of adaptation, with the consequent problem that the removal of the child created for the rendering of folds along the right leg. Most recently, emphasis has been placed on the stylistic elements which mark the Pergamon piece as later than the Prokne; see especially M. Gernand, *AthMitt* 90 (1975) 23-24, pl. 7, and H. Knell, *AntP* 17 (1978) 15-16, figs. 11-14, with notes and bibliography. Schuchhardt, *Alkamenes,* 17, has summarized the controversy and finds the Pergamon piece too close to the Athenian one to be anything other than an intentional adaptation into a different personage. Since the Pergamon figure raises a tip

of the short mantle above the right shoulder, she is probably Aphrodite or Hera. The statue was found together with the so-called Myronian Athena (*Severe Style,* figs. 159-60), which was itself considered a copy: hence Winter's label for the peplophoros; Gernand argues that both figures are Hellenistic creations after Classical prototypes. While a true Fifth century work is hard to visualize behind the Athena, the peculiarity of the folds over the right ankle makes it plausible that the peplophoros, although by no means a copy, is a learned quotation of the Prokne. The Pergamene sculptor has increased the metallic character of the rendering and altered some elements of the costume, e.g., the length of the shoulder mantle, and the pattern of kolpos and overfold. It is interesting that the peplophoros type is repeatedly used in Hellenistic and Roman times to convey the same message of established respectability and religious importance which—on a slightly different level—imbues contemporary Archaistic statuary.

FOR PAGE 159

For a criticism of Plutarch's statement and a discussion of Pheidias' role in the Parthenon see N. Himmelmann in *Festagabe J. Straub (Bonn-Jbb* BH 39, 1977) 67-90.

FOR PAGE 161

No recent book devoted entirely to Pheidias exists; the most useful summary remains G. Becatti, *Problemi Fidiaci* (Milan and Florence 1951); recent but superficial, B. Gavela, *Altertum* 19 (1973) 207-21.

For some of the literary sources on Pheidias see F. Preisshofen, *JdI* 89 (1974) 50-69.

On the Athena Parthenos, see especially the book by Leipen, which lists all replicas known up to 1971; for an additional statuette in Konya see R. Fleischer, *ÖJh* 49 (1971) 68-72.

Gold and ivory statues from Delphi: remains of three almost life-size images were published in a preliminary report, *BCH* 63 (1939) 86-106; see also E. Vanderpool, *Archaeology* 2 (1949) 66-67; J. Boardman, *Greek Sculpture, the Archaic Period* (London 1978) 77, fig. 127. A publication of the total finds is announced as imminent by P. Amandry in an article where he discusses a silver bull from the same deposit, which may give some clues as to the chryselephantine technique: *BCH*, suppl. 4 (1977) 273-93. Other comments in Leipen, with bibliography.

FOR PAGE 162

For the molds of the Zeus at Olympia see E. Kunze in *Neue deutsche Ausgrabungen in Mittelmeergebiet und im vordern Orient* (Berlin 1959) 277-91; also A. Mallwitz and W. Schiering, *Die Werkstatt des Pheidias in Olympia* (*OlForsch* 5, 1964).

On repairs to the Parthenon and the suggestion that the cult image may have been entirely replaced in Roman times, see, e.g., J. Binder, in *Festschrift Brommer*, 29-31; W. B. Dinsmoor, Jr., *Hesperia* 43 (1974) 132-55, esp. p. 147; Travlos, *Pictorial Dictionary*, 444. Cf. also A. Frantz, *AJA* 83 (1979) 395-401, esp. n. 54.

FOR PAGE 163

Athena Parthenos as a cult image: even Leipen

(p. 17) calls it "a splendid votive offering rather than a cult image." See her n. 2 on p. 21, for additional bibliography; as a work of art, F. Schiff, *AntK* 16 (1973) 4-44 (a poetic interpretation).

On the inventories see, G. Donnay, *BCH* 92 (1968) 21-28.

FOR PAGE 164

Nike on the hand of the Parthenos: for a possible identification see Appendix to this chapter. On the question of the support under Athena's hand see H. Williams, *Summaries of Papers Delivered at the 76th Meeting of the AIA, 1974*: relief from near Adana, Turkey, showing no column, Nike holds a wreath in her right hand, a palm branch in her left.

Gods hostile or at least aloof: suggested by P. von Blackenhagen in a series of lectures on the Parthenon, of forthcoming publication (The Mellon Lectures); cf. supra, ch. 2, n. 11.

FOR PAGE 165

Latest discussion of the Parthenos' base (critical of the Neo-Attic reliefs): W.-H. Schuchhardt, in *Wandlungen, Festschrift E. Homann-Wedeking* (Waldsassen/Bayern 1975) 120-30, pls. 26-27. Possible attribution: J. Dörig, *Art Antique* (Geneva and Mainz 1975) no. 243. For the gesture of lifting mantle associated with Demeter and Kore see A. Peschlow-Bindokat, *JdI* 87 (1972) 60-157, esp. figs. 34-35. For the Frejus Aphrodite see ch. 8.

Centauromachy in Madrid: Leipen, p. 30, n. 58, figs. 73-75; on the Pasquino helmet: the most explicit description remains the original publication: B. Schweitzer, *Das Original der sogennanten Pasquino-Gruppe* (*AbhSäh* 43:4, 1938) 1-164, esp. pp. 104-15 on the Centauromachy and helmet. On the Sperlonga replica, see *AntP* 14 (1974) 36-38 (B. Conticello) and 87-95, esp. 92 (B. Andreae).

For an actual find of Tyrrhenian shoes see *Deltion* 28 (1973) 116-37 and English summary on pp. 252-54, pls. 68-81.

Amazonomachy of the shield: besides Leipen, pp. 41-50, see T. Hölscher and E. Simon,

AthMitt 91 (1976) 115-48; E. B. Harrison has refined her initial suggestion in *Hesperia* 35 (1966) 107-33, and an *AJA* article by her is forthcoming: cf. *AntK* 21 (1978) 114, summary of a lecture delivered in June 1978. The Peiraeus reliefs have just been republished by Th. Stephanidou-Tiveriou, *Neo-Attika—Hoi anaglyphoi Pinakes apo to Limani tou Peiraia* (Athens 1979) 113-38.

FOR PAGE 166

On Assyrian city reliefs and their influence on later Greek and Lycian art see W.A.P. Childs, *The City-Reliefs of Lycia* (Princeton 1978) esp. p. 65 for a mention of the shield, but with skepticism.

The theory that the battle did not take place on the Akropolis is by Hölscher and Simon.

Kenan Erim has shown photographs of the sarcophagus at the Seventy-eighth and Seventy-ninth Meetings of the AIA; a brief mention is printed in *AJA* 80 (1976) 277-78; it will be published by Harrison in *AJA*.

Gorgoneion from Cyrene: J. Floren, *Boreas* 1 (1978) 36-67, with discussion of the entire composition.

FOR PAGE 167

Athena, fold motif on right side: cf. F. Noack, *JdI* 45 (1930) 198-217.

Olympian Zeus: for the molds see bibl. for p. 162. The story of the stolen locks is in Lucian, *Timon*, 4 (SQ 750); Lucian, *Iupp. Trag.* 25 (SQ 751).

FOR PAGE 168

On the throne of Zeus: J. Fink, *Des Thron des Zeus in Olympia* (Munich 1967).

On the Ephesos groups of Sphinxes and Theban Youths see F. Eichler, *ÖJh* 45 (1960) 5-22; Fink, 57-64.

On the Niobid frieze, besides Becatti and Fink, see also G. Hafner, *Ein Apollon-Kopf in Frankfurt* (Baden-Baden 1962) 33-35 and reconstruction on pp. 40-41, figs. 13-14; cf., however, the new suggestion by G. V. Gentili, *BdA* 54 (1974) 101-105. References to the style and composition of the Niobid frieze occur throughout C. A. Picón, *AJA* 82 (1978) 47-81, esp. 61 and n. 50.

Kneeling Nike near leg of throne: K. Stähler, *Boreas* 1 (1978) 68-86, pls. 11-13; cf. *Severe Style*, p. 73, no. 9.

FOR PAGE 169

Athena Promachos: the most extensive recent discussion is by E. Mathiopoulos, *Zur Typologie der Göttin Athena im fünften Jahrhundert vor Christus* (Bonn 1968) 7-47; she includes the ancient sources, reflections in the minor arts, and a study of the bronze statuette of Athena in New York (Athena Elgin) as a contemporary echo of the Promachos. See also W. Gauer, *Weihgeschenke aus den Perserkriegen* (*IstMitt*—BH 2, 1968) 103-105; on the problem of Parrhasios making the drawings for the shield see his n. 483. For the base of the Promachos on the Akropolis see the extensive bibliography in Travlos, *Pictorial Dictionary*, 55. For the dates here quoted see Becatti, 165, Mathiopoulos 11.

Athena Medici: see G. Despinis, *Akrolitha* (*Deltion* suppl. 21, 1975), which includes colossal "akrolithic" replica in Saloniki. But see also M. Gernand, *AthMitt* 90 (1975) 37-40.

FOR PAGE 170

Marathon bronze group: Kron, 215-27; note that the location of the group along the Sacred Way has been disputed in recent years; the pertinent bibliography is given by Kron, nn. 1037-38.

Athena Lemnia: the Dresden statues, or rather, a composite cast, are illustrated in all general books on Greek sculpture and Pheidian art, but the Athena type itself is not extensively published and analyzed. Besides Becatti, see most recently G. Gualandi, *Carrobbio* 2 (1976) 205-24, on the Bologna head. The Karyatid of Kriton and Nikolaos, usually considered a Roman adaptation of the Lemnia, is discussed by H. von Steuben in Helbig[4], no. 3218.

FOR PAGE 171

The Bologna head is often compared with the "Anadoumenos Farnese," generally considered a copy of a work by Pheidias; it has, however, been clearly recognized as a Classicizing adaptation of Polykleitos' Diadoumenos by Zanker, 13-14, no. 11. In general, Classicizing renderings of the Diadoumenos increase its similarity to the "Lemnia": for good illustrations cf. Zanker, pls. 12-15, and the illustrations to an article by H. Marwitz, *AntP* 6 (1967) 31-36, pls. 15-21.

Agorakritos: the major work is now by Despinis, after the identification of the Nemesis. For a review of the book see, e.g., J. M. Cook in *JHS* 93 (1973) 264-65. For a detail of the Nemesis' diadem—the Nikai fighting stags mentioned in the sources—see E. Simon, *AntK* 3 (1960) 3-26, esp. 17-19, using the Panaguriste Treasure for comparison.

FOR PAGE 173

On the Nemesis' base, besides Despinis, see Dohrn, 30, and Robertson, 352. The basic reconstruction remains at present L. Pallat, *JdI* 9 (1894) 1-22; good illustrations in K. Schefold, in *R. Boehringer, Eine Freundesgabe* (Tübingen 1957) 543-72. Just appeared: B. G. Kallipolitis, *ArchEph* 1978, 1-90, pls. 1-32.

Dresden Zeus: cf. ch. 8; for illustration see also *Severe Style*, fig. 20.

Athena Hope-Farnese: for an illustration see Lippold, *Handbuch*, pl. 66:4. The type has been discussed in all its ramifications by E. Mathiopoulos, *Zur Typologie der Göttin Athena im fünften Jahrhundert vor Chr.* (Bonn 1968) 48-69, 102-108.

On the Eleusis Demeter see Appendix 5:1.

FOR PAGE 174

Alkamenes: the most recent work is by W.-H. Schuchhardt, *Alkamenes* (*BerlWinckProg* vol. 126, 1977; edited posthumously by R. Preisshofen-Kabus, who completed footnotes and bibl.). An important study on the style of Alkamenes centers on his cult statues for the Hephaisteion: E. B. Harrison, *AJA* 81 (1977) 137-78, 265-87, 411-26.

For Alkamenes' influence on the Erechtheion Karyatids (Kore C, probably by a pupil) cf. Lauter, *AntP* 16, and here ch. 5.

On the new dating of the Temple of Dionysos in Athens, see Travlos, *Pictorial Dictionary*, 537.

Hermes Propylaios: Schuchhardt, *Alkamenes*, 30-33; E. B. Harrison, *Agora* 11 (Princeton 1965) 86-98, 122-24; D. Willers, *JdI* 82 (1967) 37-109; id., *Zu den Anfängen der archaistischen Plastik in Griechenland* (*AthMitt* BH 4, 1975) 33-47; A. Hermary, *BCH* 103 (1979) 137-49, who reaches conclusions opposite to Willers's on the basis of a Delian herm dated 341/40.

Hekate: Schuchhardt, *Alkamenes*, 27-30; see also Harrison's discussion in *Agora* 11 and, for the question of Archaistic sculpture, see *Archaic Style*, ch. 11.

FOR PAGE 175

On the Aphrodite of Frejus see ch. 8; Schuchhardt does not discuss the Aphrodite in the Gardens.

Prokne and Itys; the official publication is now by H. Knell, *AntP* 17 (1978) 9-19; Schuchhardt, *Alkamenes*, 9-22; Adam, *Technique*, 89-92.

FOR PAGE 176

Hephaistos and Athena Hephaistia: Schuchhardt, *Alkamenes*, 37-48, the Athena type here favored is the Cherchel Athena, and this theory has been recently repeated by W. Fuchs, *Boreas* 1 (1978) 32-35, pls. 7-8.

On the possible confusion between Hephaistos and Odysseus see, e.g., B. Freyer-Schauenburg, *BonnJbb* 177 (1977) 185-97, esp. 186.

On the Velletri Athena see E. B. Harrison, *AJA* 81 (1977) 150-55 and 164-74; a list of replicas of the type is given on pp. 175-78. This Athena has also been discussed recently by E. Berger, *AntK* 17 (1974) 131-36, and G. Traversari, *Sculture del V° e IV° Secolo del Museo Archeologico di Venezia* (Venice 1973) nos. 16-17, pp. 44-47.

On the base for the Hephaisteion statues see E. B. Harrison, *AJA* 81 (1977) 265-87; F. Brommer, *Hephaistos* (Mainz 1978) 45-46.

FOR PAGE 178

Ares Borghese: A monograph is forthcoming in *AntP* (by B. Freyer-Schauenburg); see also Schuchhardt, *Alkamenes*, 33-37; T. Lorenz, *Polyklet* (Wiesbaden 1972) 49-52; an earlier contribution by B. Freyer is in *JdI* 77 (1962) 212-26. For the statue as stock body for Roman emperors and in group with Aphrodite type, see Freyer, p. 214, nn. 7-8, and Bieber, *Ancient Copies*, 43-45, figs. 107-109.

FOR PAGE 179

On the concept of historical portraits, see Hölscher, *Historienbilder*, 207-11; related works are D. Pandermalis, *Untersuchungen zu den klassischen Strategenköpfen* (Diss. Freiburg 1969), and, more recently, B. Dontas, in *Festschrift Brommer*, 79-92.

Themistokles from Ostia: *Severe Style*, 99-100,

108, fig. 137; for recent bibliography see J. Klein, *Untersuchungen zur Chronologie der attischen Kunst von Peisistratos bis Themistokles* (*IstMitt* BH 8, 1973) 133-42; H. Hiller, *Ionische Grabreliefs der ersten Hälfte des 5. Jahrhunderts v. Chr.* (*IstMitt* BH 12, 1975) 65-67. For Harrison's theory see *Abstracts of Papers Presented at the 79th AIA Meeting, 1977*, 17.

Bronze head from Cyrene: latest discussion in L. Beschi, *ASAtene* 34-35 (1972-73) 501-502, where it is attributed to Amphion of Knossos; see also G.M.A. Richter, *The Portraits of the Greeks* (London 1965) 104-105, figs. 453-55.

FOR PAGE 180

For the "Philosopher" from the Straits of Messina see ch. 5.

On the portrait of Pheidias see F. Preisshofen, *JdI* 89 (1974) 50-69.

I do not know a monograph on Kresilas; see, however, the entry in the *EAA*, s.v. Kresilas (P. Orlandini).

Perikles: a study of its setting and its significance has been made by T. Hölscher, *WürzJbb* n.s. 1 (1975) 187-218; cf. also A. Raubitschek, *ArchCl* 25-26 (1973-74) 620-21, on the inscription (perhaps the statue was dedicated by Perikles' son).

For the various replicas see G.M.A. Richter, *Portraits of the Greeks*, 102-104, figs. 429-47.

FOR PAGE 181

On the Ephesian Amazon see B.S. Ridgway, *AJA* 78 (1974) 1-17; also *AJA* 80 (1976) 82; a more recent study of all four types of Amazons, with lists of replicas, is by M. Weber, *JdI* 91 (1976) 29-96; she attributes the Mattei Amazon to Kresilas. See also Appendix 9:5.

Protesilaos in New York: attributed to Kresilas by J. Frel, *BMMA* 39 (1970) 170-77; rebuttal by E. Langlotz, *AA* 1971, 427-42; rebuttal by Frel, *AA* 1973, 120-21; rebuttal by Langlotz, *AA* 1977, 84-86.

Wounded warrior from Bavai: illustrated in G.M.A. Richter, *Sculpture and Sculptors*, figs. 127, 625, p. 235 and n. 151. The pastiche theory is mentioned by P. Orlandini in *EAA*, s.v. Kresilas. The official publication of the bronze is G. Faides-Feytmans, *Recueil des Bronzes de Bavai* (*Gallia* suppl. 8, 1957) no. 104, pp. 69-71, pls. 24-25, where the piece is called an Amazon, later changed into a lamp support; see also Weber, *JdI* 91 (1976) 89-94.

For a comparison of the New York Protesilaos with the Marsyas "by Myron" see R. Carpenter, *MAAR* 18 (1941) 5-18.

CHAPTER 8

Copies of Fifth Century Works

THE important sculptors reviewed in the previous chapter had one feature in common: they were all known to have made at least one cult statue or divine image each. We come now to consider another situation: divine images of some artistic importance that cannot be connected with specific sculptors, and the unusual case of a most famous sculptor who probably never made a cult statue: Polykleitos. In all cases we shall be dealing exclusively with copies, and it is therefore essential to define what is meant by that term.

Strictly speaking, a *copy* is an identical reproduction, obtained through mechanical means, of an original creation which was made in only one exemplar. Such accurate duplication was rare in ancient times; more often the same original was copied only along general lines, more or less mechanically, and in different periods, according to the stylistic and technical preferences of the time. Therefore, we may have several *replicas* of the same statue, each of them distinguished by its own peculiarities despite the fact that they all go back to the same prototype. For instance, one replica may simplify some details, one may omit one or more, one may introduce a form of support that did not exist in the original, and still others may also use supporting elements but of different shapes and positioning, according to the individual requirements of their medium. While all these works are regarded as *copies* insofar as they depend from the same prototype, they are called *replicas* when considered in their individuality; the two terms are basically interchangeable, but *replica* is—or should be—used in a more restrictive sense than *copy*. For instance, among the many copies of the Athena Parthenos, we should speak about the replica in the Louvre or the one from Pergamon, to suggest two specific versions and technical renderings after the same original. Considerable difference and variation, especially in scale, may occur in fact from replica to replica.

It used to be taken for granted that reproduction of Greek originals started during the Hellenistic period, more specifically during the last century before Christ, at the behest of a Roman clientele who could either not afford or not find Greek original sculptures on the market, yet wanted to own their own pieces at a time when statuary had become mainly decorative and inspirational. Somewhat the same phenomenon is observable today, when museum shops make brisk sales of reproductions from the famous originals in their collections. Similarly, such reproductions in ancient times were not all in the same medium as the original, for comparable economic reasons, nor of the same size: bronze or chryselephantine statues were copied in cheaper material, usually marble, and colossal scale could be brought down to statuette format.[1] Since, moreover, many of these pieces were made for

---

[1] Not all bronze originals were translated into marble copies. For a bronze copy of a bronze original see C. Mattusch, *AJA* 82 (1978) 101-104. In the case of recasts, total duplication was possible. Of

an architectural setting, the proper finish of their backs was often neglected and mirror images were created in order to produce a balanced effect on either side of a pool, for instance, or at the top of a flight of stairs. The Romans seem to have continued their love of Greek copies for at least four centuries, certainly down to the time of Constantine, though the greatest period for such copying may have been the Second century A.C., under the Antonine emperors. Because of this historical phenomenon, "copies" has usually been synonymous with *Roman* copies—meaning reproductions of Greek originals made for Roman patrons, or at least during the period of Roman political supremacy, regardless of the nationality of the sculptors who actually produced such copies. Today it seems obvious that the meaning of our terminology should be expanded.

CULT STATUES AND THEIR COPIES

Attention has been drawn in recent years to groups of marble works, usually of modest size, which were undoubtedly made during the Classical or Hellenistic period for Greeks and in Greek marble, in imitation or more or less faithful reproduction of larger Greek originals.[2] Single pieces have also been found, not so modest in size, which themselves stood as cult images in local shrines but imitated a more famous prototype elsewhere. Some works, because of peculiar circumstances, seem to have had "doubles" that can be inferred, if not materially proved. Some major statues were "copied" in more or less contemporary reliefs, and finally even reliefs themselves are known in more than one replica, as we have already discussed, or make use of single figures that occur in a variety of contexts but seem

special interest for the history of copying are also the plaster casts found at Baiae: *AA* 1974, 631-35; *AJA* 74 (1970) 296-97; *AntK* 21 (1978) 108-10.

[2] A list of works that can be considered contemporary copies of famous originals is given by S. Karouzou, *JHS* 92 (1972) 68 n. 26, and forms the basis for the following:

a. Grimani Statuettes, Venice: R. Kabus-Jahn, *AntP* 11 (1972); G. Traversari, *Sculture del V° e IV° Secolo del Museo Archeologico* (Venice 1973); S. Karouzou, *AthMitt* 82 (1967) 158-69;

b. Peiraeus Maiden, Athens Nat. Mus. 176: S. Karouzou, *AthMitt* 82 (1967) 158-69;

c. Frejus Aphrodite, small head, Athens Nat. Mus. 3569: S. Karouzou, *AthMitt* 89 (1974) 151-72;

d. Frejus Aphrodite, limestone head in Conservatori Museum, Inv. 2646 (less than life-size): E. La Rocca, *ASAtene* 34-35 (1972-73) 419-50.

e. Athena Velletri type, statuette, Athens Nat. Mus. 4486: S. Karouzou, *AntP* 12 (1973) 37-45, pls. 6-7; E. B. Harrison, *AJA* 81 (1977) p. 153 fig. 12, p. 150 n. 64.

f. Hekataion in the British School in Athens: S. Karouzou, *JHS* 92 (1972) 68; F. Eckstein, *AntP* 4 (1965) 27-36.

g. Cybele from Moschato, early Fourth century replica of Agorakritos' statue for the Agora Metroon (life-size): V. Papachristodoulos, *ArchEph* 1973, 189-217, esp. p. 202.

h. Female figure Akr. 1310: see here, ch. 5, bibl. for p. 114.

i. Aphrodite in Berlin from Tarquinia (South Italy?): see here, ch. 5, bibl. for p. 116.

j. Barberini Suppliant, Louvre, as marble copy of contemporary bronze original: S. Karouzou, *AntK* 13 (1970) 34-47.

k. Group in Kos of seven statuettes, Fourth century: R. Kabus-Preisshofen, *AntP* 15 (1975) 31-64.

l. Aphrodite from Daphni, Athens Nat. Mus. 1604: A. Delivorrias, *AntP* 8 (1968) 19-31; S. Karouzou, *Catalogue*, 96-97.

m. Statue from near Olympieion, Athens Nat. Mus. 4762, A. Delivorrias, *AntP* 9 (1969) 7-13 (but see also Delivorrias, pp. 168-69).

Not all items listed are undisputed Greek work; in each case, the authors quoted in the bibliography are responsible for making the suggestion that the piece be considered "a contemporary copy." For Greek copies of reliefs see S. Karouzou, *ArchEph* 1956, 154-80; V. M. Strocka, *JdI* 94 (1979) 143-73.

dependent on a single prototype or model. It is, to be sure, very difficult to distinguish between categories and to determine the exact date in which a replica was made. By and large, we seem able to distinguish a Roman copy from one made during the Greek period because of technical features; however, when the copy was made in Greek marble and during the First century A.C., before the introduction of distinctive carving mannerisms, discrimination is somewhat more difficult. It is very difficult indeed to decide when a Greek work is a true original or a more or less contemporary copy, and complete certainty is impossible; probabilities increase, however, when more than one piece is found and the group appears technically homogeneous but without stylistic or chronological coherence. It is nonetheless still hard to assess the correct geographical affiliations of the styles, especially when the pieces were removed from their original setting during the Renaissance or later. A case in point is that of the so-called Grimani statuettes.

The Grimani Group

These ten marble pieces in Venice had been recognized as Greek originals by Furtwängler, but they had received little attention since, despite the fact that four among the ten were entirely preserved, a rare occurrence. Only one figure, for instance, the so-called Hera, was illustrated in that great photographic catalogue of Greek originals, the book by Lullies and Hirmer. In recent years, however, the statuettes have attracted interest from many quarters and have even been fully published as a group, with ample commentary on stylistic parallels and possible identification. Given the early arrival of the figures in Venice, probably during the Sixteenth century, it is impossible to prove that they came from a single site, but their technical similarity, the use of the same type of marble, the comparable dimensions and, above all, the fact that each statuette can be connected with a famous cult statue, either through reproduction in votive reliefs or through Roman copies in the round, lend a high degree of probability to the assumption.

R. Kabus-Jahn believes that the Grimani pieces all represent either Demeter or Kore (since this is the conjectured identity of their parallels), that they therefore derive from an Eleusinian sanctuary, and that they were made within one generation from their prototypes, approximately between 420 and 360 B.C. The way for this solution had been paved by S. Karouzou when she published a comparable statuette, probably representing Kore, from the Peiraeus (fig. 125) as another contemporary variant. She considered the original of its Grimani counterpart a cult image for the Thesmophorion at Peiraeus, made presumably by an Argive sculptor working in Athens.

On the strength of this undoubtedly Attic figure, Kabus-Jahn attributed the entire Grimani group to the same sanctuary, which she therefore localized in Attica. After her careful publication, however, L. Beschi made a thorough investigation of Venetian archives and documents and reached a different conclusion. Historical circumstances indicate that the most probable source for the Grimani pieces is the island of Crete, which in the Sixteenth century was under Venetian control, while no contact, except for a single raid in 1464, can be documented between Venice and the Peiraeus. Even the Grimani label is a misnomer (albeit a convenient one), since the statuettes entered the Venice Museum from various collections, but this does not affect their original provenience from the Aegean island; Beschi suggests that they came specifically from Knossos. In recent years other votive deposits and groups of statuettes have been found at that site, although not all have been published; this abundance of finds makes Beschi's suggestion plausible.

The Cretan provenience is important on many counts. On the one hand it explains, as Beschi pointed out, that mixture of Attic and island Ionic traits which Furtwängler had already noticed. Yet it is probably risky to attribute a chronological value to these stylistic differences and to assume that Attic influence spread to the island toward the end of the Fifth century, supplanting the previous Cycladic *koine*, since some of the Grimani figures with Ionic features seem to me later than the Atticizing ones. As a second point, the group documents beyond doubt the diffusion of Attic styles and motifs over a wide area, and this very consideration raises an important question: did the Grimani statuettes reproduce cult images standing on Cretan soil, in the very sanctuary in which the smaller replicas were presumably dedicated, or did they imitate more or less freely some important statues in Athens? Since Kabus-Jahn assumed a Peiraeus provenience, correlation with Attic reliefs presented no problem for her; but how are such similarities to be explained once a Knossian origin is accepted for the statuettes? Given the technical similarities over a span of circa sixty years, the workshop that produced the Grimani marbles was local; it seems logical, therefore, that it reproduced local statues to satisfy the demands of local worshipers. In that case, influence from Athens must have extended to the Cretan prototypes themselves, and the Attic votive reliefs must be imitating other statues elsewhere. In other words, certain major types probably occurred in more than one version, in more than one place, made by more than one master, and perhaps representing more than one deity. This point can be best exemplified through the problem of the Kore Albani and the so-called Abbondanza among the Grimani statuettes.

The Abbondanza (Kabus-Jahn, no. 1) has been considered the earliest figure within the Venetian group and dated to ca. 420. It represents a young woman, probably Kore, standing with her weight on her left leg, the right slightly trailing. She wears a long-sleeved chiton with overfold and a mantle draped over the left shoulder and around the hips; the mantle is folded double so as to form a triangular apron in front. The general pattern is similar to that of the Velletri Athena except that a thin chiton replaces Athena's heavier peplos; even the mannerism of having some folds of the undergarment bend over at the point of contact with the mantle is repeated in both types. The Abbondanza finds another replica within the same Grimani group, but this latter (Kabus-Jahn, no. 10) is greatly simplified and seems later; it is also headless and of lesser quality. Equally simpler is another headless figure in Athens, which was at first published as a cult image but has now been reclassified by the same author as pedimental and tentatively attributed to the Hephaisteion. Finally, the Peiraeus statuette already mentioned (fig. 125) repeats the same general schema in reverse stance and is responsible for the divine identification of the entire group on the basis of a comparison with a contemporary votive relief to the Eleusinian goddess. All four statuettes were made during the Greek period, three of them probably still within the Fifth century.

By contrast, the Kore Albani is a Roman copy of large scale. Its similarity with the Grimani Abbondanza is undoubted, but differences exist in the stance, more restful in the former, more chiastic in the latter. Both figures retain the original heads, but these are not alike: the Kore Albani wears a sakkos, which imparts a touch of severity to the rather heavy face; the Grimani statuette has soft, rounded waves gathered into a simplified chignon high over the nape, and the shape of her face seems different, with different proportions to its features. Finally, the chiton of the smaller marble has fewer folds with wide, flat ridges, like ribbon drapery but without its transparency. The Kore Albani has instead a series of closely spaced folds ("vermicelli" drapery) which are equally opaque but form a dense and calligraphic pattern all over the chest.[3]

It is difficult to decide whether any chronological value should be attached to such differences. Since the many-ridged chiton with short overfold and the doubled mantle appear on a figure of the Parthenon metopes (S 19, fig. 2) we could assume that the Kore Albani, with her almost cubic appearance and her sober headdress, reflects an earlier prototype than the Grimani piece, or that the latter has been modernized in keeping with the style of her own period of manufacture. But both statues show the same mannerism of folds bending over in contact with the himation, which seems to appear only around 420. By contrast, neither the supposedly pedimental statue nor the Peiraeus maiden retain this detail, although stylistically they seem definitely later. Finally, one replica of the Kore Albani type, in the Villa Doria Pamphilj, though extensively restored, shows in her original portions an adherence to the same general drapery pattern together with a slipped-strap effect over the left breast, which recalls Figure M of the Parthenon East pediment, and a different arrangement of the mantle along the left side.[4] The chiton is here rendered in yet a third manner, halfway between that of the Kore Albani and those of the Fifth century statuettes: a copyist's variant, a pastiche, or a different prototype?

In summary, and given the long stylistic life of this general type, within which both the chiton and the peplos variants should be included, we can assume that the *drapery schema* originated early in the Fifth century and that it was copied and imitated over and over again with modifications, for both statuary in the round and in relief, for cult images of Kore and also other personages, both in Attica and elsewhere. If this position is correct, it could explain why it is so difficult to pinpoint the exact prototype and, incidentally, its sculptor. The main feature is the schema of the two garments, each setting off the other in its contrasting lines: vertical the chiton, horizontal the mantle, and also oblique in its triangular apron.[5]

Each successive phase introduced its peculiar mannerisms or stylistic traits, such as the ribbon drapery in the 430s, the bending folds in the 420s, the adhering and transparent cloth in the 410s. The Velletri Athena type changed the chiton into the peplos probably because the latter had been Athena's dress par excellence. Yet the system of contrasting

[3] It is difficult to parallel this precise rendering of the chiton in Classical originals, though it occurs in other Roman copies, e.g., a replica of Agorakritos' Nemesis in Albania (Despinis, pl. 43). On a Greek original, perhaps the closest rendering is that of the seated goddess in Parthenon metope N 32 (figs. 3-5), but there with a Lingering Severe effect as against the very Classical appearance of the pattern on the Kore Albani. The dense spacing of the folds in the latter is almost Archaistic and may have been introduced by the copyist, who nonetheless retained the stylistic trait of the bending folds.

[4] This modest piece forms a link between the Kore Albani type and that of the Hera Borghese or the

Aphrodite Doria, which in their lively and wind-blown effect are related rather to the original Aphrodite from the Athenian Agora. In these latter pieces, the triangular pattern of the doubled mantle is greatly underplayed (cf. Appendix 8:6).

[5] Basically, this drapery schema occurs also on the Nemesis of Rhamnous, where, however, the chiton is belted just below the overfold, thus creating a more complex system of bending folds, and the mantle lacks the triangular apron. The similarity with the general type is so strong that Despinis (pp. 190-92) has eventually commented on all the monuments that have been discussed so far in this chapter.

folds between upper and lower garment was retained; this may explain why the aegis was made so short or even reversed—so that its horizontal accent could not disturb or cover the vertical lines of the torso.[6] The aegis was entirely eliminated in the statuette Akr. 1310, (figs. 89, 90), although the peplos was retained. The sculptor of the Peiraeus maiden utilized the chiton but reversed the stance, so that the triangular apron adhered to the raised left thigh and some of the contrast was toned down. In this last piece scholars have seen traces of Agorakritos' style; the Grimani statuette has been atttributed to an Argive bronze sculptor active in Athens; the Velletri Athena has been given either to Kresilas or, more recently, to Alkamenes, the Kore Albani to Kalamis or to the Pheidian circle, the Parthenon South metope obviously to Pheidias.

This wealth of attributions convinces me that we should study styles rather than sculptors, and that even the so-called great masters adopted and elaborated current motifs and patterns without specifically striving for originality in our sense of the word. If specific works were copied, as they undoubtedly were, even during the same generation, it was probably because of their religious significance as cult images rather than because of their artistic value; but the identity of the type would change from sanctuary to sanctuary and from imitation to imitation. Regional boundaries were easily crossed.

Both the Grimani Abbondanza and the Peiraeus maiden have been compared, either directly or indirectly, with the so-called Dresden Zeus, who has a similar triangular apron to his mantle, although combined with a bare torso. Despinis' reconstruction of Agorakritos' Nemesis has led him to identify this well-known male type with the Hades made by Pheidias' pupil for the sanctuary of Athena Itonia at Koroneia, presumably around 440-430, and the suggestion is plausible, although our interpretation of the diffusion of patterns and styles makes it both questionable and unnecessary. Underworld divinities were not often represented in cult images, and indeed the Koroneia statue that Strabo calls Hades is called Zeus by Pausanias; a replica of the Dresden type has been found in Olympia, thus suggesting that the major god of that site was meant.[7] It is more important to note that, although the Zeus/Hades is only preserved in Roman copies, the typical rendering of its wet drapery over the advanced right leg, with oval patches defined by sharp ridges, can be paralleled in a Greek original: the youth of the Cat Stele. The relative accuracy of the Roman copies is therefore assured, together with the variation in stance, which recalls that of the Ares Borghese but with a fully frontal position as befits a true (or perhaps just an earlier?) cult statue.

To return to the Grimani statuettes, they are not of such outstanding quality that they need be reviewed further. Only one more piece (Kabus-Jahn, no. 2) calls for a few comments, to identify other stylistic components within the group. This headless peplophoros has been connected with the so-called Capitoline Demeter, but its general rendering is non-Attic and may exemplify Ionic drapery. A certain heaviness in the appearance of the cloth translates itself into a confused pattern between the breasts, which does not succeed

---

[6] If this is the main explanation for the rendering of the aegis, one of the reasons for considering the Velletri Athena as the Hephaistia by Alkamenes may be weakened.

[7] To be sure, Zeus and Hades were considered brothers, thus physically similar. It is also assumed likely that the Athena Itonia herself had a certain chthonic aspect. Nonetheless, it is possible that the Dresden type was created as a free-standing version of the Zeus from the East Pediment at Olympia, and for that site. On the iconography of Hades see R. Kabus-Preisshofen, *AntP* 15 (1975) 58-59.

in modeling the torso. The folds are broad-ridged without having the sharpness of ribbon drapery and look tubular and doughy. At the same time the short mantle worn on the back comes forward over the right hip with a wind-blown effect of its folds, which contrasts with the static appearance of the whole. The almost decorative cast of patterns that in Attica would have had sharper clarity and function suggests Ionic influence at work, but the general schema is Attic or rather international.[8] The same review that we briefly attempted for the Abbondanza could be made for this figure, but with even greater spread, since the peplophoros type occurs with endless minor variations in a whole range of types. Note how many of the statuettes within the Grimani group wear this voluminous peplos belted under the overfold, with low kolpos; this is, one suspects, the already old-fashioned version of the garment which is used to impart a matronly and venerable identity to its wearer, be it Hera or Demeter or, later on, maternal personifications like Eirene with the child Ploutos. As such, the peplophoros type continues well into the Hellenistic period and is revived to great favor under the Romans, as an antiquarian trait.

The Frejus Aphrodite

Like the Velletri Athena, another statue is known through many Roman replicas, allusions in Fifth century reliefs, and contemporary variants in the round: the so-called Frejus Aphrodite (figs. 126, 127). The name derives from the alleged provenience of the replica in the Louvre, which has now been shown erroneous since the figure comes from the neighborhood of Naples. Some scholars therefore call her the Louvre/Naples type, but even this terminology is ambiguous, given the amount of sculptures in both museums. The name "Venus Genetrix" is often used in connection with the same figure because Roman coins with this legend illustrate a very similar type. This is usually taken to be the statue of the ancestor of the Julian family that Caesar commissioned Arkesilaos to make in 46 B.C. If this numismatic identification is correct (and indeed at least one scholar disputes it) we would have to assume that the artist produced an imitation of an earlier work rather than an outright creation, or, as one author has suggested, that the Aphrodite as we know it through the many replicas only imitates Classical styles but originated in fact during the Late Hellenistic period. However, since many of its stylistic traits can be found in Fifth century originals, it is more likely that the traditional dating is correct and that the sculptors of the early Roman Empire did not hesitate to adopt the general lines of the Classical prototype for their own purposes. That this was the case at least with the pupils of Pasiteles can easily be shown through the group of Orestes and Elektra in Naples, where the female figure, although a pastiche of several styles, displays the drapery pattern of the Aphrodite with only minor additions and variations. For convenience sake we shall continue to call this type the Frejus Aphrodite.

That this statue was quite popular in Roman times is shown by the large number of replicas extant, including mirror images and adaptations. Since many Roman matrons utilized the type as a stock body for their portraits, slight changes and additions were made for the sake of modesty, so that the left breast could appear covered by some invented garment, although the entire figure was suggestively revealed through the transparent

---

[8] Note the effect of the folds emerging from some of the ridges in the overfold, a trait that recalls the mannerism of the Rhamnous Nemesis—Parian or Athenian?

drapery. These modifications are easily recognized and disregarded, so that the original appearance can be visualized. The goddess stood in a completely chiastic pose, her weight on the left leg with the right foot trailing, her left arm bent and probably holding an apple. This fruit functioned as an attribute, since it alluded to the Judgment of Paris, who had awarded the Apple of Discord "to the fairest" among the three major Olympian goddesses. With her right hand the figure lifted a tip of her mantle above her shoulder, and this gesture has been variously understood. According to some scholars, Aphrodite is adjusting, therefore putting on, her cloak; according to others, she is letting it drop behind herself, so that the thick garment forms a virtual background wall and acts as a foil for the extremely transparent chiton, which enhances rather than hides her bodily forms. In addition, by raising her right arm and lowering her left, the goddess causes her "strap" to slip, thus uncovering her left breast. The mannerism had originated with Figure M of the Parthenon East pediment (fig. 24), where, however, the cloth, through artistic license, still clung modestly to the flesh; in later statues the neckline slipped farther and farther, and in this Aphrodite the revealed body became as much an attribute as the apple itself. In addition, the single source of folds over the one shoulder lent itself to an ever-spreading pattern of divergent lines, as in the Nike of Paionios or the Sandalbinder from the Nike Balustrade. Paradoxically, in the Frejus Aphrodite this opportunity for pattern has been virtually by-passed in favor of an increased transparency through the almost total elimination of folds; only here and there do a few flat "ribbons" articulate the torso, so as to show that it is not entirely naked. Obviously, in antiquity the dress was painted, and the impression of nudity was therefore lessened.

But the major pattern of the drapery occurs from the waist down. The thin garment clings to the body and falls in a major gather between the legs; at the same time the roundness of the thighs pushes the cloth to the sides, so that the figure seems virtually supported by the long folds which outline her, evenly spaced in a tripartite rhythm.[9] The underlying principle is still that of the modeling line, as is visible from the side view; there, long folds terminate in sweeping curves bending at the knee in the typical pattern meant to suggest the articulation, and a system of quasi-catenaries gives volume to the leg like dotted lines onto the drawing of a cylinder. Somewhat the same modeling principles had been used for the Nike alighting in front of Athena on the Nike Balustrade, with the difference that her drapery is sucked between the thighs as if by a rushing wind and therefore lacks the strong vertical accent of the Aphrodite (figs. 76, 77). In this latter, however, the compositional principles are more complex: the eye is led from the raised mantle tip, diagonally along the neckline, down to the lowered arm, and into the mass of folds which has been channeled from both hips to cascade between the legs down to the ground. The unevenness of these curving lines as they part over the thighs emphasizes the slant of the hips and the weight distribution of the body.

This descending, continuous line is something new. Other statues had provided horizontal accents or contrasting patterns of horizontals and verticals, but the total appearance of the figure was still made up as if with building blocks, whether of drapery or of

---

[9] The long folds by the right leg are mainly visible in profile. They exist nonetheless and are echoed and reinforced by the fall of the mantle on that side. See Hiller, pl. 1:1. The main garment should be a chiton, and the buttons of the sleeve, unfastened, may be visible along the right side of the Louvre statue; however, the rendering is unclear and the lack of an overfold is surprising.

anatomy. With the Ares Borghese the continuous compositional line was introduced, of which this Aphrodite is the draped counterpart; but while the Ares obtained its effect through a diagonal pose, the Aphrodite can remain fully frontal and even in chiastic stance, but with a dominant system of lines along which the eye travels from top to bottom. What is remarkable is that the full volume of the body is nonetheless acknowledged by the pattern. By contrast, the Este Aphrodite reveals her Hellenistic date, to my mind, by emphasizing a linearity that denies modeling; her long folds cross the entire body and equally lead the eye along the garment, but with no respect for the underlying forms.

The gesture of the Frejus Aphrodite, of raising the mantle behind her, has a long history in Classical sculpture, and we have already sketched it elsewhere. For present purposes, note that it is found in the so-called Pheidian circle of works: from the Parthenon to the Nike Temple and its balustrade, which have been connected with Agorakritos. Yet the Frejus Aphrodite has been considered a reaction to Agorakritos' style, because the simplicity of her drapery contrasts with the textured surfaces of the Nemesis and other related statues. On this basis, and on the strength of a Roman comment about the fussiness of his perfectionism, the Frejus Aphrodite has been attributed to Kallimachos, a master singularly slighted by the ancient sources. Of him we are told that he made an elaborate oil lamp for the Erechtheion and that he was the "inventor" of the Corinthian capital; as a sculptor he is credited with the "Lakonian Dancers," which have not been identified, unless they are the Maenads of the Maenad Reliefs to be discussed later. The suggestion that the Frejus Aphrodite is the Ourania of the temple near the Hephaisteion, which Pausanias attributed to Pheidias, would imply that ancient confusion about sculptural styles was as great as ours or worse. In addition, if the connection with Pheidias implies also a connection with the Periklean building project, the cult statue should be no later than ca. 430; the Frejus Aphrodite type should, however, be dated as late as possible within the Fifth century, certainly after the Nike Balustrade.

Despite slight variations in the binding of the headdress, a small head in the National Museum in Athens has been published as a contemporary replica of the Frejus Aphrodite and dated to ca. 410-400.[10] I assume that this is the very date of the "prototype," even if its echo can be found in the amphiglyphon of Echelos and Iasile on the divine-assembly side. Definite similarities exist also between the young maid of the Hegeso gravestone (fig. 107) and the Aphrodite. One more comparison may help define the difference between true Attic style and its Ionic imitation. A fragmentary gravestone from Stryme (?) in Komotini (Thrace) preserves the figure of a young man in profile standing near a much larger, frontal, and now headless male dressed in a chitoniskos and chlamys. In the latter, two folds tend to merge between the thighs, while the rest of the costume flattens itself against the background. The effect should be comparable to that of the Frejus Aphrodite but is instead quite different: the figure looks almost naked, because the curving folds have been entirely eliminated and only the long sweeping verticals remain; as a result, the outline of the body appears almost independent of the costume, yet at the same time it lacks articulation. In

[10] For a second head replica of the Frejus Aphrodite, of the same size as the one in Athens, but surprisingly in limestone, see E. La Rocca, *ASAtene* 50-51, n.s. 34-35 (1972-73, published 1975) 418-50, especially p. 413. A third head replica may exist on the Akropolis (Akr. 244; *ArchEph* 1957, pls. 1-5) and would reveal the proper head inclination. S. Karouzou believes that the original prototype also was smaller than life-size.

the young attendant the himation is draped with tension lines at knee and ankle, but no other folds are marked over the entire length of the leg. Once again, the outline of the body from above the buttock to below the calf has been drawn as if free from any drapery, and the front of the leg with the prominent knee has been carved deeply into the area of the mantle. The effect recalls some figures on White Ground lekythoi, especially those by the Achilles Painter, presumably because the creative process was virtually the same: conceiving a human body and then adding the drapery above and around the preestablished outline.[11]

POLYKLEITOS

From the previous discussion it would appear as if only cult images were copied, whether created by famous or by less renowned masters. But the most copied statues of antiquity probably belonged to the one sculptor who never made a cult image: Polykleitos.

To be sure, Pausanias credits the Argive master with several statues of divinities, and in particular with the chryselephantine Hera of the Argive Heraion. But this attribution is not repeated by Pliny,[12] and even Strabo, who mentions Polykleitan statues in the Argive temple, does it in ambiguous terms which do not suggest that he is referring to the cult image. In addition, the temple itself has now been dated to the very end of the Fifth century and a good argument has been made for the possibility that Polykleitos was no longer active at that time. A Polykleitos the Younger might have produced some of the works that were later confused with those of his more famous predecessor; but it is also possible that the great name attracted completely unrelated attributions, made simply to add grandeur and importance to certain pieces in the eyes of the Romans who obviously greatly admired the Argive master. Be that as it may, the Argive Hera is known only through numismatic reproductions and literary descriptions. Its sculptural type has not been identified with any assurance, and even a head in the British Museum (fig. 147), which seems to correspond to the profile on the coins, stylistically is either far too early or far too late (Classicizing) to belong with the redated temple. Not one of the other divine statues connected with Polykleitos by Pausanias has been even conjecturally identified.

Undoubtedly, the master excelled in athletic statuary and his medium par excellence was bronze. This explains why no originals by him have survived, and it is ironical that what the Romans and later art critics considered the greatest Greek sculptural achievement, the naked athletic statue, should be known to us only through marble copies. At Olympia three statue bases have been found inscribed with Polykleitos' name, but none of the corresponding figures has been recognized. Conversely, a base that carried the dedication of the boxer Kyniskos has a distinctive set of footprints, which have been connected with the so-called Ephebe Westmacott type on the strength of its stance; however, this fragmentary base does not preserve Polykleitos' name.[13] The question should indeed be

[11] G. Bakalakis, *AthMitt* 77 (1962) 197-206, esp. 200 and 202, dates this stele to the first quarter of the Fourth century, but he recognizes the affinities between the heroized deceased and late Fifth century Attic works that he compares, including the Frejus Aphrodite.

[12] It is repeated by Plutarch, *Life of Perikles*, 2.

[13] The attribution rests on Pausanias (6.4.11), who mentions Polykleitos as the sculptor. Since the writer's report that Polykleitos made the statues of Pythokles, Xenokles, and Aristion has been confirmed by the finding of the pertinent bases with the sculptor's name, his statement about Kyniskos may also be correct, but the base gives no evidence, in its

raised whether monuments in the major Panhellenic sanctuaries could be copied; at the present state of our knowledge the answer must remain tentative and perhaps in the negative. Conversely, we cannot tell where the Doryphoros stood[14] or whether it represented a mortal or a hero. Some scholars have suggested that its superhuman size is not appropriate for a common man and have identified it as Achilles; Roman sources in fact speak about athletic statuary in stadia that was called Achillean.

But a Fifth century Greek would have needed more specific attributes to recognize the hero: some armor, or at least long hair, to judge from other contemporary representations. Quite probably the Doryphoros did not represent a particular individual but the athlete or the Olympic victor par excellence, with the heroic connotation attached to such feat; it seems certain that it represented also the embodiment of the *Canon*, a book written by the sculptor in which the theoretical basis for his method was propounded. This is the epitome of idealization, since the body is seen as a sequence of interrelated measures that create the total harmony of the figure, as numbers create the harmony of a song. As such, no human being could ever look like the Doryphoros, and the statue assumes the value of a Platonic idea, of which this world can afford only vague copies.

While these philosophical speculations are quite possible for Polykleitos' times and undoubtedly were shared by many, there is no question that the primary consideration behind the canon was the establishment of a method which enabled the sculptor to proportion a statue easily and safely. Such techniques had been in use since the earliest days of Greek sculpture, inherited from the Egyptians, be they the grids applied to the marble block or comparable systems for the casting of large-scale bronzes. Polykleitos, being a practicing sculptor, needed to combine theory with both practice and practicality; therefore, any method involving a great deal of measuring and variation in the measuring unit employed can be considered improbable. In a way, to pinpoint Polykleitos' canon is secondary in respect to the understanding that his system was proportional, theoretical, and functional, meant to achieve the perfect human body in its various aspects.[15]

We cannot know Polykleitos through any of his originals: being in bronze, they are long since lost. But the many replicas of the Doryphoros, and its correspondence with what the literary sources tell us about Polykleitos' principles and the appearance of his statues, confirm the identification. Modern analysis of the figure is therefore justified, given the strong similarity among Roman replicas (fig. 128). The Doryphoros is the exemplification of the chiastic principle. The term is derived from the Greek letter *chi* (χ) which is formed

present damaged state. Note that Pausanias specifically mentions also statues by a Polykleitos the Younger, which stood in the same sanctuary (6.6.2).

[14] The fact that a funerary (?) relief from Argos reproduces the Doryphoros is not in itself enough assurance that the statue stood in that town. By the same token, it could have stood in Athens, since it is echoed in the Parthenon frieze and by some funerary reliefs. Obviously, popular types were copied everywhere. On the other hand, if the Doryphoros is truly the material embodiment of the canon, it may have been made by Polykleitos for his personal satisfaction, without a proper commission. Argos would therefore be a logical place for its setting.

We may also have to question how closely the Doryphoros was copied, since it has now been claimed that some of the Baiae casts reproduce a Doryphoros quite different from the extant Roman copies: A. F. Stewart, *JHS* 98 (1978) 123-24 and n. 17.

[15] I personally believe, however, that a sound solution, or at least a step in the right direction toward breaking the code of the canon, has been found by R. Tobin, *AJA* 79 (1975) 307-21. My conviction stems from the fact that Tobin, himself a sculptor, has shown me how to work out all the dimensions of an over-life-sized statue with the simple help of a knotted cord and in a very short time.

by two lines crossing obliquely, but the stroke descending right to left is straight while the other is, like a reversed S, curved at both ends. Thus the upper curve on the left corresponds to a mirror-image curve on the lower right and two straight halves face each other across the sinuous divide.

The principle can therefore be stated as the attempt to give two versions of the same element (two lines, one curved, one straight) which are opposite when side by side, but equal on a bias. When applied to the statue of a man the principle works as follows: utilizing the bilateral symmetry of a human body, each element is shown in one of its two possible states, so that when one is tense, the other is relaxed and vice versa.[16] In the Doryphoros, the right arm is loose, the left is bent at the elbow; the right leg is tense, supporting the weight of the body, while the left trails free. This stance affects the alignment of hips and shoulders: the right shoulder dips while the hip muscle rises, so that the entire right side of the figure is compressed; on the other side of the median line, the left shoulder rises while the hip is lowered, thus producing the greatest possible stretch of the torso on that side within a quiet pose. The same "dissimilarity" principle applies to other elements of human anatomy: note the different shape of the two pectorals, the two collar bones, the two neck muscles. Even within the arm itself, when the biceps is flexed the muscle of the lower arm is relaxed and vice versa. The analysis could be continued for the legs; note in particular that the trochanteric depression, so deep and distinctive in Polykleitan statues, is deeper on the side of the weight leg, while the genitals swing toward it, at the end of the curve formed by the median line; the head turned toward the side of the weight leg caps the upper end of that same curve.

Four main elements of the human body describe an invisible *chi* across it: the raised left shoulder corresponds to the raised right hip, the lowered right shoulder is balanced by the lowered left hip. This position established a secondary pattern of lines along the figure. If we visualize imaginary spikes thrust through the body at key points, the entire balancing system of the statue is revealed. One spike through the ankles would slant from top (viewer's) right to lower left; one through the knees would move the opposite way (from viewer's left to right); one through the hips would parallel that latter, to be counterbalanced by one through the shoulders, which would, once again, go from right to left. Thus a system of four diagonals would be revealed, the top matching the bottom line, the two central ones parallel. This visualization makes apparent the inner statics of the body: given the horizontal as the perfect balance, equilibrium is lost as the shoulders slant, it is recovered by the counteraction of the hips; this movement is then exaggerated by the knees to be again counterbalanced at the ankles. It is thus superfluous to ask wether the Doryphoros is walking or standing: his pose is thoroughly artificial and only made to look

[16] This is also often referred to with the Italian word *contrapposto*, which, however, does not carry the descriptive precision of the Greek term.

Mark Fullerton has pointed out to me that a chiastic principle of sorts is already embodied in the so-called Zeus/Poseidon from Cape Artemision. The straight left arm corresponds to the tense right leg, while the bent left knee balances the right elbow; an attempt at contrapposto might indeed explain why the right arm is so extended, as if to throw a long-shafted weapon, and why the left arm is stretched out. Though usually explained as a "sighting arm," this is not a common position for a javelin-thrower and the total schema seems to respond exclusively to aesthetic rather than to practical and realistic needs. The secret of success of Greek sculpture lies primarily in the fact that such artistic dictates can be made to look so natural and convincing. In the Severe bronze, however, the chiastic rendering is limited to the extremities and does not extend to the parts of the torso.

plausible; it is actually slightly uncomfortable, with the trailing leg too far displaced for proper poise, yet elegant and convincing from an aesthetic point of view.

Within this framework, individual forms are massive, heavy. The musculature is so pronounced that the sheer outline of the torso invites the use of a template; the Iliac crest projects like a molding.[17] Horizontal accents are strongly articulated, especially at the end of the rib cage, despite the fact that no actual bending of the torso is attempted; but this effect is different from the breath-intake of some contemporary architectural figures. By comparison, the Doryphoros looks fleshier, more mature. His entire body appears built in sections, with the legs almost fitted into the strong groove of the groin, which is in turn echoed in reverse by the wide curve of the epigastric arch; this latter resembles a bracket lying prone, its peak on the median line, and is in turn repeated by the hair division over the forehead.[18] Like the body, a Polykleitan face is distinctive; flat cheeks, heavy jaws, rounded chin, bulging eyes. In profile, the cranium is rather flat and elongated from front to back, curving low above the nape with an indentation in the hair from ear to ear, as if a fillet had rested there at length. Yet the hair has little volume, the long wisps adhere to the skull so that only minute tips break the outline. The pattern is quite artificial, starting from a starfish motif displaced to the rear of the crown, toward the point of greatest curvature. Over the nape the curls are combed forward toward the face: a distinctive feature of Julio-Claudian portraits, and it is difficult to tell whether they imitate the Doryphoros or whether the Roman copyists of the Polykleitan statue have introduced a motif of contemporary sculpture.

As already mentioned, a relief from Argos and the many Roman replicas of the Doryphoros assure us that we have a correct indentification of Polykleitos' work, probably to be dated around 440-430. Another work attributed to him by the sources and recognizable in Roman copies through definite stylistic similarity with the Doryphoros is the Diadoumenos; the stance and the chiastic principles are the same as for the Doryphoros, but both arms are raised, though to different levels. The presence of the fillet (broken in the marble replicas, where it required the introduction of unseemly struts sprouting from the shoulders), stretching from hand to hand in the bronze, created a large area of enclosed space around the head, thus making the composition top-heavy but in a balanced and graceful way. The eye travels along these unbroken lines, almost in a circle, before coming down the curve of the median line to the weight leg and finally to the ground. The turn of the head to the figure's right is logical and uncontrived; proportions and musculature are close to those of the Doryphoros, though the head with its indented hair mass may suggest that the Diadoumenos is later than the Canon, of which it creates a variation.

How many variations are admissible, before casting doubt on the attribution? The third best known Polykleitan statue is the above mentioned Westmacott Athlete, usually iden-

---

[17] The very pronounced musculature may have been required partly by the medium. Over the shiny surface of a newly cast bronze statue, the diffusion and reflection of light would have made any but the strongest articulation invisible, so that a marble replica, which lacks the blurring of the original shine, appears overbuilt. Closer to the original is probably the black basalt torso in Florence, which has a comparably polished surface against which the light breaks.

[18] This last comparison may seem far-fetched but is supported by the very artificiality of the hair arrangement on the Doryphoros. This is briefly described below, but finds excellent analysis in von Steuben, *Der Kanon des Polyklet* (Tübingen 1973), who seeks to find one of several measuring units for the statue among the locks.

tified with the Kyniskos because of its unusual stance. As noticeable from the imprints on the statue base, the figure rested its weight on the left leg and had the right foot trailing. This corresponds to the statue in the British Museum (known also through several other replicas): the athlete turns his head toward the side of the free leg and raises his right arm to put a crown on his head, which therefore bends in the same direction. Thus, although the chiasmos is respected within the torso, the basic rhythm of the composition is reversed, while the arm raised and the head turned on the side of the free leg produce an impression of imbalance. An area of space is enclosed once again near the head, but the dominant pattern is the wide curve visible in silhouette from right hand to right foot. Anatomy and facial features are Polykleitan, although the body build is somewhat attenuated, more youthful. If the original had not stood at Olympia, I would perhaps be more confident in considering the statue the Kyniskos; at present, I am inclined to think that the correspondence between the footprints on the statue base and the stance of the Westmacott Athlete is fortuitous and only tells us that Polykleitos could reverse his poses—if the Kyniskos was surely by Polykleitos. As for the Westmacott Athlete type, he is either a replica of an original by the master himself or by one of his followers.

It is more difficult to decide about other attributions. The other signed statue bases at Olympia show that Polykleitos could make figures resting their weight on both feet (bases for Ariston and Xenokles), perhaps before perfecting his canon. The so-called Diskophoros (probably a Hermes, according to Zanker) is usually considered the earliest among Polykleitan works because of this early stance. The youthful figure, the definite similarity with the Doryphoros, make me wonder whether this is not rather an adaptation of later times, as Zanker, for example, argues cogently for the so-called Diadoumenous Farnese. Similar cases have been made for the Herakles and another Hermes type, which may not have existed as separate entities in Greek times. The so-called Narkissos (or Hyakinthos), known through a remarkably large number of replicas, returns to the stance with both feet flat on the ground, but the pose is rendered off balance by the fact that the youth leans with his left hand against a support; his head turns toward the left free leg, but the curvature of the body is almost eliminated by the fact that the foot does not trail. There is a romantic quality in this piece which had suggested to some scholars that its original was a Classicizing rather than a Classical creation. The latest analysis, by Zanker, accepts an attribution to the very end of the Fifth century, within the school of the Argive master. A recent find of original Greek marbles from a Classical shrine in Thessaly includes a statue in a similar, though reversed, pose, which makes the suggested chronology for the Narkissos more plausible.[19]

According to the ancient sources, Polykleitos had many pupils, who surely elaborated on the findings of the master. In addition, the Romans' demand for Polykleitan replicas created a large market for Polykleitan adaptations or even for creations in approximate Polykleitan manner. Some of them are veritable pastiches and mixtures of different styles, others come so close that it is impossible to be sure. In general, Polykleitan originals could be changed into funerary monuments by the addition of appropriate attributes; identities

[19] Milojčic, *AAA* 7 (1974) p. 66 fig. 30. The site in question is Soros (Amphanai) in Thessaly. The headless marble statues represent plump children and would seem more Hellenistic or Roman than Classical, but, according to this preliminary report, nothing later than the third quarter of the Fourth century was found in this shrine, and the pottery is well dated, because it includes some Panathenaic amphorae.

could be changed with similar additions or subtractions. By and large, Roman copyists tended to make the bodies less mature, more typically adolescent, and to introduce romantic elements in the faces or the turn of the heads. In other cases, a true Polykleitan body could convey a heroizing effect and be used for portrait heads. A recent masterly study of Polykleitan creations and imitations has been made by Paul Zanker and is as important for the study of Greek as for that of Roman art and taste. Many pseudo-Polykleitan attributions, like the Idolino or the Benevento Head, have been finally put to rest and our conception of Polykleitan style is much clearer.

COPIES OF FIFTH CENTURY RELIEFS

Like statuary in the round, Classical reliefs could be copied almost immediately after their creation, or even be made in more than one exemplar. They could also be copied in Roman times, especially for decorative purposes. We have already mentioned some of the Roman copies after the shield of the Athena Parthenos, the armrests of the throne of Zeus at Olympia, or the friezes on the bases of the major cult statues. We can here discuss only two basic and problematic groups: the so-called Three-Figure Reliefs and the Dancing Maenads.

The Three-Figure Reliefs

As already seen in chapter 5, many Greek reliefs are limited to three figures, in a compositional arrangement particularly suited to an approximately square plaque, like a metope. However, in 1938 a major article by H. Götze grouped together four such pieces, each known from at least two replicas, which appeared similar both stylistically and chronologically and which probably belonged to a single monument. Since the mythological subject matter of the reliefs seemed appropriate for theatrical works, it was first assumed that the plaques had adorned a choragic monument celebrating a victory in a trilogy, but this theory was somewhat weakened by the fact that four, and not three, reliefs existed and that no direct connection could be established between the relief topics and any known tragedy. Other suppositions seemed equally improbable: that the reliefs adorned the walls of a Classical building, like Roman paintings; or that they filled the intercolumnia of a monopteros. In 1952, H. A. Thompson noted the correspondence between the dimensions of the plaques and the spaces near the two openings into the precinct surrounding an altar in the Agora, which he considered the Altar of Eleos as well as of the Twelve Gods. Interpreting Eleos as Pity, Thompson suggested that all four episodes represented pitiful situations: Orpheus losing Eurydike after having received permission to bring her back from the Underworld (fig. 129); Theseus leaving Peirithoos in Hades since Herakles had succeeded in freeing only one of the two friends; the Peliads losing their father since Medea had deceived them into killing him, thinking to rejuvenate him (figs. 130, 131), and Herakles leaving the Hesperides, who had fallen in love with him, after obtaining the Apples of Immortality. Götze had also emphasized the theme of tragic partings as the topical link among the four scenes, but Thompson highlighted instead their effect arousing compassion for reversals of human fortune.

The theory was criticized both in terms of interpretation and of placement of the reliefs.

206

It was pointed out that Eleos is not Pity but rather Mercy, and that it is unlikely a single altar served two functions: as a place of ritual for the Twelve Gods as well as for Eleos, and therefore as a place of asylum and the city's milestone. Recent topographical studies have proposed different locations, and this double identification for the altar in the Agora should probably be dismissed. E. B. Harrison circumvented the iconographical objection by suggesting that the four scenes represented instead the quest for eternal good—two frustrated and two achieved—in the world of heroes: a subject that might have been appropriate for the Twelve Gods. A slight variant of this thought was independently introduced by L. Beschi, who saw in the four panels four different attempts to obtain immortality. Among them, only one succeeded (that of Herakles), while the other three represented intermediate stages, from a totally negative one (Medea never meant to rejuvenate Pelias) to a possible one (Orpheus *could* have brought back Eurydike if he had not looked back too soon) and to a partial success (Theseus, if not Peirithoos, was freed by Herakles from his imprisoning seat in the Underworld). Both Harrison and Beschi, therefore, saw the Hesperides panel as a scene of joy rather than as a painful parting.

A more fundamental objection has recently been raised by Langlotz. He has pointed out that the entire reconstruction of the precinct around the Agora altar is largely hypothetical and that a symmetrical arrangement with two openings was excluded by the first excavator on the evidence of the remains. He has also criticized the attempts to correlate the dimensions of the relief plaques (all different because of the different replicas and the various states of preservation) with those of the intervals between the posts of the altar precinct and, in general, also the way in which relief slabs would have been set up in an unprecedented arrangement for Greek-mainland altars. Langlotz concludes that the four slabs did in fact belong together, but that they represented the four sides of a funerary monument, perhaps marked by piers at the four corners, and cites appropriate parallels from Athens and other areas of the Greek world. This cubic structure might have served as independent marker or as support for a lekythos or a funerary statue; it was obviously meant for an important man whose fame rested on his connection with tragic myths. Sophokles or Euripides are two possible candidates for a grave monument to be dated in the last decade of the Fifth century, a date which Harrison also now supports.

Langlotz has attributed the originals of the four plaques to three sculptors, among whom the Orpheus master is the best and the possible leader; his art is comparable to that of the man who carved the North frieze of the Parthenon. The master of the Medea relief he compares to that of the South Parthenon frieze, while the Theseus relief has affinities with the West frieze. Since the Hesperides scene is the most extensively damaged and restored, judgment is difficult, but Langlotz places it closer to the Orpheus and the Theseus than to the Medea relief. Similarities between the plaques and architectural monuments like the Erectheion frieze and the Nike Balustrade are also outlined.

Since none of these reliefs is preserved in the original and since some of the fragmentary replicas were extensively integrated or recut by modern restorers, it is impossible to make precise stylistic judgments. In particular, the Roman copies of the Great Eleusinian Relief have shown that modernization was possible in reproducing an original work. I have the impression that this may also be the case with the Three-Figure Reliefs and that our tendency to group them together may be influenced by a common late Fifth century flavor imparted to them by the copyists. It has already been pointed out by Hausmann that original votive reliefs have similar composition and characteristics, including the upward taper of the slabs, and some Attic funerary stelai provide good comparisons except for the mythological content. Undoubtedly, some of the figures and concepts of the four panels under discussion were adapted for other purposes, and it is almost impossible to determine in what context the idea for a specific figure originated. To be sure, none of the comparisons is known through as many replicas as our four scenes, or even through any replica at all; this interest in reproduction during Roman times singles out the Three-Figure Reliefs as having special importance. Nonetheless, I still hesitate in dating them together, even making allowance for different hands.[20]

Specifically, the Hesperides and the Theseus reliefs seem to me earlier than the other two and perhaps hardly later than ca. 430; in the Theseus slab the seated Peirithoos does not cross his legs and sits in an awkward pose, which should produce a torsional rendering but remains instead flat and without depth.[21] The indentation at his wrist, as well as the fine wrinkles, are mannerisms to be found also in the Hephaisteion and the Parthenon frieze, while the standing Theseus has been convincingly compared to some of the water carriers on the North Parthenon frieze. The Herakles behind Peirithoos has a Polykleitan pose and anatomical details. From replica to replica the rendering of drapery varies without necessarily being coherent; in the fragmentary plaque in the Louvre, for instance, the mantle over Peirithoos' lap is confusing in its pattern of folds and recalls some of the seated gods of the Parthenon East frieze; by contrast, the standing Theseus has almost cobwebby drapery, with folds looping across the legs that are fully visible beneath the transparent cloth. Since these two renderings should be chronologically incompatible, it seems more likely that an earlier rendering should be modernized rather than a later one be made old-fashioned and perhaps less comprehensible.

Compositionally, the Hesperides relief is so close to the Theseus panel that one is likely to have been the inspiration for the other, but it is difficult to say whether this means contemporaneity or intentional imitation within a relatively short time span. The subject of the

---

[20] It has been pointed out that the four plaques are linked also by intentional variations in the possible combinations of figures: three men in one, three women in another; one man between two women in the Hesperides scene, one woman between two men in the Orpheus relief. But these may be fortuitous arrangements. The existence of other Three-Figure reliefs has been postulated by Möbius and suggested by Dohrn (p. 20). One such is the relief in Ince Blundell with three heroes, or that of a hero (?) Asklepios and Hygieia illustrated by Hausmann, fig. 37 (Athens Nat. Mus. 1388). The Attic grave stele of Sosias and Kephisodoros in Berlin (Blümel, no. 17, pp. 25-26, fig. 25; K 29) has somewhat the same language of hands and glances as the Orpheus relief. G. Carettoni, *BdA* 52 (1967) 148-51, figs. 31-35, has assigned a fifth relief to the established series, a panel with three women, because it was found on the Palatine in Rome together with a copy of the Orpheus relief. Technically, the fragmentary plaque is so similar to the Orpheus replica that un-doubtedly the two were set up together in antiquity, but there is no assurance that the three-women composition was not created specifically to serve as pendant to the genuine copy. Stylistically, the new addition does not appear as coherent as the other four reliefs; the central woman has Archaizing traits and the whole may have been patterned after the Three Graces reliefs. No other replica of this specific panel is known.

[21] Contrast, for instance, the Tyche of Antioch and her much more three-dimensional pose. Note, however, that advocates of different dates for the panels can reach opposite conclusions. K. Schefold, in *R. Boehringer. Eine Freundesgabe* (Tübingen 1957) 544 n. 7, places the Orpheus and the Peliads reliefs around 420, the other two in the last decade of the Fifth century. Prof. Harrison has pointed out to me that the Theseus has the same "dripping hair" of the Ares Borghese, which belongs at the end of the century.

young Herakles rejoicing in the Garden of the Hesperides is known only through vase painting. In sculpture, this is usually the last of Herakles' labors, and the hero is shown mature, bearded, and tired—in the late Fourth century even exhausted. Given the fragmentary state of the replicas, I wonder if the original scene might have represented Triptolemos between Demeter and Kore, perhaps seated on his winged chariot. A comparable relief base for a funerary lekythos from Moschato (Athens) suggests that the Elysian Fields were equated with the Garden of the Hesperides, but vegetation and immortality are common concepts appropriate within both the Eleusinian tradition and the funerary repertoire.

The Medea relief (figs. 130, 131) is known in fewer replicas[22] and is also problematic in its interpretation. The daughter with the knife is in the typical pose of anguished puzzlement, like the Prokne or the woman on Parthenon metope S 19 (fig. 2); could the Peliad on the relief represent, with proper modifications, a mirror image of Alkamenes' work? The hand under the drapery, cushioning the right elbow, is unusual and recalls the hidden hand of Hermes in the East Parthenon frieze. The Peliad behind the cauldron is in a peculiar pose, not very successful in its spatial treatment. If the transparent drapery of the two girls is to be believed, the date of the relief should not be far from that of the Nike Balustrade, but the Medea looks more sober and earlier.

Finally, the Orpheus relief (fig. 129). This is the most famous of the series and the most precisely known, given the relative coherence of all replicas. If this is indeed the second separation of Orpheus and Eurydike, it would be the earliest documentation of this version of the story, which we first learn from Vergil. In fact, it has been suggested that the plaque depicts the first parting, in order to reconcile the apparent discrepancy; but the language of gestures is unmistakable: Orpheus is removing the veil from his bride's face, to catch that glimpse of her which will spell her eternal loss. Since art often preserves themes unknown from contemporary written versions, there is no reason to doubt that this interpretation is correct, and future discoveries may give us the missing literary link.

The relief is a masterpiece, and even viewers ignorant of the myth sense the mood of sorrow and love conveyed by the lowered heads, the crossing glances, the eloquent hands. Compositionally, the long garment of Eurydike, with its folds massed over the weight leg, creates a strong central axis to the scene, balanced on either side by the trailing leg of the two male figures. These are turned inwards, so that they form a virtual frame to the panel despite their slightly different poses; the tripartite rhythm is subtly altered by the closer spacing of the two lovers, which corresponds to the emotional ties, while Hermes' right leg parallels the lines of Eurydike's as if to convey the direction of their future movement away from Orpheus. Stylistically, the Hermes finds a good parallel in one of the men near the chariots on the South frieze of the Parthenon (fig. 44). Eurydike in the swinging folds of her apoptygma recalls the Karyatids of the Erechtheion in a later version, with drapery as transparent as that of the frieze on the same temple. Her pose (but not her costume) has been compared in mirror image to that of Myrrhine on a large marble lekythos of ca. 400, showing the deceased being led away by a more active and frontal, but not entirely dissimilar, Hermes. Much heavier in features and garment but comparable in pose is a female figure on a relief in Cyrene (figs. 132, 133) being led by Herakles, perhaps in a depiction

---

[22] One, highly fragmentary, comes from Corinth and is the only one of the series found in Greece proper: *Corinth*, 9, 121, no. 246.

of the Alkestis myth. Finally, general parallels can be established with several other votive and funerary reliefs, as pointed out by many scholars.[23] Here we shall mention only one, in Berlin, because of its unusual provenience.

This votive relief was found on the Quirinal in Rome and it has therefore been suggested that it comes originally from Magna Graecia. It is certainly influenced, however, by Attic Nymphs reliefs, since it shows a small worshiper at the extreme left confronted by the much larger figures of Hermes leading three nymphs while the river god Acheloos appears at the right edge of the plaque in his traditional protomelike form, part bull and part man. The remains of a rock near the edge of the break at the right upper corner of the plaque show that Pan was perched on a ledge watching the dance. That the nymphs are dancing is suggested by their fluttering drapery, their linked hands, and the traditional iconography of similar reliefs, but the frontal pose of the central nymph recalls the conventions of the Three Graces series. However, the bent head of the first nymph, combined with the gesture of Hermes, who holds her wrist, give the impression that she is being led away mournfully rather than in joy. The similarity with the Myrrhine lekythos, and therefore with the Orpheus relief, is puzzling, since the plaque in Berlin may not be an Attic monument. Once again we are confronted with evidence for the diffusion of single motifs as well as style. This Berlin relief is also important because the linear drapery of the dancing nymphs (perhaps more linear than an Attic master would have carved) recalls in its patterns another highly discussed series of ancient reliefs known only through Roman replicas: the so-called Dancing Maenads.

The Dancing Maenads Reliefs

Known through so many reproductions that they could be called the most widely known monument of Greek art during Roman imperial times together with the Doryphoros, these striking figures (figs. 134, 135) highlight one of the major problems inherent in copies, when no part of the original is preserved. Highly decorative in their flowing garments and frenzied poses, the Maenads appear on large flat slabs, large curved slabs, marble vases, sarcophagi, gems, terracotta reliefs, and Arretine bowls, in a variety of sizes ranging from natural to diminutive. They occur singly, in groups of three or more, or together with satyrs and other figures, so that it is difficult to reconstruct their original context. Most scholars agree that two streams of movement are represented, some Maenads being shown consistently facing to the right while others face left; but some among them are so similar that the possibility of intentional duplication of certain types cannot be excluded, and no agreement exists as to the total number of the original figures. As common in Neo-Attic workshops, the material at hand could be stretched to suit the need of the object or area to be decorated, and new figures could be created along the lines of the others, with a minimum of variation and additions; or a preexisting figure, for instance a dancer, could be turned into a Maenad by giving her a thyrsos or a dismembered animal.

[23] Note in particular the similarity between the Hermes of the Orpheus scene and the Artemis (?) of the divine gathering on one side of the Echelos and Iasile amphiglyphon (supra, ch. 6, p. 133). If the latter is properly dated around 400, the date of the Orpheus relief cannot be brought as far down as the last decade of the Fifth century.

Thus some scholars claim that the original monument comprised six, some eight, and some as many as nine Maenads.

More important is whether the original belongs to the late Fifth century or whether it is a Classicizing creation. The linear drapery of the figures, the flamboyant movement of their garments, the decorative effect of the whole combine with the cold appearance of the Neo-Attic rendering to raise a legitimate doubt. With the Three-Figure reliefs we could suspect modernization on the part of the individual copyists; with the Maenads the difference in time is not limited to one or two decades but to three centuries or more. Our earliest dated replica of the Maenads occurs on a marble krater from the Mahdia shipwreck, off the coast of Tunisia, which is dated around 100 B.C. This, however, does not exclude the possibility that the original was only slightly earlier than that date. The other replicas are not so closely dated, and none seems to belong within the Classical period. Yet a bronze krater in Berlin (of unknown provenience), which seems to date from the very end of the Fifth century or only slightly later, is adorned with several comparable, if not identical, Maenads, two holding a kid between them: a motif not attested in the Neo-Attic series. In addition, several other figures, both in relief and in the round, can be adduced as genuine Fifth century parallels, and even that linearity which is thought to be the main responsibility of the later copyists can to some extent be found in the above-mentioned original relief in Berlin. It would therefore seem certain that the Maenads truly belong at the very end of our period. They provide, then, a good example of the stylistic excesses possible around 400, when the modeling and motion lines conquered by the previous generation took the upper hand and ran free with baroque abandon.

Not all the replicas of the Maenads are shallow and predominantly linear. Though the individual folds and patterns in the drapery remain the same, some marble slabs, being curved, produce an impression of greater depth and volume to the bodies. Carpenter has suggested that the original monument was a round pedestal and that the disturbing calligraphy of the flat versions stems from the difficulty of transposing the linear design without reproducing the original depth. In his opinion, the (nine) Maenads were created by the same group of sculptors who carved the Nike Balustrade and decorated a tall pedestal over which stood the over-life-sized chryselephantine statue made by Alkamenes for the Temple of Dionysos in Athens. We have already noted the recent down-dating of that temple on the basis of excavational evidence and the question it raises about Alkamenes' statue, but this is here of secondary importance. The assignment of the Maenads to a late Fifth century prototype is primary. Where that prototype stood cannot be determined on the basis of the distribution of the copies. Many of them are of unknown provenience, although some come from Italy, including Rome, and several were found in North Africa, especially the remarkable curved series from Ptolemais. Some are said to be in Greek, even Pentelic, marble, while others are in Italian stone. Given the great disparity in size, medium, and date among the replicas, a single center of production and shipment seems unlikely, but Athens remains the best possibility.[24]

[24] A fragmentary female head crowned with ivy has recently been found in the area of the Theater of Dionysos: *BCH* 90 (1966) 729 fig. 11, text on p. 727; *Deltion* 19:2, A (1964) pl. 29:6. Although the published reports do not specify whether the fragment comes from a relief, nor attempt identification or dating, the piece could possibly reproduce one of the famous Maenads. Together with it a

The frenzied Maenad was popular in early Red Figure vases but is not attested in sculpture in the round before Skopas and the Fourth century.[25] Our relief Maenads could exemplify the chorus for Euripides' *Bacchai*, but they are unusually elegant and civilized. Animal skins are omitted or, when present, inconspicuous; there is only one knife in the series, and the four dismembered kids are virtually lost in the swirling drapery. Some Maenads wear their hair long but not entirely loose, others have it rolled up or even covered by a *sakkos*, like an Aphrodite: yet this last rendering belongs with the most original figure, known through the highest number of replicas. If any of these Neo-Attic reliefs copies a true Greek original of the Classical period, this Kid-Slayer (Hauser, no. 23) has the greatest probability of all. Her pose recalls Harmodios, but her inclined head gives her an appearance of grace and fatigue absent from the defiant attitude of the Tyrannicide, or from the ecstatic mood of her fellow Maenads with head thrown back. Another well-known Maenad from the group has been labeled "la Stanca" (the Weary) because of her similarly inclined head and her bent leg which give the impression the figure is near collapse. There is in them that suggestion of sadness which is typical of Classical works but seems surprising in dancing Maenads.

However, the most remarkable feature in these reliefs is the treatment of the drapery. Through their Neo-Attic versions it is impossible to say whether different hands could be recognized in the original, as for the Nike Balustrade; at present, they all seem alike or at least coherent within their individual monument, whether a marble vase or a relief slab. The Maenads are shown in very transparent costumes, though some wear a sleeved chiton and some a peplos, in two cases even belted over the overfold. They also wear a mantle, mostly used scarflike. In the various replicas the costume is often poorly differentiated, mantle and skirt merging together; in some cases the copyist has even eliminated the cloak from the background but has omitted to remove it as well from around the arm of the Maenad, which appears illogically covered. Yet, whether peplos or chiton, properly or incorrectly rendered, these garments in all replicas have in common the transparency, the linearity, the flamboyancy, the emphasis on pattern. Folds are very long and tubular, following the contour of the legs and billowing around the ankles, often in sanguisuga curves (fig. 135). In many points omega folds appear at the bottom of pleats and zigzags cascade at the edges of mantles and overfolds.

One Maenad has such an elaborate swirl to her skirt that a large ivy-leaf pattern is formed against her body. She finds a good parallel in the round in the Nike-Akroterion from the Agora (fig. 37), despite her different pose. The Nike is fully frontal, with legs wide apart, so that the drapery, dipping in between, supports her while at the same time forming an ivy-leaf. The Maenad is in profile but the treatment of the skirt suggests that she has been spinning around rather than moving in one direction. This greater compositional freedom is permitted by the relief technique, but stylistic mannerisms, including the excessive transparency and the overall flamboyancy, are quite similar in the two

---

Lapith torso from one of the Parthenon South metopes was found, therefore the pieces come from a mixed context. For a Maenad from Corinth see, lately, *BCH* 90 (1966) 765 fig. 25. For Maenads among the Peiraeus reliefs see now Th. Stephanidou-Tiveriou, *Neo-Attika—Hoi anaglyphoi Pinakes apo to*

Limani tou Peiraia (Athens 1979) nos. 54-55.

[25] The same situation applies to satyrs, and explanations have therefore been sought for the Marsyas of Myron: either a political allusion to Thebes or to a contemporary play.

works. Another Maenad, la Stanca, with her drapery clinging in between her legs, recalls the alighting Nike from the balustrade (figs. 76, 77) and, to some extent, the Frejus Aphrodite (figs. 126, 127), largely because of her quieter pose, where only her drapery moves. Although the main purpose of such drapery is decorative, it is clear that modeling principles are still in use. As a whole, however, the Maenads look more like works of painting and drawing than of sculpture. Those who believe in a true Fifth century prototype have usually attributed it to the sculptor Kallimachos because ancient sources mention his excessive elaboration; this attribution must remain pure speculation.

SUMMARY

Our brief review of copies has revealed some of the problems inherent in working with them. Both with sculpture in the round and in relief, we often find it hard to tell whether we are dealing with variants introduced by the copyists or with different prototypes, with true reproductions of a Classical work or with Classicizing creations. Even when overall similarity exists among the replicas, it is difficult to assess the correct date and style of the original, which can be modernized in some reproductions, simplified in others. Finally, in the case of reliefs, it is often impossible to visualize the original monument to which they belonged and to determine where that monument might have stood. This situation occurs also with sculpture in the round, yet one of the most important sculptors of the period, Polykleitos, would remain entirely unknown to us were if not for the world of copies.

The strictures of Roman copies have been often discussed and we are becoming increasingly aware of the ways in which copyists approached and altered their models. Several questions remain to be answered, and we may summarize a few here.

How Were Copies Made? In Roman times, mechanical means probably prevailed: either the pointing system or the use of plaster casts, which allowed reproduction either in marble or in bronze.[26] During the Classical period itself copying must have been more approximate, perhaps inspired by direct examination of the original and with proper "modernization" according to the style prevalent at the time of copying. Workshops may have had "monopoly" over certain figures, which appear both on votive and on record reliefs or on gravestones, presumably because made by the same carvers. In some cases, however, the distance involved in geographical and/or chronological terms is so great that, during the Greek period, we may have to postulate the use of pattern books, since only the linear design is respected or the iconographic trait, but the actual rendering has local peculiarities and the chronological gap can be wider than a single generation. What form these pattern books may have taken is problematic.

What Was Copied? Primarily cult statues or images of divinities, and athletic figures, these last, it seems, only in late Hellenistic or Roman times. Architectural sculpture could

[26] A rudimentary pointing system probably existed already in Greek times, for the enlargement and duplication of architectural sculpture from models, as postulated, for instance, for the pedimental figures at Olympia. The practice undoubtedly continued as architectural compositions became more complex, and was certainly adopted to produce the statues of the Parthenon gables, even if traces of the technique have not been detected.

also be copied; some instances, like the Barberini Suppliant, are debatable, but others are clear, like the Erechtheion Karyatids or the Ilissos frieze. In many cases we cannot speak of true copies but of adaptations, such as those from the Nike Balustrade. Statue bases and other famous reliefs, like the shield of Athena Parthenos, were often reproduced in decorative form. Even votive reliefs seem to have been copied, not only contemporaneously but even in Roman times. Since the true nature of the Three-Figure Reliefs and of the Dancing Maenads has not been satisfactorily determined, it is impossible to tell what type of monument was being copied. Gravestones, as far as we know, were not copied mechanically, and certainly not in Roman times, but motifs and iconography were widespread during the Greek period, with Athens seemingly providing the greatest inspiration.

Why Were Fifth Century Originals Copied? During the Classical period, the intent was obviously religious: to reproduce cult images or to provide votive offerings in the shape of the cult image itself. Some divinities seem to have been copied more often than others, especially goddesses and, among these, especially Demeter and Kore.[27] In Roman times, these divine images were often used as stock bodies for portrait heads, so that their original connotation added beauty and importance to the person portrayed. The same applies to athletic bodies, which were used for their heroizing quality. To some extent, some works were copied because made (or thought to have been made) by famous masters, but this consideration does not always hold true, as in the case of the Athena Promachos. Availability of the prototype, or even the practicality of reproduction, seem to have been definite factors. Few seated statues, in fact, are known among the copies in comparison to the many standing figures. Among the originals themselves, decorative parts, such as statue bases or shield devices, lent themselves particularly well to what was perhaps the primary function of Roman sculpture: the embellishment of buildings and gardens, but this function was often extended to statues that had originally served entirely different purposes.

Where Were the Monuments Being Copied? Undoubtedly some of them were in Athens and Attica, probably even the majority. We are less sure about other areas, and are especially uncertain about the great Panhellenic sanctuaries, Delphi and Olympia, since, at the most, adaptations but not true copies have been recognized. This is particularly true of the athletic statues by Polykleitos and the many other bronze sculptures at Olympia, or the many political and historical votive offerings at Delphi. We cannot say much about the Peloponnesos, thought it is likely that the Doryphoros stood in Argos. Magna Graecia and East Greece are largely blank areas in our knowledge. This is perhaps the topic in greatest need of further study, and its difficulty is made greater by the uncertainty in our attribution or identification of the various copies.

[27] To my knowledge, no *contemporary* copy of a   male cult image has as yet been recognized.

1. *Athletic statues from the Samian Heraion.* Despite the general lack of Classical statuary from the Heraion at Samos, two pieces have been recently published. Both cannot be clearly categorized as either originals or copies and both have been considered works by Samian sculptors in imitation of mainland Greek styles. The first is the under-life-sized head of an athlete, his comma locks bound by a fillet knotted over the nape, which strongly recalls Polykleitan originals in the rendering of the hair but differs in the proportions of the face: H. Kyrieleis, *AthMitt* 93 (1978) 171-79, pls. 51-54. The second is an over-life-sized torso, which probably held mantle and an attribute over its missing left arm: E. Homann-Wedeking, *AA* 1965, col. 438, fig. 12, *AA* 1969, 556-58, fig. 6. Both pieces show traces of repairs, both have been dated approximately around 450-440, although the torso had at first been considered close to the style of Myron. The practice of setting up victors' statues within the Heraion is attested for Roman times, but evidence is lacking for the Greek period. The Samian head, although of excellent execution, recalls some Roman copies of the Doryphoros and Diadoumenos. If both these marbles are of Roman date, they should be considered adaptations of Classical styles, since no specific prototype can be cited at present.

2. *Headless statue of youth, Bowdoin College Museum of Art 1961.97* (figs. 136, 137). This under-life-sized statue is known only through the entry in K. Herbert, *Ancient Art in Bowdoin College* (Cambridge, Mass., 1964) 40-41, no. 97, pl. 14, where it is described as a "refashioning" of a Polykleitan model. With both its feet on the ground and a pronounced curve of the median line toward its right, the figure strongly recalls the so-called Diskophoros usually attributed to Polykleitos himself. Two elements are of interest. Along the right leg of the figure stands a tree trunk of the type commonly used as statue supports; however, in the Bowdoin piece a snake is depicted coiling *within* the tree itself. Its tail emerges from an opening at the bottom, while the head protrudes from an upper hole and is directed forward, toward the viewer. Snakes and tree trunks are often used in connection with representations of Apollo, but in those the animal appears alongside the stump, not within it. See,

e.g., the Apollo/Commodus Corsini: G. De Luca, *I monumenti antichi di Palazzo Corsini* (Rome 1976) no. 38, pl. 63, and further discussion on the type by E. Paribeni, *RivIstArch* 1, ser. 3 (1978) 5-10. Perhaps the rendering of the Bowdoin piece is meant to suggest a chthonic rather than an Apolline connection.

A second point of interest is the presence of struts along the entire left side of the youth: stumps remain at mid-calf, mid-thigh, and at the level of the pubes. A scar on the left shoulder may be a later damage, but could perhaps be connected with the series of supports. In that case, a long object must have rested on the shoulder and continued down to the ground, where it joined the base. A large circular scar on the top surface of the latter suggests that the object was, at least in its lower portion, of considerable thickness and not spearlike as, for instance, in the Meleager type, which nonetheless vaguely recalls our figure. More pertinent is the fact that R. Fleischer has recently presented a torso from Ephesos, of the Diskophoros type, with traces of a stafflike object along the left shoulder. On these grounds Fleischer has suggested that the "Diskophoros" should be reconstructed neither as a discus carrier nor as a Hermes but rather somewhat along the lines of the Doryphoros, the staff continuing downward, since the Ephesos torso has a strut on the calf along the same line of the upper one: *Final Programme*, 66. Fleischer's suggestion seems to conflict with the composition, in that it would require a long vertical accent on the side of the bent leg, while the figure turns its head in the opposite direction. E. Berger, on the basis of a bronze statuette in Basel, suggests that the original work represented Theseus looking toward a sword held in his right hand: *AntK* 21 (1978) 51-54, esp. nn. 4-5. But the marble torso in Basel that is considered a replica of the same type (pl. 15.6) shows stronger musculature and more mature forms, which may indicate a contamination with the so-called Polykleitan Herakles. At least one marble head, from Corinth, which is said to be of the Diskophoros type, seems to me to have portrait features: *BCH* 90 (1966) 756, fig. 9.

The Polykleitan "Diskophoros" is known in a

variety of sizes. Several bronze statuettes with attributes of Hermes occur, especially in Gaul, and S. Boucher has argued that this distribution suggests a true dependence from a Greek, not a Roman, original: *BCH* 100 (1976) 95-102, and *Recherches sur les bronzes figurés de Gaule préromaine et romaine* (Rome 1976) esp. map 13. Most of the stone replicas are under-life-sized, including the new torso from Ephesos. Finally, a large-scale bronze from the Sebasteion in Boubon, Turkey, has been compared in general stance, although the face has been given a fine beard; head and one foot are now in the J. Paul Getty Museum, Malibu, while the body is in the Burdur Museum. See J. Inan, *IstMitt* 27-28 (1977-78) 267-87, esp. 285, no. 15, and pls. 93-94. From its provenience and through the existence of the inscribed base, the Boubon statue is firmly dated to 254-268 A.C.

The Bowdoin torso is obviously of Roman date. Because of the unusual rendering of the snake, it is perhaps to be considered a funerary statue, in which case the long object on its left side may be a downturned torch or a similar funerary symbol: cf. the so-called Ildefonso group and other possible reconstructions and suggestions in E. Berger, *AntK* 21 (1978) 55-62 and sketches on p. 60 (on the Westmacott Athlete).

3. *Polykleitan Youth, Carnegie Institute Museum of Art, Pittsburgh* (figs. 138-141). The Polykleitan nature of this Roman statue is enhanced by the head, with its carefully detailed hair and the strong indentation on the nape so typical of the Doryphoros. The forms of the body are softer than in true Polykleitan works, and the age depicted is appropriate for an adolescent, as also suggested by the delicate face. The statue, allegedly found near Olympia, was published by D. T. Owsley, *Carnegie Magazine* 46 (Jan. 1972) 16-22, as a copy of a Polykleitan bronze ca. 440-435 B.C. made around 130-138 A.C. Owsley interpreted the two large cuttings over the shoulders as points for the attachment of the statue to a niche made by a later owner. It seems more probable that these deep and long cuttings on the back of the figure served for the fastening of separately carved wings turning the figure into an Eros. This interpretation accords well with the adolescent and rather romantic appearance of the statue and may strengthen the suggestion that the work is a Roman creation in Polykleitan style comparable to the Ikaros: Zanker, 23-24, no.

20, pl. 23:5-6. As in the latter, the head of the Carnegie youth seems patterned after that of the Westmacott Athlete; however the stance is different, with both arms lowered and weight on the right leg.

4. *Hermes Ludovisi Type.* The name comes from the best replica, in the Terme Museum, but several others exist. Also well known is a statue in the Louvre signed by Kleomenes, a sculptor of the Augustan age who gave the torso a portrait head; the statue has therefore been known as the "Germanicus." The Hermes Ludovisi type has been attributed to various sculptors of the mid-Fifth century, primarily Myron and Pheidias. S. Karouzou has suggested that the bronze original represented not Hermes Logios but Hermes Psychopompos and that it stood on the official monument for the dead at the Battle of Koroneia in 477 B.C.: *AthMitt* 76 (1961) 91-106. This theory is still being debated, and D. W. Bradeen has stressed the lack of evidence for *public* funerary monuments of the Fifth century decorated with sculpture (see ch. 6, Bibl. for p. 144). Attention has also centered on the so-called Germanicus, which has been independently identified as M. Claudius Marcellus, Augustus' nephew, by G. Säflund (*OpRom* 9 [1973] 1-18) and J. Ch. Balty (*AntK* 20 [1977] 102-18, esp. 108-16). The statue would have been erected posthumously and the choice of a famous type of Hermes Psychopompos made to heroize the deceased.

A fragmentary replica of the Ludovisi type from Side has provided new evidence for the position of the raised right arm, which parallels that of the Germanicus. J. Inan has suggested that the original was by the same hand as the Kassel Apollo and therefore by Pheidias: *AntK* 13 (1970) 26-32, and *Roman Sculpture in Side* (Ankara 1975) 32-40, no. 6. Strongly against an association with that Apollo type is E. A. Arslan, who has identified a replica of the Hermes Ludovisi in Genoa: *BdA* 51 (1966) 133-48, figs. 45-49. His position agrees with that of H. von Steuben who, in discussing the Terme replica (Helbig[4], no. 2326), doubts both the Myronian and the Pheidian attribution but gives the type to a sculptor of the mid-Fifth century.

Since the body was used for the funerary portrait of a member of Augustus' family, it seems likely that the original was truly a Fifth century statue of some prominence, but the superimposition of the face of the Kassel Apollo to that of the Side Hermes (as attempted by J. Inan in *AntK*) shows that the contour of the Hermes is wider and only the side locks of the Apollo blur the difference. The stance of the Hermes is more stationary than that of the Apollo (perhaps because the head is turned in the opposite direction) and conforms to our understanding of Severe/Classical poses—the so-called Attic stance. The meaning of the raised right arm has not yet been satisfactorily explained, but a gesture of farewell or summoning seems plausible and in keeping with Hermes' function as Leader of the Dead, whether the statue was originally intended as a funerary monument or, what is more likely, as a private dedication.

5. *Aphrodite with the Turtle in Berlin (K 5)*. This slightly over-life-sized statue has often been considered a Greek original by Pheidias (the Aphrodite Ourania), or at least by a member of his circle, and as such it was included in Blümel, *Berlin*, 91-93, no. 109, figs. 161-69. A subsequent study has attempted to associate a head type to the Berlin torso, here considered a copy: F. Croissant, *BCH* 95 (1971) 65-107. The theory is based on the peculiar form of a female "bust" from the theater at Arles, which would correspond to the distinctive slip of the chiton in the Berlin statue. Croissant would date the original composition early in the first quarter of the Fourth century, coming perhaps from Praxitelean circles and inspired by such earlier works as the Aphrodite Valentini. He further stressed the "Classicizing" character of the statue, which he would ascribe to the stylistic trends of the early Fourth century.

Traditionally, the Berlin statue has been compared to the reclining Figure M from the Parthenon East Pediment: Schrader is supposed to have exclaimed: "One of the *Tauschwestern* has stood up!" when first confronted with the piece. The similarity is especially apparent in the curving folds rippling concentrically away from the rounded salience of the stomach, below the kolpos, and in the motif of the sleeve slipping off the shoulder. Another frequent comparison is with a figure from the Erechtheion frieze, Akr. 1077, most recently discussed by P. N. Boulter, *AntP* 10 (1970) 9-10, pls. 3-4, which is, however, considered earlier except by Croissant. In all these types the sliding of the sleeve is caused by the leaning position; the Berlin statue is supposed to have rested the left elbow on an Archaistic idol.

From personal examination, I am inclined to believe that the Berlin statue is a copy rather than a Greek original, not only because of the many attachments, but also because of a certain harshness and simplification in the treatment of the chiton folds. The Berlin Museum acquired the statue from a Venetian collection (Palazzo Brazzà), and perhaps the piece, rather than having been brought in from Athens by Morosini as usually surmised, may have come from Crete, as did many of the Venetian antiquities. The stiffness of the pose despite the leaning motif, and the advanced left leg, which seems to be stepping forward rather than simply resting on a turtle (restored, but probably correctly), are perhaps too awkward for a true Fifth or even Fourth century creation and more in keeping with Classicizing art: a conclusion that does not necessarily exclude the connection of the Berlin torso with the Arles bust. No true replica of this statue is known (perhaps only one adaptation), but the motif is certainly popular during the late Fifth century and continues well into the Hellenistic period.

6. *Aphrodite Doria and Ariadne Valentini*. The Doria statue, known in only three replicas, has been recently published by B. Palma in R. Calza, ed., *Le Antichità di Villa Doria Pamphilj* (Rome 1977) 44-45, no. 12, pls. 10-11. The general type is related to the Aphrodite with the Turtle in Berlin (supra, no. 5), except in details: the mantle is longer and curves up above the left hip, thus covering more of the stomach area; the chiton slides toward the right shoulder rather than the left; the statue does not lean on a support and the advanced left foot rests level with the right, in a static pose, although the drapery in general is lively and windblown, as contrasted with the stately fall of folds in the Berlin statue. The Doria type has been attributed to the period 430-420, within the circle of Agorakritos or to the master himself (Despinis, 159-61 and n. 267 with bibliography).

This creation is closely related to other types, specifically the Hera Borghese, which has also been given to the same sculptor (Despinis, 156-58) and which is in turn comparable to the Aphrodite from the Athenian Agora (supra, ch. 5). One more figure, known from seven replicas, is the so-called Aphrodite Valentini, which E.

Bielefeld claims is an Ariadne on the evidence of a wreathed copy of the head and a Dionysiac scene on an Attic vase: *AntP* 17 (1978) 57-69. The type differs from the Doria statue in having no belt to the chiton and a mantle that falls along the left leg after crossing the thigh, without visible support. Bielefeld ascribes the Valentini type to a master of the Pheidian circle and dates the original to ca. 421-415. In the Late Hellenistic period the composition was "re-created" by Neo-Attic sculptors, but it had already served as the foundation for the style of the sculptor Timotheos. An article on the Leda assigned to this Fourth century master stresses, in fact, the parallelism between the copies of the Aphrodite Valentini and those of the Leda: A. Rieche, *AntP* 17 (1978) 21-55, esp. 44-45.

The similarity among these statue types—all representative of the transparent ribbon-drapery /flamboyant-costume manner—underlines the stylistic koine already noted for works of the Quiet Style. Some of the liveliness in the wind-blown folds may have been added by Roman copyists and some variants may be imputed to later sculptors as "new creations."

FOR PAGE 192

The problem of copies has received sporadic treatment but still demands attention. Among recent works on the subject see Bieber, *Ancient Copies*, and her historical analysis of the approach to copies, ch. 1, pp. 1-9. On the arrangement of copies within a Roman context see recently C. C. Vermeule, *Greek Sculpture and Roman Taste* (Ann Arbor 1977). A technical discussion on the methods of reproduction can be found in G.M.A. Richter, *The Portraits of the Greeks* 1 (London 1965) 24-27, figs. v-vii and no. 26 on p. 115, fig. 527; cf. also id., in *Studi in onore di Luisa Banti* (Rome 1965) 389-91.

FOR PAGE 193

For works with "doubles" see, e.g., the so-called Penelope, *Severe Style*, 101-103; a general discussion by F. Brommer in *Studies Presented to D. M. Robinson* 1 (St. Louis 1951) 675-82, with mention of statues on reliefs. For copies of reliefs, see ch. 6, and here n. 2.

FOR PAGE 194

Grimani Group: the most complete publication is R. Kabus-Jahn, *AntP* 11 (1972); see also G. Traversari, *Sculpture del V° e IV° Secolo A.C. del Museo Archeologico di Venezia* (Venice 1973) 52-70, nos. 20-26; on their provenience see L. Beschi, *ASAtene* 50-51, n.s. 34-35 (1972-73) 494-502; stylistic discussion in S. Karouzou, *AthMitt* 82 (1967) 158-69. "Hera" in Lullies and Hirmer, fig. 206 (labeled Demeter). Cf. also E. La Rocca, *ArchCl* 28 (1976) 225-34, pl. 87. On the Peiraeus Kore see ch. 5.

FOR PAGE 195

Other deposits of sculpture from Knossos: cf., e.g., G. Waywell, *BSA* 72 (1977) 91-99 (perhaps a private collection of sculpture from a villa?), note mention of forthcoming publication of a shrine. See also J. N. Coldstream, *Knossos, the Sanctuary of Demeter* (*BSA* suppl. 8, 1973) 180-85. For a similar sanctuary group from Kyparissi, Kos, see R. Kabus-Preisshofen, *AntP* 15 (1975) 31-64; there see also mention of another group, still unpublished, from Macedonia.

Abbondanza Grimani: Kabus-Jahn, no. 1; Traversari, *Venezia*, no. 24, pp. 60-65, with new list of replicas of the Kore Albani (updating Hekler's original list). Traversari considers the statue a Parthenonian creation.

Velletri Athena: see ch. 7.

Headless figure in Athens, Nat. Mus. 4762: Delivorrias, 168-69, pl. 60; id., *AntP* 9 (1969) 7-13 (considered the cult image of the Ilissos Temple).

Kore Albani: Helbig⁴, no. 3342 (W. Fuchs)—considered a copy of a bronze original of the circle of Pheidias, ca. 440-430.

For the type reproduced in a relief see Helbig⁴ no. 3229.

FOR PAGE 196

Villa Doria Pamphilj statue: R. Calza, ed., *Le Antichità di Villa Doria Pamphilj* (Rome 1977) 42, no. 8, pl. 8—so-called Flora.

Peiraeus Maiden: traces of Agorakritos' style are suggested by S. Karouzou, *AthMitt* 82 (1967) 158-69; *contra* see Despinis, 190-91 and n. 445.

Grimani statuette by Argive sculptor: Karouzou, *loc. cit.*

Velletri Athena by Alkamenes (with discussion of previous attributions): E. B. Harrison, *AJA* 81 (1977) 150-55, 164-74.

Kore Albani: to Pheidian circle, Fuchs in Helbig⁴, no. 3342; to Kalamis: lecture by E. B. Harrison; Delivorrias, *AthMitt* 93 (1978) 17-18.

Dresden Zeus: Despinis, 132-42; replica in Olympia, P. Mingazzini, *ASAtene* 47-48, n.s. 31-32 (1969-70) 71-84, esp. p. 73 n. 3; Mingazzini dates the prototype to ca. 370-360.

Capitoline Demeter: Helbig⁴, no. 1387 (von Steuben); most recently discussed, in connection with the Prokne and Itys, by Schuchhardt, *Alkamenes*, 11-13, n. 8 and fig. 9 on p. 15. On the Hellenistic revival of the peplos see M. Gernand, *AthMitt* 90 (1975) 1-47; H. Jung, *JdI* 91 (1976) 97-134.

FOR PAGE 198

Frejus Aphrodite: illustrations of the name-piece and of many replicas and variants conveniently collected in Bieber, *Ancient Copies*, figs.

124-57, pp. 46-47; Bieber had once considered the possibility that the type was created in the early imperial period: *RömMitt* 48 (1933) 261-76; for the discussion of the Venus Genetrix type see W. Fuchs, in *Festschrift B. Schweitzer* (Stuttgart 1954) 206-17. For a possible Hellenistic adaptation see B. S. Ridgway, *Classical Sculpture* (Catalogue of the Museum of Art, RISD, Providence, 1972) 40-42, no. 14.

Orestes and Elektra in Naples: see *Severe Style*, 135, fig. 175.

FOR PAGE 199

For an eclectic Roman creation (Neronian) that starts from the Frejus Aphrodite type, see a statue from Rethymnos, Crete, D. Papastamos and K. Stähler, *KrChron* 1972, 93-106.

That the Aphrodite is dropping her mantle is suggested by Hiller, 3-7, on the basis of a new, unpublished, replica of the type in Saloniki. His text gives a detailed stylistic analysis.

FOR PAGE 200

Este Aphrodite: Lippold, *Handbuch*, pl. 104:2, see also ch. 3:63-64 and n. 30.

Frejus Aphrodite as reaction to Agorakritos' style: S. Karouzou, *AthMitt* 89 (1974) 151-72. For the suggestion that she is the Aphrodite in the Gardens by Alkamenes see G. Siebert, *BCH* 90 (1966) 718-20, pls. 8-9. The latest defense of the often-repeated attribution to Kallimachos is by Karouzou, *loc. cit.*, who, however, wants the statue to be also the Ourania that Pausanias (1.14.6) attributes to Pheidias. G. Becatti, *Problemi Fidiaci* (Milan and Florence 1952) 207-12, states that the Temple of Aphrodite Ourania was part of the Perikleian building program, but gives no authority for his statement, and I have not been able to substantiate it.

Head in Athens, Nat. Mus. 3569: S. Karouzou, *AthMitt* 89 (1974) 151-72, with comparison to the Hegeso stele.

Gravestone from Stryme (Thrace): G. Bakalakis, *AthMitt* 77 (1962) 197-206.

FOR PAGE 201

Polykleitos: a useful collection of ancient sources, including drawings of the extant signed bases, remains R. Bianchi Bandinelli, *Policleto* (Quaderni per lo Studio dell'Archeologia 1, Florence 1938). For a compendium of modern

literature see also P. E. Arias, *Policleto* (Florence 1964). See also T. Lorenz, *Polyklet* (Wiesbaden 1972), and H. von Steuben, *Der Kanon des Polyklet* (Tübingen 1973). Important considerations on true Polykleitan traits in Zanker. Cf. also *EAA*, s.v. Policleto (L. Beschi).

Head of "Hera" in British Museum: see ch. 9. On Polykleitos the Younger as the maker of the Hera see A. Linfert, *Von Polyklet zu Lysipp* (Diss. Giessen 1966) 2-8.

FOR PAGE 202

That statues in Panhellenic sanctuaries may not have been copied is mentioned by Kron, 223.

The latest suggestion on Polykleitos' canon is A. F. Stewart, *JHS* 98 (1978) 122-31. According to him, the Baiae casts reveal an angular Doryphoros quite different from the Roman copies.

For a rebuttal of von Steuben's theories on the canon see H. Philipp in *Wandlungen* (Festschrift Homann-Wedeking, Waldsassen/Bayern 1975). On the Doryphoros as Achilles: Zanker, 7.

FOR PAGE 204

Diadoumenos: Zanker, 11-13.

Westmacott Athlete: Zanker, 19-21; E. Berger, *AntK* 21 (1978) 55-62.

FOR PAGE 205

Diskophoros: Zanker, 4-5; for a new replica from Ephesos see R. Fleischer, *Final Programme*, 66, to be published in forthcoming *ÖJh*. See also Appendix 8:2.

Diadoumenos Farnese: Zanker, 13-14, no. 11.

Herakles: Zanker, 17-19, esp. 19.

Hermes: D. K. Hill, *AJA* 74 (1970) 21-24.

Narkissos: Zanker, 26; recently, also S. Hiller, *AntK* 19 (1976) 38-40.

On the school of Polykleitos, besides Linfert, *op. cit.*, see also D. Arnold, *Die Polykletnachfolge* (*JdI—EH* 25, 1969).

FOR PAGE 206

Three-Figure Reliefs: H. Götze, *RömMitt* 53 (1938) 189-280.

H. A. Thompson, *Hesperia* 21 (1952) 47-82. For a criticism of Eleos as Pity, cf. G. Zuntz, *ClMed* 14 (1953) 71-85. On the possible location of the altar and its independent existence from the Agora altar see, e.g., E. Vanderpool, *Hesperia* 43 (1974) 308-10.

FOR PAGE 207

Harrison: *Hesperia* 33 (1964) 76-82.

Beschi: in *Sculture Greche e Romane di Cirene* (Padua 1959) 76, n. 40. ˙

Langlotz, in *Bonner Festgabe J. Straub* (*BonnJbb* BH 39, 1977) 91-112. For E. B. Harrison's acceptance of a lower date see *AJA* 81 (1977) 421 n. 67: contemporary with the Erechtheion frieze.

Great Eleusinian Relief and its copies: see ch. 6.

Hausmann: pp. 48-50.

FOR PAGE 208

Peirithoos/Theseus: see E. Langlotz, *AntP* 12 (1973) 91-93.

FOR PAGE 209

Moschato base, Athens Nat. Mus. 4502, *BCH* 85 (1961) 604; the point was noted both by Harrison and by Langholtz (*Festgabe Straub*, p. 103 n. 18).

The Medea relief has been analyzed in particular by R. Carpenter, *MAAR* 18 (1941) 62-70. Cf. also C. Hofkes-Brukker, *BABesch* 42 (1967) 38-48.

Orpheus relief: on the literary aspect of the story see J. Heurgon, *MélRome* 49 (1932) 6-60; for the theory that the relief does not represent Orpheus' second loss see L. M. Owen, *Hesperia* 33 (1964) 401-404. The relief has been the subject of a small monograph by W.-H. Schuchhardt, *Das Orpheus-Relief* (Opus Nobile, Reclam no. 102, Stuttgart 1964).

Parthenon frieze parallel: Brommer, *Fries*, pls. 144-45, slab S XXV, 62.

Lekythos of Myrrhine: Athens Nat. Mus. 4485; S. Karouzou, *Catalogue*, 47; for illustrations see, e.g., Harrison, *AJA* 81 (1977) 271, fig. 8, and bibl. in n. 28; latest, Ch. Clairmont, in *Studies von Blanckenhagen*, 103-10.

Cyrene relief: L. Beschi, in *Sculture Greche e Romane di Cirene*, 57-90.

FOR PAGE 210

Relief from the Quirinal in Berlin, K 83: Blümel, *Berlin*, 60-61, no. 69, fig. 101. H. P. Isler, *Acheloos* (Bern 1970), 31 and cat. no. 1, p. 123, considers the relief Attic, taken to Rome by an ancient art-lover.

Dancing Maenads Reliefs: perhaps the most extensive study is by W. Fuchs, *Vorbilder*, 72-91; for an additional Neo-Attic relief in Geneva see J. Dörig, *Art Antique, Collections privées de Suisse romande* (Mainz 1975) no. 3; cf. also Helbig[4], no. 159 (W. Fuchs). The costumes are analyzed by Bieber, *Ancient Copies*, 110-14, figs. 495-507. For the opinion that they are the most widely known monument see Carpenter, 157.

FOR PAGE 211

Berlin bronze krater: W. Züchner, *BerlWinkProgr* 98 (1938) 3-27.

Carpenter, pp. 156-59; he expanded his comments during a lecture in 1955.

For the series from Ptolemais see G. Caputo, *Lo scultore del grande bassorilievo con la danza delle menadi in Tolemaide di Cirenaica* (Rome 1948).

FOR PAGE 212

The suggestion that the Maenads could have exemplified the chorus for the *Bacchai* is made by Züchner, *loc. cit.* The original numbering of the figures goes back to F. Hauser, *Die neu-attischen Reliefs* (Stuttgart 1889) 7-17.

"Ivy-Leaf Maenad": Hauser, no. 28; Carpenter, pl. 27.

For the Nike Akroterion from the Stoa of Zeus see ch. 3.

FOR PAGE 213

Attribution to Kallimachos: see, e.g., G. Gullini, *ArchCl* 5 (1953) 133-62.

CHAPTER 9

Echoes of Fifth Century Styles in Later Periods—
Roman Creations

TENTATIVE CHRONOLOGICAL OUTLINE OF TRUE FIFTH CENTURY STYLES

THROUGHOUT the preceding chapters we have discussed the various sculptural styles that developed in the period between 450 and 400 B.C.; they were examined at first in original works, both in relief and in the round, and then in copies, either approximately contemporary or of Roman times, which gave sufficient assurance of reflecting Classical Greek originals. We come now to the most difficult task of determining when evidence of such Fifth century styles in later, and especially in Roman, works should be interpreted not as slavish dependence from a Greek prototype but as imitation of the styles alone, in new creations which may resemble Fifth century sculpture but which differ from it in spirit, coherence, purpose, or other aspects. This enormous task necessarily involves a great deal of subjectivity and can only be touched upon in this context. Before beginning, however, it seems expedient to review what we can distill from our previous analyses and discussions. The traits of Classical sculpture had already been outlined at the beginning of our survey, but they were intentionally expressed in such general terms as to apply to any of the various stylistic manifestations within the period under review. We can now attempt a more or less chronological sketch of the different trends.

Drapery

The beginning of the period sees the last manifestations of the Severe style at work. Garments are still heavy and doughy, though with increased richness of patterns, especially where the edges of mantles or peploi cascade along the bodies or are held by belts. Selvage is introduced. Variations in surface treatment are attempted, so that the thinner chiton can be differentiated from either the himation or the peplos that covers it. Two major interests therefore develop in the period 450-435: (1) *Interest in texture.* It promotes the reintroduction of the chiton and its crinkly folds, not in the artificial patterns of the Archaic period but in more naturalistic renderings albeit dependent on the same principles of a multiplicity of lines often branching off from buttons or seams. (2) *Interest in modeling.* Since the heavy peplos and the sober taste of the Severe style had virtually hidden the body except for key points of protrusion or articulation, a system of folds is now devised to allow the rendering of volumes under the garments. This attempt had begun with the sculptures of the Olympia pediments; its purpose is now fully achieved through the gradation of depth and the use of tension lines cutting across forms. Two styles of drapery develop: (a) the heavy, opaque kind, which differs from the Severe only in the greater amount of its folds, the sharpness of the ridges, and the depth of the valleys in between. Since this heavy cloth has a consistency of its own, motion lines can be introduced to convey the impression that movement is pushing the drapery off the body. Thus, in heavy drapery the motion lines are almost always moving away from the figure rather than around it. (b) the thin, transparent drapery, which clings to the body, even in unnatural ways or, when away from it, falls in flat pleats very closely spaced, usually pulled by gravity. A good amount of incision helps in the textural effects. Only relatively small areas of the body are left free of folds where such thin drapery is adopted. Both types of drapery are fully exploited within the sculptures of the Parthenon, which form our best evidence for this period.

Between 435 and 425 a transformation takes place. The desire to combine modeling lines with motion lines and the increased interest in the effects of transparency induce the sculptors to forego coherence and to use heavy drapery as if it were light. Garments move up as well as away from the body, as if carried by individual upsurging drafts, which produce sanguisuga folds at ankles and waists. Peploi can also cling as if made of silk and yet retain their thickness when away from the figure, so that the same garment can at once appear both thin and heavy. This ambiguity of rendering has created some confusion in the definition of the costumes: these are not chitons worn in peplos-fashion, as sometimes stated, but peploi treated as if they were chiton-thin;[1] the real differentiation should be made on the basis of mode of fastening and width, the chiton being much larger and having sleeves, the peplos being pinned only over the shoulders. But texture, which was once the main indication of a costume, is now no longer a valid criterion. In addition, mantles are shown worn with the peplos and similarly treated. This rendering is the logical development of the heavy drapery style used in the preceding phase. The thin drapery develops into ribbon drapery: the ridges become flatter and wider, their edges sharper and undercut, but no real valleys separate the folds from each other. They lie close to the body, which they reveal.

Around 420 several styles are current simultaneously: a "quiet style," fairly opaque and sedate, which models with only moderate elaboration; a "ribbon style," which becomes increasingly transparent, with fewer and fewer folds; a "flamboyant style," which goes beyond the expression of movement and transparency and delights in decorative effects; finally, all sorts of combinations of the above occur, in various degrees. Drapery clings in ogival patches rimmed by sharp edges; large areas of the body may be left free of folds, but very rich effects are also prevalent. Contrasts of vertical, horizontal, and oblique lines are favored, often to stress the pose.

The last two decades of the Fifth century see a slightly more unified style. Transparency is the order of the day, with drapery that occasionally looks almost cobwebby and loops across virtually naked limbs, fully outlined within their clothes. Transparency can also be accompanied by simplicity, with very few lines forming patterns at articulation points. Folds, which had already been used for compositional effects, lead the eye in certain directions and emphasize stance, act as foils or visual supports, outline limbs. Parallelism

---

[1] A precedent for this treatment occurs already during the Severe period, in the Nike from Paros, that is, in an area of Ionic influence where decorative effects have precedence over structure. An aid to the distinction may be given by the presence or absence of selvage, which should appear only on the heavier cloth of the peplos or the himation.

of lines often results in a "railroad tracks" effect across some smooth surface as folds tend to pair off rhythmically. Flamboyancy can assume baroque overtones, without following true modeling or motion principles but aiming at purely decorative and chromatic effects of light and shadow. Textural renderings seem largely irrational and selvage virtually disappears. Outside of Attica, similar developments can be noted, perhaps slightly later. In Ionic territory the lack of a strong body support under the drapery creates a more decorative effect from the beginning. In the north of Greece, linearity predominates and a certain harshness of forms, which can be found also in the Peloponnesos but without the Ionic touches. From Magna Graecia there is little evidence, but baroque taste seems in favor at least by the end of the period.

Anatomy and Poses

In the Severe period naked bodies had looked almost pasty, solid, undifferentiated except in major areas. Conversely, lean renderings looked harsh and built up in sections, with little modulation between planes. Torsos were wide and fairly static, except for the slanting of the hips. In cross-section, a Severe-style body would appear as two fairly uniform curves dipping in the center to mark the median line in front, the spinal furrow in the back. This rendering continues after 450, but around 440 the Doryphoros of Polykleitos brings in the chiasmos (contrapposto), and bodies receive a much greater articulation, flat areas being balanced by swellings, stretched muscles alternating with compressed ones. In Attica a peculiar mannerism appears, perhaps in an attempt to convey effort and motion: the rib cage is made to protrude as if for an intake of breath, creating a sharp indentation at or slightly above the waist; in some figures wrinkles, often near the navel, suggest loose skin rippling above the skeletal frame or the flesh.

Musculature in Attic figures is moderate, in "Polykleitan" figures enormous, perhaps because the former have survived in marble, but the latter were in bronze, where light diffusion and reflection would blur articulation unless emphasized. Knowledge of anatomy seems too great to be limited to direct observation in the palaestra. Perhaps the answer lies in the concomitant development of the medical schools. But artistic interest focuses on the front, which in free-standing statues is almost never hidden from view by limbs or attributes.

The so-called Attic stance continues the Severe tradition of one foot forward or to the side, but flat on the ground, although the weight of the body is largely supported by the other leg. The Peloponnesian stance, probably perfected if not initiated by Polykleitos, has the free leg trailing and even at some distance from the body, the heel off the ground. The chiastic balance occurs in some Parthenon figures, so the diffusion of the style must have been rapid.

Around 425, bodies become leaner, and some differentiation between youths and men is favored, but evidence is uneven and largely derived from copies. Poses begin to emphasize continuous lines from head to extended foot and "heroic diagonals" both in relief and in free-standing sculpture. Whatever the pose, the body gives the impression of being a coherent whole, with arms and legs not as mere appendages but as integrated elements of a functioning machine.

I have not been able to obtain a clear idea of the male naked figure around 400.

224

Head and Hair Treatment

Heads are large in proportion to the bodies, even in female figures: jaws are heavy, in continuation of the Severe style, but features become larger within the face and the rather vacant expression of the earlier style disappears. Characterization is introduced and goes from extremes of linear pattern to modeling and naturalism, from old age to youth, if not to true rendering of adolescence and childhood. Portraiture begins, but more as idealized depiction of character than as close imitation of individual features.

Attic heads tend to be oval, "Peloponnesian" (or rather Polykleitan) heads are flatter on top, with greater depth to the skull. Eyes are large, slightly bulging, with prominent lids, which slope downward like flat shelves, and which may have sharp edges rather than the rounded contours of the Severe renderings. The "rosebud" mouth occurs in the Parthenon frieze, Polykleitan faces seem to have straighter lips, though fleshier, especially the lower one. Male hair is no longer impressionistically rendered, as is often the case in the Severe period; locks are longer and more detailed, as befits the engraving possible in bronze, but arranged according to a radiating pattern and closely adhering to the skull, with little protrusion and mass. Their volume increases toward the end of the period.

Female hair is parted in the center and waves away from the temples in rounded shapes with considerable undercutting. It is usually worn in a chignon over the nape or (more rarely) gathered on top of the head in a spray of strands (the *lampadion* coiffure), but it can also fall down in a large mass over the shoulders, in slightly Archaizing fashion. Long locks over the chest are also an antiquarian trait and may suggest a matronly character. Braids are rare but can encircle the head as well as originate in the area of the central part. *Sphendonai* (wide bands that support the hair over the nape) and *sakkoi* (wide bands covering the entire head) are commonly used for Aphrodite or Kore, but while the Severe sakkos compressed and hid the hair from view, the Classical rendering allows wisps of hair to emerge and suggest a springy mass. Faces tend to become rounder and less heavy toward the end of the century, but the pointed oval of some Roman replicas may be due to the romanticizing intent of the copyist.

ECHOES OF THE FIFTH CENTURY IN LATER PERIODS

The Fifth century ended on a note of flamboyance and virtuoso carving, which the Fourth century continued with abandon for at least twenty more years. The sculptures from Epidauros exemplify the development of some trends that had begun in the previous phase, and the Nereids from Xanthos (figs. 142-144) are so similar to true Classical work that until recently they were dated around 400. Since they are at least one generation later, they are an obvious case of Lingering Fifth century styles. They reproduce both the transparent drapery, which here is literally engraved onto the body of one figure, and the heavier, opaque type on which S-folds run parallel courses forming the typical railroad tracks.

Another clear case of Lingering styles, the Lycian sarcophagus from Sidon, has already been discussed in chapter 6. The many friezes of the Heroon at Gjölbaschi Trysa could provide many more examples. These works have received attention in recent publications pointing out the links with Fifth century Athens and therefore need no further discussion here. It may be worth noting, however, that of the many Classical mannerisms the non-Greek territories of Asia Minor adopted one in particular and turned it into a virtual hieroglyph for movement: the billowing skirt. The most obvious Fifth century example for this motif is Figure G on the Parthenon East Pediment (fig. 23), where the saillike area of the peplos flattening out from the left knee is actually not a very successful attempt at conveying speed, since it does so at the expense of modeling. Under its flattening effect the left leg is all but lost. In East Greek renderings this curving section of fluttering drapery is added to the rear of the skirt in a more plausible arrangement, but it is made so mechanical and symbolic that it is difficult to see it as an imitation of those motion lines which were so effective in true Fifth century sculpture. The motif occurs throughout the Fourth century: in the friezes of the Nereid Monument, in those of Gjölbaschi Trysa, in the hunt frieze of the Sarcophagus of the Mourning Women, and elsewhere, despite chronological differences. What is unusual is that these motion lines are applied to male garments, as contrasted with true Fifth century practices.

Lingering Fifth century styles may not be surprising in areas outside the Greek world proper; to some extent they are not surprising in provincial areas of Greece itself, such as Thessaly or Macedonia. They are more remarkable in Epidauros, since the Peloponnesos, and especially the sanctuary of Asklepios, succeeded Athens as the seat of strong artistic activity and development. However, the reasons behind the adoption of such styles may be different. In the case of the pedimental or akroterial figures from the Asklepieion it is clear that the trends are being developed further, not just imitated or repeated; in other cases stylistic conservatism seems intentional, perhaps for religious reasons. A good example is provided by the two famous reliefs from Epidauros, which have been traditionally thought to represent Asklepios, perhaps even the cult image by Thrasymedes of Paros, but are instead different depictions, one of Asklepios, bearded and with short hair, and one of Apollo, with long curls and beardless. Poses and garments are comparable (although the Olympian is given a more elaborate seat), but the drapery of Asklepios has the irrational bunching of folds typical of its period, while Apollo's mantle is arranged with all the regularity of a Parthenonian figure.

In nude male figures Fifth century echoes and forms are fewer. The Diskobolos usually attributed to Naukydes, a pupil of Polykleitos, bears a surprising resemblance to the pose of the Ares Borghese, presumably a typically Attic work. Lysippos could claim that the Doryphoros of Polykleitos was his teacher, but he certainly developed his own canon and a different set of human proportions. Poses and facial features undergo the greatest changes, and the Fourth century can rightly be seen as the harbinger of the Hellenistic period. Although some peplophoroi revive the composure of the Erechtheion Karyatids, enough variations in proportions and renderings clearly mark them as the product of a later phase. Textural effects and interest in clothing reach naturalistic levels never attained by the intellectual Fifth century patterns.

The Third century, as far as I can judge, is almost entirely immune from Classical influence, but the trend starts again in the following period, for a variety of reasons. Primary among them is the prestige that Athens had achieved through the greatness of its philosophical schools and the flourishing of its arts. The Perikleian period and, in general, the entire span from 450 to 400 were justly seen as a peak in civilization: to share in that culture and to emulate it became the aim not only of other areas within the Hellenistic world but also of Athens itself, which had lost its political prominence and now attempted to strengthen its shaken self-confidence by harping on the conquests of its past. We therefore have in Athens such Classicizing works as the Nike of Euboulides, which combines Fifth century transparent drapery with later proportions and high belting; or the Athena by the same master, with a heavy face comparable to the Pheidian Parthenos.

Another factor in the Pheidian revival may have been the need to restore the great gold and ivory images that had been damaged by time and man. Damophon of Messene is known to have repaired the Olympia Zeus and to have made statues of his own with strong Classicizing overtones. In these latter, Hellenistic elements are obvious, but so are the Classicizing quotations.

The area with the greatest interest in Fifth century Athens is Attalid Pergamon. A free replica of the Athena Parthenos stood in the Library, an adaptation of the Prokne stood nearby, and the Gigantomachy frieze of the Great Altar was carved with many allusions to the Parthenon and Fifth century styles.[2] For instance, the skirt of Athena in combat with her giant has the long S-lines that suggest movement, and the inflated folds bend with nicks and curves like those of Paionios' Nike. The pose itself has been used to reconstruct the missing figure from the center of the East Parthenon Pediment, and some scholars advocate the presence of a Nike crowning Athena on the temple, because a Nike occurs in this context within the Great Altar frieze. The supposition might be strengthened by the fact that many Roman historical reliefs utilize the same motif, which is likely to have been copied from the more famous Parthenon rather than from the less well known Pergamene Altar.[3]

Throughout the Gigantomachy frieze, patterns of folds and anatomy recall Classical prototypes, but with a rendering of texture and coloristic contrasts entirely alien to the Fifth century. Valleys between the folds form enormous pockets of shadow, and deep channels outline limbs in an exaggeration of transparent drapery; hems lift and fly out with violent movement, so that the total effect is the epitome of baroque. But the baroque style, in Rhys Carpenter's penetrating conception, is simply the utilization of functional devices, such as the modeling or the motion line, for dramatic purposes. In other words, what had been invented by Fifth century sculptors for practical reasons—to convey the movement or the volume of bodies under heavy drapery—is now used to produce an emotional response through overemphasis and surface differentiation. Were we to reproduce the Great Altar frieze as a linear design, many patterns would clearly resemble those of the Fifth century, although their execution varies enormously. Beyond the language of folds and garments anatomical details bear similar comparison; the great Zeus on the East side of the frieze, for instance, has the same prominent sternum in his chest, the same hollow

---

[2] It has recently been suggested that the monument is not a true altar but an elaborate Heroon over the mythical tomb of Telephos, the founding Hero of Pergamon: K. Stähler, in *Studien zur Religion und Kultur Kleinasiens* (Festschrift K. Dörner, Leiden 1978) 838-67. In either case, the monument would embody an allusion to the victories of the Attalids over the Gauls, and the epic overtones of theme and style would be equally appropriate to a Heroon as to an altar.

[3] To be sure, the same crowning Nike occurs on one of the Parthenon East metopes, in conjunction with an Athena victorious over her giant; perhaps we are less inclined to consider this prototype because of the poor state of preservation of the East metopes.

beneath it, as the heroic Poseidon of the Parthenon West Pediment. But the powerful structure of the latter turns into overdeveloped and almost flayed musculature in the former.

The same comments can be extended to some Pergamene sculpture in the round. Carpenter has analyzed the great male figure from the temple of Hera (either Zeus or one of the Attalids: the so-called Zeus/Hero in Istanbul) against Fourth century works, and indeed the pose, with arm raised on the side of the weight leg and highly trailing left foot, is nonchiastic and momentary, as contrasted with that of the Doryphoros. But the arrangement of the mantle recalls the Dresden Zeus or the Velletri Athena. To be sure, the lines are more irregular and the tension folds around the weight leg stop at the triangular apron instead of continuing under and with it. The roll across the waist is more voluminous and twisted; transparency is obtained through different effects, not with flat ogival patches, and the one irregular valley between the legs, below the tip of the apron, achieves unprecedented texturing and depth. Yet some of the folds along the right leg, in their shelf-like projection, recall the flying-Nike akroterion from the Agora and the massive fall of the mantle edges along the left side retains the zigzags of the Classical works.

One more statue may be briefly mentioned: the dead Amazon in Naples, which probably copies one of the Attalid dedications on the Athenian Akropolis. The entire problem of this group of sculptures needs reexamination; supposedly more than one victim represented each category of defeated enemy—the Giants, the Amazons, the Persians, and the Gauls—and scattered examples of Gauls and Persians in our museums seem to bear this supposition out. But dead Giants and Amazons are only known through one replica each, in the Naples museum, and it may be argued that no great room was available on the Akropolis wall, near the Parthenon, for more than a token representation. Be that as it may, this single Amazon seems a close reproduction of a figure from the shield of the Parthenos: the dead woman lying at the bottom of the various Neo-Attic replicas and consequently the various modern reconstructions. The close proximity of the Pergamene dedication to the Parthenon would have made the comparison obvious and the allusion to Pergamene greatness transparent. But the Amazon in Naples looks Fifth century only in her pose and general attire. Her expressive face and the texture of her chitoniskos are certainly Hellenistic. Once again, the design is Classical but the rendering is contemporary.

Classicizing creations of the First century B.C. are best analyzed together with purely Roman works, since the artistic limits between the two worlds during that period are entirely blurred and the great era of copying and adapting begins.

FIFTH CENTURY TRAITS IN ROMAN WORKS

Books on Roman sculpture usually illustrate historical and funerary reliefs and a series of portrait statues, imperial or otherwise, but almost entirely omit sculpture in the round. This situation is largely the result of a peculiar slant in modern art-historical studies, whereby we are willing to credit the Romans with originality and ability in the former two areas but, when confronted with a free-standing sculpture, we always look for a Greek prototype. Recently an increased appreciation of Roman art and a greater understanding of Roman taste and methods have resulted in the proper assessment and evaluation of some Roman creations. Outstanding in this field has been the work of Paul Zanker, and his book on Classicizing statues, though limited to the naked male figure and to Fifth century styles, has broken important new ground. Since such stylistic analysis cannot be reduced to a scientific formula, however, a certain amount of disagreement is bound to exist in every such attempt to "give Caesar what is Caesar's."

Fifth century traits permeate many Roman historical reliefs, especially in the rendering of divinities, and we shall examine briefly a few safely dated examples to determine what can be expected from comparable Roman creations when executed in the round.

Perhaps the best known and most frequently illustrated among Classicizing Roman reliefs is the Tellus panel from the Ara Pacis (13-9 B.C.), and its similarity to figures from the Parthenon East Pediment has often been pointed out. But the style incorporates renderings which, in a Greek work, should belong to different stages. In the main figure, for instance, the transparency of the chiton with its clear indication of the navel belongs to the very last decade of the Fifth century, yet the treatment of the mantle around the legs is more Parthenonian, therefore earlier. At the same time, the contrast between mantle and chiton is not emphasized as much as in the Parthenon, and there is less depth to the valleys between the folds in the roll over the thighs. Definitely more advanced than on the Parthenon, perhaps even greater than on Fifth century drapery as a whole, is the effect of impressionistic softness conveyed by the mantle tip where it falls against the inner face of the left thigh, between the knees. A comparable use of the drill cannot be found before the pedimental statues from Epidauros in 375 B.C.[4] In the chiton only one sleeve slips, yet both breasts are encircled by the transparent drapery in curving patterns, regardless of the single source of folds, which a Greek would have exploited. In the hair, the drill has been used to separate the strands of a coiffure which recalls that of the Prokne or of the Nemesis, but two long locks have been added, coming from the nape rather than the sides as in the Karyatids. These differences are not "mistakes," since the sculptor of the Tellus was trying not to be correct on antiquarian grounds but simply to produce an impression of grandeur and dignity by alluding to major Greek sculptures: the *aemulatio* of the ancient sources.

A clearer indication of this approach is given in the Julio-Claudian relief in Ravenna (ca. A.D. 40?). The fragmentary figure at the left edge is seated, yet the folds of her chiton are rendered as if in active motion. The omega pattern at the end of the folds is eliminated or attenuated in favor of a squarish opening that reveals the inside of the "tube," as it were. The sharpness of the tension folds in the himation and their looping around the leg suggest transparency, yet the body is not outlined. By contrast, the upper torso is clearly rendered in the most advanced Fifth century style of sheer drapery, with a single sharp fold marking the roundness of the abdomen; however, proportions are rather elongated, more than we would expect in a Classical piece. The individual details are therefore consonant with Fifth century modes, but the total appearance is not.

In the cuirassed figure within the same relief, note also the dichotomy between the vertical folds over the weight leg and the curving lines over the free leg: because of the

[4] These comments are perhaps difficult to credit without proper comparison or contrast. Consider, therefore, the corresponding mantle tip of the Nike leading a bull by Master B on the Nike Balustrade. Although, admittedly, this is a figure in action while the Tellus is static, note that, were we to draw both, in the Nike the pattern of the folds could be reproduced as a logical, linear design which accounts for every course and turn of the cloth, while in the Tellus the appearance of the material could be conveyed only by shading and the design is definitely less "logical."

apparent lack of transition, it looks almost as if two independent garments were rendered. The youthful man to the right wears his mantle as no Greek would wear it: short, almost skirtlike, and circling the back without visible mode of support, but the torso above it and the general pose are Polykleitan, and the tripartite arrangement of the drapery recalls the Aphrodite of Frejus with which it shares also the curving lines across the thighs and the long channel of shadow outlining the figure.

One last example, from the frieze of the Basilica Ulpia in the Forum of Trajan (ca. A.D. 113) may stand for all. One of the Victories kneeling on the back of a bull, ready to sacrifice the animal, is in the familiar pose of a victor overtaking an enemy. Her drapery is transparent when on her legs, heavy and flamboyant when away from the body, with nicks to the tubular folds, and a wavy hem that reveals the interior of pleats. An upward draft lifts a section of the cloth just above the ankle, in a familiar Fifth century pattern. But the rolled mantle slashed by dark channels provides too great a contrast with the underlying areas, such as only the Fourth century or the Hellenistic period produced, and the total nakedness of the torso is in contrast with Fifth century practices.

In summary, although many Fifth century motifs and styles are used in these Roman sculptures, they are often combined with anachronistic renderings or proportions, which betray the artists' awareness of later periods and styles. Modeling and motion lines are used without proper regard for their initial function, and not even for emotional effect, as in the baroque style, but simply as pattern. Technical contrast is either toned down or emphasized in more naturalistic ways than the Fifth century knew. True ribbon drapery is not in great favor, and in general the middle stylistic phase of the Fifth century seems bypassed, while Parthenonian motifs are combined with the decorative and transparent effects of the end of the period. The vocabulary is Fifth century Greek, but the syntax is Roman and includes other idioms. Finally, technical features, such as the extensive use of the drill, can be cited, but they are less compelling since a *bona fide* Roman copy of a Greek original could also display them.

To be sure, once we venture into the field of sculpture in the round, our analysis is complicated by the fact that a whole range of possibilities exist. We could be dealing with a true copy romanticized or rejuvenated by the copyist; or with a copy of an original adapted to a different medium or for a different purpose and therefore with additions or change of attributes; or with such a poor and modest work that the traits of the original are all but lost. However, we could also be confronted with a true creation in Classical style, or with a pastiche making use of different parts from different works, or with an eclectic statue that derives its inspiration from different styles and periods. Finally, there is also the danger of evaluating a statue on the basis of an appearance produced by extensive Roman reworking or repairs, if not by a Renaissance or Eighteenth century restoration. All the suggestions that follow should therefore be considered as tentative: open questions rather than dogmatic pronouncements.

ROMAN CREATIONS

Statues of Old Women

An almost life-size sculpture in Pentelic marble now in the Metropolitan Museum in New York (fig. 145) was found in Rome and, according to the technique of its workmanship, may date from early Flavian times, around A.D. 70. It represents a woman bent over with age, carrying a basket of fruit and chickens, presumably on her way to the market. Her "peplos" (?), which dips so low as to leave her right breast uncovered, is belted at the waist both above and below the kolpos, in the fashion of an Amazon.[5] A long mantle wraps around her back: it is stretched forward by her right arm and is tucked under her belt on her left side, so that part of her skirt on the front is covered by it. On her head is a kerchief that falls down her back and is held in place by an ivy wreath. Her face appears wrinkled and emaciated, a study in ugliness and old age. In keeping with it is the rest of her body: angular shoulders, withered neck and chest, pendulous breasts. This statue has usually been considered a copy of a Hellenistic original, but in a paper delivered in 1948 Rhys Carpenter suggested that it is instead a copy of a Hellenistic pastiche which utilized a contemporary head over a body copied from a Fifth century original.[6] From the excessive thinness of the statue when viewed in profile, he argued that the monument copied was in relief rather than in the round, since the Hellenistic sculptor was unable to supply sufficient depth to the composition. The bent pose he attributed to a definite action, such as that of restraining a bull or working on a trophy, and the Classical prototype he assigned to a monument comparable to the Nike Balustrade. Carpenter's observations focused primarily on the drapery: the use of catenaries, modeling lines, sharp and narrow ridges, central gather of folds on the axis of the body, and great transparency where the cloth adheres to the body. In addition, he pointed out that only the exposed flesh looks wrinkled and emaciated; under the garment the hanging breasts are full and rounded and the body is that of a young girl.

As usual, Carpenter's appreciation of style is masterly and only his conclusions may need modification. Compared to the many similar works representing old people, the New York woman seems to belong to another world. Even her costume is Classical, in contrast to the amorphous rags of the others. Only two other old women have related attires of "peplos" and himation. One is the so-called Drunken Woman of Myron, which Carpenter would attribute to the great Myron himself, in the Severe period. The second, in Basel, is the headless body of a peplophoros with deep kolpos, symmetrical mantle over both shoulders and down her back, feet flat on the ground but knees bent, and a definite inclination of the upper torso at the waist, which identifies it as an old woman.

This last sculpture has been recently published and has since attracted some attention. E. Berger has suggested that the body should be completed with the head of an old woman in Fifth century style known through two replicas, one in the British Museum (fig. 146) and one in Rome. Because realistic depictions of old women (as contrasted with dignified old men or old centaurs) are highly unusual during the Classical period, this head type has often been identified with the portrait of Lysimache, priestess of Athena for sixty-four years, which Demetrios of Alopeke, according to Pliny (*HN* 34.76) and Pausanias (1.27.5), made for the Akropolis, presumably during the last decades of the Fifth century.[7] Berger

---

[5] The dress may indeed be the sleeveless chiton or chitoniskos of an Amazon, but worn long and rather incongruously.

[6] Carpenter, *AJA* 53 (1949) 149. His theory was not accepted with favor and he never published it fully, so that only the brief summary of his paper remains in print. However, he expanded on it in his sculpture classes at Bryn Mawr College.

[7] Another theory would identify the head as the portrait of a Delphi prophetess, Charite, made by Phradmon, for which an inscribed base has been found at Ostia: F. Zevi, *RendPontAcc* 42 (1969-70) 95-116, esp. 114. Kron, 27-72, Cat. ?Ak 17, dissociates the head, but dates the Basel woman ca.

has joined the Basel body to a cast of the London head and has suggested a date of ca. 430 for the original. This theory has been rejected by Hilde Hiller: according to her, the British Museum head should not go with the body, and the old figure should portray not a respected and venerable priestess but Eurykleia, Odysseus' nurse. Her suggestion stems from a remarkable representation on a Campana plaque known through several replicas. It shows a Penelope of the well-known Persepolis type confronted by an old woman who is undoubtedly close to the headless sculpture in Basel. Hiller suggests that the originals of the two statues are contemporary and were set up as a group in antiquity, thus providing inspiration for the Roman makers of Campana plaques.

The similarity between the sculptures and the terracotta reliefs is so great that Hiller, understandably, tries to downplay the stylistic differences between the Severe Penelope and the Classical "Eurykleia." This discrepancy has been noted, however, by W. Trillmich, who offers a different solution: the statues do date from two different periods and once stood independently; they were grouped later, either as originals or as copies, in a Classicizing arrangement that was copied by the makers of the Campana plaques. Thus Roman Classicism can produce not only eclectic statues but even eclectic groupings by putting together heterogeneous, if genuine, Fifth century works.

One more possibility remains: that all these representations of old women are neither copies of Fifth century works nor replicas of eclectic Hellenistic originals, but rather Classicizing Roman creations, which can therefore utilize any previous style. The relative anachronism of having a genre statue in Fifth century styles would only add to its attraction for a jaded Roman clientele who also welcomed the Aphrodite of the Esquiline type with a naked body incongruous for the Severe period. That the inspiration for the various features came from genuine Fifth century originals should perhaps not be doubted, but the combination of these features, as for the Roman imperial reliefs, is a contemporary and spontaneous creation.

Stylistically the most coherent of the three pieces is the old woman in Basel. Even a hint of selvage appears at the edge of her mantle and minor omega folds punctuate the rim of the full kolpos, while the tripartite rhythm of the skirt goes back to the Aphrodite of Frejus, so that a date around 420 would be plausible for this style. However, the lack of overfold is most unusual,[8] and the arrangement of the skirt is here rendered without subtlety or those slight variations that make the Aphrodite's pattern clear only from different viewpoints. Since, moreover, both the woman's knees are bent, no tension folds can form, yet neither does the cloth fall vertically down according to the law of gravity, but it bends back in pleats that cling to the leg in an impossible fashion. The Fifth century sculptors used catenaries or tension folds, therefore horizontals or diagonals, to outline the body underneath the cloth, but they respected the straight course of vertical folds from the point of greatest projection, therefore away from the body where necessary, to

---

460-450 and identifies her as Aithra, from a group with her grandchildren. For a summary of the problems on the Lysimache see Robertson, 504-506.

[8] It could be argued that the upper torso shows an overfold and not a kolpos, but several reasons militate against this theory: (1) If the rendering is truly Classical, an overfold without kolpos would be equally unusual, since the peplos is obviously belted. (2) An overfold would end in a sharp edge with undercutting and perhaps swing forward because of the bent pose. The Basel statue shows instead the typical thickened edge of doubled-up cloth. (3) A plain overfold would adhere more closely to the chest and be open under one of the arms.

the extent that some renderings look almost like struts for the bent knee. Although the Basel woman supports herself more or less evenly on both legs (in itself a surprising stance for a period so concerned with chiastic poses), her right foot is sufficiently forward of the left that some differentiation should have been introduced into the skirt, even had the sculptor decided to be strictly realistic and logical. The symmetry of the arrangement is un-Classical but completely in keeping with Roman practices, which used the same motif for the tunics of their cuirassed statues.[9]

The Basel woman, moreover, gives the impression of being built from two different halves, the lower covered by thin and transparent cloth, the upper totally hidden by heavy material. This irrationality in itself can easily be paralleled within the Classical period, but the Greeks usually differentiated between cloth on and off the body. Here no hint of adherence to the stomach or the chest is given, as one would expect from a Fifth century work. The upper part therefore appears as if earlier, stylistically, than the lower one and almost at the cubic stage of the Severe style, were it not for the close spacing and the subtle intricacy of the folds.[10] Finally, the pose itself is peculiar, since a bend at the waist should not automatically indicate old age. Classical old men lean, but because they seek support from their staffs. The even bend of the Basel woman is more a hieroglyph of weakness than a true rendering of it.

It could be argued that the Fifth century was not capable of, or interested in, producing a more naturalistic effect and that therefore this pose is an argument in favor of a true Classical prototype. On the other hand, Roman sarcophagi including depiction of old nurses consistently show the bent pose and the kerchief, although the former is often justified by the action. The point, I believe, is clarified further by the statue in New York. Here too the bent pose is unnatural, and Carpenter's observation is undoubtedly correct. A striking resemblance between the Old Market Woman and the Peliad working at the cauldron in the Medea relief of the Three-Figure group (fig. 131) emphasizes the impression that the sculptor who made the New York statue took his inspiration from a similar relief.[11] But he did not produce an outright copy: his rendering of the drapery is excellent and quite similar to the stylistic phase of the Nike Balustrade, however the mantle tucked under the belt is not common in the Fifth century and recalls Archaic korai from East Greece. The intended effect, however, is not to produce contrast of textures, as in the korai or even in Classical works, but rather to obtain a central gather of folds as the vertical axis of the composition, with the natural symmetry typical of Roman works.

Other traits may also be significant. The bared-breast motif, so closely connected with female allure and specifically with Aphrodite, in these old women becomes definite and ferocious satire. On the New York statue, however, the garment is not pinned but tied together with flaps or strings, a rendering that is, to my knowledge, unparalleled in Greek art. If the detail means to convey the poverty or the sloth of the Old Woman, it is certainly not part of the Fifth century protoype, but I suspect that the separate straps are part of a

[9] This same motif occurs on Classicizing Amazons, not only the universally accepted Doria-Pamphilj statue, but also the so-called Lansdowne type, which is here discussed in the Appendix to this chapter.

[10] I omit comments on the advanced texture of the cloth because the surface treatment could be imputed to the copyist.

[11] Note that the Peliad also wears a mantle which falls with zigzags between her legs, but her garment must be coming from the back around the right hip, although its arrangement is obscured by the cauldron.

Hellenistic or Roman costume. Wider and more detailed straps appear in similar position on the dress of the Drunken Old Woman, whose drapery is, I must agree with Carpenter, stylistically close to Severe renderings.

A broader question can be raised at this point. Are any of the statues representing old men and women definitely known to copy a Hellenistic prototype? None of those extant are Hellenistic originals, and they were found throughout the Roman Empire, but especially in Italy. Several replicas of a single type were also excavated at such different sites that the suggestion has been made of a single center of manufacture in a Roman workshop which could utilize the resources of Roman export and trade.[12] Recent studies have emphasized the propensity for the ugly inherent in Roman sculpture, and the setting for such realistic portrayals of old age can be more readily visualized as a Roman estate than as a Greek sanctuary, agora, or private house. Were it true that such genre sculptures were not produced before the Roman period, the proper place of the three old women under review would automatically be found within the Classicizing movement.

Be that as it may, I believe that a similar case can be made for the head in the British Museum, the so-called Lysimache (fig. 146). To be sure, the rendering of old age in the face is limited to a linear system of wrinkles and bags under the eyes, without the excessive realism of the toothless hags in New York or Munich. However, protruding cheekbones and deep eye cavities show that the depiction of old age is not limited to superficial indications but affects the bone structure itself. A contrast with the bronze old man from the Porticello wreck (figs. 94, 95), or with more safety dated Fifth century works such as the old men of the Parthenon frieze, clearly points out the differences. In addition, the hairstyle is definitely appropriate to a younger figure, and it has all the artificiality of attested Classicizing renderings of the Severe style, such as the bronze lamp-bearer from Pompeii or the Munich "Orpheus." A certain similarity with the hairstyle of the Cherchel Demeter type or the Barberini Suppliant (figs. 86-88) suggests the ultimate inspiration for the rendering, but the linearity and symmetry of the London head betrays the Classicizing origin and cannot be imputed to a copyist. That the so-called Hera head (fig. 147) also in the British Museum, usually considered a replica of the Polykleitan statue for the Argive Heraion, has a rendering comparable to that of the "Lysimache" does not make the latter more Classical but casts doubts on the correct interpretation of the Hera, which I would consider Classicizing.

One more matronly statue can be included here, although this time my suggestion is very tentative indeed. The so-called seated Aphrodite or Olympias is known through at least eleven replicas, among which the best known is probably in the Capitoline Museum. It has always been considered a copy of a Fifth century orginal by a major master, and it has occasionally been identified with the Aphrodite in the Gardens by Alkamenes, or the Aphrodite Ourania by Pheidias. The type was so often used as a stock body for Roman

---

[12] This theory has been advanced by Adrienne Rossner Long in an unpublished honors paper written for Bryn Mawr College in 1969. She made the interesting observation that Hellenistic genre terracottas from Alexandria or Asia Minor emphasize deformity and disease, with age only a secondary feature, as contrasted with the healthy and normal, if emaciated, renderings of old age in stone and large scale. She did not, however, commit herself to a Roman date for all statues of old people, although she seriously considered it a possibility. Note that Tanagra figurines depicting old nurses include the child and clearly suggest a theatrical character, underplaying the ravages of old age. There is, moreover, no iconographical parallelism between terracottas and major statuary.

ladies, especially the mothers of emperors, that the original head type is not known; Becatti (following an earlier theory) has attempted to identify it in the so-called Aspasia or Sappho head, which has survived in a considerable number of replicas and variants, one at least of colossal size; he has exemplified this conception through a cast that combines the Capitoline body and a herm replica of the head in Naples. The total effect is pleasant but not attested through any ancient evidence. The connection has nevertheless been accepted by the most recent reconsideration of the problem.

This new study stems from Delivorrias's discovery of a fragment in Parian marble in the Akropolis Museum. Its findspot is unknown, but its present location suggests that it may have come from nearby. It comprises part of the right shoulder of a female figure wearing a sleeved chiton, and although the front surface is largely missing, part of the cavity for the insertion of the head is visible, while the back retains a portion of the backrest of a klismos. Comparison of this fragment with replicas of the seated "Olympias" has prompted Delivorrias to claim that we have here a piece of the original statue, which was therefore in marble; he also believes that the finish of the back implies all-around viewing and therefore precludes a temple setting. He suggests that the work dates from ca. 440, or at least from before 438, since the Aphrodite of the Parthenon East frieze seems inspired by the statue in the round; this should also represent Aphrodite and was probably meant originally for the unconventional setting of the sanctuary on the North Slope of the Akropolis. It may have been later moved to the Roman rearrangement of the Propylaia, where it was seen by Pausanias, who refers to it (1.23.2) as a work by Kalamis dedicated by Kallias.

Despite Delivorrias's careful analysis, a Fifth century dating for the composition remains, to my mind, in question. Omitting from the discussion the head, which represents merely an attribution, however plausible, we shall focus on the body as known through the Roman copies, since the Akropolis fragment is too small for stylistic analysis. We may also have to disregard the specific treatment of the folds, which in some replicas are almost ribbonlike, in others either denser or shallower and flat. Equally imputable to the copyist may be the overly ornate proliferation of omega folds at the edge of the apoptygma, which do not appear in all versions of the statue.[13] What cannot be so easily dismissed, however, is the seated pose, which is definitely part of the prototype, whatever its true date.

To my knowledge, no Greek Classical figure sits in such stretched-out fashion: it resembles that of the Hellenistic Sleeping Ariadne, and has forced the sculptor to use the heavy fall of the chiton as a veritable strut under the legs. The type of chair (the *klismos*) is similar to that of the Hegeso stele (fig. 107), where the lady of the house stretches her feet to the very edge of the slab; her pose is nonetheless more compact, and not simply because of the format of the stele or the presence of the maid with the jewel box. A seat of that type, comfortable as it may have been, was not meant to be used as a chaise longue,[14] and the

---

[13] A stylistic analysis of the composite cast created by Becatti reveals a certain discrepancy between the tubular ridges, which bend with "Paionian" nicks and the great amount of incisions that occur over flat areas and are not always parallel to the primary folds. The irregularity of the lines over the stomach and the deep depression for the navel are surprising, and a few other details seem too advanced for a Fifth century statue, such as the texture of the chiton over

the feet, which recalls much later works like the Artemis of Versailles or the Fanciulla d'Anzio. The excessive mannerism of the omega folds increases the Classicizing effect. However, the cast is largely based on the Capitoline replica, which Becatti considered the best, while Delivorrias prefers, rightly, the copy in Verona (his pl. 3), which seems somewhat more coherent and less ornate.

[14] This type of chair is discussed by G.M.A. Rich-

result is to make the "Olympias" seem excessively elongated and disproportioned. In particular, her knees are a considerable distance from the edge of the chair, which Fifth century sculptors had utilized so effectively as a catch point for angling the drapery. Other Classical seated figures usually have at least one leg retracted to provide variety, including the Barberini Suppliant (fig. 86), who is perhaps the most stretched out of them all, given her unconventional seat. An illuminating contrast is provided by the seated Athena on the Nike Balustrade (fig. 74) who resembles the "Olympias" because of the raised arm; yet her seat is not a standard klismos and her legs are closer to it. Comparison with the Aphrodite on the Parthenon frieze, supposedly so closely connected to the statue in the round, reveals the same discrepancy. The goddess there sits on a backless stool and the relative lassitude of her pose is permitted by the fact that she leans against Artemis' legs. Nonetheless, her knees are closer to the edge of the seat and her feet can rest naturally on the ground line, as contrasted with the almost dislocated ankles of the "Olympias."

Parallels on vases are not more convincing. Those adduced by Delivorrias definitely show a more compact rendering, with the klismos reaching just behind the bent knees, and a general review of other Fifth century representations has yielded no closer analogies. Yet the seated matronly figure, often with right arm outstretched holding an attribute (as the "Olympias" probably did) and the left draped over the backrest, seems popular during the last quarter of the Fifth century and the early Fourth and is known through many examples, both in painting and in sculpture, whether in relief or in the round.[15]

Because of this excessive elongation, and despite the postulated turn of the head toward her right, the "Olympias" remains, at least in the Roman versions, a one-sided composition to be viewed exclusively from the side. The Roman masters may have enhanced this trait, but they cannot have introduced it entirely, given the consistency among the replicas. The analogy with the Parthenon Aphrodite, rather than proving the priority of the sculpture in the round, may in fact suggest the opposite: that the free-standing sculpture was derived from a relief, as indeed seems to have been the case with several Hellenistic works inspired by the Parthenon frieze, including the Ares Ludovisi. One more suggestion may therefore be tentatively advanced.

The fact that this body was so frequently used for matronly portraits—for the mothers of the emperors rather than for their wives—may suggest that the prototype was an equally maternal or elderly figure, although not necessarily a mythological personage to be viewed in a narrative context. Roman ladies were notoriously eager to be identified with famous statues of heroines or goddesses, but they might have equally coveted association with a Roman creation made famous by its original purpose. The prototype of the "Olympias" may therefore have have been a Classicizing Hellenistic or early Roman portrait, perhaps Livia, the mother of Tiberius, intentionally imitating the Parthenon Aphrodite if first set up on the Athenian Akropolis. The Greek workmanship would ensure excellent quality to

---

ter, *The Furniture of the Greeks, Etruscans and Romans* (London 1966) 33-37, as a typical Greek invention, which she defines as an easy chair. However, she also states (p. 34) that the equation between the name in the literary sources and the visual examples in art is not universally accepted. For the continuation of the type in Roman times see her

p. 102; her example of a Roman matron (fig. 513) is the Uffizi replica of the "Olympias."

[15] It may be argued that the very appearance of so many representations on vases and reliefs speaks for inspiration from a major prototype in the round. However, the inspiration may come equally well from the Parthenon frieze, rather than vice versa.

Delivorrias's fragment despite a Roman date, while the method of attachment of the head may confirm a late chronology.[16] A Julio-Claudian original may even be suggested by the fact that one of the replicas of the "Olympias" portrays Helena, Constantine's mother, since her period witnessed a conscious revival of early imperial iconography and style.

Male Classicizing Figures

Leather (?) straps similar to those of the Drunken Old Woman or the Old Market Woman in New York appear also on a statue known from two replicas, one greatly restored in Salerno, Palazzo d'Avossa (figs. 148-150), and another, headless and armless, in Berlin. They have been identified by Jose Dörig as the Dionysos (probably bearded) made for Tanagra by Kalamis; I think once again of a Classicizing creation. The stance, even disregarding the restored lower legs of the Salerno replica, is uncertain and disjointed, with shoulders thrown back like those of the Stephanos Athlete. The bent knee of the forward (right) leg does not produce the pose of the Ares Borghese because the torso is more frontal rather than turned. The chitoniskos covers a soft body which seems to lack articulation; the garment is also draped in a peculiar fashion, with a strange dip over the area of the genitals that cannot be explained in sartorial terms. Equally strange is the apparent split in the skirt, which adheres to the advanced right thigh in a series of ribbon catenaries and hangs lower than the section on the left thigh, which is instead windblown, with a pattern of vertical folds in the back. The stone-studded belt with a Gorgoneion as a buckle may perhaps be compared with some renderings on South Italian vases, but it seems non-Classical, like the above-mentioned straps. The body build and the fine lines over the entire surface of the garment recall Ionic renderings, so that the apparent strangeness of the copies may stem from our relative ignorance of non-Attic works; however, the non-Greek details of the attire may be more in keeping with a non-Classical prototype.

Two important statues that are as yet imperfectly published are the over-life-sized bronze warriors recovered off the coast of Calabria (Riace Marina) from an uncertain context (figs. 151-153). The two figures appear different at first, since one is bare-headed but for a fillet and has long locks framing his face, while the other is helmeted and wears his hair short. Yet they are remarkably similar in build, stance, and details, such as the distinctive rendering of the feet widening out just before the small toe. Both warriors stand with their weight on the right leg, left leg forward and bent, left arm supporting a now lost shield. The published photographs of the entire statues show them before cleaning, and preliminary notices place them within the Fifth century, but a detail of the cleaned face of the long-haired warrior has appeared (fig. 151). To my mind, its heavy-lidded eyes, engraved, projecting eyebrows, and long locks of that nature are Classicizing traits of the First century B.C./A.C., but the dating of one figure should carry with it that of the companion piece. Proportions seem also rather elongated, and the head of the short-

[16] None of the pieces mentioned by Delivorrias (p. 3, no. 5) as parallels for the method of insertion of the head can be considered an undisputed Greek original. As to the lack of traces of the running drill on the Akropolis fragment, it could be argued that the finish of the back did not require it. In general, however, copies of Roman times made in Greece have been found to be of such good quality that their nature as copies has often gone undetected, witness some of the replacement figures for the Erechtheion frieze and other major monuments over which controversy is still rife.

haired warrior, perhaps because it lacks the curly frame of its mate, appears too small for the body. The rendering of the hair over the forehead of the bare-headed man has that calligraphy which is usually a trait of Classicizing styles. Newspaper accounts of teeth lined with silver foil increase the impression that the statues are late.

Long locks appear also on the so-called Tiber Apollo type, after a replica found in that river and now in the Terme in Rome. Several other examples of the type are known, including a head in much reduced scale and with a romantic expression, which have both been rightly imputed to the changing influence of a Roman copyist. The anatomy, the hairstyle, and the "Attic" stance with the level shoulders have usually been considered traits of the Severe period, and I have myself briefly discussed this type in my *Severe Style*, where I accepted it as a genuine reflection of an early Fifth century work. Zanker includes the Apollo in his review of Severe head types and their transformation in imperial times; he points out that the relative dryness of the statue from the Tiber is the effect of its underwater sojourn and that other replicas show a more powerful torso and developed anatomy.

After years of thinking and looking, I find myself reverting to a certain skepticism: should the type be considered a Roman Classicizing creation? There would be no point, however, in including the Tiber Apollo in a book on the Fifth century, were it not for the fact that it has repeatedly been attributed to the young Pheidias, although one scholar has ascribed it to Kalamis. The Pheidian attribution has been recently rejected by Uta Kron in her discussion of the Marathon Dedication by the Athenians at Delphi, which included an Apollo, since the Tiber type is self-contained and does not presuppose a group arrangement. The objection is secondary to the proper assessment of the statue and its chronology, and it is significant that Zanker hesitates in evaluating the prototype, thus confining his comments to the Roman traits of the replicas. I would tentatively suggest that the original is a Classicizing creation of relatively early date, perhaps contemporary with the Stephanos Athlete with which the Apollo shares the awkward attachment of arms to torso, in an almost Archaic rendering. The ephebic youthfulness of the god is also surprising, even in less weathered copies, since the impression is largely conveyed by the long locks, the rounded face, and the relatively small and soft mouth. Were this low dating of the Apollo accepted, we would know that Classicizing creations, and not only Classical originals, could be copied in reduced scale like the famous cult statues of the Fifth century.[17]

Similar to the Riace bronze warriors in general stance is the Mars from the Canopus at Villa Hadriana in Tivoli. Once again, we are dealing with a type usually dated early in the Classical period. Berger has suggested that the prototype was the Theseus of the Marathon Group, but the hypothesis is weakened by the presence of a second, though headless, replica from the same context, which still retains the attributes of Hermes/ Mercury. Jale Inan, considering the Hermes to be the original type, attributes it to Kresilas

[17] Of course, nothing precludes the possibility that the Tiber Apollo type was created as a cult image in Roman times, perhaps under Augustus, thus explaining its popularity in areas of Augustan patronage like Cherchel. The Classicizing style would therefore be a symptom of religious *decorum* and conservatism rather than of lack of artistic creativity. After these lines were written, Erika Simon informed me that she had reached my same conclusions and had included the Tiber Apollo in her entry on Roman representations of that god for the *Iconographic Lexikon of Classical Mythology* (*LIMC*) vol. 1, forthcoming. She considers the statue as one of many examples of Augustan household Apollo statues, which Tibullus calls *nititus et pulcher*.

on the strength of a good copy from Side. Trillmich cites both statues from Villa Hadriana as examples of the duplicating practices of Roman copyists, although he seems to favor the theory that they are Classicizing adaptations of Severe Greek types—a point of view supported by Zanker and most recently by Uta Kron. One more opinion, by F. Hiller, is worth noting, since it is the only one to advocate a date as late as the third quarter of the Fifth century for the Greek original from which the Tivoli warrior was supposedly copied. This situation reflects our difficulty in dating male figures to the late Fifth century when they are not in an obvious Polykleitan pose or tradition. Yet I see stronger Polykleitan than Severe traits in the two Tivoli figures.

To be sure, both feet are almost evenly aligned and also that of the bent leg rests flat on the ground, but the torso follows the chiastic arrangement, the right hip muscle is enhanced, and the median line curves strongly in the direction of the weight leg, where the knee pattern appears quite pronounced. In fact, the Hermes figure, which lacks the distracting elements of helmeted head and shield, is fairly close to the so-called Polykleitan Diskophoros in its more Classicizing forms, like the bronze statuette in the Louvre or the marble replica in Basel. This similarity strengthens my suspicion that "Polykleitos' Diskophoros" may also be a Roman creation. We would then have another instance of the preference in that period for statues in the "Severe" pose and, when preserved, with a Severe-inspired head but a body that conforms to chiastic compression and distension, statues which can, with proper alteration of attributes, represent different gods or heroes. The two sculptures from Villa Hadriana are also good examples of how duplication can be disguised by changing the position of the tree-trunk support and the shape of the attributes, so that two figures with the same stance can actually seem to be mirror images.

A final comment on the so-called Diadoumenos Farnese may conclude this section on Classicizing male figures. Usually attributed to Pheidias and considered the Attic counterpart to the Polykleitan Diadoumenos, the statue in the British Museum has been convincingly shown by Zanker to be an Antonine copy of a Classicizing original, probably of the First century B.C., made in imitation of the Polykleitan Diadoumenos and of which small replicas also exist. Once again, the name of the great Attic master had been made (in this case by Furtwängler, but again as late as 1951 by Becatti) especially because of the stance with level feet, while the undoubted similarity of the London statue to the Polykleitan creation could go undetected because of minor variations in the position of head and arms. It seems worth stressing that all the above-mentioned examples of Classicizing works—the Diadoumenos Farnese, the Mars and Mercury from Villa Hadriana and, if accepted, the "Polykleitan" Diskophoros, the Tiber Apollo, the bronze warriors from Riace, and the Dionysos Salerno/Berlin—have combined Fifth century chiastic principles with the "Attic," or more correctly the Severe, stance, in keeping with the predilection for mixing anachronistic traits that seems a hallmark of the Classicizing workshops. Other distinctive features, in some cases, are: the tendency to rejuvenate the types or to make them look more adolescent, and the corresponding reduction in size, from slightly over- to slightly under-life-size, as appropriate for a developing youth. The consequent softening of the musculature increases our difficulty in dating the "prototypes" correctly. That so many of these Classicizing creations could be considered works of the young Pheidias or be attributed to other Fifth century masters should make us more cautious with attributions.

Classicizing Herms

This topic is vast and cannot be explored adequately here. Only two examples can be mentioned, to complete our survey of Fifth century style. The first is the famous bronze head of an ephebe in the Louvre, the so-called Benevento Youth, which we now know is from Herculaneum. This provenience alone is sufficient to suggest that the head could not be a Classical Greek original, and Zanker has rightly dated it around 50 B.C.

After Zanker's analysis, it is redundant to repeat what are the Polykleitan and what the later features of the face. He has properly stressed the discrepancy between the hair within the wreath and that framing the face, as well as the difference between nose and mouth (after Peloponnesian renderings) and eyes (more Attic). We may add here the shape of the face itself: broad at the temples and tapering rapidly toward a small and delicate chin, as contrasted with the oval faces of Polykleitan statues and their pronounced chin. Three points should however be made: (1) A Classicizing creation can be of outstanding quality. We automatically react as if a date within the First century B.C. or the Roman period were shameful and demeaning to the value of a sculpture. To be sure, some of the Pasitelean figures or other Roman adaptations and pastiches are mediocre or even slightly disturbing for an eye accustomed to Greek proportions and styles. However the undoubted beauty of the "Benevento" Head can assure us that masterpieces could also be created; many of them are probably so good that we are still considering them copies of Greek originals and it will take added work and refined analysis to spot them. (2) Feminine traits almost always occur in these Classicizing heads of youths, often adding to their beauty. In the Benevento Head the frame of writhing curls around the face seems endowed with an animal life of its own and sets off most effectively the smooth treatment of the face, in coloristic contrast. Yet a truly Fifth century female face does not possess the delicacy of these Classicizing works. Comparison between the Benevento Head and the Athena Lemnia head in Bologna (fig. 112) which have been made to confirm the classical date of the bronze, may instead suggest that a revision of the "Lemnia" head type is needed. (3) A Classicizing creation need not always be a full statue or represent a mythological character; it can also, as in this case, belong to a herm. This was perhaps the most popular form of adornment for Roman gardens and peristyles, and the great demand must have prompted a variety of creations, of which the Benevento Head is a good example.

In keeping with this last point is the suggested grouping with Classicizing creations of a second herm: the Aspasia in the Vatican. This marble bust is inscribed with the name of Perikles' famous lover, and the inscription is ancient, although some suggest that it is not contemporary with the sculpture. The literary sources make no mention of a portrait of this prominent woman in Fifth century Athens, and indeed the chances of such a portrait being made at the time are tenuous. The position of women in Athens was not prominent enough to justify it, and Aspasia's privileged status and association with Perikles are likely to have brought her more animosity than admiration. Even as a private dedication, a statue of her is improbable. In later times Aspasia became famous, and it is quite understandable that Romans who wanted a portrait of Perikles in their homes also commissioned one of his companion.

That the extant herm was created then, to supply this demand, has been suggested but not generally accepted; Richter is not against an actual Fifth century date for the prototype, and others, who object to the distinctive hairstyle (the *Melonenfrisur*) as a Fifth century feature, would not oppose a Fourth century date. I am convinced of a Roman date for two reasons: (1) The face is round and full, rather than modulated as in the Fourth century, and its features—the large eyes, the closed mouth—are in keeping with general Fifth century renderings. (2) The drapery covering the upper part of the herm has been treated as if it were part of a Fifth century statue, with engraved lines curving over the breasts and folds in V-pattern channeled in between. Yet this is not a Fifth century face, nor is that true Fifth century drapery: the vocabulary is correct but the accent is alien. In this context the hair arrangement acquires greater weight and can definitely be considered anachronistic.

SUMMARY

Traits of Fifth century styles have been here considered in a variety of forms: as eclectic quotations within a different and vigorous stylistic current, as learned allusions to confer dignity and religious connotations, as conservatism or provincialism. We have reviewed direct copies, adaptations, pastiches, new creations in approximate Fifth century styles. Discrepancies in the renderings have alerted us to the possibility of dates considerably later than the Classical period, but the very skill of the sculptors has often made such chronological revisions difficult and tentative. In general, however, we have seen that the Romans tended to romanticize and rejuvenate the Classical ideal, unless they wanted to establish a direct correlation between a portrait and a famous prototype used as a stock body. Other changes introduced by the later sculptors were part of a consistent attempt to use earlier (Attic) poses in combination with Peloponnesian chiastic musculature. Perhaps the often-advocated Attic influence on the Polykleitan or Argive school should instead be attributed to the Romans. To be sure, Attic styles spread throughout the Greek world after the great conquests of the Athenian building program, but when undoubted Greek originals do not confirm a mixture of traits present only in Roman "copies," this label ought to be reexamined with care.

Roman creations may have made use of Fifth century styles to create genre subjects that would have been unthinkable during the Classical period. We may have to consider seriously the possibility that all statues of old people and peasants go back to Roman rather than to Hellenistic prototypes, but in particular we should acknowledge that at least a few of them, whether truly Hellenistic or later, intentionally use Fifth century motifs and drapery styles. More often, however, subjects are loftier and dignified, as befits the styles of a period which saw the height of Greek creativity and sculptural beauty. That later periods acknowledged this achievement so thoroughly and in so many different ways may make the analytical task of the modern art historian difficult, but it is proper tribute to the greatness of that art.

1. *Seated Hermes Akr. 1346.* This headless marble torso with traces of bronze attachments is traditionally considered a Greek original of the third quarter of the Fifth century, of which two Roman copies are also known, one in Leningrad and one, heavily restored, in the Palazzo Corsini, Florence. M. Bieber has called attention to the piece: *AthMitt* 37 (1912) 174-79, pl. 13, the Leningrad copy illustrated in her fig. 4; more recently, *Ancient Copies*, 27-28, fig. 26 (the Corsini replica: *EA* 318). Robertson (191, 473, 560, n. 59 on p. 648; pl. 60a) agrees with Bieber in considering the figure a Classical anticipation of a motif popular in the Hellenistic period, as exemplified by the seated bronze Hermes from Herculaneum. However, the Akropolis statue is not included (perhaps significantly) in Brouskari, while it appears instead in B. Kapossy's list of fountain figures: *Brunnenfiguren der hellenistischen und römischen Zeit* (Zurich 1969) 27. Both the Athenian and the Leningrad statues served in fact as fountains, the former through a hole in the rocky seat so that the flow of water fell behind the crossed legs of the god, the latter through the mouth of the turtle on which Hermes rested his right hand. The Florence replica has a similar arrangement, but the turtle is restored; however, the similarity of this detail in both Roman copies suggests that the restorer might have correctly interpreted some ancient clue.

By this inclusion Kapossy may imply that a Classical piece was adapted into a fountain at a later time, but Bieber suggests that the water arrangement is original, on technical grounds. The early date of the sculpture seems to depend largely on the treatment of the Hermes' drapery, which adheres to the left side, leaving the rest of the body bare; the cloth is rendered as thick and doughy, almost in Severe style, except over the upper arm, where its transparency resembles late Fifth century patterns. Moreover the figure as a whole, especially in its outstretched pose, strongly recalls the statues of seated philosophers from the Hellenistic period, which are at times rendered with heavy and simplified, if more voluminous, drapery (cf., e.g., G. Dontas, *Eikones kathemenon pnevmatikon anthropon*

[Athens 1960] pls. 17, 19b, 21, 28a, 29). The wrinkle over the navel, while common in the Classical period, is also apparent on many Hellenistic works, and the more complete version of the Hermes in Leningrad seems to have a definitely Roman head. The work may therefore be a Hellenistic or Roman creation in Classicizing (and eclectic) style; the Akropolis torso (which may not have originally stood on the citadel) may have escaped detection because of its location, better quality, and mutilated state. In this respect, note the similar case of a crouching marble groom in the Ny Carlsberg Glyptothek, Copenhagen (Inv. 1185), usually considered a Fifth century pedimental figure, but recently redated to the Hellenistic period: W.-H. Schuchhardt, *AntP* 17 (1978) 89 n. 40, fig. 20. Instructive is also the fact that the "Lysippan" Hermes from Herculaneum finds a remote mirror image in a much poorer statue which has been given a Polykleitan/Julio-Claudian head, from the House of the Camillus in Pompeii: Naples Nat. Mus. 4892, E. J. Dwyer in *Pompeii and the Vesuvian Landscape* (AIA, Washington, D.C., 1979) 63 and fig. 20 on p. 75.

2. *Head of an Athlete, Metropolitan Mus. 11.120.2* (figs. 154, 155). Because of its replicas, this head type is known as the New York/Petworth/Abbati/Riccardi/Trier athlete. The New York piece was published by Richter, *MMA Catalogue*, 34, no. 45, pl. 61, as a copy of a work from the third quarter of the Fifth century. G. Becatti, *Problemi Fidiaci* (Milan and Florence 1951) 151-55, pls. 80-82, argued that the original could not have represented Kresilas' Doryphoros (as suggested by Furtwängler) nor Pheidias' Anadoumenos, because the remains of a strut in the center of the head were the support for the raised right hand, indicating an athlete resting after a competition rather than in the act of tying a fillet. Becatti thought that the beauty of the figure made it a possible candidate for the statue of Pantarkes (presumably Pheidias' favorite and a winner in the Olympic games of 436 B.C.), which Pausanias saw in the Altis (6.10.6) but for which he did not name a sculptor. Affinity with the head of the "Lemnia" in Bologna has been considered a supporting argu-

ment, as well as the fact that in Trier a copy of this head type was found in the same building as a replica of the Mattei Amazon, usually attributed to Pheidias.

The Trier head has been most recently published in R. Schindler, *Führer durch das Landesmuseum Trier* (Trier 1977) 57, fig. 169 (G 46), and explained as part of a relief, probably from a wall revetment, in the Baths of St. Barbara, while the Amazon from the same building, fully in the round, would have stood in a niche as part of the decoration of the north façade of the frigidarium. The two sculptures were therefore visually unconnected. The thermae were built around the middle of the Second century A.C.

The very beauty of the New York head type, the refined oval, the coloristic treatment of the hair and, if correctly restored, the languorous gesture of the raised arm suggest that the prototype may have been a Classicizing creation. Note the similar comments in connection with another statue of a youth in the Metropolitan Museum (Richter, *MMA Catalogue*, 27, no. 33, pl. 31) by E. Pochmarski, in *Classica et Provincialia* (Festschrift E. Diez, Graz 1978) 159-67. Except for the pattern of the spiralling curls, the New York head also recalls some romanticized heads of the Polykleitan Diadoumenos and the Diadoumenos Farnese (Zanker, pls. 12:1, 13:3), so that it combines Attic and Polykleitan traits in a typical Classicizing mixture.

3. *Bronze Herakles with the Boar, Istanbul Museum* (figs. 156-159). This fragmentary statue comes from Tarsos in Cilicia and has been dated to the mid-Fifth century. Recomposed from several pieces, the largest portion shows the upper torso of a youth with left arm raised above the level of the head holding an object. The right arm, also raised, is now missing—only an unattachable fragment remains—together with most of the body on that side. Additional fragments from both legs cannot be joined either to the torso or to a part of the base plinth still extant. The position was first considered that of an athlete pouring oil on himself; it was later accepted as that of a man lifting an animal high over his head, tail held in the left hand, and therefore recognized as a youthful Herakles preparing to throw down the Erymanthian boar. The most extensive discussion of the statue is by P. Devambez, *Grands Bronzes du Musée de Stamboul* (Paris 1937) 35-49, pls. 7-12. He notes

that the piece is Myronian in subject, Polykleitan in conception, Archaizing in the treatment of hair and ears and, in sum, is the powerful creation of a good Greek master of the mid-Fifth century B.C. who made the statue for the city of Tarsos. Lippold, *Handbuch*, 139 and n. 4, more simply attributes the work to Myron but considers it a Roman copy.

Devambez's comparison of the head of the Herakles to that of the Idolino is significant. The Tarsos figure is likely to be a Classicizing eclectic creation of the Roman period. To this conclusion lead not only the history of the city, fully Hellenized only in later times and prosperous under the Romans, but also the features of the head. The rosebud mouth and the tapering oval contrast with the simplified treatment of the ear and the calligraphic curls closely adhering to the cranium, but separating in the center of the forehead in a mannered pattern that recalls Archaic renderings.

4. *Artemis of Ariccia, Terme Museum.* This colossal statue (H. 2.86m. without base) was found in a Roman villa of Trajanic date between Albano and Ariccia. It stood in a niche, on a tall pedestal, so that it could only be seen from the front and mostly from below. It has usually been considered a Roman copy of a Greek original in bronze, probably representing Artemis because of the peplos belted over the apoptygma and the long hair over the shoulders, supposedly a youthful coiffure. No true replica of the type is known, although the head is similar to that of the Hera Farnese in Naples (BrBr 414) and exists in various copies. Attribution of the type to Kresilas on the basis of an alleged similarity to the Velletri Athena has recently been discounted in favor of a date before 440 and certainly before the Athena Parthenos: H. von Steuben in Helbig[4], no. 2130. See also text to BrBr 756/7 (by P. Arndt and G. Lippold, 1934).

The very massiveness and stiffness of the statue, which have been adduced in support of a divine identification, seem to me indicative of a Roman creation. The head type is so generically Fifth century that it can be found with other bodies and is therefore proper to none. The richness of the kolpos over the hips (which prompted the comparison with the Athena) is in stylistic contrast with the relatively Severe course of the folds and stiff pattern of the skirt. Moreover, representations of Artemis during the Fifth century seem confined to reliefs, and I have been unable to find a true Fifth century type in the round except the statue under discussion. Although this last argument cannot be considered probant, I am inclined to see in it further support for the possibility that the Ariccia statue is a completely Roman work in Classicizing style and probably patterned after an Athena type.

5. *The Berlin/Lansdowne/Sciarra Amazon type*. This figure is usually considered a Fifth century creation, either by Polykleitos or by Kresilas, according to the information given by Pliny (*HN* 34,53) on a group of bronze Amazons set up in Ephesos. I have ventured to suggest that the type dates instead from the Augustan period and is therefore Classicizing rather than Classical: *AJA* 78 (1974) 1-17. This conclusion is reached on the basis of the mannered drapery with Archaistic overtones, the gesture of the right hand, the leaning position requiring a support unnecessary in a bronze composition, and the elongated proportions, which are only superficially Polykletan. I also called attention to the strange belt present on several replicas of the type but unparalleled on other statuary: *AJA* 80 (1976) 82. Although I have since noticed a remotely comparable rendering on the Roman Eros riding the Old Centaur in the Louvre (Bieber, *Hellenistic Age*, fig. 583), the puzzle of the Amazon has truly been solved by J. Boardman, who has identified the "belt" as a horse's bridle pressed into service as a girdle: *AJA* 84 (1980) 181-82. This explanation, however, carries with it no specific chronological indication.

Numerous articles have appeared in recent years, rejecting a Classicizing date for the Lansdowne type. P. Devambez has examined the literary sources and concluded that only the Greek mainland and specifically Athens were interested in Amazonian legends, primarily after contacts with the Persians during the wars; Asia Minor seems to have developed interest only in the Classical period, as a result of Athenian influence: *RA* 1976, 265-80, and *CRAI* 1976, 162-70. Note, however, that two other examples can be added to those mentioned by Devambez for the mainland: a terracotta pedimental composition in Corfu (*Archaic Style*, 191 and 219; *BCH* 90 [1966] 838, fig. 9), and a terracotta rider from the Athenian Agora, which M. Goldberg has identified as female because of its white-painted

flesh, and which may have been an akroterion for the Royal Stoa: T. L. Shear, Jr., *Hesperia* 42 (1973) 401-402, pl. 75a-b. Both these examples have been dated to the late Sixth century, therefore presumably before the Persian wars. An Amazonomachy has also been postulated as the subject of the frieze of the Treasury of Massilia in Delphi (E. Langlotz, *Studien zur nordostgriechischen Kunst* [Mainz 1975] 56), therefore on a building from a Phokaian colony, around 500 B.C. It may simply be that the scant evidence from Asia Minor should be explained in the light of the considerably narrower knowledge we have of Asia Minor sculpture, and the relative Ionic lack of interest in narrative iconography in comparison with the mainland.

A. Bammer has also discussed the Amazons' connection with the Artemision, and illustrates the relief of the Lansdowne Amazon type, which he connects with the altar: *RA* 1976, 91-102; cf. also E. La Rocca, *ASAtene* 34-35 (1972-73) 425, fig. 8, and note the heavy lids of the face in the relief. M. Weber has written an extensive analysis of all Amazon types, suggesting new restorations and attributions: *JdI* 91 (1976) 28-96. According to her, the Mattei type holds both ends of a bow, not a spear, and was made by Kresilas; the Lansdowne type (which she calls Sciarra) leans not on a pier but on a weapon, a double-axe or more probably a bow, and was made by Polykleitos; the Doria-Pamphilj type is only a variant of the latter; the Capitoline (which she calls the Sosikles) type, the only one truly leaning on a spear, she attributes to Pheidias. In a recent addendum, *JdI* 93 (1978) 175-83, Weber also connects a fragmentary head in the Milles collection, probably from Ephesos, with the Mattei Amazon, whose head type has long been problematic. Her positions (and mine) are rejected by T. Dohrn: *JdI* 94 (1979) 112-26, with extensive bibliography. He believes that the Ephesian priesthood ordered the statues at the time of completion of the temple construction, choosing to turn to Athens for both subject matter and sculptor (Pheidias, perhaps as creator of the models only) because of the political moment.

I have asked Richard Tobin to apply his conception of the Polykleitan canon to the examples of the Amazons for which measurements were available. Although the published figures do not always correspond to the dimensions needed by the system, Tobin tentatively tells me that the Capitoline type employs the Polykleitan canon, the Mattei uses an entirely different system, the Lansdowne seems to reflect a conscious influence of the canon with reference to height only (not to widths, which is responsible for the elongated effect), while the Doria-Pamphilj type is also non-Polykleitan. I think the question should remain open.

BIBLIOGRAPHY 9

FOR PAGE 222

The best analysis of drapery development during the Classical period is still Carpenter. Hiller offers the interesting features of *sections* of draped statues, which therefore demonstrate the ins and outs of folds. However, he does not distinguish between Greek originals and copies. The viewer will note the difference between the straight U-cuttings of the latter as against the Ω undercutting of the former.

FOR PAGE 225

Epidauros, sculpture from Temple of Asklepios: good, recent photographs in B. Brown, *Anticlassicism in Greek Sculpture of the Fourth Century B.C.* (New York 1973).

Nereids from Xanthos: see, e.g., Bieber, *Ancient Copies*, fig. 191; A. H. Borbein, *JdI* 88 (1973) 104-13, figs. 13-22.

Reliefs of the Heroon from Gjölbaschi Trysa: the most recent discussion of some scenes from the cycle is by W. Childs, *The City-Reliefs of Lycia* (Princeton 1978) with all previous bibl.

FOR PAGE 226

Hunt frieze, Sarcophagus of Mourning Women: see detailed photographs in F. Hiller, *MarbWinckProg* 1960, 1-12, pl. 1.

Reliefs from Epidauros: B. S. Ridgway, *AJA* 70 (1966) 217-22.

On Lysippos and his canon see, most recently, A. F. Stewart, *AJA* 82 (1978) 163-71, 301-13, 473-82.

FOR PAGE 227

A new role for Athens in the Hellenistic period has been recently advocated by A. F. Stewart, *Abstracts of Papers presented at the 80th AIA Meeting, 1978*, p. 6; an extensive monograph on this subject by the same author has just appeared as *JHS* suppl., vol. 14 (1979).

Nike by Euboulides: BrBr 49; on the sculptor (fourth of that name) see *EAA*, s.v. The Athena by him is supposed to be a variant of the Velletri Athena; for illustrations see Bieber, *Hellenistic Age*, fig. 669; cf. G. Waywell, *JHS* 92 (1972) 246-47.

Damophon of Messene: the repairs to the Olympia Zeus are mentioned by Pausanias, 4.31.6; a recent attempt to date the artist's career to the Hadrianic period (G. Donnay and E. Lévy, *BCH* 91 [1967] 518-45, 546-51) has now been discounted by the authors: cf. E. Lévy and J. Marcadé, *BCH* 96 (1972) 967-1004, esp. 986, 1003.

On the Athena Parthenos replica in Pergamon see, most recently, M. Gernand, *AthMitt* 90 (1975) 1-47.

Most recently, on the Gigantomachy frieze, with updated illustrations, E. Simon, *Pergamon und Hesiod* (Mainz 1975).

FOR PAGE 228

Carpenter, p. 203, for a definition of baroque style; for a stylistic analysis of the Zeus/Hero see pp. 204-205 and pl. 38.

Attalid dedications in Athens: for illustrations of the group of replicas in Naples see Bieber, *Hellenistic Age*, fig. 435; for the Amazon, Lippold, *Handbuch*, pl. 127:4. Less useful than Zanker, but well illustrated, is G. Traversari, *Aspetti Formali della scultura neoclassica a Roma dal I al III Sec. d.C.* (Rome 1968).

FOR PAGE 229

Ara Pacis, Tellus panel: Strong, pl. 39.

On *aemulatio, imitatio*, and *interpretatio* see the comments by R. Wünsche, in *Festschrift L. Dussler* (Berlin 1972) 45-80, esp. 62-68.

Ravenna relief: Strong, pl. 46.

FOR PAGE 230

Frieze from Basilica Ulpia: Strong, pl. 67.

Old Market Woman in New York: Richter, *MMA Catalogue*, 222, no. 221, pl. 115.

FOR PAGE 231

A collection of what Bieber calls "old derelicts" can be found in her *Hellenistic Age*, figs. 385-95, and cf. her p. 141.

Drunken Old Woman "by Myron": see, e.g., *Severe Style*, 131 and bibl. on p. 146.

Basel peplophoros: E. Berger, *AntK* 11 (1968) 67-70, pls. 31:1, 33. The identification as Lysimache and the connection of the head with

246

the Basel body have been accepted by Robertson, 505, although he dates the whole to the early Fourth century and briefly considers the possibility of a Hellenistic Classicizing work.

FOR PAGE 232

H. Hiller, *AA* 1972, 47-67; for the Campana plaque see her pp. 49 n. 9, 51, fig. 3, 63, fig. 15. A recent illustration and discussion of a similar plaque is in J. Dörig, *Art Antique* (Geneva/Mainz 1975) no. 2. On the Penelope see *Severe Style*, 101-105.

W. Trillmich, *JdI* (1973) 266-67.

For the Esquiline Aphrodite and its meaning in terms of Roman taste, see *Severe Style*, ch. 9, passim, and bibl.

FOR PAGE 233

On the old nurses of Roman sarcophagi see the enlightening comments by H. Sichtermann, *JdI* 83 (1968)180-220, esp. 207 and n. 84. He illustrates several details of Niobids sarcophagi, where the bent nurse is a standard feature. For the Peliad relief see the discussion of the Three-Figure Reliefs in ch. 8.

FOR PAGE 234

For the ugly in Roman sculpture see A. F. Stewart, *JRS* 67 (1977) 81 and n. 50; Stewart quotes M. Fuhrmann in *Die nicht mehr schönen Kunste* (ed. H. R. Jauss, 1968) 23-66 for the theme in Latin poetry.

Head in the British Museum: G.M.A. Richter, *The Portraits of the Greeks* 1 (London 1965) figs. 878-79, pp. 155-56.

Bronze man from the Porticello wreck: see ch. 5.

Lamp-bearer from Pompeii: Zanker, pp. 87-89, no. 3, pl. 68:1-4, see esp. p. 89 and n. 136.

Orpheus, basalt head in Munich: Zanker, pp. 84-86, no. 1, pl. 64

Cherchel Demeter: see Appendix 7:5.

"Hera" head, B.M. 1972: see, e.g., A. Linfert, *Von Polyklet zu Lysipp* (Diss., Giessen 1966) 9-11, where it is attributed to Polykleitos the Younger.

Aphrodite/Olympias (also called Agrippina): the most recent study by A. Delivorrias summarizes previous positions: *AthMitt* 93 (1978) 1-23. The identification as the Aphrodite in the Gardens is by E. Langlotz, *SBHeid* 1953-54; as the Aphrodite Ourania by Pheidias, Becatti,

most recently *StMisc* 15 (1970) 35-44, with list of replicas and a plaster-cast reconstruction with the so-called Sappho head, on which see now N. Himmelmann-Wildschütz, in *Studies von Blanckenhagen*, 99-101.

FOR PAGE 235

The Akropolis fragment identified by Delivorrias has now the Inv. no. 6692; he illustrates it on pls. 6:1, 8:1, 10.

Besides the vases quoted by Delivorrias, cf. also some examples that Mark Fullerton kindly researched for me: Meidias Painter: *ARV²*, 1314, no. 16 (Ruvo, Jatta, 1538); *ARV²*, 1312, no. 2 (Florence, MA 81947); also *ARV²*, 1179, no. 3 (Louvre Ca 1679). Eretria Painter: *ARV²*, 1247, no. 1 (Berlin·2471) and others. None of these parallels can duplicate the position and elongation of the legs.

FOR PAGE 237

Dionysos Salerno/Berlin (this latter, K 4): see J. Dörig, *JdI* 80 (1965) 177-92, figs. 24-30, 38, 41, reconstruction on p. 187, fig. 37; a later discussion by E. Pochmarski, *Das Bild der Dionysos in der Rundplastik der klassischen Zeit Griechenlands* (Diss. Graz, Vienna 1974) 28-31, leaves the identification uncertain and points out the vast chronological distance between this type and the next representation of a bearded Dionysos.

On the Stephanos Athlete see Zanker, 49-70.

Bronze warriors from Riace Marina: the long-haired statue is illustrated in *JHS—AR* 23 (1977) p. 63, fig. 29 (note the contrast with the Porticello-wreck head illustrated on the same page, fig. 30); G. Foti, *Il Museo Nazionale di Reggio Calabria* (Naples 1972) pl. 57 and p. 78 (short-haired warrior). Id., *Atti 12° Convegno Studi Magna Grecia* (Naples 1973) 311-52, pls. 31-32; *Calabria Turismo*, 6:18 (Oct.-Dec. 1973), cover ill. and pp. 9-15 (on both wrecks, with various ills.); *Magna Graecia* 10:11-12 (Nov.-Dec. 1975) cover ill., and several accounts in Italian magazines and newspapers. The *Gazzetta del Sud*, Nov. 3, 1978, has published a recent interview with Dr. Foti which mentions that the statues are still at the Istituto Restauri in Florence, that their teeth are lined with silver, and that they date from the Fifth century.

FOR PAGE 238

Tiber Apollo: *Severe Style*, 71, no. 2; head in reduced scale: W. Trillmich, *JdI* 88 (1973) 274 and figs. 29-30 on p. 275. Zanker, pl. 71:4, p. 92; on the type, pp. 91-92, no. 6.

Attributed to Pheidias: see bibl. in Kron, 220-21, nn. 1067-70, who disagrees with the attribution.

Attributed to Kalamis: J. Dörig, *JdI* 80 (1965) 230-36.

Mars from Villa Hadriana, Tivoli: E. Berger, *RömMitt* 65 (1958) 6-32; Kron, *loc. cit.*, rejects the possibility.

On the Hermes see J. Inan, *AntK* 13 (1970) 21-26; id. *Roman Sculpture in Side* (Ankara 1975) 19-29, no. 3.

FOR PAGE 239

Trillmich, *JdI* 88 (1973) 276-77 and esp. n. 99.

Zanker: in Helbig⁴, vol. 4, no. 3198, pp. 161-62. I understand that the Tivoli Mars is the object of a forthcoming article by E. Minakaran-Hiesgen in *Tainia* (Festschrift R. Hampe). She considers the type Severe, a reproduction of the Epicharinos by Kritios. I owe this information to E. Simon.

F. Hiller, pp. 12-13, fig. 3.

On Polykleitos' Diskophoros see ch. 8.

Diadoumenos Farnese: cf. ch. 8; Zanker, 13-14, no. 11, pls. 8-10.

FOR PAGE 240

Benevento Youth: Zanker, 32-33, no. 29, pls. 34:1; 36:1, 4, 7.

Vatican Aspasia: Richter, *Portraits of the Greeks* (London 1965) 154-55, figs. 875-76; *EAA*, s.v. Aspasia (Siena-Chiesa).

Index

Architectural sculpture has been grouped with the building to which it belonged, whenever possible, under the place of origin, since the decoration of a single structure is often scattered through many museums. Sculptural types have been entered under their most common name, when more than one replica is involved, although some cross-referencing by museums has been attempted. For any entry, when the page cited refers to the main text, the bibliography for that page should also be checked, for frequent additional information.

I gratefully acknowledge much help by George Szeliga in the preparation of this index.

PLATES

1. Parthenon metope S 17

2. Parthenon metope S 19

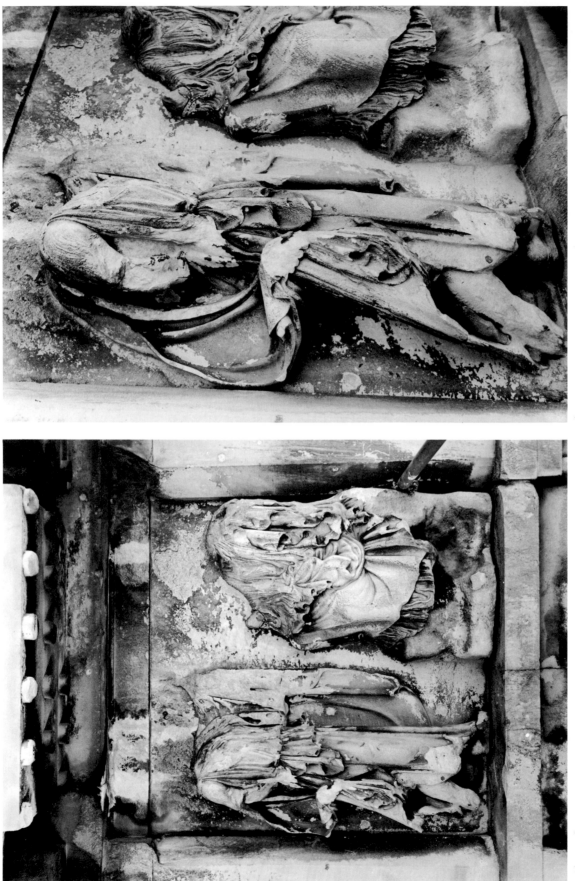

4

3-5. Parthenon metope N 32

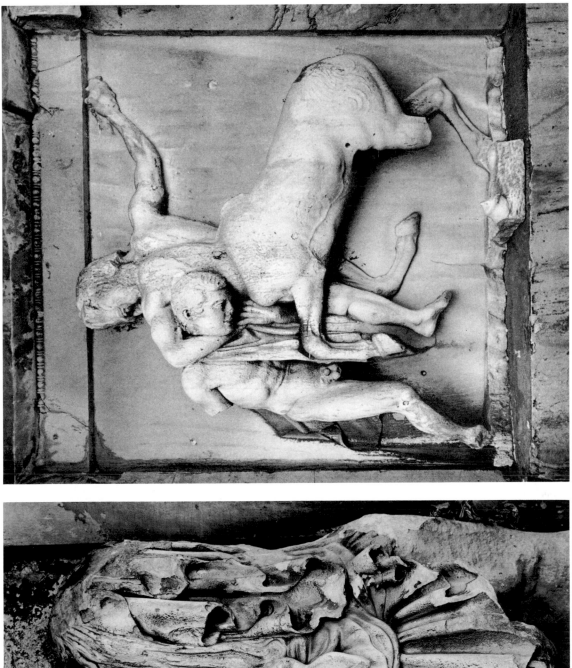

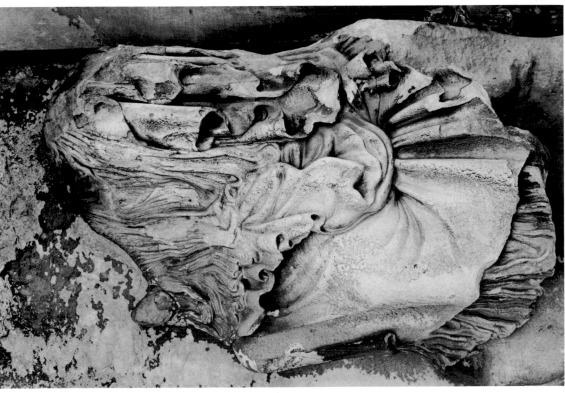

6. Parthenon metope S 1

5

7. Hephaisteion metope, Theseus and Skiron

8. Hephaisteion metope, Theseus and the Marathon Bull

9. Hephaisteion metope, Theseus and the Minotaur

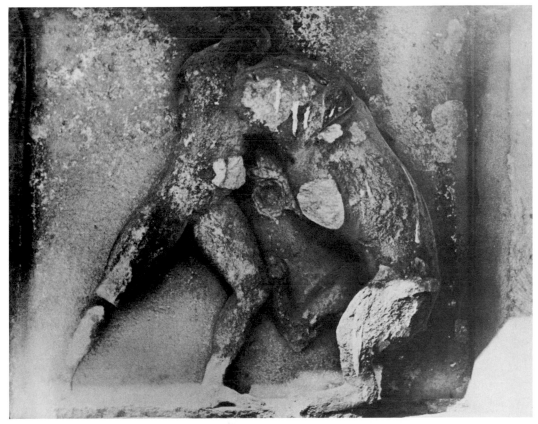

10. Hephaisteion metope, Herakles and the Lion

11. Rome, Villa Albani, metope

12. Thasos, Gate of Hera

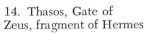
14. Thasos, Gate of
Zeus, fragment of Hermes

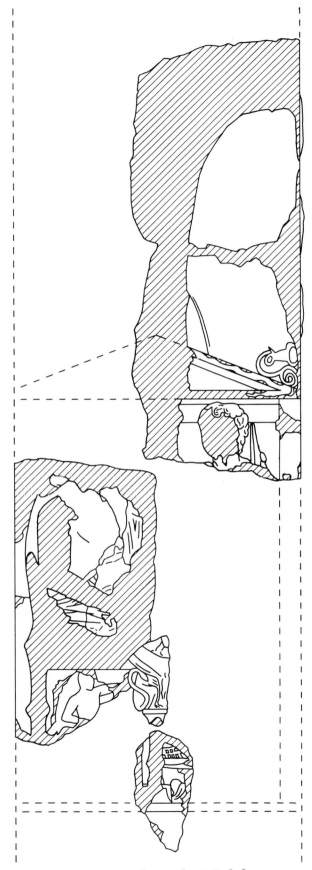

13. Thasos, Gate of
Zeus, fragment of Zeus

15. Drawing of Gate of Zeus, by P. Rehak,
after P. Bernard

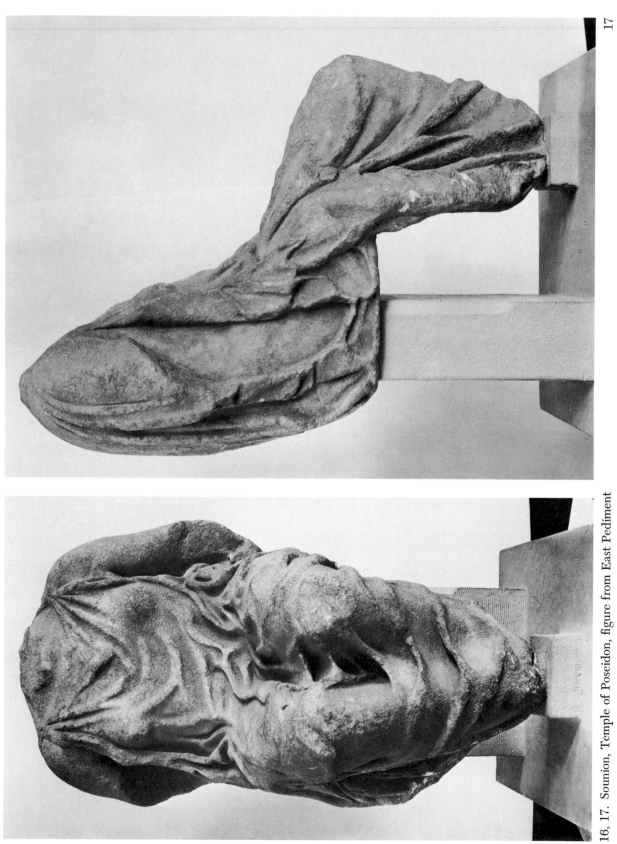

16, 17. Sounion, Temple of Poseidon, figure from East Pediment

17

18. Parthenon, East Pediment, Figure D

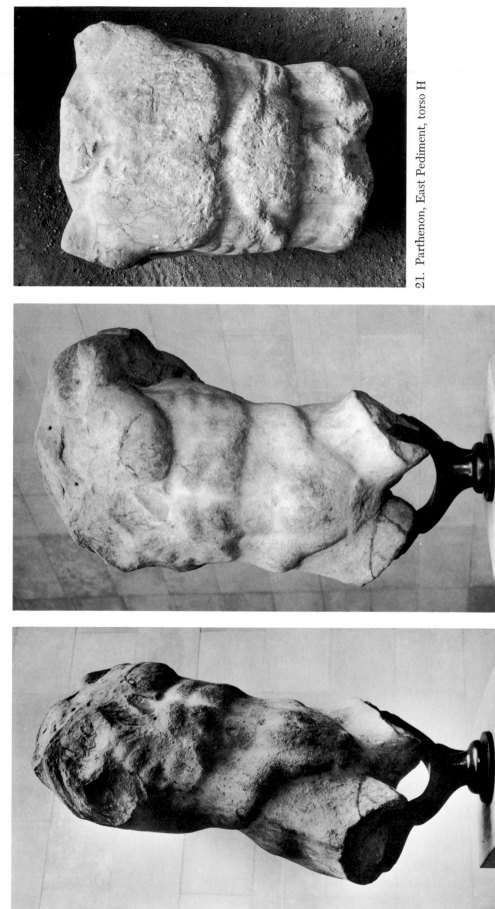

21. Parthenon, East Pediment, torso H

19, 20. Parthenon, West Pediment, torso H

20

22. Parthenon, East Pediment, Figures E, F

23. Parthenon, East Pediment, Figure G

24. Parthenon, East Pediment, Figures K, L, M

25. Rome, National Museum, Stumbling Niobid

26-30. Copenhagen, Ny Carlsberg Glyptothek, Reclining Niobid

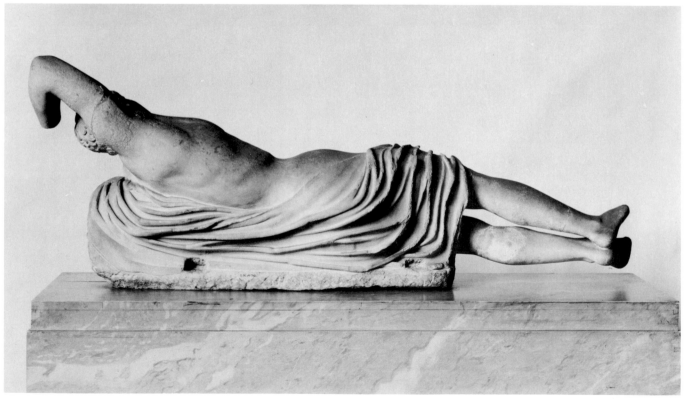

30

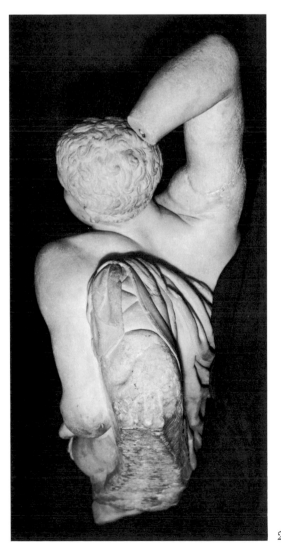

29

28

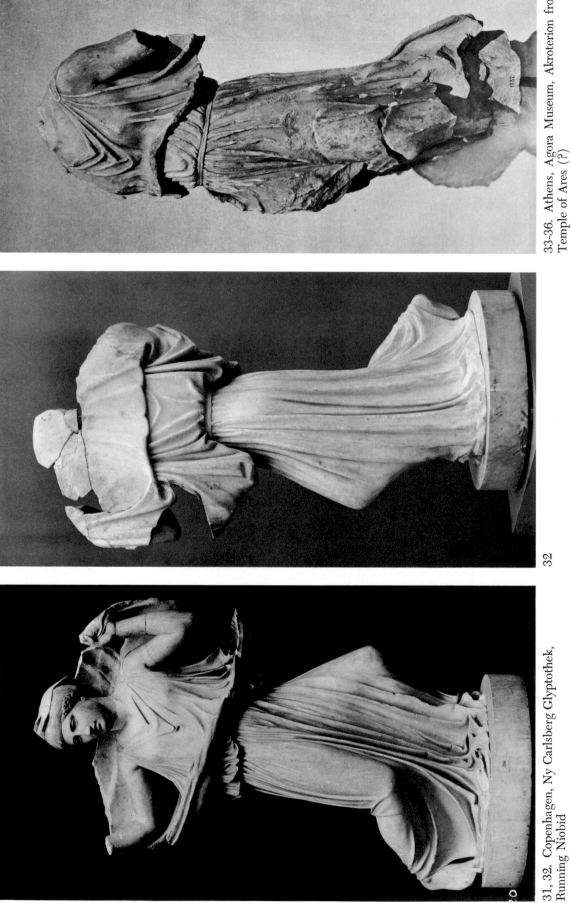

33-36. Athens, Agora Museum, Akroterion from Temple of Ares (?)

32

31, 32. Copenhagen, Ny Carlsberg Glyptothek, Running Niobid

36

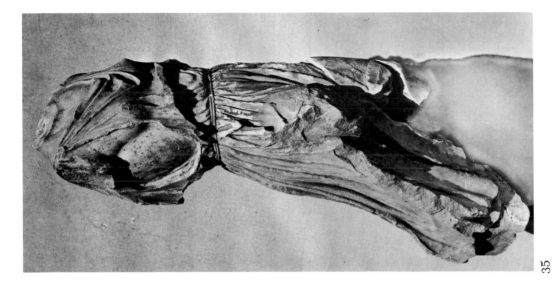

35

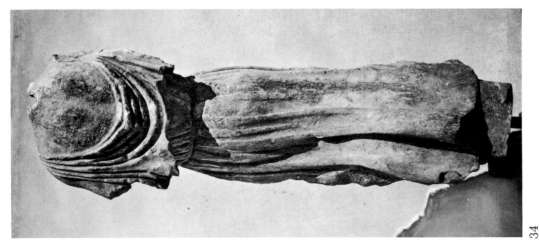

34

37. Athens, Agora Museum, Akroterion from Stoa of Zeus

38. Oxford, Ashmolean Museum, Metronomic Pediment

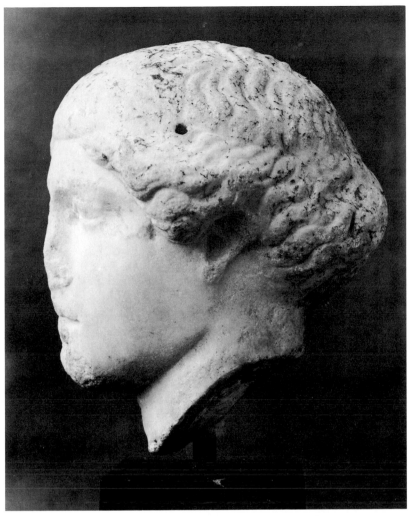

39. Providence, RISD Museum of Art, head from a pediment

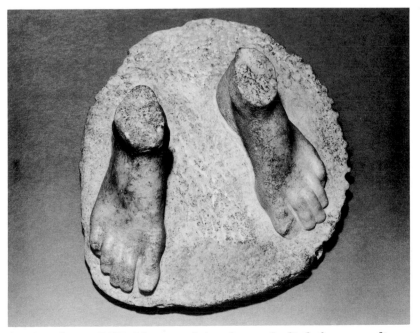

40. Providence, RISD Museum of Art, feet and plinth from a pediment

41, 42. Boston, Museum of Fine Arts, Akroterion (Leda/Nemesis)

43. Parthenon, frieze W XII, from a cast

44. Parthenon, frieze S XXV

45. Parthenon, frieze S XL

46. Parthenon, frieze N VI, detail of Figure 18

47. Hephaisteion, East frieze, slab 1

48. Hephaisteion, East frieze, slab 1

49. Hephaisteion, East frieze, slab 2

50. Hephaisteion, East frieze, slab 2, detail

51. Hephaisteion, East frieze, slab 4, detail

52. Hephaisteion, East frieze, slab 4, detail

55. Vienna, Art Museum, relief from Ephesos, copy of Ilissos frieze

53. Berlin, National Museum, Ilissos frieze, slab D

54. Vienna, Art Museum, Ilissos frieze, slab E

56. Nike Temple, South frieze, block *g*

57. Nike Temple, South frieze, block *o*

58. Nike Temple, South frieze, block, *a*, from a cast

59. Nike Temple, South frieze, block *i*

60. Nike Temple, South frieze, block *k*

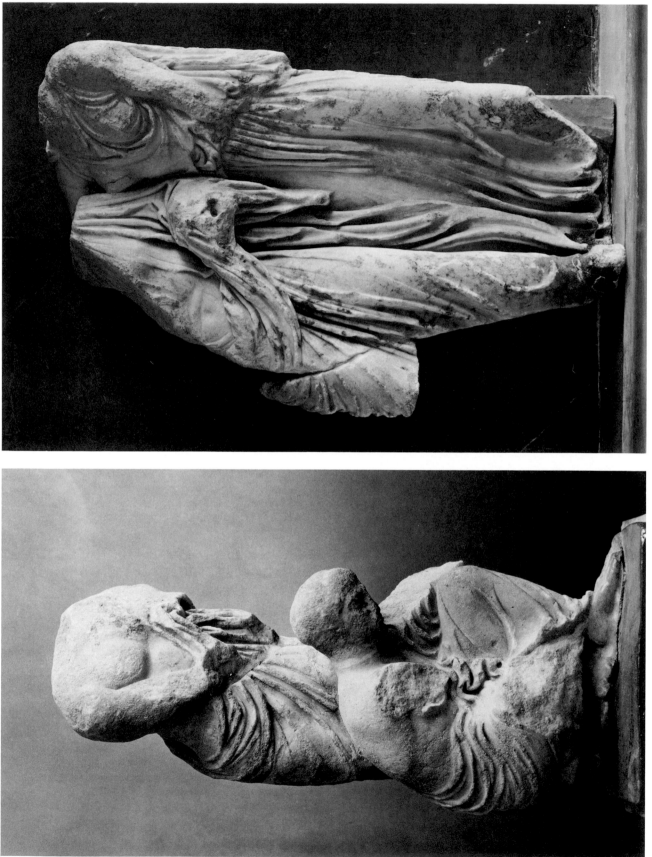

62. Erechtheion frieze, Akr. 1071

61. Erechtheion frieze, Akr. 1073

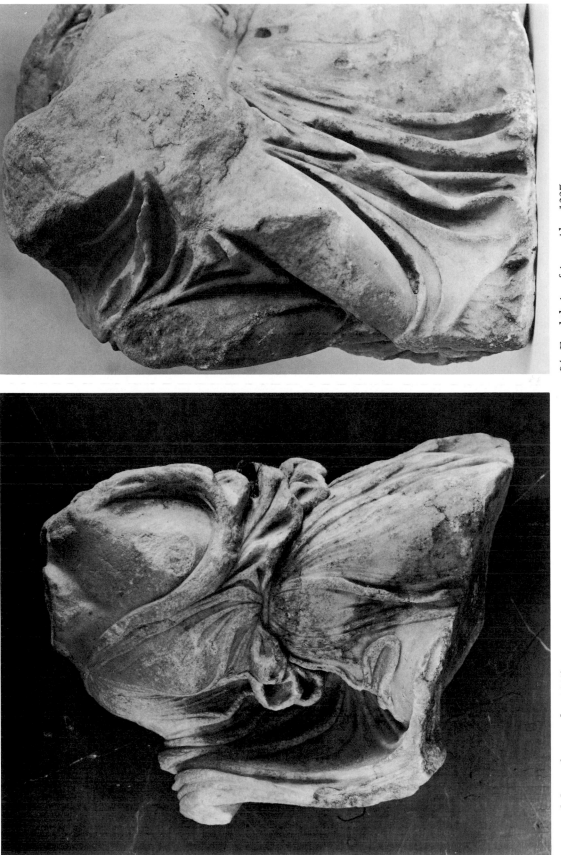

64. Erechtheion frieze, Akr. 1237

63. Erechtheion frieze, Akr. 2835

65. London, British Museum, Bassai frieze, B 542

66. Nike Balustrade, Nike mounting step

67. Nike Balustrade, detail of chiton of Nike restraining bull

68. Nike Balustrade, example of quiet drapery

69. Nike Balustrade, head of Nike

70. Nike Balustrade, detail of sanguisuga fold

71. Nike Balustrade, detail of nicked folds

72. Nike Balustrade, detail of butterfly (binocular) fold

73. Nike Balustrade, detail of ribbon drapery

74. Nike Balustrade, seated Athena (note for gesture and catch of folds at knee)

75. Nike Balustrade, detail of seated Athena (ribbon drapery below mantle)

76. Nike Balustrade, Nike alighting

77. Nike Balustrade, detail of Nike alighting

78. Nike Balustrade, detail of Sandalbinder

79. Nike Balustrade, detail of drapery on wing, upswept overfold

81. Nike Balustrade, Akr. 1013, 1003

80. Nike Balustrade, Persian trophy

82. Athens, Erechtheion, Karyatid Porch, detail (opposing curves at knee, alternation of stance)

V.P.

83. Erechtheion, Karyatid C

84. Nike of Paionios, Olympia Museum

85. Head of Vatican Herm after Paionios' Nike   86. Paris, Louvre, Barberini Suppliant

87, 88. New York, Love Collection, head of Barberini
Suppliant type

88

89, 90. Statuette Akr. 1310, two views   90

91. Sorrento, statue of Artemis (?) on animal

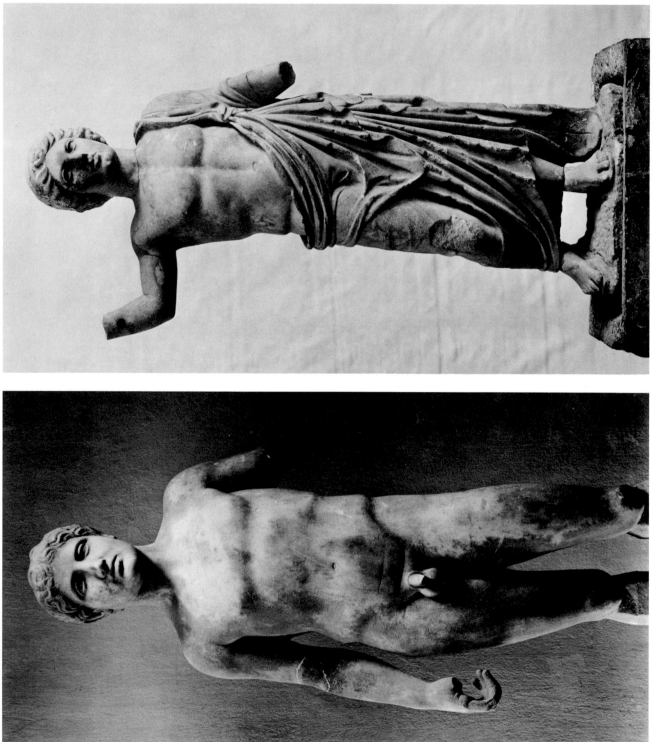

92. Peiraeus Youth

93. Athens, National Museum, Youth from Rhamnous

96. Demeter (?) from Eleusis

95

94, 95. Reggio Calabria Museum, head of bearded man from Porticello wreck

97. Athens, National Museum, Xenokrateia relief

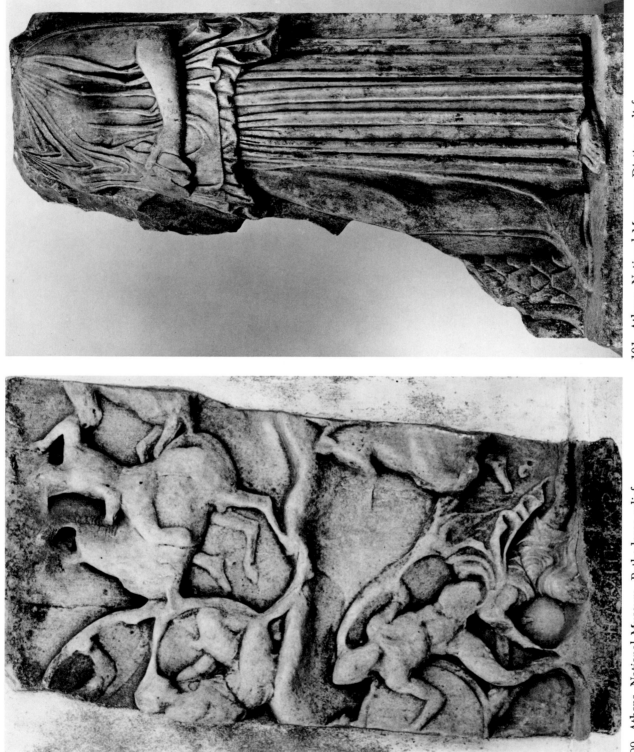

101. Athens, National Museum, Diotima relief

99. Athens, National Museum, Pythodoros relief

100. Rome, Torlonia relief

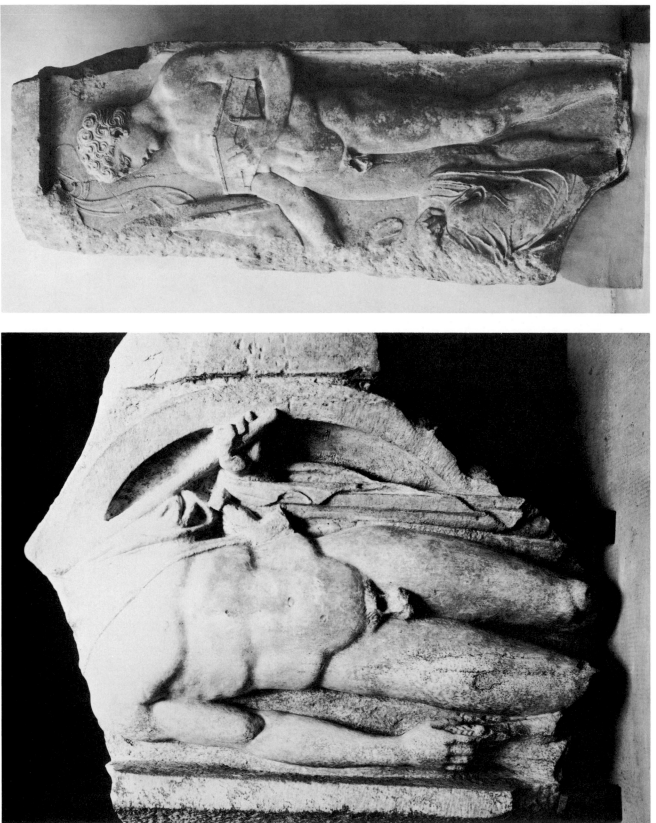

103. Samos Museum, funerary relief

102. Cyrene Museum, stele of a warrior

104 Rome, Albani Relief, detail

105. Rome, Albani Relief, detail

106. Athens, National Museum, Stele from Aegina

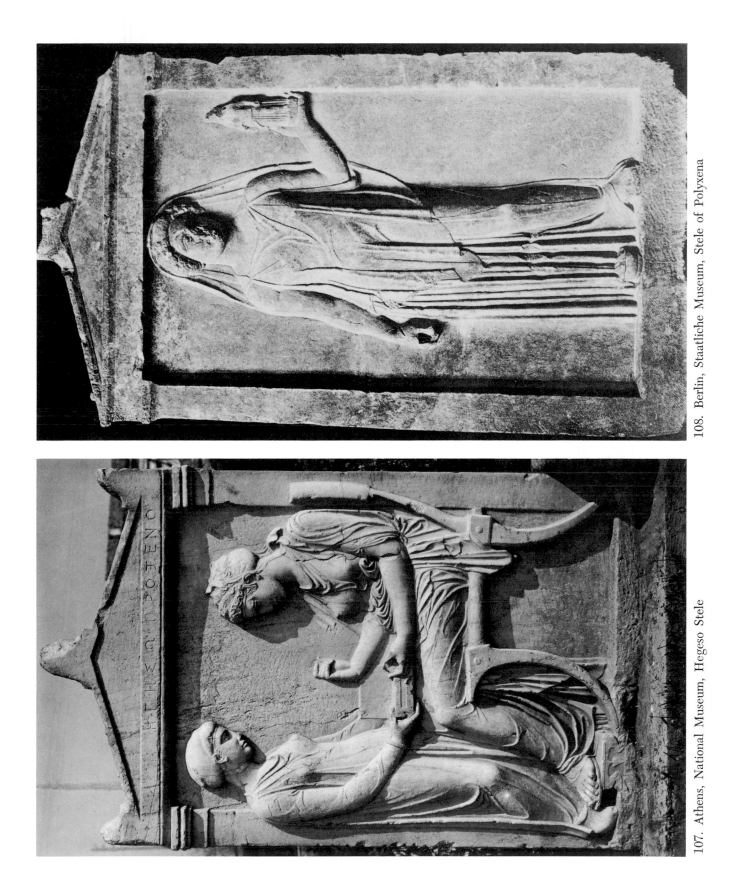

108. Berlin, Staatliche Museum, Stele of Polyxena

107. Athens, National Museum, Hegeso Stele

109. Rhodes, Museum, Stele of Krito and Timarista

110. Athens, Kerameikos Museum, Stele of Eupheros

111. Athena Medici (Louvre, after cast in Dresden)

115. Yale University Art Gallery, Velletri Athena

112. Bologna, Head Palagi (Athena Lemnia ?)

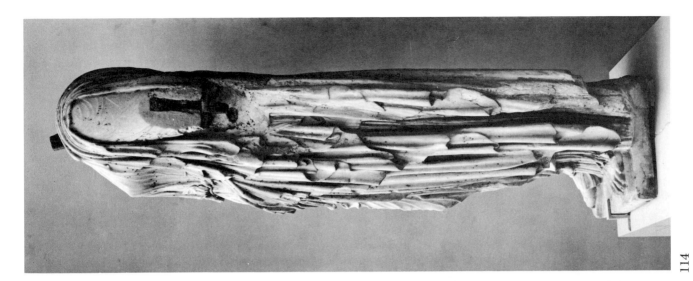

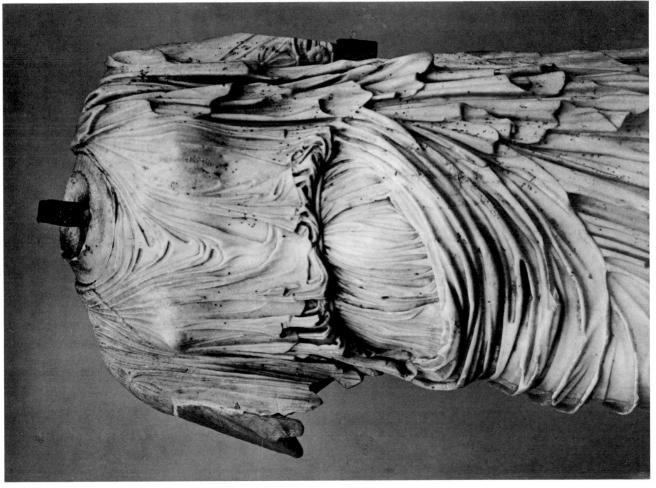

113, 114. Copenhagen, Ny Carlsberg Glyptothek, Nemesis by Agorakritos

114

116-118. Cyrene, bronze head (Arkesilas IV ?)   117

118

122

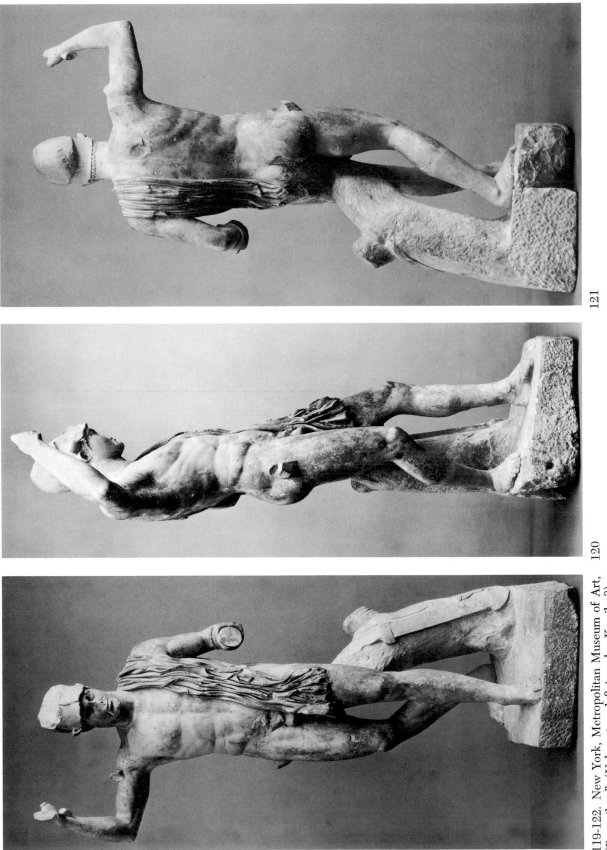

119-122. New York, Metropolitan Museum of Art,
"Protesilaos" (Volneratus deficiens by Kresilas?)

120

121

125. Maiden from the Peiraeus

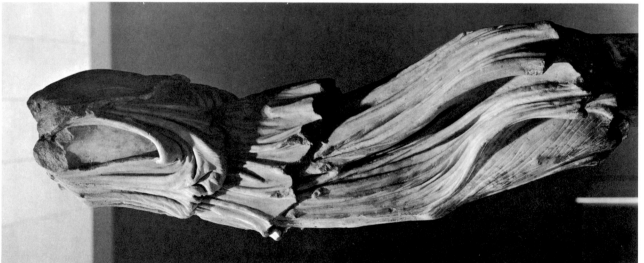

124

123, 124. Philadelphia, University Museum,
Pitcairn Nike

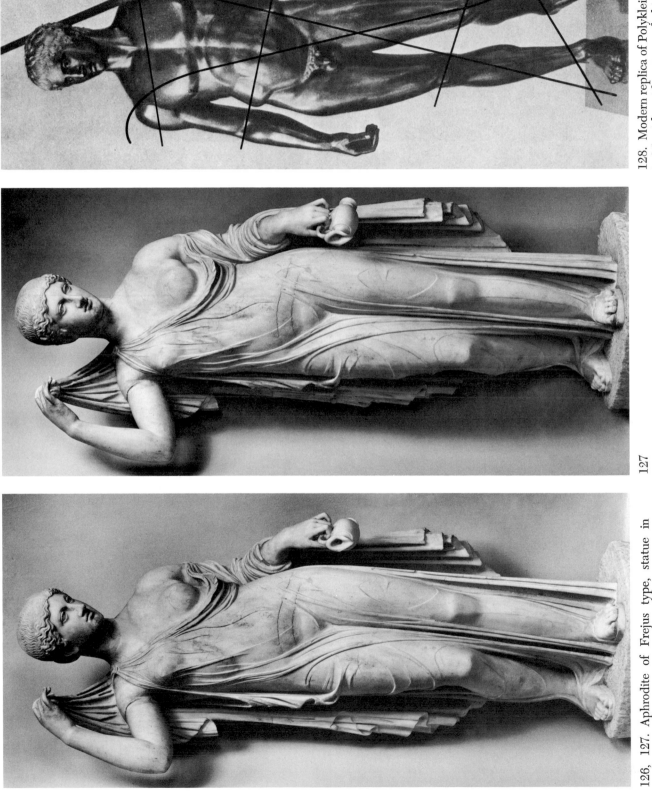

128. Modern replica of Polykleitos' Doryphoros in Munich, with pattern of chiasmos superimposed

127

126, 127. Aphrodite of Frejus type, statue in Holkam Hall

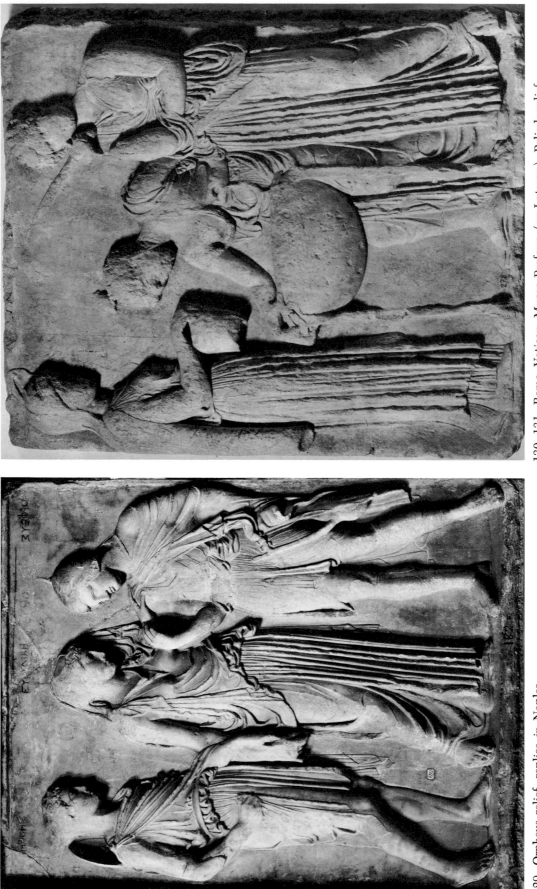

129. Orpheus relief, replica in Naples

130, 131. Rome, Vatican, Museo Profano (ex Lateran), Peliads relief

132, 133. Cyrene Museum, funerary reliefs (Herakles and Alkestis?)

133

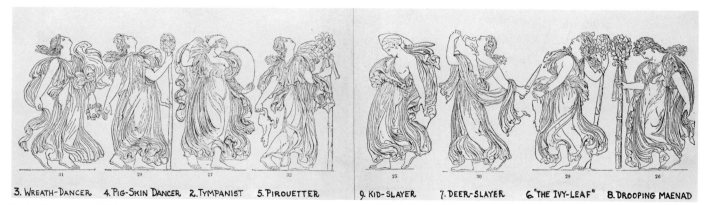

3. WREATH-DANCER   4. PIG-SKIN DANCER   2. TYMPANIST   5. PIROUETTER   9. KID-SLAYER   7. DEER-SLAYER   6. "THE IVY-LEAF"   8. DROOPING MAENAD

134. Drawing of Maenads, arrangement by R. Carpenter, after patterns by Hauser

135. Florence, Uffizi, Neo-Attic relief with three Maenads, detail

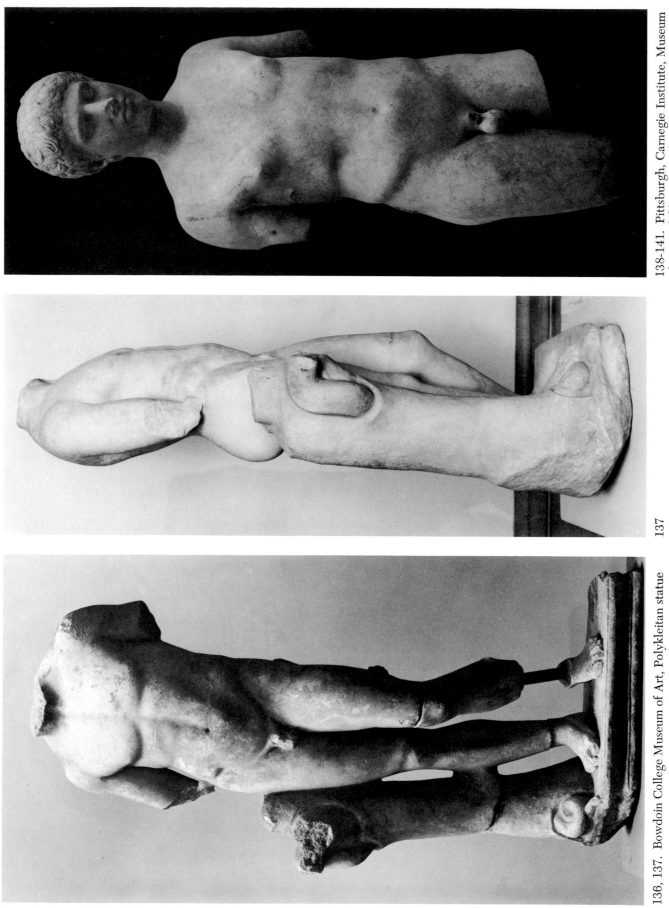

138-141. Pittsburgh, Carnegie Institute, Museum of Art, Polykleitan Youth

137

136, 137. Bowdoin College Museum of Art, Polykleitan statue

141

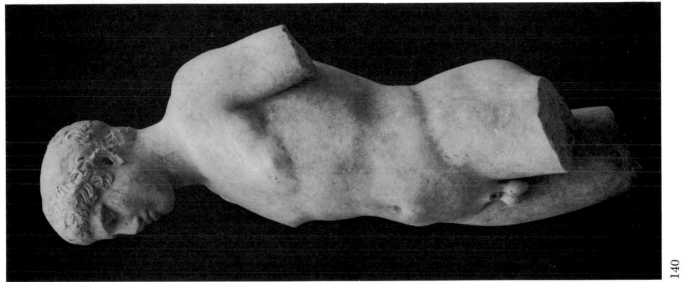

140

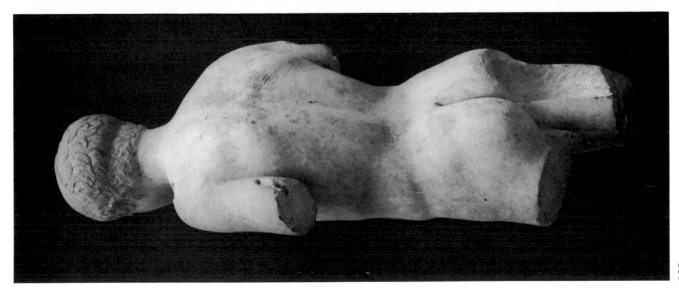

139

142. London, British Museum, Nereid from Xanthos   143, 144. London, British Museum, Nereid from Xanthos

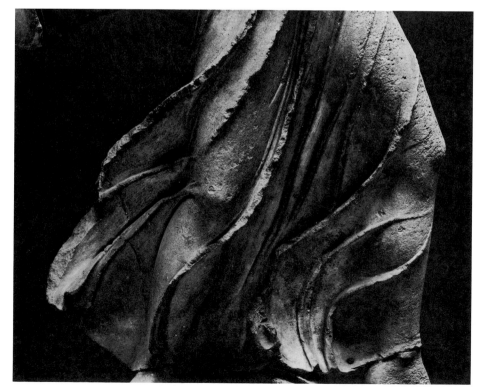

144

145. New York, Metropolitan Museum of Art, Old Market Woman

147. London, British Museum, so-called Hera by Polykleitos

146. London, British Museum, so-called Lysimache

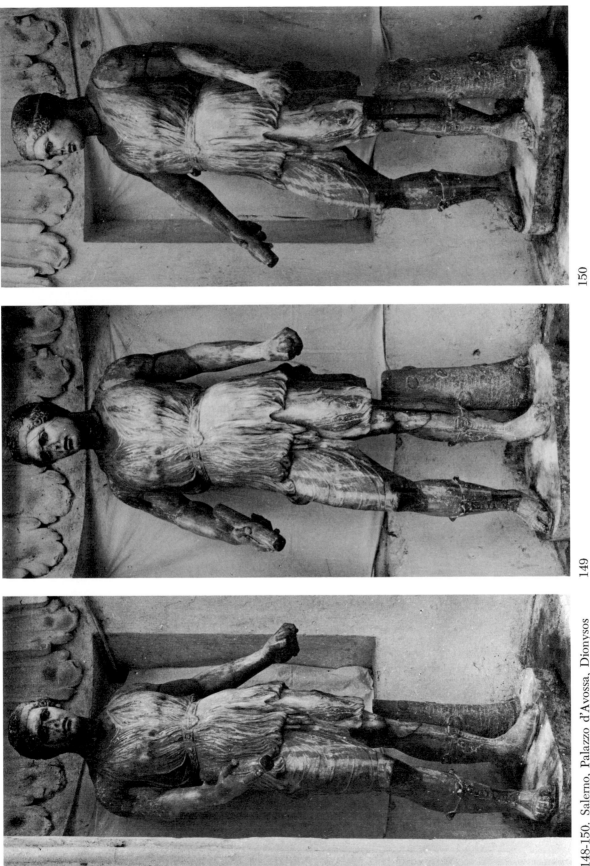

150

149

148-150. Salerno, Palazzo d'Avossa, Dionysos

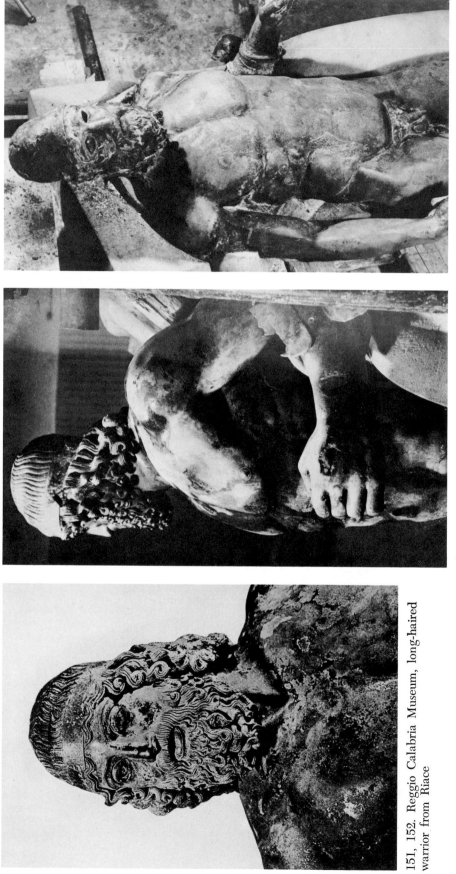

153. Reggio Calabria Museum, short-haired warrior from Riace

152

151, 152. Reggio Calabria Museum, long-haired warrior from Riace

154, 155. New York, Metropolitan Museum of Art, Head of Athlete

156-159. Istanbul Museum, bronze Herakles from Tarsos   157

158

159